CONFESSIONAL LUTHERAN DOGMATICS

Gifford A. Grobien, Editor

Theological Anthropology and Sin

by

Klaus Detlev Schulz

Published by
The Luther Academy
Ft. Wayne, Indiana

Thank you to The Roy D. and Ingaborg G. Randolph Memorial Endowment Fund for supporting the publication of this work through their gifts.

Jennifer H. Maxfield, Technical Editor

Luther Academy books are available through www.logia.org.

Library of Congress Catalog Number: 89-84112

ISBN: 978-1-935035-45-9 (Volume V, hardcover)
978-1-935035-46-6 (Volume V, paperback)
978-0-9622791-0-2 (13-Volume Set)

Published in the United States of America

To my family
Cornelia, Julia, and Sophie

CONTENTS

PREFACE TO THE GENERAL INTRODUCTION

by Gifford A. Grobien, General Editor
Confessional Lutheran Dogmatics

A contemporary publication expounding upon anthropology runs the risk of being passed by the quickly moving stream of public opinion. Perhaps no other current questions fall victim to the whims of human imagination more than those about nature, personhood, sex, and identity. Among secularists the concept of nature has become so fluid as to be meaningless. "Trans-" refers not only to sex but to nature itself, so that in our evolutionary-dominated landscape transhumanism has become the longed-for destination. The goal is to set my own parameters of what it means to be me. The goal is—as it always has been after all—to become a god on my own terms.

Likewise, long gone are the days when Christian apologists could claim that sin is empirically demonstrable. Secularism short-circuited that argument by simply denying that there is any kind of God who would make sin a category. Without sin and without the restrictions of nature, I have nearly become my own god already.

Theology that becomes enamored with such ever-moving targets would have little to say of enduring value. However, theology that resets the questions and themes according to Scripture contributes and confesses faithfully, not only to this generation but for the future generations of the church. Speaking out of Scripture and the Lutheran Confessions, Detlev Schulz has provided us with a volume on anthropology and sin which is able to set right the confusion and error of the current age while contributing to the doctrinal theology of the evangelical Lutheran church for generations to come. Human nature, the image of God, the corruption of sin, and the responsiveness of human existence are deftly applied against the spirit of the age, while finding their steadfast ground in biblical teaching.

I am thankful for this resource for seminaries, pastors, and scholars around the world, this ninth of thirteen volumes to be published in the Confessional Lutheran Dogmatics series.

GENERAL INTRODUCTION

by
Robert D. Preus, General Editor, 1984–95
Confessional Lutheran Dogmatics

For some time now those of us in the Lutheran church who have interested ourselves in the Lutheran Confessions, taught from them, and conducted research in these great symbolic writings have recognized the need for a dogmatics resource based upon the outline and thought pattern of the Lutheran Confessions. Such a resource, heretofore available only in Leonard Hutter's little *Compendium Locorum Theologicorum*, would address theologians of our day with a truly confessional answer to the theological issues we are facing in Christianity and in our Lutheran Zion today. We were in no way interested in replacing as a textbook in our Lutheran Church—Missouri Synod Francis Pieper's monumental *Christian Dogmatics*, which has served students in our church body and others for three generations. Such an endeavor would have been unnecessary and unproductive. The authors of the various monographs in this Confessional Lutheran Dogmatics series come at their respective subjects from somewhat different vantage points and backgrounds and personal predilections as they practice dogmatics. It was decided, therefore, to issue a series of dogmatics treatises on the primary articles of faith usually taken up in traditional dogmatics since the sixteenth century—the Augsburg Confession, Phillip Melanchthon's *Loci Communes*, and Martin Chemnitz's *Loci Theologici*, for example.

But why the approach from the Lutheran Confessions? Are not these musty old creeds and symbols irrelevant to our day, and would not a series of monographs written from the point of view of confessional Lutheran theology be equally irrelevant to the theological issues presently confronting the church? It is because we must respond to such a question with an emphatic *No* that we presume to issue the forthcoming volumes. The Confessions, whose theology is taken directly from the Scriptures, are indeed relevant to our day, just as are the Scriptures themselves which are always "profitable for doctrine, for reproof, for correction, for instruction in righteousness" (2 Tm 3:16). There has been a real call and need for just the kind of dogmatics series here proposed, that is, a confessional Lutheran dogmatics. First of all, no dogmatics book of any kind has been published by orthodox confessional Lutheran theologians (along the lines of Elert, Pieper, Hoenecke, and Hove) within the last generation. During the same time, however, there has been a renewed interest in the Lutheran Confessions, in their function in giving form to our Lutheran presentation of doctrine, and to some extent even in norming that doctrine: note the excellent studies of Edmund Schlink, Holsten Fagerberg, Leif Grane, Peter Brunner, Wilhelm Maurer, Friedrich Mildenberger, Hermann Sasse, and others as well as the many recent books and studies written in connection with anniversary observances of the Book of Concord, the Augsburg Confession, etc. Thus, it would appear that there is need not only for a dogmatics resource in our day, but one that is strictly and consciously confessional in its presentation of doctrine and its assessment and analysis of modern theological trends throughout the Christian church. This series, of which the present volume is a part, is written to fill this need, and it is the hope and prayer of the editors that the present volume will to some extent accomplish this aim.

The volumes making up Confessional Lutheran Dogmatics are not a theology of the Lutheran Confessions; they are rather a series in dogmatics. They differ from other dogmatics books in that they are patterned strictly after the theology of the Book of Concord as they address the issues of today. They follow not only the theology of the Book of Concord, as the texts of Francis Pieper and Adolf Hoenecke and other confessional Lutheran dogmaticians have done, but, unlike these dogmaticians, the authors of the present volumes follow the actual pattern of thought (*forma et quasi typus*, ὑποτύπωσις) of the Lutheran Confessions. Such a procedure is according to the principle of the Confessions themselves; creeds and confessions are indeed a pattern and norm according to which all other books and writings are to be accepted and judged.[1] This fact will account for the agreement in both doctrine and formulation that the reader will observe within the present entire dogmatics series; the authors bind themselves not only generally to the theology of the Book of Concord, but to its content and terminology (*rebus et phrasibus*).[2]

There is another reason for the doctrinal agreement which will be apparent among the authors of the Confessional Lutheran Dogmatics. It is this: all the authors share the concept of doctrine, unity of doctrine, consensus in doctrine, and purity of doctrine consistently articulated in our Confessions. All of the Lutheran Confessions see doctrine as a singular, organic whole. Christian doctrine is like a body (*corpus doctrinae*) with parts (*partes*) or joints (*articuli*) and ligaments and members (*membra*). The plural "doctrines" is rarely used in the Confessions, as in Scripture, but rather the singular "doctrine." In the church, if one member suffers the whole body suffers; according to the organic, unitary nature of Christian doctrine, if one article or member fails, the whole body of doctrine is adversely affected. Luther said, "One article is all the articles, and all articles are one."[3]

As a confessional Lutheran dogmatics, the present volume will consciously and scrupulously draw its doctrine from Scripture. All the Confessions, beginning with the creeds and concluding with the Formula of Concord, claim

1. See SD RN.10.

2. Preface, *The Book of Concord: The Confessions of the Evangelical Lutheran Church*, trans. and ed. Theodore G. Tappert (Philadelphia: Fortress Press, 1959), 13.

3. *Lectures on Galatians*, 1535 (AE 27:38; WA 40/2:47.32–33).

to be and are direct explications of Sacred Scripture. As such, their purpose is never to lead us away from Scripture, nor to summarize the Scriptures in such a way as to make their further study unnecessary. They are written to lead us *into* the Scriptures. This is exactly what their function has been in the history of the church, whether we think of the many commentaries written on the early creeds by the church fathers or the expositions of our Confessions by the reformers and their successors. The reader will therefore notice that the present work in dogmatics engages in much more direct and extensive exegesis than other works in dogmatic theology of our day, except the immense *Church Dogmatics* by Karl Barth. This is altogether proper and called for in a confessional Lutheran dogmatics text.

The present work is a kind of *loci communes*, the recapitulation of the main themes of Scripture on the basis of the confessional Lutheran outline and pattern of thought. The Lutheran Confessions themselves never claim to be the final work on the understanding and exegesis of the Scriptures; we recall Luther's statement on *oratio, meditatio, tentatio*[4] with its blasts against theological know-it-alls and how often this statement of Luther's was repeated by the post-Reformation theologians in their dogmatics works. The Confessions always lead deeper into the Scriptures, especially as new issues arise in new cultures and succeeding generations which must be faced only with theology drawn from the Scriptures and patterned after the Lutheran Confessions.

The volumes in this series are dedicated to Francis Pieper, a great confessional Lutheran dogmatician of our church, in the hope and prayer that they will help to achieve what he did so much to accomplish in his day—namely, doctrinal unity and consensus in the doctrine of the Gospel and all its articles among all Lutherans and a firm confessional Lutheran identity so sorely needed in our day.

4. *Preface to the Wittenberg Edition of Luther's German Writings*, 1539 (AE 34:285; WA 50:659.4).

PREFACE

A number of years ago at the symposium for the pastors of the Evangelical Lutheran Church of Kenya (ELCK) at Matongo Lutheran Seminary in Kenya, the Executive Director of the Luther Academy approached me to ask whether I had any interest in taking on the project to write the volume on anthropology and sin for the Confessional Lutheran Dogmatics series. After accepting his offer, I immediately delved into the material, reading, gathering and sorting data, writing, speaking, and teaching on this subject. Now the volume has finally come to completion, and thanks are due to many people who accompanied me on this path and who have been instrumental in helping me produce this volume. First, however, I should briefly explain the structure and purpose of this book.

As the late Robert Preus points out in his General Introduction, the volumes of the Confessional Lutheran Dogmatics series are to be "patterned strictly after the theology of the Book of Concord as they address the issues of today" (ix). I have tried to accomplish that purpose. This book accordingly is not a repetition of previous systematic treatments of anthropology and sin. Standard presentations abound. This volume is also not focused wholly on contemporary concerns. Its purpose lies somewhere in between. It draws from traditional information, particular the Lutheran Confessions, but also integrates into the discussion contemporary issues and alternative theological perspectives. I thus present an anthropology that goes beyond what students of theology usually encounter in traditional dogmatics texts. For as this project progressed, I realized that in the light of contemporary theological discussions on the status of humans, there is an urgent need for us to revisit what it means to be human. While the traditional two-pronged foci remain central to theological anthropology—sin's impact on humanity and then the solution found through Christ's redemption and one's justification—we must also draw in other important issues that are crucial and require clarification. What continually surface today are not only the traditional hot-button topics on the origin of humans, their relationship with one another, and their status with relation to the rest of creation, but also issues relating to the human self, one's identity, personhood, and structure. Discussions on human identity elicit strong emotional reactions; they have become contentious and divisive in all spheres of life, in the social, cultural, and political arenas. Christians are not immune to these external influences, and so they need to (re)conceptualize theological anthropology in order to understand who they are and how to live out their daily lives with others in today's context. Theology must not remain silent in the public discourse on what defines human beings; it can and should speak to all realms of human life, as Martin Luther has done in the Large Catechism's explanations on the three articles of the Apostles' Creed, and as this volume explores further. Theological anthropology has to do with one's relation to God, to the neighbor, to the environment, and lastly to the self. For human beings are exceptional in this world, created by God, and exist as conscious beings, each endowed with a particular personality and actively engaging his own subjective self, other humans, and the material environment.[1]

To that end, the reader will notice three themes or parts: first, the status given to humans at creation, or the relationship with God; second, the downfall which depicts the loss of that status, or the loss of the relationship with God, which then is corrected through Jesus Christ, the Son of God; third, the restored relationship as viewed from a functional perspective, or the relationship with the world—those *coram Deo* relations with the creator God, with spouse, family, creation, government, and the self. Here a description of this restored relationship does not rely on a static definition but draws out humans' engagement as stewards of this world.

When I took on this project for the Confessional Lutheran Dogmatics series, little was I aware of the vast literature on the subject of anthropology, even excluding treatments of cultural anthropology. Thus, for me the selection, sorting, and exclusion of information became one of the most challenging tasks in this project. Not everything that could be said on the subject is included in this volume. It is my hope, however, that readers will discover many things of value in this volume and will reach the conclusion after studying the material that the Lutheran narrative on what it means to be human is both biblically founded and relevant for today.

The testing field to which I first exposed my findings was pastors, who at various conferences gave valuable feedback and insights into their own struggles at the parish level. To me it became evident that the question "Who is man?" is not a speculative or cerebral topic but is fundamentally connected to the realities and struggles of everyday life resulting from the ever-present force called sin. As God's created beings, humans are capable of doing a lot of good, but they are just as much able to cause their own downfall and that of others. In that context, God's Word does not promise a world of utopian dimensions but rather one of redemption and forgiveness. Thus, "getting it wrong" in the area of anthropology—describing humans in an unrealistically optimistic light—compromises the gifted character of the Gospel. My interaction with pastors, colleagues, and friends, too many to mention here by name, has enabled me to add, remove, and reformulate the material along the way. I want to thank all of

1. Even sociologists such as Christian Smith and philosophers such as Mortimer Adler who do not take a deliberate theological line in their treatments on anthropology have committed themselves to an exceptional status of humans. See Christian Smith, *What Is a Person? Rethinking Humanity, Social Life, and the Moral Good from the Person Up* (Chicago and London: The University of Chicago Press, 2010), and Mortimer J. Adler, *The Difference of Man and the Difference It Makes* (1967; reprint New York: Fordham University Press, 1993).

them, including all the students who in the classroom and through independent studies opened for me the forum to teach and discuss this subject matter more deeply.

A special thanks goes to Pastor Tom Sabel, who in spite of his pastoral commitments volunteered to read and critique the manuscript. A final thanks to Jennifer Maxfield, the final editor, under whose close watch this volume received its present form. Her guidance and assistance have been invaluable.

Klaus Detlev Schulz
Ft. Wayne, Indiana
12 June 2023

ABBREVIATIONS

References to versions of the Bible:

LXX	Septuagint
NIV	New International Version

References to the Book of Concord:

AC	Augsburg Confession
Ap.	Apology of the Augsburg Confession
SA	Smalcald Articles
LC	Large Catechism
SC	Small Catechism
FC	Formula of Concord
	Ep. Epitome of the Formula of Concord
	SD Solid Declaration of the Formula of Concord
	RN Rule and Norm of the SD

References to the editions and translations of the Book of Concord:

K-W *The Book of Concord: The Confessions of the Evangelical Lutheran Church*. Edited by Robert Kolb and Timothy J. Wengert. Minneapolis: Fortress Press, 2000.

References to the Book of Concord are to the confession, article, and paragraph number.

References to Luther's works:

WA	*D. Martin Luthers Werke. Kritische Gesamtausgabe*. 69 vols. Weimar: Hermann Böhlaus Nachfolger, 1883–1993.
WABr	*D. Martin Luthers Werke. Briefwechsel*. 15 vols. Weimar: Hermann Böhlaus Nachfolger, 1930–78.
WADB	*D. Martin Luthers Werke. Deutsche Bibel*. 12 vols. Weimar: Hermann Böhlaus Nachfolger, 1906–61.
WATr	*D. Martin Luthers Werke. Tischreden*. 6 vols. Weimar: Hermann Böhlaus Nachfolger, 1912–21.
AE	*Luther's Works*. American Edition. 82 vols. Edited by Jaroslav Jan Pelikan, Hilton C. Oswald, Helmut T. Lehmann, and Christopher Boyd Brown. St. Louis: Concordia Publishing House, 1955–86.

Other references:

ANF *The Ante-Nicene Fathers: The Writings of the Fathers Down to A.D. 325*. Edited by Alexander Roberts and James Donaldson, 10 vols. Peabody, MA: Hendrickson Publishers, 1994.

BWA *The Basic Works of Aristotle*. Edited by Richard McKeon. New York: The Modern Library, 2001.

LSB *Lutheran Service Book*. Prepared by the Commission on Worship of The Lutheran Church—Missouri Synod. St. Louis: Concordia Publishing House, 2006.

NPNFa *Nicene and Post-Nicene Fathers*. 14 vols. First Series, edited by Philip Schaff. Peabody, MA: Hendrickson Publishers, 2004.

NPNFb *Nicene and Post-Nicene Fathers*. 14 vols. Second Series, edited by Philip Schaff and William Wace. Peabody, MA: Hendrickson Publishers, 2004.

WSA *The Works of Saint Augustine: A Translation for the 21st Century*. Edited by John E. Rotelle. Hyde Park, NY: New City Press, 1990–.

PART ONE

HUMAN EXISTENCE UNDER GOD

1

THE QUEST FOR A NORMATIVE ANTHROPOLOGY

NAVIGATING THE VIEWS OF MAN

For as long as humanity has existed, philosophers and theologians have thought, debated, and written about human origins, purpose and destiny. Dietrich Bonhoeffer explored his own identity with the famous question "Who am I?" while in Tegel Prison. The answer he discovered is that identity is found not in the opinions of other people or in what he makes himself out to be, but rather in an external source: "Whoever I am, thou knowest, O God, I am Thine."[1]

The theologian Jürgen Moltmann posits that questions about one's identity are unique to humans:

> A cow is always simply a cow. It does not ask, "What is a cow? Who am I?" Only man asks such questions, and indeed clearly has to ask them about himself and his being. This is his question. His question follows him in hundreds of forms.[2]

Today, multiple narratives describing humans exist. The biblical and theological account lies alongside alternative sources stemming from philosophy, medical sciences, and social sciences. For those who are guided by theology, this profusion of sources means that prevailing descriptions of humans are indeterminate, or at best offer only a part of the whole, a *pars pro toto*. The philosopher and anthropologist Max Scheler (1874–1928) touched on this very issue of multiple parallel interpretations in 1927 in his lecture "The Human Place in the Cosmos":

> Ask an educated European today what his thoughts are when one uses the term "human being" [*der Mensch*], and he will just about always find three irreconcilable ideas about the term, which are in continuous conflict with each other.
>
> 1. There is the thought of the Jewish-Christian tradition about Adam and Eve, and of creation.
>
> 2. There is the thought stemming from the ancient Greeks when the human being's consciousness of himself raised him for the first time into a special place, realizing that the human being is what he is through his possession of what is variably called "reason," *logos*, *phronesis*, *ratio*, *mens*—"logos" meaning here the possession of speech as well as the ability to grasp the "what" of each and every entity. Closely connected with this view is the theory that there is also a reason

1. Dietrich Bonhoeffer, *Letters and Papers from Prison*, ed. Eberhard Bethge, trans. Reginald Fuller et al., First Touchstone ed. (New York: Simon and Schuster, 1997), 347–48.

2. Jürgen Moltmann, *Man: Christian Anthropology in the Conflicts of the Present*, trans. John Sturdy (London: SPCK, 1974), 1.

> above the human being that underlies the whole universe and with which the human being alone is in a state of participation.
>
> 3. There is the thought of natural science and genetic psychology, today already a tradition. According to this theory, the human being represents a late stage in the evolution of our planet. He distinguishes himself only by degrees of complexity of the energies and abilities that he has inherited from ancestors in the animal world and that are found in subhuman nature.
>
> These three ideas lack any underlying unity which could provide us with a common foundation. Thus, we have a theological, philosophical, and a scientific anthropology before us but which, as it were, have no concerns with each other: *yet we do not have one uniform idea of the human being.* The ever-growing number of special disciplines which deal with the human being conceal, rather than reveal, his nature, no matter how valuable these disciplines may be. Furthermore, the said three ideas are severely shaken today, especially Darwin's solution of the origin of the human being. Hence, one can say that in no historical era has the human being become so much of a problem to himself as in ours.[3]

These three accounts demonstrate that the interpretation of what it means to be human is diverse, and each offers a distinct view of the status of humans. The widely published German theologian Helmut Thielicke addresses this issue in *Being Human—Becoming Human.*[4] He observes that over the last few centuries three humblings or humiliations of man have occurred: cosmological, biological, and psychological. In the cosmological sense, the astronomer Nicolaus Copernicus (along with Johannes Kepler) was responsible "when he showed that the earth and humanity are not the center of the universe. He forced upon us the startling insight that we are an insignificant marginal phenomenon, mere dust set on a particle of dust."[5] Biologically, the natural historian Charles Darwin "brought the second humbling when with his theory of evolution he demonstrated our animal ancestry,"[6] for with that claim humans lost the privilege of being special, created in the likeness of God, and instead assume the status of mere "higher animals." The third, psychological humbling was caused by Freud, "for he had made it plain to us that from the root up we are not under the control of the self and its will but of a complex of subconscious impulses."[7]

---

3. Max Scheler, *The Human Place in the Cosmos*, trans. Manfred S. Frings (Evanston, IL: Northwestern University Press, 2009), 5. Emphasis original.

4. Helmut Thielicke, *Being Human—Becoming Human: An Essay in Christian Anthropology*, trans. Geoffrey W. Bromiley (Garden City, NY: Doubleday & Company, 1984), 29. Thielicke cites Sigmund Freud as having made this observation first.

5. Thielicke, *Being Human—Becoming Human*, 29. Similarly, Ian G. Barbour on Galileo's impact on man's status: "Galileo's metaphysics left man a stranger in the universe of particles-in-motion which was increasingly taken to be the real world." Ian G. Barbour, *Issues in Science and Religion* (Englewood Cliffs, NJ: Prentice-Hall, 1966), 33–34.

6. Thielicke, *Being Human—Becoming Human*, 29: "This seemed to demand the conclusion that we are no longer privileged as compared with the animal kingdom, that we no longer enjoy the prerogative of divine likeness, but that we have to regard ourselves as higher animals."

7. Thielicke, *Being Human—Becoming Human*, 29.

Since philosophy, neuroscience, psychology, and other social sciences have entered the debate, theological anthropology must now respond both critically and constructively. Within this ongoing debate the pluralistic horizon keeps expanding. The previous generation of theologians, like Karl Barth, Werner Elert, Paul Althaus, and Paul Tillich, were attuned to what was presented on anthropology in the world around them, and each offered his own responses.[8] This conversation remains important, even pivotal. The theological account, unlike all the contemporary sciences relating to anthropology, engages a universal and unchanging truth delivered to humanity via revelation and not through empirical observation alone. Theology thus represents a unique stance in that discussion, as the Italian Renaissance philosopher Giovanni Pico della Mirandola (1463–94) in *Oration on the Dignity of Man* reminds us:

> Natural philosophy, therefore, cannot assure us a true and unshakable peace. To bestow such peace is rather the privilege and office of the queen of the sciences, most holy theology. Natural philosophy will at best point out the way to theology and even accompany us along the path, while theology, seeing us from afar hastening to draw close to her, will call out: "Come unto me you who are spent in labor and I will restore you; come to me and I will give you the peace which the world and nature cannot give."[9]

Anthropology is the Enlightenment's birth child, a child which began a noticeable and irreversible trend: humans have created for themselves a field of study in its own right, in which they strive for independence from God.[10] Consequently, the prospect of engaging the public with a theological and biblical understanding of humanity finds only limited acceptance. Particularly alarming are perspectives on gender and sex, and on ethics and morality, that no longer embrace revelatory truths about humans.[11] Instead, the apotheosis of humanity in this field—a striving for autonomy, rights, and freedom—provides a blanket endorsement for humans to fashion their existence in the limitless pursuit of their own dreams and desires. Toward that goal, no one and no organization should posit caution, set limits, or suggest humanity's potential for failure. The biblical worldview, however, expresses precisely such a caution by referring all humans to someone outside of themselves, that is, their Creator, not only for accountability but also for dignity and value which are bestowed on each human. In other words, theology engages the metaphysical reality or the a priori facts, namely that God exists, and the Christological dimension of a

8. Albrecht Peters, *Der Mensch* (Gütersloh: Gütersloher Verlagshaus Mohn, 1979), 21.

9. Giovanni Pico della Mirandola, *Oration on the Dignity of Man*, trans. Robert Caponigri (Chicago: Henry Regnery Company, 1956), 21.

10. John Monaghan and Peter Just, *Social and Cultural Anthropology: A Very Short Introduction* (Oxford, UK: Oxford University Press, 2000), 1.

11. On 27 June 2015 the Supreme Court, in the case *Obergefell v. Hodges*, ruled by a 5–4 margin in favor of same-sex marriage nationwide. For an explanation of the developments leading up to that decision, see David Von Drehle, "How Gay Marriage Won," *Time*, 8 April 2013, 18–24.

human's identity. This reality serves as the foundational and definitive premise for theological anthropology.

The church has a missionary obligation to demonstrate that the answers given from outside the biblical narrative about the identity of humans are inconclusive and limited. What appears to others an antiquated story is a timely and truthful alternative response to those seeking life's meaning and purpose.[12] Where the world either elevates a human's status to god or angel or reduces him to a mere animal, theology does more than navigate between the Scylla and Charybdis of an unrealistic optimism on the one hand and a nihilistic shadow cast over human existence on the other. The biblical worldview offers a realistic, sobering, and hopeful understanding of a meaningful dependency on the triune God.

Our culture's pluralism entertains multiple accounts of human identity as equally true. This lack of a common story that would provide normative standards is disturbing to many. This is so for three apparent reasons. First, humans generally long for a normative and comprehensive account, a base from which they can assess themselves and judge others. Often humans express assumed values about something that is ethically unacceptable with exclamations such as "That is inhumane!" This is a natural reaction even if the source of such normativity is unclear.[13] Second, human beings are social beings and therefore live as individuals together with others. Aristotle's definition of a human being as a social or political being is a truthful depiction of most humans, other than those who deliberately choose a life of isolation from others.[14] Within communities humans seek to establish common standards that bring individuals together and allow them to coexist peacefully. Third, leaving humans as an undefined group or vague mass does not satisfy those who pursue a coherence theory that assumes it should be possible to define human life within some reasonable, specified set of sentences, propositions, or beliefs rationally acceptable to all—for such coherence will never exist. This frustration echoes Francis Schaeffer's "line of despair" in *The God Who Is There* (1968), which maintains that Western culture's loss of absolutes can be remedied only through a return to a belief in the absolute God of Christianity.[15] The American

12. Here apologists step to the fore, attempting to make a difference in the public discourse by arguing the reasonableness of faith and the absurdity of a life without God. See Alister E McGrath, *Mere Apologetics: How to Help Seekers and Skeptics Find Faith* (Grand Rapids: Baker Books, 2012), 93ff.; William Lane Craig, *Reasonable Faith: Christian Truth and Apologetics* (Wheaton, IL: Crossway Books, 2008), 65–88.

13. An opening point of discussion for C. S. Lewis, *Mere Christianity* (New York: HarperCollins, 2000), 3–8.

14. "Man is by nature a political animal. And he who by nature and not by mere accident is without a state, is either a bad man or above humanity." Aristotle, *Politics* 1.2.1253a3, trans. Benjamin Jowett, in *The Basic Works of Aristotle*, ed. Richard McKeon (New York: The Modern Library, 2001), 1129 (hereafter cited as BWA).

15. Francis A. Schaeffer, *The God Who Is There: Speaking Historic Christianity into the Twentieth Century* (Chicago: InterVarsity Press, 1968), 43.

theologian and ethicist Reinhold Niebuhr in *The Nature and Destiny of Man* also calls for a Christian narrative that offers a logical account "against the constant peril of confusing admixtures from other, partially contradictory, views of man."[16]

THE MISERY OF A LIFE WITHOUT GOD

From the perspective of theology, a life without God is inconceivable and impossible. The only correct understanding of human life and practice is one that affirms an existence under God. Thus, the alternative proposal that there is a life without God is treated in Scripture as absurd, for it lacks ultimate meaning; it has no ultimate value and no ultimate purpose. The Christian philosopher Blaise Pascal (1623–62) describes in his *Pensées* the misery of a life without God and the happiness of man with God. The nineteenth-century Russian writer Fyodor Dostoyevsky (1821–81) echoes a similar thought in his novels *Crime and Punishment* and *The Brothers Karamazov*,[17] demonstrating that a life without God ends in complete relativism. Pascal's observations still ring true for the life of many people today:

> On this point, therefore, we condemn those who live without thought of the ultimate end of life, who let themselves be guided by their own inclinations and their own pleasures without reflection and without concern, and, as if they could annihilate eternity by turning away their thought from it, think only of making themselves happy for the moment.[18]

In a post-theistic or "post-Christian" context, alternative "-isms" and "-ologies" prevail, all of which dismiss the human relation to the universal foundation in which God assumes the definitive role. The attempt to isolate human existence from God and universal destiny represents the tragedy or pathos of human existence. The Old Testament accounts of Babel and Sodom and Gomorrah reflect that tragedy, and in the history of secular literature pathetic antiheroes abound, like Oedipus of the Greek tragedies or the protagonists of American playwright Arthur Miller (*Death of a Salesman*) and French philosopher and author Albert Camus (*The Stranger*).[19] In the end, human tragedy culminates in hubris (self-pride), which drives a person toward self-determination and away from outside authorities, especially from God.

16. Reinhold Niebuhr, *The Nature and Destiny of Man: A Christian Interpretation* (New York: Charles Scribner's Sons, 1964), 1:150–51.

17. Fyodor Dostoevsky, *Crime and Punishment*, trans. Constance Garnett (New York: Random House, 1956); Fyodor Dostoyevsky, *The Brothers Karamazov*, trans. Constance Garnett (Chicago: Encyclopædia Britannica, 1955).

18. "Pensées. Fragment 195," in Blaise Pascal, *Pensées. The Provincial Letters*, trans. W. F. Trotter (New York: The Modern Library, 1941), 72.

19. Arthur Miller, *Death of a Salesman: Certain Private Conversations in Two Acts and a Requiem* (New York: Viking Press, 1958); Albert Camus, *The Stranger*, trans. Stuart Gilbert (New York: Vintage Books, 1946).

This trajectory brings to mind Luther's description of the human as someone who is curved in on himself (*homo incurvatus in se*) instead of being focused outwardly toward his Creator and fellow humans.[20]

A life of incurvature, which dismisses one's createdness from the hands of God and shuns a destiny molded and guided under Him, has disastrous consequences for human existence, society, and culture.[21] Two terms in theology are particularly useful to defining human life under God. One is the destiny (*Bestimmung*) God has marked out for humans and the other is the relationship (*Beziehung*) He has with them.[22] Already in his *Outlines of a Philosophy of the History of Man* the philosopher Johann Gottfried Herder places humans on a forward path, stating that "we are not yet men, but are daily *becoming* so."[23] Wolfhart Pannenberg identifies Herder as the watershed figure in philosophical anthropology for articulating this eschatological perspective that places humanity's destiny in its outward focus to the outside world in anticipation of interacting with events in history, and finally in the end with God.[24]

Humanity's destiny and relationship with God may not be forgotten, and for this reason Christian philosophers and theologians have stepped up to defend Christianity's point of view. The Danish existentialist Søren Kierkegaard (1813–55) argues for a life under God by dismissing alternative approaches as hopeless and meaningless. He advances this point by describing three stages in which life can be and commonly is structured among humans: the aesthetic stage, the ethical stage, and the religious stage. For Kierkegaard only the last stage arranges life sensibly and properly. In the aesthetic stage, human life is focused on bringing instantaneous pleasure to the self. This pursuit through the senses for material things or experiences provides little meaning and no long-lasting satisfaction.[25] In the ethical stage, a human pursues doing good and attempts to conform to objective or universal standards of the good. But in this approach, as with the first, life is incomplete and leads in the end to guilt and despair. "For the more one tries sincerely to bring one's life into conformity with the objective standards of the good, the more painfully aware one is that one cannot do it," argues Kierkegaard.[26] Only the third stage, the religious stage, offers a fulfilled life within a personal relationship with God

20. We shall return to this point in chapter 9, under "The *Homo incurvatus in se*."

21. See here Craig, *Reasonable Faith*, 65–90.

22. These terms are used heavily in Pannenberg's anthropology and therefore worth noting. Wolfhart Pannenberg, *Anthropology in Theological Perspective*, trans. Matthew J. O'Connell (Philadelphia: Westminster Press, 1985), 45.

23. Johann Gottfried Herder, *Outlines of a Philosophy of the History of Man*, trans. T. Churchill (New York: Bergman Publishers, 1966), 229.

24. Pannenberg, *Anthropology in Theological Perspective*, 45.

25. "The self-centered, aesthetic man finds no ultimate meaning in life and no true satisfaction. Thus, the aesthetic life finally leads to boredom, a sort of sickness with life." Søren Kierkegaard, *Either/Or: A Fragment of Life*, trans. David F. Swenson and Lillian Marvin Swenson (Princeton: Princeton University Press, 1944), 1:69.

26. Kierkegaard, *Either/Or* 1:70. The ethical stage is also described in volume 2 of *Either/Or*.

and therein finds forgiveness of sins. Abraham was such a person who moved from the ethical stage to the religious stage, recognizing that the relationship with God requires more than a cognitive act or ethical decision but an actual "leap of faith," which leads to a life of total dependency on God.[27] Thus, all the good things we love in life, which in Abraham's life are represented by his love for Isaac, are qualified and defined "not from the mere fact that they exist and can be valued, enjoyed, delighted in, but from the source of existence itself."[28] In affirming and committing himself to the source of all good things in life, namely God, and renouncing his love for Isaac, Abraham goes through infinite resignation and rises as the knight of faith.[29]

Many like Kierkegaard have defended the Christian faith in their own ways to argue for an existence under God, and to warn of the disastrous consequences of a life without God. Aleksandr Solzhenitsyn spoke critically of the West's blindly following the ideals of a "despiritualized and irreligious" humanism and the Enlightenment at his 1978 Harvard Laureate Award speech, entitled *A World Split Apart*.[30] After fleeing from Nazi Germany to Paris in 1938, the Jewish-Christian author Franz Werfel gave a presentation entitled "Without Divinity, No Humanity" (*Ohne Divinität, keine Humanität*). His message expressed a similar concern, that when humans dismiss God's presence from their lives, when they take God's actions into their own hands, and when they exist without knowledge of Him, they are in danger of losing their humanity.[31]

27. Craig, *Reasonable Faith*, 69–70. The "leap of faith" is a term scholars ascribe to Kierkegaard's description of Abraham's faith, which according to Kierkegaard "admits the impossibility and at the same time believes the absurd." Søren Kierkegaard, *Fear and Trembling*, trans. Alastair Hannay (Harmondsworth, England: Penguin Books, 1985), 77.

28. Alastair Hannay, "Introduction," in Kierkegaard, *Fear and Trembling*, 21.

29. Kierkegaard, *Fear and Trembling*, 75.

30. "There is a disaster, however, which has already been under way for quite some time. I am referring to the calamity of a despiritualized and irreligious humanistic consciousness. To such consciousness, man is the touchstone in judging everything on earth—imperfect man, who is never free of pride, self-interest, envy, vanity, and dozens of other defects. We are now experiencing the consequences of mistakes which had not been noticed at the beginning of the journey." Aleksandr Solzhenitsyn, *A World Split Apart: Commencement Address Delivered at Harvard University, June 8, 1978*, trans. Irina Ilovayskaya Alberti (New York: Harper & Row, 1978), 52.

31. Alma Mahler-Werfel, *Mein Leben* (Frankfurt/M: Fischer Verlag, 1960), 289–94.

2

EXAMINING THE LIFE LIVED UNDER GOD

THEOLOGICAL STRUCTURES AND SCHEMES

Specialized approaches to anthropology developed only after the Reformation and the time of Martin Luther. Luther was aware of multiple perspectives on the nature of man, however. First, a philosopher such as Aristotle approaches the matter from nature: "philosophy or human wisdom defines man as an animal having reason, sensation, and body."[1] Second, a lawyer looks at man as a being with possessions and as lord of his fortunes. Third, a medical doctor sees man from the point of view of health or illness.[2] Luther realized that, depending on the field of expertise and the relationships in which man finds himself, different perspectives and discussions are offered on who man is. Because of these approaches, Luther posited that while it is possible to speak of "different truths," some truths are contradictory.[3]

Luther and the reformers entered that dialogue with their own contributions toward a theological anthropology. They treated the theological subject of anthropology as a separate locus prior to soteriology in order to extol the work of Christ as the solution to a problem. In a lecture on Psalm 51 Luther discussed the proper subject of theology, which "is man guilty of sin and condemned, and God the Justifier and Savior of man the sinner. Whatever is asked or discussed in theology outside this subject, is error and poison."[4] The problem or tragedy is that man, whom God created, succumbed to temptation, failed to fulfill God's will, and was thus rejected by his Creator. Since then the relationship between God and humanity has been broken irreparably, as are also the relationships among humans themselves. Controlled by original sin and an incessant desire

1. *The Disputation Concerning Man*, 1536 (AE 34:133; WA 39/1:175.34–35). Aristotle, *On the Soul* 2.1.412a2–412b9, trans. J. A. Smith, BWA 554–55.

2. *Commentary on Psalm 51*, 1532 (AE 12:310; WA 40/2:328.15–16). *Die Promotions Disputation von Palladius und Tilemann*, 1537 (WA 39/1:231.1–33.40); Peters, *Der Mensch*, 30.

3. "Denique aliquid est verum in una parte philosophiae, quod tamen falsum est in alia parte philosophiae" (While something is correct in one part of philosophy, it, however, is false in another part of philosophy). Thesis 36 in *Die Disputation de sententia: Verbum caro factum est (Joh. 1,14)*, 1539 (WA 39/2:5.27–28).

4. *Commentary on Psalm 51*, 1532 (AE 12:311; WA 40/2:328.17–20). Luther's motivation for clarity is evident: "We cannot tolerate these purely pagan teachings, because, if these teachings were right, then Christ has died in vain." SA III.i.11; Robert Kolb and Timothy J. Wengert, eds., *The Book of Concord: The Confessions of the Evangelical Lutheran Church* (Minneapolis: Fortress Press, 2000), 311 (hereafter cited as K-W).

to do what is undesirable in the eyes of God, the human's only solution now is to submit himself entirely to the gracious and salvific will revealed in Christ, who on the cross earned for all of humanity true and eternal life. Thus, in addressing who a human being is, one cannot merely go back to his creation. Rather, one must look forward to Christ and eschatology. True humanity and destiny, temporal and eternal, are Christologically defined.

The generation of Lutheran theologians after Luther made anthropology an important topic (*locus*) in their systematic treatments on theology. In *The Theology of Post-Reformation Lutheranism* Robert Preus points out that post-Reformation Lutheranism discusses anthropology under the following topics: (1) the image of God; (2) the freedom of the will; (3) the constitution of a human (dichotomy as opposed to trichotomy); (4) the origin of the soul (traducianism as opposed to creationism); (5) the immortality of the soul (that a human does not perish like an animal but has an existence after death); and (6) the state of the soul after death (blissful fellowship with God rather than soul sleep, purgatory, and so on). The topic of sin (hamartiology) is treated as a special locus, usually after the themes on anthropology.[5] In the broader scheme of theology, anthropology and hamartiology take their respective places after theology, or the discussion of who God is, and before soteriology, or how God saves the sinful human.

Theology →	Anthropology →	Hamartiology →	Soteriology
Who God is	Who man is	What sin is	How God saves sinful man

Such themes remain crucial in the theological quest to define anthropology.

From a Lutheran and Christian perspective, we posit four important theological constructs, each of which offers its own particular angle in answering who the human is and what a life under God is: the salvation history scheme, Law and Gospel, the trinitarian context, and the two kinds of righteousness.[6]

The Salvation History Scheme

The first description of humanity places it within God's salvific work in history. Beginning with creation and the Fall, salvation history proceeds to Abraham's special calling and the formation of the nation of Israel, the sending of Jesus Christ, the church—in which and through which God's salvific work continues through believers until the Lord's return—and the full revelation of His reign.[7] To highlight human existence in the context of God's salvation history, theologians traditionally have identified a number of stages. In *The*

5. Robert D. Preus, *The Theology of Post-Reformation Lutheranism*, vol. 2, *God and His Creation* (St. Louis: Concordia Publishing House, 1972), 189n70.

6. Hans-Martin Barth, *Dogmatik: Evangelischer Glaube im Kontext der Weltreligionen: Ein Lehrbuch* (Gütersloh: Christian Kaiser, Gütersloher Verlagshaus, 2001), 483–84.

7. See for example Peter Brunner, "Die Freiheit des Menschen in Gottes Heilsgeschichte," in Peter Brunner, *Pro Ecclesia*, vol. 1 (Berlin: Lutherisches Verlagshaus, 1962), 108–25.

Disputation Concerning Man (*Disputatio de homine*) from 1536,[8] particularly in Theses 21 through 23, Martin Luther divides human life into pre-Fall and post-Fall conditions. Then he notes two additional states, the state of grace in which one lives in a restored relationship with Christ through justification, and the fourth state, that of a life after death. In theological anthropology these four states have become the standard divisions among theologians, and they are, according to orthodox Lutheran theologian Johann Andreas Quenstedt (1617–88), the following:

(1) The primeval state of integrity (*status integritatis*) in which man found himself before the Fall;

(2) The state of corruption (*status corruptionis*) caused by the Fall;

(3) The state of grace (*status gratiae* or *status restorationis*), which is given through Jesus Christ to all who are baptized and converted here on earth;

(4) The state of glory (*status gloriae*) for all believers after death.[9]

Similarly, the Formula of Concord in describing the various spiritual states of man as related to the use of his free will provides the following description:

(1) The state of the will as originally created, before the Fall;

(2) The state of the free will of the unregenerate before conversion;

(3) The state of the free will of a human being after being reborn and ruled by the Holy Spirit;

(4) The state of the free will of a human being after arising from the dead.[10]

Within the state of integrity, the human being, unlike the rest of creation, is uniquely placed in a relationship with God. He was made after the image of God and this relationship with God is destined for "eternity." Juxtaposed between the image in the state of integrity and the eschatological focus on eternity, theology brings to the table information pertaining to the state of corruption. After the Fall Adam no longer had an eternal relationship with God and was subject to the power of the devil, sin, and death. Subjection under that fallen state is also eternal. Because man cannot free himself from that state, the only possibility for him to return to the state of integrity is to be freed by the Son, Jesus Christ. According to Luther that return occurs through justification, with reference to Paul (Rom 3:28): "We hold that a man is justified by faith apart from works" (Thesis 32).[11] Luther is saying that every human being lives not out of his own powers of achieving and accomplishing his own purpose, but rather by faith clinging to Christ, and only in that relationship can true destiny be found.[12] The

8. *The Disputation concerning Man*, 1536 (AE 34:139–41; WA 39/1:175–80).

9. Johann Andreas Quenstedt, *Theologia Didactico-Polemica, Sive, Systema Theologicum, In Duas Sectiones, Didacticam et Polemicam, Divisum* (Wittebergae: Johannis Ludolphi Quenstedii, 1701), II,1,1,1. Quenstedt offered also a fifth state, namely, the state of damnation (*status ignominiae aeternae seu damnationis*) for all unbelievers after death. Horst Georg Pöhlmann, *Abriß der Dogmatik: Ein Repetitorium*, 3d ed. (Gütersloh: Gütersloher Verlagshaus Gerd Mohn, 1980), 163.

10. SD II.2 (K-W, 543).

11. *The Disputation Concerning Man*, 1536 (AE 34:139; WA 39/1:176.34–35).

12. Wilfried Joest, *Ontologie der Person bei Luther* (Göttingen: Vandenhoeck & Ruprecht,

destiny or purpose of humanity, according to Luther, is clearly the relationship of a person with God through Christ. This could be said also of the image of God. In a teleological orientation, man's image finds fulfillment with God, the creator through Jesus Christ.[13]

Salvation history depicts the life of each human being progressing on a linear path. Humans have been given a destiny to pursue life on earth as God's "created co-creators."[14] Their existence is a temporal and spiritual one, and though humans are on the path of self-destruction, life under God's providential care proceeds toward a final conclusion, a restoration in Christ and life eternal. For many biologists, including those of the Darwinian bent, this scheme would prove unsatisfactory since no details are given describing each individual's biological origin and development history (ontogenesis) or the evolutionary theory of species (phylogenesis).[15] Instead, the outline relates a human being spiritually to the existence of God and addresses how that relationship plays out at a particular point in time.[16]

Law and Gospel

Key to Lutheran theology is that it connects anthropology to the distinction of Law and Gospel. This approach lets each see himself in his present condition from a dual perspective: under both the demand and the reprieve of God. God demands, but He also offers His own grace and favor (Jn 1:17; Rom 3:22–23; 2 Cor 3:6). On the one side, a human recognizes God's demand placed upon him yet fails to comply; on the other side, he is led to God's promise. In other words, failure revealed through the Law points to reprieve through the Gospel. In his *Lectures on Galatians* (1535)[17] Luther describes the true Christian outlook on human existence precisely in these categories. Here his efforts serve as a critique of earlier distinctions of theology. He begins by picking up the concepts of nature and grace as Augustine laid them out in his treatise *Nature and Grace* (415),[18] and proceeds to critique the medieval, merit-based scheme of Thomas Aquinas by distinguishing the epistemological categories of reason and revelation.[19] Luther presents his distinction of Law and Gospel as follows:

1967), 190.

13. Pannenberg, *Anthropology in Theological Perspective*, 123.

14. Carl E. Braaten and Robert W. Jenson, eds., *Christian Dogmatics* (Philadelphia: Fortress Press, 1984), 1:325.

15. Barth, *Dogmatik*, 483. The terms "ontogenesis" and "phylogenesis"were coined by the German biologist and professor Ernst Haeckel (1834–1919) in an attempt to embrace and discuss the Darwinian understanding of human genesis and development.

16. Barth, *Dogmatik*, 483.

17. *Lectures on Galatians*, 1535 (AE 26–27; WA 40/1:1–688).

18. *Nature and Grace*, trans. Roland J. Teske, in *The Works of Saint Augustine: A Translation for the 21st Century*, ed. John E. Rotelle (Hyde Park, NY: New City Press, 1997), 1.23:204–78.

19. See Jaroslav Pelikan, foreword to C. F. W. Walther, *The Proper Distinction between Law and Gospel: 39 Evening Lectures*, trans. W. H. T. Dau (St. Louis: Concordia Publishing House, 1986), xii.

> Now the true meaning of Christianity is this: that a man first acknowledge, through the Law, that he is a sinner, for whom it is impossible to perform any good work. . . . When a man is taught this way by the Law, he is frightened and humbled. Then he really sees the greatness of his sin, and finds in himself not one spark of the love of God; thus he justifies God in His Word and confesses that he deserves death and eternal damnation. Thus the first step in Christianity is the preaching of repentance and the knowledge of ourselves.
>
> The second step is this: If you want to be saved, your salvation does not come by works; but God has sent His only Son into the world that we might live through Him. He was crucified and died for you and bore your sins in His own body (1 Peter 2:24). . . . Therefore the Law only shows sin, terrifies and humbles; thus it prepares us for justification and drives us to Christ. . . . This briefly is our doctrine of Christian righteousness.[20]

On the surface level, the presentation of human life under the distinction of Law and Gospel appears to deliver a mechanical and unhistorical description of human existence. One gets the impression that it makes a blanket or universal statement on the human relationship with God without any distinctions or particularities of individual humans. That, however, is only half of the story. This is a true depiction of the human as he exists on earth, for it remains a description of every human, today and in the future. Therefore, Law and Gospel are not limited or excused by local conditions such as geography and culture. And yet this scheme presents God's dealings with the human in a very concrete way and unveils every human's particular predicament in that context and relationship with others. Applying Law and Gospel is thus not a mechanical procedure. Instead, this application reveals an inescapable reality for every human in his specific context and place in history. It thus takes hold, as Luther puts it, of a person's deeds and practice, that is, it grips his inner being of heart and conscience.[21]

Werner Elert, who places anthropology under the distinction of Law and Gospel, reiterates this insight, saying that "the most important matter is . . . that man knows during his life or death, that he has to justify himself before God, and that he understands the reason why Christ and He alone is his justification."[22] What appears mechanical is a personal discovery of who one is at a particular point in time and place. And if the nature of Law and Gospel comes across as sterile and mechanical, this problem must be attributed to preachers and

20. On Gal 2:16 in *Lectures on Galatians*, 1535 (AE 26:126–27; WA 40/1:223.29–25.1). For a comprehensive summary of Law and Gospel see Walther, *Proper Distinction between Law and Gospel*; C. F. W. Walther, *Law & Gospel: How to Read and Apply the Bible*, trans. Christian C. Tiews, ed. Charles P. Schaum, John P. Hellwege, Jr., and Thomas E. Manteufel (St. Louis: Concordia Publishing House, 2010).

21. *Lectures on Galatians*, 1535 (AE 26:117; WA 40/1:209.16–10.14–19). See also the sermon he preached 1 January 1532, on the distinction of Law and Gospel (Gal 3:23, 24), *Wie das Gesetz und Evangelion recht gründlich zu unterscheiden sind*, 1532 (WA 36:8–23).

22. Werner Elert, *The Christian Faith. An Outline of Lutheran Dogmatics*, trans. from 5th ed. by Martin H. Bertram and Walter R. Bouman (Columbus: Lutheran Theological Seminary, 1974), 29–30. See also Parts One and Two in Werner Elert, *The Structure of Lutheranism*, trans. Walter A. Hansen (St. Louis: Concordia Publishing House, 1962), 17–176.

theologians who in their sermons simply gloss over their audience's particular predicaments, failing to speak to their situation. The proper application of Law and Gospel also falls short of its purpose when the Law's negative diagnosis and indictment over human life dominates and the Gospel's positive light fails to shine. For this reason Walther argues that the Gospel must predominate in the preaching and teaching of God's Word.[23]

In the end, God's Word through Law and Gospel relates to human life by reflecting or highlighting common human experiences which some might have discovered on their own but never fully understood until Law and Gospel were applied. The concept of Kierkegaard's ethical stage recognizes that many humans are intent on fulfilling objective standards, even those they have set for themselves, yet end up in despair over their failure to realize these. This reality is uncovered so unwaveringly by the Law of God, which fact of course raises the question whether the Law places on man a demand that he is even potentially capable of fulfilling. Should a man fulfill God's demand to do good, he could conclude that he had reached the state of grace by virtue of his merits, independently, or partially apart from God's doing. Luther rules out this conclusion and posits the Law's function as always accusing the sinner (*lex semper accusat*), because, as Joest observes, "when it demands then its purpose is not to place man on the path of self-accomplishment and self-doing, but to reveal to him his sin and powerlessness."[24]

The Trinitarian Context

The third depiction of human life and existence under God is within a trinitarian context. This approach is best depicted in Martin Luther's Large and Small Catechisms, where the believer confesses his faith in the triune God and reflects upon His activity in all aspects of life:

> I believe that God has made me and all creatures; that He has given me my body and soul, eyes, ears, and all my members, my reason and all my senses, and still takes care of them. . . . I believe that Jesus Christ, true God, begotten of the Father from eternity, and also true man, born of the Virgin Mary, is my Lord . . . I believe that the Holy Spirit has called me by the Gospel, enlightened me with His gifts, sanctified and kept me in the true faith.[25]

In this context, every aspect of a believer's existence is connected to the outward economy of the triune God. The catechisms do not explain the ontological aspect of who a human is, nor do they relate to the salvation history perspective. However, they show the extent to which every aspect of life is

23. C. F. W. Walther indicates that concern in Thesis 25: "The Word of God is not rightly divided when the person teaching it does not allow the Gospel to have a general predominance in his teaching." Walther, *Proper Distinction between Law and Gospel*, 403.

24. Joest, *Ontologie der Person bei Luther*, 306.

25. Martin Luther, *Luther's Small Catechism with Explanation* (St. Louis: Concordia Publishing House, 1986), 105, 116, 144.

anchored in God's benevolent will toward humans to sustain, redeem, and preserve them all in body and soul. Humanity's entire existence is characterized by the cognitive and experiential knowledge of a dependency on God and being carried along by Him from whom "all blessings flow" and to whom he responds in praise.[26] To be truly human means to lead a life in faith under God, not in a self-centered way but responsive to the triune God as He supports the believer in all areas of his life.

The believer perceives his reality through each article of the creed. In the First Article he sees himself as a creation of God, from whom he receives all blessings and under whom he lives a responsible life in his vocation. Under the Second Article the believer attributes his salvation to the work of Jesus Christ and sees his life fashioned by the cross. In the Third Article he sees his entire life as dependent on the external means of God's delivery system, where in worship he receives the gifts through Word and Sacrament.

Some might argue that this approach focuses too much on the individual, as intimated in the first-person confession, "I believe . . ." This approach may end in subjectivism, even solipsism, if the believer sees only himself, elevated above the world, society, the church around him, and unbelievers.[27] But this danger is preempted by the key aspect of theological anthropology, which Luther affirms: every human is placed in a relationship not only to God but also to fellow humans. This second relational component is brought out already by the creation narrative: "It is not good for the man to be alone. I will make a helper suitable for him" (Gn 2:18). Theological anthropology must ward off individualistic and isolationist tendencies in its depiction of what it means to be human.

The Two Kinds of Righteousness

A fourth and final description or scheme laying out human existence under God and before the world, one which has received renewed popularity, is the two kinds of righteousness.[28] This scheme picks up a theme to which Luther often referred through his life. In his sermon on the *Two Kinds of Righteousness* (1519)[29] and then later in his *Lectures on Galatians* (1535),[30] to mention just two sources,[31] Luther points out that a human being must view his existence in terms of two relationships, one before God (*coram Deo*) and one before the world and people (*coram mundo* and *coram hominibus*).[32] Luther's intentions

26. LC II.19 (K-W, 433).

27. Barth, *Dogmatik*, 484.

28. Charles P. Arand and Joel D. Biermann, "Why the Two Kinds of Righteousness?" *Concordia Journal* 33, no. 2 (2007): 116–35.

29. *Two Kinds of Righteousness*, 1519 (AE 31:297–306; WA 2/2:145–52).

30. *Lectures on Galatians*, 1535 (AE 26:7; WA 40/1:1–688).

31. For a discussion of other sources in Luther, see Wilfried Härle, "Die Entfaltung der Rechtfertigungslehre Luthers in den Disputationen von 1535 bis 1537," *Lutherjahrbuch* 71 (2004): 211–28.

32. Wilhelm Maurer, *Historical Commentary on the Augsburg Confession*, trans. H. George

were to define these relationships in the context of righteousness. In terms of righteousness before God, a human being must regard himself as totally passive; toward the world, a believer may see himself as active in promoting righteousness in civil matters. This distinction structures itself along the lines of *sacramentum* (gift) and *exemplum* (example): the former has to do with receiving a gift through the Gospel, whereas in the latter one actively pursues God's Law. With this scheme Luther provides the believer a helpful lens through which to see and arrange his life equally around these two poles, not favoring one at the cost of the other.[33]

From the above we can see that the question "What therefore does it mean to be human?" is answered by theology in various ways. Nevertheless, all point humans toward a relationship with God and the neighbor. In so doing, each of these four approaches—salvation history, Law and Gospel, the trinitarian context, and the two kinds of righteousness—provides important insights into our human existence, who we are, and what our true destiny is. Therefore, we shall not abandon any of these four schemes but rather draw from them all as we continue.

THE STATUS OF HUMANS

In addition to schemes explaining a life lived under God, dogmatic treatments of theological anthropology must clarify humanity's status both in its relationship with the rest of creation and with God, in order to avoid a concentration on the human alone, known as anthropocentrism, even anthropomonism.[34] However, treating humans as merely a part of creation is to deny their special status and honor. Such a perspective makes it difficult to explain why a human's destruction should be of concern. The taking of human life would then seem to be as irrelevant as, or no more concerning than, the elimination of other life forms, even pathogenic agents. On the other hand, an unqualified elevation of humanity above creation easily can lead to an exploitation of creation, a reckless destruction of it, devoid of theological and ethical justification. Theological anthropology should address both concerns, speaking to the unity and diversity of all creation and marveling at how humans are an integral part of it all, while clarifying their special place and role within that unity without endorsing creation's exploitation.[35] We want to recognize both perspectives, and so we begin by connecting humans to the rest of creation.

Anderson (Philadelphia: Fortress Press, 1986), 89.

33. The Confessions follow Luther on this: SD II.32 (K-W, 567).

34. Some treatments have narrowed their study. For example, Francis Pieper, *Christian Dogmatics*, vol. 1 (St. Louis: Concordia Publishing House, 1950–57); Karl Barth, *Church Dogmatics*, 4 vols. in 12 parts, ed. G. W. Bromiley and T. F. Torrance (Edinburgh: T&T Clark, 1936–77), 3/2; Wilfried Härle, *Dogmatik* (Berlin: De Gruyter, 2000), 424–25.

35. See the statement *Together with All Creatures: Caring for God's Living Earth.* A Report of the Commission on Theology and Church Relations of The Lutheran Church—Missouri Synod (St. Louis: The Lutheran Church—Missouri Synod, 2010), 47–50.

Humans Have Much in Common with All Created Life

In the Nicene and Apostles' Creeds we confess the creation of heaven and earth (Gn 1:1). This confession acknowledges the spectrum of what God has created in both realms: grass, trees, the sun, the moon, stars, animals of the skies and the land, and finally man. Like the rest of nature, humans owe their existence to God. They are God's "offspring" (Acts 17:28), which implies that their origin is from God alone. Everything, both visible and invisible (Col 1:16), is united as God's creation, which He brought about either directly through His Word or through an act (Gn 1:3, 6, 14, 27; 2:7), or by telling one creature to bring forth another (Gn 1:11, 24; 2:9f.). God created all living things so that varied and different species fulfilled their specific roles. God expressed His satisfaction and approval over what He created by calling it "good" (טוֹב), which means perfect, in full agreement with His design and purpose. Being called "good" qualifies living things not merely for their existence but also for fulfilling the function of multiplying. All have one common purpose: to be fruitful and to pass on life. To that end, plants serve animals and humans as food (Gn 1:29f.) and animals serve humans as nourishment.[36] However, this functional service of creation, to exist as species for the survival of others, does not apply to humans. Human life may not be taken in order to serve other humans as nourishment. Humans alone have been created in the likeness of God (Gn 1:26), and for that reason their life may not be taken (Gn 9:5f.).

Likewise, inorganic materials such as light, water, and minerals serve plant life, and from there the food chain moves upward till it reaches humans.[37] But the process also occurs in reverse: not only at their death but by breathing and through their metabolism humans pass on nutrients from which other organisms live and grow. Humans thus have a reciprocal relationship with creation that proceeds not just up the food chain, from simpler organisms to more complex, but also moves "downward." This reciprocal bond reminds us that we have much in common with nature and are integrated into the broader process of life, which includes bodily decomposition, the chemical process that breaks down the main components of the body.[38] As the psalmist points out: "My days are like the evening shadow; I wither away like grass" (Ps 102:11).

In all the diversity and plurality of what has been created, humans have been placed in a field of creatureliness they share with other nonhuman life. In the Genesis account of creation (Genesis 1), God created animals and humans on the sixth day, giving both of them the "breath of life," a nephesh (נֶפֶשׁ). Humans are part of a greater nature and are subject to the broader process of existing and dying for the other, thereby safeguarding further existence. Physiologically and anatomically, man is an animal. He shares the genetic code with animals.

36. The fact that animals become food for humans is mentioned specifically after the Fall. It seems to be a consequence of sin. Be that as it may, eating meat remains a divinely supported function (Gn 9:3; Acts 10:12–13) and no one should be shamed for eating it (Rom 14:1–6).

37. LC II.14 (K-W), 432.

38. Härle, *Dogmatik*, 427.

Evolutionists would call him a human primate. That both humans and animals have the breath of life suggests a common attribute: they jointly possess, you could say, the "soul" of living creatures.[39] They share some psychic symptoms, such as anxiety and distress. We often forget this commonality between human and animal life.

An additional bond was established because of the reality of sin. The savagery and brutality seen in nature keeps us from romanticizing creation. We should see such a demonstration as the result of the curse spoken over Adam and Eve, so that the earth, according to Luther in his *Lectures on Genesis*, rewards man's toils with thorns and thistles[40] and women give birth under pain and the peril of death; and every new generation is raised with great labor and pain.[41] Once man ruled peacefully and without fear over the animal kingdom; now that rule has become a battle of cunning and abuse. The Fall affected all of creation negatively so that it groans "in hope that it [the creation itself] will be liberated from its bondage to decay" (Rom 8:21). However, humans' interaction with creation, along with their stewardship role over it, has become a mere shadow of what it was originally. Additionally, the free and unhindered relationship between the two human partners has turned into a relationship of lust and shame, where one rules and the other becomes the subject.[42] Murder entered human society and destroys relationships, resulting in God ruling with the sword.[43] In spite of all that, creation displays a splendor and grandeur at which we marvel, and which, according to the psalmist, should motivate us to praise and glorify God.[44]

In short, humans are part of created life and share with it a common creatureliness, and as humans we must come to terms with what this brings into our lives—our creatureliness itself and its mortality and limitations.[45] This reality raises a question—What is distinctive and unique to humans?—that theological anthropology must answer. Creatureliness alone is unable to provide intrinsic value and purpose to our humanity.[46] Humanity's telos must be found elsewhere, namely, in its connection to God. We may infer two points from the above discussion that will lead us forward. First, our relationship to nonhuman life is an asymmetrical one. Non-human life cannot relate with humans on equal terms or symmetrically, the way humans react to one another, as they lack faculties that are uniquely human, including the ability to use language and

39. Ray Sherman Anderson, *On Being Human: Essays in Theological Anthropology* (Eugene, OR: Wipf & Stock Publishers, 2010), 22.

40. *Lectures on Genesis*, 1535–45 (AE 1:205; WA 42/2:156.20–26).

41. *Lectures on Genesis*, 1535–45 (AE 1:198–202; WA 42/2:148.4–51.42).

42. *Lectures on Genesis*, 1535–45 (AE 1:198–202; WA 42/2:148.4–51.42).

43. *Lectures on Genesis*, 1535–45 (AE 2:142; WA 42/2:361.31–32): "But in the passage before us those who have the sword are commanded to use it against those who have shed blood." Peters, *Der Mensch*, 47.

44. E.g., Genesis 1; Job 38f.; Is 55:12; Mt 6:26–29. See Härle, *Dogmatik*, 429.

45. Anderson, *On Being Human*, 23.

46. Anderson, *On Being Human*, 25.

make choices.[47] We could say that humans make this assertion for themselves while acknowledging excellent communicative skills among animal life. Second, unlike the rest of creation, humans praise God actively, not only by their mere existence. The Genesis account of creation closes with the seventh day. This seventh day may provide a clue in our search for what makes humans distinct, for it calls humans to participate in a fellowship and relationship with God and have Him work on them through His Word. This role elevates humans above the creatureliness they have in common with nonhuman life. Humans are special in the eyes of God and have been endowed with the communicative skills through which they praise the benevolent Creator of all creation.[48]

Humans Are Special, Created by God, Yet Not God

After God had created everything else, He made man as the culmination of creation. Being last in line means not only that man stands apart from the rest of creation, but that everything before him was created for his sake. Lutherans in particular point out this anthropocentric interpretation of creation.[49] In Johann Gerhard's discussion of the biblical account of creation he refers to God's Word as authoritative for his theology of creation *ex nihilo*.[50] From Scripture we learn how God created the world, and in particular also the human, not in one moment but in six successive days, so that only after the *hexaemeron* was the world's creation, and that of the human, completed.

Theology must affirm the biblical account as God's revelation and therefore acquiesce to the counsel of God, Johann Gerhard advised, even when the depths of man and creation and the cause of the Fall transcend our own reasoning.[51] Based on this principle, Elert correctly affirms that human existence has a beginning *ex nihilo* through God's Word, the "calling-forth word of the creator," which would exclude a form of pre-existence for humans.[52]

By contrast, those who oppose the biblical narrative often do so because they see the biblical account of creation *ex nihilo* as a "science stopper," one that excludes all investigation into man's origins. Richard Lewontin's saying is representative: "If we let a divine foot in the door anything can happen—and science is doomed."[53] In response, we point to those scientists who combine their

47. Wilfried Härle, *Systematische Philosophie: Eine Einführung für Theologiestudenten* (Munich: Christian Kaiser Verlag, 1982), 212.

48. "It inevitably follows that we are in duty bound to love, praise, and thank him without ceasing." LC II.19 (K-W, 433); Anderson, *On Being Human*, 23.

49. Preus, *Theology of Post-Reformation Lutheranism* 2:189, who points to Johann Gerhard, *Loci Theologici* 11.9 (8–11:255). See Quenstedt, *Systema* I,12,1,511.

50. Johann Gerhard, *Theological Commonplaces*, trans. Richard J. Dinda, ed. Benjamin T. G. Mayes and Joshua J. Hayes (St. Louis: Concordia Publishing House, 2006–), 8.3.19 (8–11:16).

51. Gerhard, *Theological Commonplaces* 8.3 (8–11:9). Johann Gerhard was unwilling to depart from the literal sense: "But one must not depart from the letter." Gerhard, *Theological Commonplaces* 8.4.21 (8–11:17).

52. Elert, *Christian Faith*, 168.

53. Richard Lewontin, "Billions and Billions of Demons," 31.

data with their Christian affirmation of God as creator. Though Isaac Newton and Stephen Hawking studied the same subject, their findings prompted them to draw different conclusions. The same scientific data exist for all but are interpreted differently, largely according to one's presuppositions. The biblical account of *creatio ex nihilo* assumes a beginning for all life, including man. The maxim *ex nihilo nihil fit* (nothing is made from nothing) and the *kalām* cosmological syllogism, an argument now deployed by Christian apologists,[54] highlight that something that exists cannot have originated from nothing. This *ex nihilo* account thus invalidates the claim that something that exists as a part or piece of a universe can be the cause of that universe's existence. In other words, the sole cause of the universe is God, not the Big Bang argued via quantum gravity and physics or some pre-existing material.[55]

The classic texts for the argument that humans are God's creation and distinctly different from the rest of creation come from Gn 1:26–28 (30) and Gn 2:7–8, 15–25. Since God created humans, the biblical narrative rules out any thought that humans have produced themselves or are still undergoing a long sequence of evolutionary steps to become more human.[56] Many Christian theologians will attempt a conciliatory approach within this discussion by striking a balance or truce between evolution and creationism, stating that under God's watch and rule humans underwent the "evolutionary process" in which "God evolved them as co-creators."[57] The French philosopher Teilhard de Chardin (1881–1955), for example, wrote his famous piece *The Phenomenon of Man* in an attempt to reconcile his own Christian faith with paleontology and the theory of evolution by suggesting that through the evolutionary process

---

54. As far back as the ninth century *kalām* has represented the kind of Islamic scholastic theology that engages in apologetics to refute doubters and detractors of God's existence and those who doubt that He is the prime mover. For the Christian use of the *kalām* argument, see William Lane Craig, "Historical Statements of the *Kalām* Cosmological Argument," in *The* Kalām *Cosmological Argument* (Eugene, OR: Wipf & Stock Publishers, 2000), 1–50. This reasoning goes as follows: "1. What begins to exist has a cause; 2. The universe began to exist; 3. Therefore, the universe has a cause." See also Douglas R. Groothuis, *Christian Apologetics: A Comprehensive Case for Biblical Faith* (Downers Grove: IVP Academic, 2011), 214–302; Craig, *Reasonable Faith*, 111.

55. The attempts to deny God as cause refer to quantum physics, which dismisses the argument of causality or wishes causality to be understood loosely, based on the unpredictability of a subatom's coming about and location. Thus, the world is claimed to have come about without God through a Big Bang and not predictably and precisely through laws and mathematics. Paul Davies, a proponent of this position, thus symptomatically concludes: "To me, the true miracle of nature is to be found in the ingenious and unswerving lawfulness of the cosmos, a lawfulness that permits complex order to emerge from chaos, life to emerge from inanimate matter, and consciousness to emerge from life, without the need for the occasional supernatural prod." P. C. W. Davies, "Physics and the Mind of God: The Templeton Prize Address," *First Things* 55 (August 1995): 31–35.

56. God's special creation of man does not rule out the development of each kind or species within its own environment—microevolution or the process of adaptation of species—nor does it exclude extinction.

57. Braaten and Jenson, *Christian Dogmatics* 1:326.

humans leave behind their brutish nature.[58] Teilhard's position is representative of the approach of those theologians who allegorize the biblical account to allow for such a synthesis. But such a view cannot be reconciled with the fact that God created the first human parents *ex nihilo*. Neither can proponents concur with Francis Pieper that humans were created from the beginning "truly cultured, endowed not only with the ability of speech, but with an intelligence that, besides knowing God, had such a grasp of the natural sciences as is unattainable today even by the most diligent study."[59]

The creation of Adam and Eve is an act of God, who called something into being through His Word (Ps 33:9), and should be understood as *creatio immediata*, whereas we confess the continual creation of man thereafter as a creation that is mediated, *creatio mediata*.[60] The latter is indicated already in the biblical creation account: something created can bring forth something else, as God said, "Let the land produce vegetation . . ." (Gn 1:11). Similarly, now the ongoing creation of humans is attributed to a man and a woman who together bring forth another human. Nonetheless, this can happen only with God behind the process as the creator and originator. Divorced from God's creative powers, humans and all creation would be devoid of true cause and thus simply would not exist.[61] Thus we affirm two principles: first, creation still happens now; it is not limited to a time in the past. Second, the concept of creation must be applied to man and by extension to all of creation, even if his life seems to have begun "naturally" in time and can be explained by scientific observation. When Luther says "God has created me together with all that exists,"[62] he obviously knows that he, like all other humans, was conceived and born from natural parents. And certainly he knows that all the clothing and shoes, food and drink, house and property, wife and children—all these gifts from God also are produced naturally. The point is that, though we are capable of scientifically explaining the beginning of life down to the smallest detail, this ability does not change

58. He would say that creation "is still evolving and that mankind is changing with it until mankind reaches the ultimate point of consciousness; we are advancing in an interactive 'noosphere' (coming from the Greek νοῦς) of human thought through an evolutionary process that leads inexorably toward an Omega Point—Jesus Christ—that is pulling all the cosmos to itself." Pierre Teilhard de Chardin, *The Phenomenon of Man*, trans. Bernard Wall (New York: Harper & Row, 1961), 220. By accepting the concept of evolution and allegorizing the biblical account of creation, Teilhard got in trouble with the Roman Catholic Church. Interest in him is on the rise, according to David Gibson, "Jesuit Pierre Teilhard de Chardin's 'Conscious Evolution' Plays Role in American Nuns vs Vatican Debate," *Huffpost* (blog), 2 June 2014, https://www.huffpost.com/entry/teilhard-american-nuns_n_5374368.

59. Pieper, *Christian Dogmatics* 1:517.

60. Wilhelm Rohnert, *Die Dogmatik der evangelisch-lutherischen Kirche: Mit Berücksichtigung des Dogmengeschichtlichen zunächst den bekenntnistreuen Geistlichen und den Theologie-studierenden dargeboten* (Braunschweig: Wollermann, 1902), 195.

61. Härle, *Dogmatik*, 418–20.

62. SC II.2 (K-W, 354).

the fact that a higher origin, God, stands behind all creation and provides "out of pure, fatherly and divine goodness and mercy."[63]

The affirmation that God is creator also should bring the recognition of man's true purpose and destiny—how God desires him to be and for what purpose he was created. Implicit in this recognition is that humans are created and designed by God in such a way that their essential qualities are not subject to indefinite change. Nor can it be argued that human beings can be explained adequately according to the propensities and behaviors of lower animals. The theological difference hinges on the understanding that humans bear God's image and the rest of creation does not. Underscoring that humans are distinct from other animal life are profound attributes such as self-consciousness and the abilities to form and use universal concepts, create and use language, form judgments, create and use new and intuitive ideas, and the senses of self-determination, morality, religious ideas and feelings, and humor.[64]

One important point to consider is the essential or ontological difference between God and His creation, including humans. Through this distinction we understand the principle that God alone reserves the right to act in complete freedom. Werner Elert points out that God is creation's *Urheber*, its originator. However, when it comes to identifying God as its *Ursache* or efficient cause, to use an Aristotelian term, we should avoid suggesting that creation is an outflow from God, an emanation from His being, or that it is generated from God in the way in which the Son was begotten of the Father. All humans are created according to God in general (κατὰ τὸν θεόν), but they are not God and they are not Christ. Humans are not *hypostases* of God; they are not of the essence that the Son and Holy Spirit share with the Father. Philosophically, the idea of emanation finds its roots in Neoplatonic thought, which carries a divine primary principle from which, across a number of steps, the world emerges. Plotinus (204/5–70), the founder of Neoplatonism, thought of all reality as emanating from a divine source, like water from a spring.[65] This idea that the world emanates or originates from a divine entity essentially would make God and the world one, a form of monism like Eastern religions follow. And if one follows that principle to its logical conclusion, then the reverse also should be possible: creation occurs where God is born or comes from the world. God thus becomes a creation of this world. This idea is foreign to the Judeo-Christian worldview as well as to Islam, which follows a dualism in which God and man relate, yet remain ontologically separate.[66] As the apostle Paul would clarify,

63. SC II.2 (K-W, 354); Ep. I.4 (K-W, 488); SD I.34 (K-W, 537).

64. As listed in McClain and Dilling, *Theological Anthropology* (Lafayette, IN: Kensington Theological Academy, 2015), 113–14. For a discussion of intelligent design versus Darwinism, see Groothuis, *Christian Apologetics*, 266–329.

65. "It belongs to every nature to produce its posteriors and to unfold itself, as from a seed, from some undivided starting point that proceeds to an outcome in the sensible world." Plotinus, *The Enneads* IV.8(6), trans. Barrie Fleet (Las Vegas, Zurich, Athens: Parmenides Publishing, 2012), 64.

66. Härle, *Dogmatik*, 412.

"Therefore since we are God's offspring, we should not think that the divine being is like gold or silver or stone—an image made by man's design and skill" (Acts 17:29; see also Is 44:9–20).

If the concept of cause suggested that God somehow is forced to bring the world forth out of necessity, like a seed bringing forth a plant or a pregnant woman a child, then we would have to dismiss the concept. God is not bound to the laws of nature; in that case He would no longer be God but a part of the world. Johann Gerhard asserts that if God is seen as the prime cause, then He is not bound to any causal laws other than from His own freedom to act.[67] Thus, Christian faith speaks of a cosmic dualism—of the Creator and the world—and avoids a cosmic monism that would make the world one with its Creator. The finite cannot cross over into the infinite but remains finite with all its consequences. For example, no matter how hard humans strive for a body that remains ageless, they cannot succeed. The finiteness of human life remains for us as it did for humans in the past.

This cosmic dualism, with God on the one side and the world, including man, on the other, speaks to God's aseity, that is, to His eternal and unqualified self-existence and self-sufficiency. From Francis Pieper we learn that "the divine aseity [self-existence] and eternity could not have been communicated to man, and the other divine attributes, for instance, the wisdom, lordship, etc., were only reflected in man. God is wise, and man is wise; God rules, and man rules. But God possesses unlimited, man only limited wisdom, dominion, etc."[68] This truth has ramifications for how we talk about our relationship with God. The Christian faith distinguishes the world that has been created from attempts to see it born or generated from God. That distinction pertains also to the Son of God or the Logos of God, who in contrast to every human is begotten or born but not created. Thus, Christ also became flesh and human, but he did so without sin, whereas we humans exist in flesh and sin.

For this reason we must qualify what the church father Athanasius once said "For he [the Son of God] was made man so that we might be made God [θεοποιηθῶμεν]."[69] If we ever come to understand human identity and being as participation with God and sharing "in the mystery of God," in order to avoid confusions we must speak to what humans are not in their relationship with God. Here an apophatic anthropology applies, that is, we speak of man *via negationis*, of what he is not in contrast to his Creator: he is not eternal but created *ex nihilo*, and he is not sinless but sinful and corrupted.[70]

67. Gerhard, Theological Commonplaces 8.1.8 (8–11:11).

68. Pieper, *Christian Dogmatics* 1:515–16.

69. Athanasius, *De Incarnatione* 54.3, in *Nicene and Post-Nicene Fathers*, ed. Philip Schaff and William Wace, Second Series, 14 vols. (Peabody, MA: Hendrickson Publishers, 2004), 4:65 (hereafter cited as NPNFb).

70. Linda Woodhead, "Apophatic Anthropology," in *God and Human Dignity*, ed. R. Kendall Soulen and Linda Woodhead (Grand Rapids: Wm. B. Eerdmans, 2006), 243.

Augustine looks at it that way. In contrast to Plotinus and Neoplatonism, where the distinction between God and creation becomes blurred, Augustine affirms God's distinct being over against humans. He recognizes that this distinction becomes unclear in the concept of divinization as promoted by Eastern theologians—that humans have a capacity to be deified gradually. Instead, Augustine emphasizes a concept of salvation that speaks to the sinfulness and utter corruption of humans and to their total dependency on salvation from God through Christ. Luther, Calvin, and others followed Augustine.[71]

The temptation is to strike an analogy between God and His creation, which lends to the world and created things a "divine" character. Sun, moon, stars, and other created things become objects of worship. In today's worldviews, such as that advanced by the New Age movement, the self is affirmed as god, much like claims in Eastern religions such as Hinduism (or Buddhism), in which the basic scheme of Atman=Brahman suggests the deep inner self of a human being is part of the broader universe, of god himself. Thus, someone who discovers this deeper inner self, the Atman, becomes almighty, the creator of the universe, the world itself.[72]

Instead, our Christian faith "desacralizes" the world by taking the divine out of it and out of humans.[73] If the world and humans have lost their divine character, then humans are tempted to exploit one another and the world around them. While one might be inclined to blame the problem of exploitation on the dominion mandate itself or the biblical worldview or the Christian application of it, this is humanity's inclination because of sin. Scripture knows of the problem and sees it arising where humans take on an unrestricted freedom divorced from a relationship with God and from responsibility toward Him (Gn 11:1–9; Is 25:11). The dominion mandate encourages humans to live responsibly toward the world under God and not as gods themselves.

---

71. Woodhead, "Apophatic Anthropology," 237. See section on Augustine in chapter 9.
72. Barth, *Dogmatik*, 503–4.
73. James W. Sire, *The Universe Next Door: A Basic Worldview Catalog*, 5th ed. (Downers Grove: InterVarsity Press, 2009), 209.

3

WHO THEN IS THE HUMAN? INTERACTING WITH PHILOSOPHY AND SCIENCES

To a degree we have defined already who the human is. He has much in common with the rest of creation, yet he is distinctly different from it. He is placed in the middle, between God on one side and all other created beings on the other. He is not God; he is neither angel nor animal. He is human, and what that means we shall now attempt to explain in the context of multiple approaches taken in this endeavor.

THE LIMITS OF EMPIRICAL STUDIES

There are many angles from which one can enter the debate. Philosophers, sociologists, psychologists, and scientists have long turned their thoughts toward defining the human, and will continue to do so. In our own conversation we should not shy away from insights gained in other sciences as they relate to anthropology. We shall see that philosophy and also disciplines like biology, sociology, psychology, neuroscience, and cultural anthropology (which carves out the particulars of functional anthropology, the various relationships in which humans find themselves)[1] have provided important information on our topic. They are, however, guided predominantly by humanist and naturalistic principles and draw their data from empirical observation. The metaphysical realm, which speaks to God's existence, the resurrection of the dead, and the immortality of the soul, is excluded. The essential issue therefore is this: by eliminating God and metaphysics from the equation, philosophical anthropology reaches different conclusions than would a theological anthropology.[2]

1. It should be noted that certain cultural anthropologists also take a theological perspective and thus draw different conclusions than those who consider themselves secular anthropologists. See Brian M. Howell and Jenell Williams Paris, *Introducing Cultural Anthropology: A Christian Perspective* (Grand Rapids: Baker Academic, 2011), 15–16; Charles H. Kraft, *Anthropology for Christian Witness* (Maryknoll: Orbis Books, 1996).

2. Härle, *Systematische Philosophie*, 218.

MARTIN LUTHER'S *DISPUTATIO DE HOMINE*

In his *Disputation Concerning Man* (*Disputatio de homine*) Luther offers an exemplary framework for how that conversation between Christian anthropology and philosophy (and all empirical sciences) can be carried out.[3] As his only systematic treatment on anthropology, it sets the appropriate stage for pointing out the particularities of theological anthropology and philosophy, that is, vis-à-vis all other sciences.[4] In this important discussion on who man is, Luther offers his own theological explanation of the origin, purpose, and final destiny of man. He does not dismiss traditional insights. He finds the philosophical understanding of man as "an animal having reason, sensation, and body" acceptable and chooses not to debate this definition much further (Theses 1 and 2). However, he points out the shortcoming of this philosophical definition as it "describes man only as a mortal and in relation to this life" (Thesis 3). Luther is willing to acknowledge the value of reason in arranging human life as it "is the most important and the highest in rank among all things and, in comparison with other things of this life, the best and something divine" (Thesis 4). In Luther's anthropology, reason does hold an important place. Not only is a human being in possession of it, it is also put to good use: "It is the inventor and mentor of all the arts, medicines, laws, and of whatever wisdom, power, virtue, and glory men possess in this life" (Thesis 5). Because of this faculty, man "is distinguished from the animals and other things" (Thesis 6). In the execution of the *dominio terrae* (Thesis 7), reason is used positively as "a kind of god appointed to administer these things in this life" (Thesis 8).

Did man lose reason after the Fall? No, argues Luther: "after the fall of Adam" God did not "take away this majesty of reason, but rather confirmed it" (Thesis 9). As we saw in Theses 4 and 5, because of reason man is ranked above all other animals on earth, and it serves to assist in the stewardship over creation and whatever "men possess in this life."

That is as far as Luther goes in his positive assessment of reason and where it finds its place in managing worldly affairs. From there Luther proceeds to limit reason: "In spite of the fact that it is of such majesty, it does not know itself a priori, but only a posteriori" (Thesis 10). Luther borrows terms from philosophical epistemology—a priori (from before) and a posteriori (afterwards)—to show that philosophy, with its use of reason, operates differently than theology by working with information that is gained from

3. *Disputation Concerning Man*, 1536 (AE 34:139–41; WA 39/1:175–80).

4. Anthropology may seem at a glance a peripheral issue in Luther's theology. However, he comments on anthropology in other documents: *Lectures on Genesis*, 1535–45 (AE 1–8; WA 42–44); *Lectures on Galatians*, 1535 (AE 26–27; WA 40/1.1–2:184; *Lectures on Romans*, 1516 (AE 25; WA 56); *Commentary on 1 Corinthians 7*, 1523 (AE 28:4–56; WA 12:88–142); *Commentary on 1 Corinthians 15*, 1534 (AE 28:59–213; WA 36:478–696). See also his *Lectures on 1 Timothy*, 1528 (AE 28; WA 26:1–120).

observation and experience (a posteriori).[5] In other words, philosophy is knowledge of the world attained through a rational exercise working through one's senses (*sensus*) and reason (*ratio*), and not through faith;[6] that is, philosophy's epistemology arises from within itself.[7] Theology instead draws in additional factors that precede (a priori), transcend, or go beyond the observable and rationally verified. That is to say, theology draws on information about man that tells a story about who he is from revelation that goes beyond empirical verification. Luther sees that philosophy cannot accept the a priori facts of man, and therefore its epistemology can produce only a limited version of who man is. Theology tells the far greater story.

The cross in particular presents an insurmountable divide between theology and philosophy. In his famous *Heidelberg Disputation* Luther draws out this split (Theses 19–23).[8] Whereas the theologian sees God active in the cross, the philosopher or theologian of glory is infatuated with God's power and fullness of being, His majesty and glory.[9] The *theologia crucis* for which Luther pleads is the true recognition of things, that is, the wisdom that perceives invisible things and calls them what they are in contrast to a wisdom "that is completely puffed up, blinded, and hardened" (Thesis 22).[10]

For this reason Luther's invective against philosophy makes sense. Philosophy, he concludes, must be given a "bath" or "baptism."[11] In his *Disputation Concerning Man* he posits: "Therefore, if philosophy or reason itself is compared with theology, it will appear that we know almost nothing about man" (Thesis 11). Luther draws in the Aristotelian four causes which

---

5. The important point for Luther is that philosophy deals with inner-worldly things, those which are below (*infra*) and not above (*supra*), what can be seen and observed (*visabilia*), things that are apparent (*apparentia*) and present (*praesentia*). Thus, Luther sets a parameter for philosophy within which it may operate. Theology in turn deals with matters that elude the unregenerate's knowledge, and are revealed to one instead through the Word of God and understood through faith (*intellectus fidei*). Faith recognizes what is invisible (*invisibilia*), not apparent (*non apparentia*), future, eternal (*futura, aeterna*), and spiritual (*spiritualia*). Joest, *Ontologie der Person bei Luther*, 100–104.

6. The *sensus* and the *ratio* are the two means of attaining knowledge in philosophy or any human endeavor. They stand in contrast to the *intellectus fidei*, that spiritual gift of recognizing divine things that the other two cannot attain. There is also the "philosophy of faith," but that exercise presumes one is a believer already, and therefore it is really a theological effort. Luther's stance toward philosophy is fairly consistent on this point. Joest lists where he engages the topic (*Ontologie der Person bei Luther*, 89–93): *First Lectures on Psalms* (1513–15); *Lecture on Romans* (1515–16); *Operations in Psalms* (1519–21); *The Magnificat* (1521); *De servo arbitrio* (1525); *Lectures on Galatians* (1531); *Lectures on Genesis* (1535–45); theses on *The Disputation Concerning Man* (1536).

7. German: *rational autogenes Weltwissen*. Joest, *Ontologie der Person bei Luther*, 85.

8. *Heidelberg Disputation*, 1518 (AE 31:40; WA 1:354.17–26).

9. Theses 20–21: "He deserves to be called a theologian, however, who comprehends the visible and manifest things of God seen through suffering and the cross. A theologian of glory calls evil good and good evil. A theologian of the cross calls the thing what it actually is." *Heidelberg Disputation*, 1518 (AE 31:40; WA 1:354.19–22).

10. *Heidelberg Disputation*, 1518 (AE 31:40–41; WA 1:354.23–24).

11. *Die Promotions Disputation von Palladius und Tilemann*, 1537 (WA 39/1:229.24–25): "müssen wir sie erst wohl zum Bade führen"; Peters, *Der Mensch*, 31.

define something that exists: *causa materialis*, *causa formalis*, *causa finalis*, and *causa efficiens*.[12] And he points out that two of the causes elude philosophy's exercise regarding who man is, "for philosophy does not know the efficient cause for certain, nor likewise the final cause" (Thesis 13). Based on empirical observation, philosophy relates both causes inadequately to the "peace of this life" (final cause) and not to God Himself (efficient cause; Thesis 14).[13]

Based on the a priori factors, theology, according to Luther, defines man's pre-Fall condition as perfect: "Theology to be sure from the fullness of its wisdom defines man as whole and perfect: namely, that man is a creature of God consisting of body and a living soul, made in the beginning after the image of God, without sin, so that he should procreate and rule over created things, and never die" (Theses 20–21). However, Luther describes the situation after the Fall differently and negatively: "But after the fall of Adam, certainly, he was subject to the power of the devil, sin and death, a twofold evil for his powers, unconquerable and eternal" (Thesis 22). As much as one would want to think of creation after the Fall in positive terms, the fact stands: "The whole man and every man, whether he be king, lord, servant, wise, just, and richly endowed with good things of this life, nevertheless is and remains guilty of sin and death, under the power of Satan" (Thesis 25). The recognition of creation as being tainted after the Fall escapes philosophy's insights: "Therefore those who say that natural things have remained untainted after the fall philosophize impiously in opposition to theology" (Thesis 26).

Philosophy either denies the reality of the Fall (Thesis 26) or admits it and nonetheless offers the inadequate solution that man does what is in him in order "to merit the grace of God and life" (Thesis 27). Philosophy places upon either reason or the will[14] the ability to choose morality (Theses 29–30). This expectation directly opposes Luther and Paul's emphasis on salvation in the act

12. Aristotle applies the four causes to everything that exists and for each thing thus requires a fourfold explanation, including for those arising from artistic production and human action, such as a bronze statue. He recognizes four types of answers to the question "Why?": the material cause, or "that out of which" (e.g., the bronze of a statue); the formal cause, or "the form," "the account of what-it-is-to-be" (e.g., the shape of a statue); the efficient cause, or "the primary source of the change or rest" (e.g., the artisan in the art of bronze-casting the statue); and the final cause, or "the end, that for the sake of which a thing is done" (e.g., the statue is to adorn the living room). Aristotle, *Physics* 2.3.195a.6–8 and 2.3.195b.25–30, trans. R. P. Hardie and R. K. Gaye, BWA 241, 242. Cf. Aristotle, *Metaphysics* 5.1.1013b6–9, trans. W. D. Ross, BWA 753. Read Norman Melchert, *The Great Conversation: A Historical Introduction to Philosophy*, 4th ed. (Boston: McGraw-Hill Higher Education, 2002), 170–72.

13. In his *Lectures on Genesis* Luther makes similar comments, namely, what escape reason and can be recognized only through faith are the *causa efficiens* and *causa finalis*. *Lectures on Genesis*, 1535–45 (AE 1:124–25; WA 42:102.21–24); Joest, *Ontologie der Person bei Luther*, 97.

14. In referring to the will, Luther expresses his dissatisfaction with the tradition strongly associated with William of Occam, the so-called *via moderna*, in which he himself was trained. This tradition, which in essence assumed a skepticism of Aquinas's scheme of establishing analogy between man and God, found its demise in Luther's eyes by emphasizing the human will in soteriology. The emphasis on reason reflects the *via antiqua* tradition associated with the medieval scholastic theologian Thomas Aquinas.

of justification by grace through faith alone (Theses 32–33). Clearly, a return to the original state as it was before is possible only in Christ: "He can be freed and given eternal life only through the Son of God, Jesus Christ (if he believes in him)" (Thesis 23). Luther looks at anthropology teleologically by keeping an eschatological perspective on man's ultimate destiny. That final cause Luther describes in Theses 37 and 38: "And as earth and heaven were in the beginning for the form completed after six days, that is, its material, so is man in this life for his future form, when the image of God has been remolded and perfected." Here Luther has taken into account the loss of the image (εἰκών) of the spiritual and physical integrity and perfection that man once had and posits a restoration of it in the future, brought about by the Gospel, received through faith in Christ, and then restored fully at the time of our resurrection.[15]

Luther here presents a narrative anthropology, an account of humanity that draws in the following aspects with their creedal overtones: man is created in the image of God, estranged from God, called to restoration in Jesus Christ, and through justification and sanctification is brought back on the path toward the final goal, eternal life.[16]

Luther is skeptical of reason's ability to arrange life perfectly in agreement with God's will, even while he affirms that faculty as important for the arrangement of matters in everyday life. He thus acknowledges the usefulness of human reason and the use of human sciences. He sees their limited value for a theological exploration, since they are based on empirical observations and general revelation alone and therefore fall short of grasping the full biblical description of who a human is. Luther's assessment of the utility of reason and science thus falls between those of Karl Barth and Wolfhart Pannenberg, who represent opposing views about whether or not one can embrace and pair human sciences with theology. Since Christians are social beings who share the world with other people in society, Pannenberg in his trenchant work *Anthropology in Theological Perspective* seeks to engage the findings of human sciences with his theological anthropology, in order for modern man to see that the religious claims are not mere "assumptions and illusions."[17] He invites

15. In his Genesis lectures Luther affirms his teleological approach to the image of God: "But now the Gospel has brought about the restoration of that image. Intellect and will indeed have remained, but both very much impaired. And so the Gospel brings it about that we are formed once more according to that familiar and indeed better image, because we are born again into eternal life or rather into the hope of eternal life by faith, that we may live in God and with God and be one with Him, as Christ says (John 17:21)." *Lectures on Genesis*, 1535–45 (AE 1:68; WA 42:48.11–16).

16. Peters, *Der Mensch*, 31, 56.

17. He explains this as follows: "If theologians are not to succumb to self-deception regarding their proper activity, they must begin their reflection with the recognition of the fundamental importance of anthropology for all modern thought and for any present-day claim of universal validity for religious statements. Otherwise they will, even if unintentionally, play into the hands of their atheistic critics, who reduce religion and theology to anthropology, that is, to human assumptions and illusions." Pannenberg, *Anthropology in Theological Perspective*, 16.

other perspectives into the discussion of humanity. His starting point is "from below," from rational and empirical bases or observation, and he works his way upward into theology in an attempt to provide a more "rational" justification of theological anthropology. A criticism of this approach is that Pannenberg's anthropology becomes too anthropocentric, drawing too much from human sciences and general revelation, and consequently sacrifices or compromises special revelatory truths about humans.

Another theologian noteworthy for "tweaking" divine revelation is Rudolf Bultmann, with his existential interpretation of the Christian message that "demythologizes" it. Approaching the biblical narratives from the point of view of the modern "scientific" Christian, Bultmann finds Scripture's appeal not in its objective historicity but rather in what it has to say to the faith of the modern believer "in his present determination."[18]

Karl Barth, on the other hand, who admits only a single source of revelation, has an a priori bias against human sciences that borders on arrogance. He is skeptical about their value and unwilling to modify any dogmatic statements about man for the sake of engaging human sciences.[19] Unlike that of Pannenberg, Barth's approach is "from top to bottom," moving from theology to general descriptions of who man is, but the latter gets short shrift.

TWO ERRANT SYSTEMS DESCRIBING THE HUMAN CONDITION

Christianity can and should engage in a conversation with empirical sciences, rather than raising up walls around itself out of fear that its theological principles might suffer through such a dialogue. Two Christian principles worth exploring in that dialogue emerge from Luther's discussion of who man is, and from theology in general.

First, theology supports the tradition of a human as *animal rationale*, an understanding rooted in the Greek, Enlightenment, and humanist positions, and places the freedom of the will and reason in the context of daily decision-

18. "These mythologies, also, do not have their point in their objectifying representations, but have to be interpreted in terms of their understanding of existence, that is, in existentialist terms." Rudolf Bultmann, "New Testament and Mythology (1941)," in *New Testament and Mythology and Other Basic Writings*, comp., ed., and trans. Schubert M. Ogden (Minneapolis: Fortress Press, 1984), 15. See also Rudolf Bultmann, "The Meaning of the Christian Faith in Creation," in *Existence and Faith: Shorter Writings of Rudolf Bultmann*, comp. and trans. Schubert M. Ogden (Cleveland: World Publishing Company, 1960), 220, on modern science's relation to biblical narratives.

19. Pannenberg's verdict of Barth is thus as follows: "When Barth, instead of justifying his position, simply decided to begin with God himself, he unwittingly adopted the most extreme form of theological subjectivism. Nothing could show more clearly how indispensable a rational justification of theology is and in particular, given the modern situation, an anthropological justification of the mode of theological argumentation." Pannenberg, *Anthropology in Theological Perspective*, 16. See also Daniel J. Price, *Karl Barth's Anthropology in Light of Modern Thought* (Grand Rapids: Wm. B. Eerdmans, 2002), 111–16.

making in the civil realm. Second, theology also addresses a spiritual captivity or uncontrollable inclination that takes hold of every faculty of the human and causes him to rebel and resist God actively. When these two principles are not held in proper relationship, they give rise to trajectories of their own and create errant systems of thought and behavior. Especially when any accountability before God is denied or when a laissez-faire attitude is permitted toward the way humans relate to their creator and to one another, one of two things will happen: humans will either elevate themselves, in their minds and behavior, to almost angelic or royal status or lower themselves to the status of wretched animals driven by instinct and impulses. The philosopher Blaise Pascal analyzes these two philosophical errors regarding the human condition and concludes that it is preferable for one to exhibit qualities of both greatness and wretchedness:

> It is dangerous to make man see too clearly his equality with the brutes without showing him his greatness. It is also dangerous to make him see his greatness too clearly, apart from his vileness. It is still more dangerous to leave him in ignorance of both. But it is very advantageous to show him both. Man must not think that he is on a level either with the brutes or with the angels, nor must he be ignorant of both sides of his nature; but he must know both.[20]

Pascal's anthropological argument is that philosophers "either exalt greatness at the expense of wretchedness or they exalt wretchedness at the expense of greatness."[21] What this means is that, in the one approach, various strains of philosophy, including psychology, tout the human potential/self-esteem message—that we are creatures of great or even unlimited potential. The other approach views human beings as products of chance and thus nothing but animals. The almost angelic status of humans is demoted to animalism. In his commentary on Pascal, Peter Kreeft is helpful in directing our attention to past and contemporary instances of both extremes:

> Some examples of "angelism", which ignore the concrete, earthy, embodied nature of man, are Platonism, Gnosticism, Pantheism and New Age humanism. Some examples of "animalism", which ignore the spiritual nature of man, are Marxism, Behaviorism, Freudianism, Darwinism, and Deweyan Pragmatism. . . .
>
> Modern philosophy has lost its sane anthropology because it has lost its cosmology. Man does not know himself because he does not know his place in the cosmos; he confuses himself with angel or with animal.[22]

Kreeft affirms what Pascal observes in his *Discussion with Monsieur de Sacy*: that both systems are unable to see that the state of humankind at present is different from its original creation. Those that speak of its angelic status are ignorant of its corruption and see no need for any restorer, and those that

20. "Pensées. Fragment 418," 132.

21. Douglas R. Groothuis, "Deposed Royalty: Pascal's Anthropological Argument," *Journal of the Evangelical Theological Society* 41, no. 2 (1998): 301.

22. Peter Kreeft, *Christianity for Modern Pagans: Pascal's* Pensées *Edited, Outlined, and Explained* (San Francisco: Ignatius Press, 1993), 52–53.

speak of the state of humankind as wretchedness acquiesce to that state and fall into despair. Only the Christian faith, according to Pascal, offers both a realistic understanding of the state of humankind and a solution, namely, its restoration.[23]

We shall proceed to look at the disadvantages of both systems from a theological point of view; that is, we will demonstrate how the exaltation of human reason has its perils, as does the attempt to lower humans to the status of mere animals.

The Shortcomings of the Apotheosis of the Human as *Animal Rationale*

We saw in Luther's *Disputation Concerning Man* a launching platform common in philosophy, which "defines man as an animal having reason, sensation, and body" (Thesis 1) and as a living being endowed with a reason (Thesis 2).[24]

From the time of Socrates and Aristotle, the classic approach to defining who man is was to ask (1) to what genus does humanity belong, and (2) what are the differences between humanity and other things in that genus. According to Aristotle, humans belong to the genus "animal," and the difference between a human and other animals is that a human is rational, an *animal rationale* possessing and exercising thought (λόγον ἔχον).[25] To this day this understanding has formed the traditional definition of who man is: rational consciousness is "a human characteristic of singular significance, distinguishing us from other animals."[26]

Aristotle also called man a social being (ζῷον πολιτικόν), implying that humans live together and use the faculty of reason to regulate their communal life.[27] However, unlike the description of man as *animal rationale*, this definition does not necessarily imply that man is different from other animals. After all, other animals like ants and buffalo are also social. Aristotle also held that humans have in common with other beings, both animal and plant life, that they are alive, which he would associate with the "soul" (*anima vegetativa*).[28] Together with all other existing life, humans possess a physical body, though it is shaped differently. Also in common with animals, humans have the ability to use their senses, which allows them to smell and feel pain among other things.

---

23. Michael Moriarty, *Pascal. Reasoning and Belief* (Oxford: Oxford University Press, 2020), 36.

24. *The Disputation Concerning Man*, 1536 (AE 34:137; WA 39/1:175.3–4).

25. "Possessing one [rationality] and exercising thought." Aristotle, *Nicomachean Ethics* 1.7.1098a5, trans. W. D. Ross, BWA 942; Melchert, *Great Conversation*, 331.

26. John Polkinghorne, "Anthropology in an Evolutionary Context," in Soulen and Woodhead, *God and Human Dignity*, 96.

27. "Man is by nature a political animal. And he who by nature and not by mere accident is without a state, is either a bad man or above humanity." Aristotle, *Politics* 1.2.1253a3, BWA 1129.

28. Aristotle, *On the Soul* 1:5.411b27–29, BWA 554. See here the footnote commentary on Aristotle in AE 34:138.

But neither the physical appearance nor the ability to use senses makes humans unique from other life forms. The definition *animal rationale* works best.[29]

The current consensus between the Christian story and philosophy is that man is a living being in a body with senses and reason. But what does it mean to be called a rational being? Does it mean one can express one's thoughts through language, that is, that one is able to put together a number of signs and symbols into a meaningful whole so that when expressed they make sense to others?[30] If that is the case, then the ability to communicate through signs and symbols makes humans unique rational beings. This is the claim we make over and against other animals, which are not able to string together complex sentences like humans do. The philologist and Orientalist Max Müller concludes that language "establishes a barrier between man and brute" that is impassable.[31] In other words, he dismissed the Darwinian theory that human speech is a development from sounds made by animals. Human communication is far more than a mere utterance of sounds, an ability we share with other animal life. Elert points this out: "Speech is more than a technical facility, otherwise human speech would belong in the same category as the bark of a dog or the murmur of a brook."[32] On this linguistic point, theological anthropology commits to a deeper understanding of communication, pointing to the capacity unique to humans to communicate with God and He with us. This capacity must be regarded as potential because the natural communication with God has been destroyed and can be restored only in Christ through faith. Outside of this restoration, the communicative capacity still exists among humans but is limited to an interhuman event.

On that interhuman level technology has advanced, enabling computers also to accomplish the feat of communication. However, computers and robots fail in an important respect: they lack self-consciousness and an identity with personality that includes senses and the use of intellect.

Another characteristic seen as contributing to human distinctiveness and the use of rationality is the ability to project into the future and make plans accordingly.[33] There is also the intuition of right and wrong and the ability to

29. "In all animals other than man there is no thinking or calculation." Aristotle, *On the Soul* 3:9.433a12–13, BWA 597.

30. Here cultural anthropologists specializing in communication have much to offer: Eugene A. Nida, *Message and Mission: The Communication of the Christian Faith* (New York: Harper & Brothers, 1960); Lamin O. Sanneh, *Translating the Message: The Missionary Impact on Culture*, 2d ed., rev. and exp., American Society of Missiology Series 42 (Maryknoll, NY: Orbis Books, 2009).

31. Max Müller, *Lectures on the Science of Language*, 5th ed. (London: Longman, Green, and Co., 1866), 15. Similarly Polkinghorne: "The use of language is one way in which human beings exercise their considerable rational skills." "Anthropology in an Evolutionary Context," 96.

32. Werner Elert, *The Christian Ethos*, trans. Carl J. Schindler (Eugene, OR: Wipf & Stock Publishers, 2004), 26.

33. According to recent studies, crows and apes have in common with humans the ability to store food and make plans, though to a lesser degree. Robin Lloyd, "Like Humans, Other

make moral decisions, though imperfectly. In his book *A Rat Is a Pig Is a Dog Is a Boy: The Human Cost of the Animal Rights Movement*, anthropocentrist Wesley J. Smith argues that human exceptionalism gives rise to human obligations to each other, to the natural world, and to animals. Humans are unique in being able to contemplate ethical issues, to know the difference between right and wrong, and to apply their knowledge to a proper treatment of animals.[34]

Without drawing on unique Christian or theological thought, a fair though limited assessment can be made of human exceptionalism based on rational, moral, and communicative capacities. And theologians in general adopted this insight, that human exceptionalism derives from the capacity for rational powers.[35] However, defining a human as *animal rationale* entails certain problems, particularly when his rational potential elevates him to a status independent from a relationship with God and with others, in what is considered the apotheosis of man. During the Renaissance, Italian scholar Pico della Mirandola called for the secular human to rise up, initiating the humanistic tradition of elevating man to the very highest level. He argues in his *Oration on the Dignity of Man* (*De dignitate hominis*) that since a human is endowed with reason and will, he stands uniquely in the hierarchy of creation, under no one except God and the angels. With rational powers at his disposal, a human can become the "maker and molder" of himself, for good or for worse.[36]

As a theologian and philosopher, Pico della Mirandola does not go so far as to encourage humans to step away from an external relationship with their Creator, nor does he say, as theologians like Augustine,[37] Origen,[38] and Gregory of Nyssa[39] taught before him, that in this relationship to their Creator and Redeemer humans will find their true and meaningful status. For Pico della Mirandola, dignity is found *within* humans and is a quality through which they

---

Apes Plan Ahead," *Live Science Newsletter* (17 June 2008), https://www.livescience.com/2620-humans-apes-plan.html.

34. Wesley J. Smith, *A Rat Is a Pig Is a Dog Is a Boy: The Human Cost of the Animal Rights Movement* (New York: Encounter Books, 2012), 243–44. "Humans have ethical intuitions of right and wrong and they acknowledge, however imperfectly at times, the responsibilities that follow from these insights." Polkinghorne, "Anthropology in an Evolutionary Context," 96.

35. Thus even orthodox theologians like David Hollaz included these powers in their definitions: "Man is an animal, consisting of a rational soul and an organic body." Rohnert, *Dogmatik der evangelisch-lutherischen Kirche*, 191. (My translation of "Homo est animal, constans anima rationali et corpore organico.")

36. Pico della Mirandola, "Oration on the Dignity of Man," 225. Cf. Soulen and Woodhead, introduction to *God and Human Dignity*, 10.

37. In Augustine, *On the Trinity* 12.11.16, in *Nicene and Post-Nicene Fathers*, ed. Philip Schaff, First Series, 14 vols. (Peabody, MA: Hendrickson Publishers, 2004), 3:161; hereafter cited as NPNFa.

38. Origen, *De Principiis*, trans. Frederick Crombie, in *The Ante-Nicene Fathers: The Writings of the Fathers Down to* A.D. 325, ed. Alexander Roberts and James Donaldson, 10 vols. (Peabody, MA: Hendrickson Publishers, 2004), 2.6.3 (4:239–382); hereafter cited as ANF.

39. Gregory of Nyssa, *On the Making of Man* (New York: Aeterna Press, 2016), 9.

enact their own powers.[40] The Christian philosopher Blaise Pascal praises the capacity for rational agency in humans: "Man is but a reed, the most feeble thing in nature; but he is a thinking reed. . . . All our dignity consists, then, in thought. By it we must elevate ourselves, and not by space and time which we cannot fill. Let us endeavor then, to think well; this is the principle of morality."[41] But Pascal, like Pico, refrained from taking the final step of cutting the umbilical cord to God. He did not encourage man to liberate himself from God but instead posited his famous wager, arguing that a life which affirms God is more compelling logically than one which does not.[42]

The focus on man's rational capacity to grasp and shape reality began with René Descartes (1596–1650). His principle *cogito, ergo sum* (I think, therefore I am)[43] summarizes his representational theory of knowledge and perception. He separates the things in the mind from those in the world, distinguishing between substances extended in space (*res extensa*) and those that are purely mental projections (*res cogitans*, what the individual reasons about). One could argue that he became the father of modernity's subjectivism or idealism, in which a human possesses and pursues a plurality of ideas and beliefs. For subjectivism, however, the question of whether something really exists outside of the human's perception, that *res extensa*, seems quite uncertain.[44] This movement reached its zenith in the philosophy of idealism. Examples include Johann Gottlieb Fichte's premise that "I posits the not-I" (*Das Ich setzt das Nicht-ich*),[45] Georg Hegel's definition of religion as eternal consciousness (*ewigen Bewußtsein*),[46] and Friedrich Schleiermacher's appeal to the feeling

40. Soulen and Woodhead, introduction to *God and Human Dignity*, 10.

41. "Pensées. Fragment 347," 116.

42. Pascal still would make room for God with his wager: "Let us weigh the gain and the loss in wagering that God is. Let us estimate these two chances. If you gain, you gain all; if you lose, you lose nothing. Wager, then, without hesitation that He is." "Pensées. Fragment 233," 81; Soulen and Woodhead, introduction to *God and Human Dignity*, 10.

43. René Descartes, *Principles of Philosophy*, Part One, §§ 1 and 7, trans. Valentine Rodger Miller and Reese P. Miller (Dordrecht: Kluwer Academic Publishers, 1991), 2, 5.

44. This is not quite in agreement with Kant's noumenon and phenomenon: for Kant the objective reality, the phenomenon, exists and qualifies the subjective perception of it, the noumenon. Melchert, *Great Conversation*, 330–31; Horst Georg Pöhlmann, *Abriß der Dogmatik*, 164; Johannes Hirschberger, *Geschichte der Philosophie*, 12th ed. (Freiburg: Herder, 1980), 2:93.

45. Hirschberger, *Geschichte der Philosophie* 2:164. In fact, Fichte disputed the external referent, "the thing in itself," as that which produces ideas, representations, or mental images in us, but maintained that these are produced by our ego, the "I" or knowing subject. Johann Gottlieb Fichte, *Foundations of Natural Right According to the Principles of the Wissenschaftslehre*, ed. Frederick Neuhouser, trans. Michael Baur, Cambridge Texts in the History of Philosophy (Cambridge: Cambridge University Press, 2000), 42.

46. "Everything that people value or esteem, everything on which they think to base their pride and glory, all of this finds its ultimate focal point in religion, in the thought or consciousness of God and in the feeling of God" (76); and "Religion, in accord with its general concept, is the consciousness of God as such, consciousness of absolute essence" (392), in Georg Wilhelm Friedrich Hegel, *Lectures on the Philosophy of Religion*, ed. Peter C. Hodgson, trans. R. F. Brown, P. C. Hodgson, and J. M. Stewart, with the assistance of J. P. Fitzer and H. S. Harris (Berkeley, CA: University of California Press, 1984–87).

(*Gefühl*) of the divine or of immediate self-consciousness.[47] Fichte, Hegel, and Scheiermacher represent those who believe that humans distinguish themselves from animals not by their rational capacity but in having a "consciousness," "spirit," or "feeling."

This subjectivism also finds its radical replica in atheistic existentialism, which takes a naturalistic and materialistic approach. In this strain of existentialism a person is fundamentally committed to himself, to his subjective world over and against the objective world. Since "for humans alone existence precedes essence," they "make themselves who they are." And because humans exist as matter, they are complex machines and their "personality is an interrelation of chemical and physical properties."[48] By dismissing God, man has the power to move into God's position and take on a god-like status, as Jean-Paul Sartre reflects in his famous statement: "If God does not exist, there is at least one being in whom existence precedes essence, a being who exists before he can be defined by any concept, and . . . this being is man."[49]

Each person is now totally free in regard to his own destiny. It is possible for each person to think, will, imagine, dream, project visions, consider, ponder, invent. The objective world, which is alien, absurd, and without order, is the place into which a person steps and creates his own value by consciously choosing to be and to act morally—or immorally.

Human freedom and self-determination, as well as the appeal to rational powers, reach their culmination with the philosopher Immanuel Kant (1724–1804). For him reason becomes the key ingredient of anthropology: it is not conferred by God but is gained through one's own feat. The autonomous reason not only must become active but also must seek to free itself from all outside authorities. Kant defined this feat as "man's emergence from his . . . self-incurred immaturity," which is the rallying cry of the Enlightenment movement.[50]

In his *Grounding for the Metaphysics of Morals* Kant goes so far as to propose that exercising one's rational powers not only makes a person human but serves to make him free and autonomous from God. A human being is to liberate himself likewise from the laws of nature and obey only those he himself

---

47. Friedrich Schleiermacher, *The Christian Faith*, ed. H. R. Mackintosh and J. S. Stewart (London: T&T Clark, 2004), 5: "The piety which forms the basis of all ecclesiastical communions is, considered purely in itself, neither a Knowing nor a Doing, but a modification of Feeling, or of immediate self-consciousness" (*Bewußtsein* or *Gefühl*, which he uses interchangeably).

48. Sire, *Universe Next Door*, 121.

49. Jean-Paul Sartre, "Existentialism," in *A Casebook on Existentialism*, ed. William V. Spanos (New York: Crowell, 1966), 278; Sire, *Universe Next Door*, 121.

50. "Enlightenment is man's emergence from his self-incurred immaturity. Immaturity is the inability to use one's own understanding without the guidance of another. This immaturity is self-incurred if its cause is not lack of understanding, but lack of resolution and courage to use it without the guidance of another. The motto of enlightenment is therefore: *Sapere aude!* Have courage to use your own understanding!" Immanuel Kant, *An Answer to the Question: "What Is Enlightenment?"* trans. H. B. Nisbet (New York: Penguin Books, 2009), 1.

prescribes. He shapes his own moral character by his own attitude of the mind and his own will.[51] In contrast to what Scripture and theology teach (in Psalm 8, for example), Kant no longer connects the human being to the rest of creation, especially to other humans. Rather, the individual appears as sole supreme being in the universe, not in relation to others or even to God only, but as an end in and of himself. In terms of his moral status, a human being must be in control of morality in order to be completely free.[52] A foundational principle for Kant is that everyone acts out of his own freedom and uses his reason to make a rational and reasonable action. A person should not randomly choose any action but rather should ask whether the action serves as an unconditional, universal, and reasonable rule of action, in accord with the categorical imperative: "Act only according to the maxim whereby you can at the same time will that it should become a universal law [of nature]."[53] According to Kant, God should be invited in only on human terms: "The idea of God is dependent on human dignity as its source and norm, not human dignity on God."[54]

Kant's thought sets the stage for modernity's concept of how humans should perceive themselves. Under the Enlightenment's influence, secular humanists and naturalists think of humans standing alone as rational and dignified persons prior to and independent of every concept of God. The Enlightenment project began to extol the rational and cognitive powers of humans to a worrisome level by "decontextualizing" humanity, stripping a human down to his cognitive and rational powers and promoting a selfhood and individualism that land him in isolation, apart from God.[55] Those who follow Enlightenment principles have taken on a naturalistic worldview and thereby have placed themselves in a box and declared the world a closed system, outside of which is mere silence. The philosopher Charles Taylor calls this development the emergence of the disenchanted modern self who lives in his own immanent frame, in which the transcendent realm finds no place.[56]

51. See especially Section II, Immanuel Kant, *Grounding for the Metaphysics of Morals*, trans. James W. Ellington (Indianapolis: Hackett Publishing Company, 1981), 19–48; Robert L. Arrington, *Western Ethics: An Historical Introduction* (Malden, MA: Blackwell Publishers, 1998), 276–78.

52. "As Kant sees it, our moral status must be altogether within our control; it must be an expression of our status as free human beings." Arrington, *Western Ethics*, 263.

53. Kant, *Grounding for the Metaphysics of Morals*, 30.

54. With his categorical imperative Kant seems to follow a natural-law principle of morality which could invite the thought of a single, supreme "moral giver." Though Kant declares that God's existence cannot be proven from reason, he proceeds to identify Him, if He exists at all, with eternal moral principles, evading thereby the accusation of being an atheist. Soulen and Woodhead, introduction to *God and Human Dignity*, 10.

55. "The naturalists removed the 'God-given' from this conception and made 'reason' the sole criterion for truth." Sire, *Universe Next Door*, 68; Soulen and Woodhead, introduction to *God and Human Dignity*, 1–24.

56. Charles Taylor, *A Secular Age* (Cambridge, MA, and London: The Belknap Press of Harvard University Press, 2007), 542; James K. A. Smith, *How (Not) to Be Secular: Reading Charles Taylor* (Grand Rapids: Wm. B. Eerdmans, 2014), 12, 28.

Kant anticipates here the modern movement, particularly that of enlightened humanism, not only by highlighting rational freedom alone or the ability to make normative ethical reflection, but also by linking the concept of human dignity with corresponding and specific rights inherent in and belonging to the human person.[57] In the political realm those ideals continue to exist in the democratic traditions as reflected in Jefferson's rights to "life, liberty, and the pursuit of happiness"[58] and in Franklin Roosevelt's "Four Freedoms" (freedom of expression, freedom of religion, freedom from want, freedom from fear).[59] As men of the Enlightenment, Jefferson and Roosevelt turned to science and reason, and by studying human behavior and the physical universe thought these rights a reflection of the "laws of nature" that are fundamental to every individual human. John Locke's political philosophy was very influential for these men. Locke claimed in his *Second Treatise of Government* (1689) that all individuals are equal and equipped with certain "inalienable" natural rights, namely, life, liberty, and property.[60] What is common to all these men's viewpoints is that a human being now possesses inherent rights, or at least rights claimed for him, that may never be taken away. By contrast, in the Christian tradition a human being's value and dignity are derived from God, who created him in His image and likeness.

One might argue that Kant at least still holds, with the Christian tradition, the concept of human as *animal rationale* with a special status over the rest of creation, and posits a dualism in which mind is a radically different kind of substance from body, which materialists or monists deny.[61] One hundred fifty years later the *Humanist Manifesto I* (1933) continues to reflect that monistic and naturalistic tradition in its third thesis: "Holding an organic view of life, humanists find that the traditional dualism of mind and body must be rejected." The consequence of that view is to deny the possibility of a life after death: "Promises of immortal salvation or fear of eternal damnation are both illusory and harmful."[62] Moreover, the Enlightenment's insistence on the rational powers of man and autonomous reason as the sole arbiter in decision-making within social and political life, without consideration of guidelines gained from religion, has certainly found its way into today's humanist and secularist traditions.[63] Kant's presentation on who man is has mapped the

57. "For Kant, the key right and obligation was that of being treated as an end and not only as a means." Soulen and Woodhead, introduction to *God and Human Dignity*, 11.

58. The United States Declaration of Independence.

59. Franklin D. Roosevelt, "The Four Freedoms," Annual Message to Congress on the State of the Union, 6 January 1941, https://voicesofdemocracy.umd.edu/fdr-the-four-freedoms-speech-text/.

60. John Locke, *The First & Second Treatises of Government* (Monee, IL: Pantianos Classics, 2021), 104–18.

61. Melchert, *Great Conversation*, 368.

62. *Humanist Manifesto I*, in *Humanist Manifestos I and II*, ed. Paul Kurtz (Buffalo: Prometheus Books, 1973), 3.

63. "Humanism and Its Aspirations: Humanist Manifesto III, a Successor to the

course for modern humanity: a tenuous or nonexistent relationship with God, and instead an elevation of man's autonomous rational capabilities and its achievements. Moreover, lifting up "rights" and "freedom" as fundamental values in a person's existence, without considering relationality, can easily work against the successful relationship of two people. As a result of the sexual revolution of the 1960s, women defined themselves apart from men and men independently of women, "as if the sexes were independent of one another or forever antagonistic."[64]

That overestimation of the self continues in the New Spirituality, which despite its label does not function as an organized religion but offers a spirituality that draws in a hodge-podge of elements from ancient world paganism, the New Age movement, and Eastern religions. It offers a pantheistic worldview in which the universal world merges with the individual and the autonomous self becomes god.[65] God is not transcendent but imminent. The New Spirituality holds that humans are intrinsically divine, manifestations of God on earth, or that they exist together with the one divine reality that encompasses all things (pantheism).[66] Whereas in Eastern religions the self is seen to merge into the universe, in New Spirituality this order is reversed: the self is elevated to become the ultimate reality. This view follows monism in claiming that not only humans but also all nonhuman life forms share the divine substance. Unlike modernism, in which reason is considered to be the final objective arbiter of truth, the New Spirituality appeals to the subconscious psyche, to myth, to "earth-based, feminine-orientated experiences and brief spiritual encounters with non-human life forms and with the non-physical world."[67]

The foregoing evidences the many worldviews and spiritualities constituting modern-day pluralism. On the one side, secular humanists appeal to rational powers as proof for a human exceptionalism, while on the other the New Spiritualists assert this status for humans by declaring them to be divine, together with creation and the universe. In both cases, humans have claimed independence from the one transcendent God. The God of the Bible and the biblical theistic worldview have been jettisoned.[68]

This supercession is reflected as well in the recent aspirations of transhumanism, which can focus on improving present human life or creating

---

Humanist Manifesto of 1933" (Washington, DC: American Humanist Association, 2003), http://americanhumanist.org/wp-content/uploads/2018/08/HumanismandItsAspirations_jefferson1.pdf; Smith, *How (Not) to Be Secular*, 48.

64. Anthony M. Esolen, *Out of the Ashes: Rebuilding American Culture* (Washington, DC: Regnery Publishing, 2017), 93.

65. Peter R. Jones, "The New Spirituality: Dismantling and Reconstructing Reality," *Modern Reformation* 17, no. 3 (2008): 24–29.

66. Gregory A. Boyd and Paul R. Eddy, *Across the Spectrum: Understanding Issues in Evangelical Theology*, 2d ed. (Grand Rapids: Baker Academic, 2009).

67. Jones, "New Spirituality," 26.

68. Jones, "New Spirituality," 26.

a posthuman life in the form of Artificial Intelligence (AI), or combining these to create a kind of superhuman. Nick Bostrom, a strong supporter of transhumanism, explains its quest as follows:

> Posthumans could be completely synthetic artificial intelligences, or they could be enhanced uploads . . . or they could be the result of making many smaller but cumulatively profound augmentations to a biological human. The latter alternative would probably require either the redesign of the human organism using advanced nanotechnology or its radical enhancement using some combination of technologies such as genetic engineering, psychopharmacology, anti-aging therapies, neural interfaces, advanced information management tools, memory enhancing drugs, wearable computers, and cognitive techniques.[69]

As the name suggests, we see in transhumanism an affirmation of ideas stemming from existentialism and secular humanism but also going beyond them to embrace an unbridled optimism in technological advances.[70] This dangerous concoction leads proponents to "search for a way around every obstacle and limitation to human life and happiness"[71] and to challenge any perceived barriers that stand in the way of their goal to "improve" bodily existence. One of their primary goals resembles a primary aim of Mormons: to achieve longevity and immortality of the body, to transform it and have it evolve into a benevolent demigod.[72] Their quest is to go beyond humanity, to replace it, and not merely to improve the quality of human life with greater technology. Since transhumanists adopt a materialistic worldview, humans are treated as matter only and not as the crown of creation. Nick Bostrom unabashedly draws out conclusions from that premise:

> If human beings are constituted of matter obeying the same laws of physics that operate outside us, then it should in principle be possible to learn to manipulate human nature in the same way that we manipulate external objects.[73]

Futurist Ray Kurzweil also predicts that one day our bodies "may eventually become immortal, as medical science outpaces disease" or that "our corporeal

69. Nick Bostrom, *The Transhumanist FAQ: A General Introduction*, Version 2.1 (Willington, CT: World Transhumanist Association, 2003), 5–6, https://www.nickbostrom.com/views/transhumanist.pdf.

70. Another proponent of transhumanism, Max More, expresses these visionary ideals: "No mysteries are sacrosanct, no limits unquestionable; the unknown will yield to the ingenious mind. We seek to understand the universe, not to tremble before mystery, as we continue to learn and grow and enjoy our lives ever more." Max More, "The Extropian Principles, v. 3.0," *The Published Data of Robert Munafo* (blog), last updated 26 March 2020, https://mrob.com/pub/religion/extro_prin.html.

71. Nick Bostrom, "A History of Transhumanist Thought," *Journal of Evolution and Technology* 14, no. 1 (2005): 1.

72. Bostrom, *Transhumanist FAQ*, 33. Mormons are brought into this discussion since their anthropology leads them to pursue their own physical immortality according to Prophet Lorenzo Snow's assertion that "as man now is, God once was; as God now is, man may be." Eliza R. Snow Smith, *Biography and Family Record of Lorenzo Snow: One of the Twelve Apostles of the Church of Jesus Christ of Latter-Day Saints* (1884; reprint, Salt Lake City: Deseret News, 1999), 46.

73. Bostrom, "History of Transhumanist Thought," 4.

beings will one day be made inorganic."[74] Indeed, it seems aspirants to a posthuman future affirm the possibility and desirability of achievements such as "the construction of artificial intelligence to augment intellectual functions, and the use of biomedical transplants, prostheses, genetic modification, and cryonic preservation to stave off the effects of disease and aging."[75]

The overcoming of our physical limitations at first sounds like a laudable goal, but unhindered advances would open the door to many obvious dangers. Those who are concerned would object that technology is placed in the hands of a virtual elite who use it to manipulate their own power over others, and who in the name of progress and efficiency determine the direction humanity should go.[76]

Against these concerns, transhumanists defend technology's usefulness for humanity. They suggest that we rid ourselves of superstition, fear, and conservatism and instead help humanity to attain greater heights of intellectual and technological achievement. And yet fears about the misuse of AI cannot be assuaged. The issue is not simply with the quest to enhance and improve human existence on earth, which Christians certainly welcome; the concern is with an ideology that reframes what human life is all about and aims to create an entity that not only enhances but actually replaces human life. Mortimer Adler rightfully recognizes in that ideology the following danger:

> Why, then, should not groups of superior men be able to justify their enslavement, exploitation, or even genocide of inferior human groups on factual and moral grounds akin to those we now rely on to justify our treatment of the animals we harness as beasts of burden, that we butcher for food and clothing, or that we destroy as disease-bearing pests or as dangerous predators?[77]

The issue is that the definition and decision of what the human is should not be left in the hands of the few who are in power, an elite group who make themselves out to be the experts, qualified and authorized to determine how life should be gauged or valued, whether in the fields of medicine or economics or in another area. What makes us human and provides us with dignity cannot be considered simply the capacity for or use of reason, nor can it derive from what humans possess or produce or do, or from a worldview that declares humans to be mere matter. For if that were so then the weak and the underprivileged, the unborn and the aged, and those lacking rational powers would easily be exploited, marginalized, or forgotten.[78] The theological tradition points to

74. Dawn Chan, "The Immortality Upgrade," *The New Yorker*, 20 April 2016, https://www.newyorker.com/tech/elements/mormon-transhumanism-and-the-immortality-upgrade.

75. Elaine L. Graham, "The 'End' of the Human or the End of the 'Human'? Human Dignity in Technological Perspective," in Soulen and Woodhead, *God and Human Dignity*, 272.

76. Xavier Symons, "The Risk of a Transhumanist Future," *BioEdge* (blog), 5 August 2017, https://www.bioedge.org/bioethics/the-risk-of-a-transhumanist-future/12371.

77. Mortimer J. Adler, *The Difference of Man and the Difference It Makes* (1967; reprint New York: Fordham University Press, 1993), 264.

78. For a continuation of this discussion, see the final section in chapter 14, "The Threat

humans as ensouled bodies or as reflecting the image of God—grounds thought to settle the debate on human exceptionalism—but as we shall see, this demands clarification also. In response to the difficult questions of what human life is and what sort of treatment that life should receive, Wilfried Härle looks to Dietrich Bonhoeffer in his *Ethics* for a simple yet insightful point about us humans:

> The question whether in cases of congenital mental deficiency one is dealing with human life at all is so naïve as scarcely to require an answer. It is sick life, born of men, and even though it must be extremely unhappy life, it cannot but be *human* life.[79]

Bonhoeffer operates here with the important yet simple premise that "life born from humans is human life." This premise dismisses the idea that a human life is looked upon as an isolated *individum*. Rather, life must be seen in its relation to other humans as a species and especially in its relationship to God, the outside arbiter from whom that life comes: "In the sight of God there is no life that is not worth living; for life itself is valued by God."[80] A simple reality applies to Bonhoeffer's insight. Everything that comes from humans is human—from its beginning to its last moment. There is no denying that what will emerge from the womb of the mother is a human being, not an elephant or a plant for that matter. Thus, only arrogance can deny someone, even an unborn child, his or her humanity.[81]

However, is it possible for human life to find an existence here on earth that is relieved of all its frailty and limitations and replaced in the end by something far greater? This question points to the fact that humans are the crown of creation and that they should not be replaced. Since 19 October 2013 an image has circulated on the internet of an engineer at the Smithsonian National Air and Space Museum in Washington, DC, making adjustments to a robot known as the Incredible Bionic Man. The robot is the world's first-ever functioning bionic man made of prosthetic parts and artificial organ implants.

Such goals of an enlightened humanism with existential aspirations emphasizing personal liberty, free inquiry, and self-determination have long been part of society. The apprehension here is over an approach that may seem at first altruistic and of benefit to human life on earth, but which upon closer inspection jeopardizes basic human values that treasure and support the vulnerable and the weak, and which affirms a bodily existence that, simply put, has its limits this side of heaven. In the end we must rejoice in our createdness and not bemoan it. Humans are created with finitude; the Christian

---

to One's Own Existence."

79. Dietrich Bonhoeffer, *Ethics*, ed. Eberhard Bethge, trans. Neville Horton Smith (New York: Simon & Schuster, 1995), 163. See Härle, *Dogmatik*, 433–34.

80. Bonhoeffer, *Ethics*, 162.

81. In that discussion prediagnostic examination of fetuses is mentioned critically, for it makes their value as humans conditional on how the results of tests turn out. Kerby Anderson, "Arguments Against Abortion," *Probe for Answers* (blog), 1 October 2014, https://probe.org/arguments-against-abortion.

understanding of salvation (Rom 8:18–27) is that it "will be an affirmation of the essential finitude of human nature, not an escape from it."[82] The biblical lesson is that life should be treated for what it is and not for what it will be or can become. There is a createdness belonging to all humans that should prohibit any from charging forward unconstrained toward a hyperhumanism[83] and even in the name of progress being willing to turn against one another or to manipulate human genetic material in order to achieve the greater goal of a few. To be sure, Christians have accepted and embrace positive technological advances. Certain devices such as cochlear implants, intraocular lenses, pacemakers, and artificial organs have become permanent parts of human physiology. Other technologies like cellular and computer-mediated communications have been assimilated into everyday life and have become a "natural" part of human existence, of organic life itself. All these developments make it increasingly complex for Christians to know which advances in technology should be embraced and which rejected.[84] Technology in the service of humans forms, and will continue to form, an integral part of our life. To turn a blind eye to all these benefits is unrealistic. Yet we cannot ignore the volatile situation in which technology has begun to encroach on the sphere of what traditionally has been thought of as natural and essential to our human existence. Today a human being sees himself existing not only as a biological being but increasingly also as a *techno sapiens* and *homo cyberneticus*,[85] and who knows what comes next.

However, the theological concerns focus especially on the ideas that drive such developments: an existential naturalism that fails to treasure the createdness of man, to affirm the special and unique status of humans, and to honor human life as God's gift.[86] Humans perceive and respond to reality on

---

82. David H. Kelsey, "Human Being," in *Christian Theology: An Introduction to Its Traditions and Tasks*, ed. Peter C. Hodgson and Robert H. King (London: SPCK, 1998), 144.

83. Graham, "'End' of the Human," 279.

84. "One of the issues about the impact of technologies is thus their impact on personal identity, and in particular whether new technologies can facilitate a better quality of life or unleash Promethean powers which threaten our very humanity. Much of that attention and anxiety has come to be focused around the integrity of the body, and whether it is appropriate to dream of transcending the frailties of the flesh to embrace new physical forms, or whether the end of the embodiment would fatally compromise our essential humanity." Graham, "'End' of the Human," 270; Langdon Winner, "Resistance Is Futile: The Posthuman Condition and Its Advocates," in *Is Human Nature Obsolete? Genetics, Bioengineering, and the Future of the Human Condition*, ed. Harold W. Baillie and Timothy K. Casey, Basic Bioethics (Cambridge: MIT Press, 2004), 392, http://site.ebrary.com/id/10225264.

85. Yuval Noah Harari, *Homo Deus. A Brief History of Tomorrow* (New York: Harper, 2017), 268, 273. A leading anthropologist in that area is Amber Case. See her article "Cyborg Anthropologist: We Can All Be Superhuman," *CNN Business* (blog), 5 December 2012, http://www.cnn.com/2012/12/05/tech/cyborg-anthropology-amber-case/.

86. "We deny that any part of creation, including any form of technology, should ever be used to usurp or subvert the dominion and stewardship which has been entrusted solely to humanity by God; nor should technology be assigned a level of human identity, worth, dignity, or moral agency." *Artificial Intelligence: An Evangelical Statement of Principles* (Nashville: Ethics & Religious Liberty Commission of the Southern Baptist Convention, 2019), https://erlc.com/resource-library/statements/artificial-intelligence-an-evangelical-statement-of-principles.

two levels simultaneously: with rational faculties (intelligence) on the one hand and with subjective consciousness on the other. A conscious individual needs rationality or intelligence to play chess and subjective consciousness to respond to events in a personal, emotionally and morally informed way. In economic and military spheres, however, subjective consciousness no longer is seen as necessary, which de facto means that a human is not needed to accomplish important tasks. In his recent book *Homo Deus* Yuval Harari observes: "It is sobering to realise that, at least for armies and corporations, the answer is straightforward: intelligence is mandatory but consciousness is optional."[87]

The Shortcomings of Casting Humans in a Negative Light as Mere Brutes

Not all depictions of humans stand in the tradition of the Enlightenment that combines existential and humanistic ideals and promotes man's distinctive position. Some philosophies and worldviews undermine the confidence in a human's self-consciousness or rational capability in the light of the discovery of the unconscious (subconscious) realm, a development that now seems to steer humans almost uncontrollably. According to Sigmund Freud, the human mind is structured into two main parts: the conscious and the unconscious. The unconscious mind includes all those things a conscious person is not aware of: his wishes, emotions, dreams, urges, and memories. Yet the unconscious mind influences a person's behavior because he is driven by his emotions and drive, the libido (*Trieb*), which is a primitive psychic urge or energy. An iceberg provides an apt analogy: the visible tip of the iceberg represents a human's self-consciousness and reason, while the larger portion of the iceberg, which lies hidden beneath the water, represents the subconscious realm and influences the conscious mind.[88]

The philosopher and materialist Thomas Hobbes (1588–1679) holds that all our voluntary actions are governed by passion—by our desires and aversions, our loves and hates. In this view humans are natural competitors, who seek satisfaction of their desires over those of their neighbors, and left unchecked turn against the others. According to Hobbes, this is man's natural state or condition before any artificial arrangements or agreements among humans are made. The reality of life, without the intervention of the state's authority, which he calls *Leviathan* (1650), is nothing but sorrow and pain:

> Every man is Enemy to every man . . . In such condition, there is no place for Industry; . . . no account of Time; no Arts; no Letters; no Society; and which is worst of all, continuall feare, and danger of violent death; And the life of man, solitary, poore, nasty, brutish, and short.[89]

87. Harari, *Homo Deus*, 314.

88. Kendra Cherry, "An Overview of Sigmund Freud's Theories," *Verywellmind* (14 February 2022), 3–4; Pöhlmann, *Abriß der Dogmatik*, 164.

89. Thomas Hobbes, *Leviathan* (Minneapolis: Lerner Publishing Group, 2018), 115.

Hobbes represents a materialistic and naturalistic determinism, in which one thinks that in every event and action humans take "there is a set of sufficient conditions guaranteeing its occurrence."[90] Thus, "left to their own devices, the theory says, individuals will always act egoistically for their own good, and the inevitable consequence is a state of war [Hobbes coins the phrase *bellum omnium contra omnes,* the war of all against all]—each of us fearing our neighbor and striving to extend our sphere of control at our neighbor's expense."[91] The laws of nature, he observes, "(as Justice, Equity, Modesty, Mercy, and (in summe) Doing To Others, As Wee Would Be Done To,) . . . are contrary to our naturall Passions, that carry us to Partiality, Pride, Revenge, and the like"; without a strong power intervening, humans will not reliably choose to follow them.[92] This intervening power is the government, which Hobbes legitimatizes. Government is the only way to provide man's peace and security among other humans and the only way to escape the dreaded effects resulting from human nature. Through a mutual contract, moral and political obligations arise for humans that ensure their own survival and a contented life. For Hobbes, contracts are essential to prevent people from warring against each other.[93]

Hobbes highlights the aspect of the human being that theological anthropologists identify as egotism resulting from sin. According to some sociologists, however, his depiction of humanity is far too negative: it overlooks the fact that humans are also social beings, not just egotistically driven beings, who actually desire to make things work out with one another and naturally resist rivalry and egotistical orientations. Hobbes, a recent journal article would argue, has something in common with the television series "The Walking Dead," in which zombie-like humans seek their survival by one simple quest: to devour others. Both Hobbes and this series fail to consider the more positive aspect of human cooperation, in which individuals come together in a common quest to help one another, working against a destructive individualization in favor of a constructive collectivization.[94] Humanity has the potential to act more collaboratively but must decide to do so. This was the argument Jean-Jacques Rousseau (1712–78) leveled against Hobbes in writings such as *The Social Contract*: humans should not be considered solely as bad and brutish, resorting to war of all against all, but as savages who can be ennobled, freed from sin, and able to discern right from wrong.[95]

90. Melchert, *Great Conversation*, 370.

91. Melchert, *Great Conversation*, 373.

92. Hobbes, *Leviathan*, 156.

93. Hobbes, *Leviathan*, 156.

94. David Fraissl, "Horro Sapiens: Was Thomas Hobbes und die Fernsehserie 'The Walking Dead' gemeinsam haben—und was der große englische Philosoph vergaß," *Hohe Luft*, May 2016: 88.

95. Jean-Jacques Rousseau, *The Social Contract* (Harmondsworth, England: Penguin Books, 1978), 65.

Where humans are governed by their egotistic passions and their own pursuit of happiness—and that certainly happens often enough—Lutherans as well would consider the state and the first (civil) use of the Law as important means to curb excesses of human behavior. For the sake of creating a communal coexistence among humans, the law establishes and enforces morality by the fear of punishment. For Lutherans, the Law of God applied through state authorities (Rom 13:1–7) serves as an objective measure to regulate the communal life of individual human beings, instead of each human deciding what is best for himself and/or for others. Even what science determines as "human flourishing and well-being" may not be so good for humans after all. The anthropologist Scott Atran raises that point:

> Nobel Prize–winner Daniel Kahneman studies what gives Americans pleasure—watching TV, talking to friends, having sex—and what makes them unhappy—commuting, working, looking after their children. So this leaves us where . . .?[96]

Hobbes's materialism is reflective of many English Deists of his time and also of contemporary naturalists' view of anthropology. The Deists' approach certainly laid the foundation for Darwinism to emerge.[97] Hobbes was not impressed with any dualism, such as that of Descartes, and accepted instead that humans exist simply as bodies, as matter, and that all thoughts, emotions, imaginations, and memory are just matter in motion.[98] Not only is his rejection of dualism disconcerting in that it paved the way for Darwinism and naturalism, but so also is its consequence, as seen in his explanation of the origin of morality. For according to Hobbes, if materialists appeal to morality, it is merely intuitive and culturally defined. Yet that makes the moral arrangement of life on earth seem rather subjective, slippery, and unstable, a concern that theological anthropology has with naturalism as a whole.[99] On this point theological

96. Scott Atran, "Sam Harris's Guide to Nearly Everything," *National Interest*, no. 112 (March/April 2011): 59.

97. In England the term "Deist" first appeared in 1624 in Robert Burton's *The Anatomy of Melancholy* (ed. Thomas C. Faulkner, Nicolas K. Kiessling, and Rhonda L. Blair, 6 vols. [Oxford: Clarendon Press, 1989–2000]). Edward, Lord Herbert of Cherbury (1582–1648) is generally considered the father of English Deism and his 1624 book *De veritate* (reprint; ed. Günter Gawlick, 3d ed. [Stuttgart–Bad Cannstatt: F. Frommann, 1966]) the first major statement of Deism. Deism flourished in England between 1690 and 1740, at which time Matthew Tindal wrote *Christianity as Old as the Creation* (1730; reprint, Stuttgart–Bad Cannstatt: Frommann-Holzboog, 1967), known as "the Deist's Bible." Of course, Deism spread to all parts of the world, first to France, notably through the work of Voltaire, then to Germany, then to the United States.

98. "The activities of thinking, feeling, and willing are no more than motions of the physical body, movements that occur as a result of the body's interaction with the objects in the surrounding physical world." Arrington, *Western Ethics*, 157.

99. Sire, *Universe Next Door*, 78. Instead of claiming that morality comes from God and Scripture, "from a voice in a whirlwind," naturalists like Sam Harris claim that science actually provides the answer, and objective stability, to the question of what morality is. In this view, science can determine which values have led and still lead to human flourishing and well-being, and therefore it is able to posit a normative morality. Sam Harris, *The Moral Landscape: How Science Can Determine Human Values* (New York: Free Press, 2010), 2.

anthropology posits God Himself as the source of values and morality and asserts that He provides them their objective character, having hard-wired these into humanity in the form of natural law, which is retained even after the Fall (Rom 2:15). Under this premise, humans ordinarily are capable of making acceptable moral decisions, however incomplete, even if they live practically as atheists.[100] And yet thinkers like Hobbes and Freud affirm one important truth about humanity's uniqueness in the negative sense: that humans are inherently sinful, with passions and urges that cannot be controlled fully, which left unbridled give rise to forces and destructive intents directed both inwardly and against others and the animal world. But these thinkers and those who follow them fail to affirm God's existence in defining the nature of reality in society today,[101] because the common claims and desires of individuals to be in sole control of their own destiny apart from God leads to a total subjectivism or solipsism.[102] A person must recognize an ultimate authority or cause external to himself or risk falling into an abyss of subjectivism, or the delusion of self-made reality.[103]

Fyodor Dostoyevsky shows clearly in his novel *Crime and Punishment* how the exclusion of God as moral lawgiver inevitably leads to practical atheism, a denial of any accountability before God. For Elert, practical atheism takes on a number of attitudes or postures: first, one may be adamant that God does not exist. Second, one may show an indifference to His existence, a position we would call agnosticism. Third, one may affirm that God exists but live out one's life without Him. "Believing in God" means that we consciously act under God's mandate, at His behest, attribute to Him all success, and hope that He will deliver us from our tiring labors.[104] Theoretical questions that cast doubts on God's existence have practical and ethical consequences.

In addition to being driven by internal and often negative impulses, humans encounter external influences as they engage with the world around them and assume roles they choose or are placed into, such as spouse, parent, friend,

100. In other words, "to some extent human reason naturally understands [the Law] since reason contains the same judgment divinely written on the mind, that is, the natural law that agrees with the Mosaic Law, or the Ten Commandments." Ap. IV.7 (German; K-W, 121); *The Natural Knowledge of God: In Christian Confession & Christian Witness*. A Report of the Commission on Theology and Church Relations of The Lutheran Church—Missouri Synod (St. Louis: The Lutheran Church—Missouri Synod, 2013), 30; Pieper, *Christian Dogmatics* 1:521.

101. Polkinghorne, "Anthropology in an Evolutionary Context," 97. See also John C. Polkinghorne, *The Faith of a Physicist: Reflections of a Bottom-Up Thinker* (Princeton: Princeton University Press, 1994), 52. Theologian Anthony Kenny (b. 1931), though turned agnostic, still argues for God's existence: "After all, if there is no God, then God is incalculably the greatest single creation of the human imagination." Anthony Kenny, *Faith and Reason* (New York: Columbia University Press, 1983), 59.

102. This is the so-called "view that each of you (if there is anyone out there!) must state for yourself in this way: 'I am the only thing that actually (formally) exists; everything is only real *for me*.'" Melchert, *Great Conversation*, 334.

103. Melchert, *Great Conversation*, 335.

104. Elert, *Christian Faith*, 43; Peters, *Der Mensch*, 141.

employee, and so forth. Next to psychological factors, which lead a person for the first time to assume the self-conscious "I" at a certain young age, and biological factors, which are mainly genetic influences, there is a sociological context in which the self assumes roles and functions in relation to others. The individual's self-identity is a product of many influences, an idea called the bundle theory, which means that it undergoes multiple changes, continually developing for the duration of one's life.[105] And all these influences, according to Bruce Hood, must be gathered and sorted in the brain to play out as patterns of neuronal activity that create one's self-identity.[106]

Neuroscientists, who study the activities of the brain, claim the brain strongly influences or largely directs human behavior so that humans do not act completely freely. The brain is the organ that steers a person's decisions in all three categories mentioned above—psychological, biological, and sociological. According to Hood, "our self is a product of our mind . . . As the brain develops, so does the self. As the brain deteriorates, then so must the self."[107] The brain gathers, processes, stores, and computes all influences; memory is especially crucial for one's own personal existence and identity.[108]

If human behavior is shaped or directed largely by chemical and physical reactions in the brain, however, it would seem there is little freedom to make decisions for oneself. Studies of the brain have shown that mechanical or chemical reactions in the brain influence body movements and senses. The neuroscientist Oliver Sacks (1933–2015) depicts people, often his patients, in their struggle with neurological conditions or injuries of the brain that influence their perception, memory, and individuality. In *The Man Who Mistook His Wife for a Hat*[109] Sacks discusses a man's struggle with visual agnosia, a condition in which the brain loses the ability to decipher what he sees with his eyes. Studies such as those of Hood and Sacks raise questions about the freedom humans think they have.[110]

Neuroscientists are treading a path that has been explored already in the psychological studies of Sigmund Freud and those of fellow observers

105. This idea represents a departure from the traditional thought about who one is, the conventional ego theory or pearl theory, which "is the common notion that our self is an essential entity at the core of our existence that holds steady throughout our life." Bruce Hood, *The Self Illusion: How the Social Brain Creates Identity* (Oxford: Oxford University Press, 2013), x.

106. Hood, *Self Illusion*, 122.

107. Hood's position is that a human being's behavior is steered by the brain, often in deterministic ways. In this emerging field of neuroethics, the brain becomes the basis of one's morality and how one should behave. He mentions the example of a forty-year-old man who developed an interest in child pornography because of a tumor in the prefrontal cortex; once the tumor was removed the man's sexual urges declined. This raises the question of culpability and determinism. Hood, *Self Illusion*, 117–18.

108. Hood, *Self Illusion*, 290.

109. Oliver Sacks, *The Man Who Mistook His Wife for a Hat: And Other Clinical Tales* (New York: Simon & Schuster, 1998).

110. Hans Schwarz, *The Human Being: A Theological Anthropology* (Grand Rapids: Wm. B. Eerdmans, 2013), 125.

such as Carl Gustav Jung and Erich Fromm. All in their particular theories concluded that humans are led toward evil by an unconscious drive.[111] Indeed, neuroscientists, sociobiologists, and psychoanalysts affirm in varying degrees the reality of evil in humans alongside the good; their self-destructive inclinations continually destroy the good. However, it is impossible to identify the origin of such evil from a purely deterministic perspective. Humans have shown deliberate inclinations and abilities to pursue evil willfully. Personal responsibility and accountability for such acts remain, which leads to an important principle of theological anthropology: humans are culpable for the evil in which they participate.[112]

If matter and nothing else comprises our being, if "sensation, thought, motivation, and voluntary action are all analyzed in terms of matter in motion,"[113] what does that portend for the estimate of man? We may recall Charles Darwin's own evaluation. In *The Descent of Man,* published in 1871, Darwin describes humankind as descending from "a hairy quadruped, furnished with a tail and pointed ears, probably arboreal in its habits."[114] Darwin lost confidence in human reasoning. Who could trust, he would ask, "our powers of thought" if these have evolved from the minds of lower animals! In his old age Darwin wrote to a friend and expressed his doubt in epistemology: "With me the horrid doubt always arises whether the convictions of man's mind, which have been developed from the mind of the lower animal, are of any value or are at all trustworthy."[115]

Darwin's teaching that humans descended from prosimians through natural selection eventually emerged as the dominant hypothesis among biologists[116] following the publication of *On the Origin of Species* (1859) and *The Descent of Man* (1871).[117] He had based his ideas about the survival of the fittest and natural

111. Schwarz, *Human Being*, 139.

112. Schwarz, *Human Being*, 155, 166.

113. Melchert, *Great Conversation*, 375.

114. Charles Darwin, *The Descent of Man, and Selection in Relation to Sex*, vol. 2 (London: John Murray, 1871), 389; Polkinghorne, "Anthropology in an Evolutionary Context," 89.

115. Charles Darwin to William Graham, 3 July 1881, in *The Life and Letters of Charles Darwin*, ed. Francis Darwin, vol. 1 (London: John Murray, 1887), 316; Polkinghorne, "Anthropology in an Evolutionary Context," 89; Michael Ruse, *Can a Darwinian Be a Christian? The Relationship between Science and Religion* (Cambridge: Cambridge University Press, 2004), 107.

116. The protoevolutionary thinker and botanist Joseph Gottlieb Kölreuter (1733–1806) first uses the term "transmutation" in his *Vorläufige Nachricht von einigen das Geschlecht der Pflanzen betreffenden Versuchen* (Leipzig: Gleditsche Handlung, 1761) to refer to species that undergo biological changes through hybridization. Around that time discussions on the origin of humans also emerges, for example with Gotthold Ephraim Lessing's *Die Erziehung des Menschengeschlechts* (1780; reprint, Leipzig: Evangelische Verlanganstalt, 2018) and with Johann Gottfried Herder's *Ideen zur Philosophie der Geschichte der Menschheit*, vols. 1–4 (1784–91; reprint, Darmstadt: Melzer Verlag, 1966).

117. Charles Darwin, *On the Origin of Species* (London: John Murray, 1859) and *Descent of Man.*

selection on patterns he had observed in wild populations of flora and fauna,[118] an area of inquiry that seems to have been influenced by Thomas Malthus's *Essay on the Principle of Population* (1798).[119] Malthus had proposed the idea that if humans continued to populate the world at a geometric rate, many would die and only a few would survive. Darwin interpreted the variations he noticed among the wild populations as demonstrating that some species are better equipped than others to survive and reproduce under given conditions, and that their traits thereby become dominant.

With the rise of the theory of evolution, pessimism about man's existence and his limited agency against the broader evolutionary progress of time and space became part of many materialists' worldview. Such a philosophy terminates in nihilism.[120] Friedrich Nietzsche (1844–1900) merely reflects the assessment of human existence that is implicit in Darwin's theory: he denies the dignity and uniqueness of humans.[121]

In his philosophy Nietzsche denigrates any traditional valuation of human life to advance the ideal of the Übermensch (the overman), a brutish being who applies his will over others with no clear objective standard to guide him except his will for power.[122] Beset with this negative estimate of the human, Nietzsche argues (against Kant's postulate) that people are not able to secure access to universal truths. His skepticism of that capacity dethrones the human's scientific and moral reasoning, reducing it to merely his particular and partial perspective of truth; he maintains that "reason tends to be nothing but a cover up for deeper instincts, prejudices and emotions, and strategies of control."[123] Science is just an attempt to interpret and arrange the world but not an explanation of it, and morality seeks to hide emotions such as "hatred, envy, covetousness and lust for domination."[124]

---

118. Darwin borrowed the phrase "survival of the fittest" from the English philosopher Herbert Spencer, who in that context also used the term "evolution." Herbert Spencer, *Principles of Biology*, vol. 1 (London: Williams and Northgate, 1864), 444. Darwin adopted the phrase survival of the fittest in his fifth edition of *On the Origins of Species* (1869). Since his day the term evolution has been linked with the theory of natural selection as the primary cause of species changing over time. Darwin still preferred to speak of the "descent with modification" to describe how living things changed over time or passed their characteristics on from one generation to the next.

119. Thomas Malthus, *An Essay on the Principle of Population* (London: J. Johnson, 1789).

120. Sire, *Universe Next Door*, 94–116.

121. "Alas, the faith in the dignity and uniqueness of man . . . is a thing of the past—he has become an animal . . . he who was, according to his old faith, a child of God. . . . Now he is slipping faster and faster away from the center into—what? Into nothingness?" Nietzsche, quoted in Soulen and Woodhead, introduction to *God and Human Dignity*, 8.

122. "*I teach you the overman.* Man is something that shall be overcome. What have you done to overcome him? . . . Behold, I teach you the overman. The overman is the meaning of the earth. Let your will say: the overman *shall be* the meaning of the earth!" Friedrich W. Nietzsche, *Thus Spoke Zarathustra: A Book for All and None*, trans. Walter Kaufmann, Modern Library Edition (New York: Random House, 1995), 12, 13.

123. Soulen and Woodhead, introduction to *God and Human Dignity*, 12.

124. Friedrich Nietzsche, *Beyond Good and Evil: Prelude to a Philosophy of the Future*, trans. R. J. Hollingdale (Harmondsworth: Penguin Books, 1979), 26, 35; Soulen and Woodhead,

Nietzsche's message is anti-Christian: he believes Christians have created their God to affirm their own value. In contrast, he points the human to himself and the earth and not to the true self in Christ, the true dynamic of Christian hope. Humanity, he says, must escape its previous bondage to the conventional morality, the common good, and the constraints of believing in a god. Though he dethrones human reasoning, Nietzsche appeals to human freedom and the autonomous human will (that overman or superman) to transcend conventional norms, free himself from bondage to any higher authority, and realize his true individuality.[125] All this is disconcerting for many reasons, particularly because humans are asserted to be similar to animals, impotent "to comprehend or control the deep and often unconscious drives and emotions which shape lives and behavior."[126] Taken to its logical conclusion, a human being's life if created by mere evolutionary mechanism is no different from that of the elephant, cow, or pig.[127] Without an external, objective moral referent, the value of human life derives from standards humans create for themselves. These standards may change over time, making the value attached to human life fleeting and vacuous.

Here theological anthropology raises two critical points. First, because God created humans as His counterpart, He is the external moral referent determining a human's value. Second, we cannot reduce the argument for the value of human life to a mere listing of the genetic congruence between humans and, say, primates and conclude that because of this similarity distinctions do not exist. This small genetic distinctiveness bears enormous implications for who humans are in contrast with other created life forms, an argument made by a former atheist, now a theistic existentialist, Francis Collins.[128] Thus, humans are not different from other animals merely in degree, as Darwin's materialist theory about the origin of human nature implies, but also in kind, a point to which we shall return.

Theological anthropology can now recognize the fact that the philosophical description of the human as an *animal rationale* is not the only factor defining what a human being is. The belief that a human being can elevate himself above all things by the feat of his rational powers stands next to the research that reveals man as an uncontrollable being subject to passions or emotions. However, these philosophical descriptions share a trait that is theologically

---

introduction to *God and Human Dignity*, 12.

125. Peters, *Der Mensch*, 162.

126. Soulen and Woodhead, introduction to *God and Human Dignity*, 13.

127. Sire, *Universe Next Door*, 123.

128. See his best-selling book: Francis S. Collins, *The Language of God: A Scientist Presents Evidence for Belief* (New York: Free Press, 2006), 140–41, 263. Similarly, Howell and Paris, *Introducing Cultural Anthropology*, 8, and Polkinghorne: "The issues cannot be settled by crude genetic calculation. It is no doubt the case that human beings share about 98.4 percent of their DNA with chimpanzees, but the observation only exhibits the fallacy of genetic reductionism. These apparently small biological differences are correlated with immense metaphysical variation. The same is clear within humanity itself." Polkinghorne, "Anthropology in an Evolutionary Context," 98.

disturbing: each has lost sight of the influences of sin and evil and the need for personal accountability. Whereas one view places great confidence in the individual's ability to choose a right moral act over an immoral one, the other holds that a person encounters evil passively and cannot escape it by rational feat or choice. The idea that one can fashion one's existence by freely made decisions reaches its breaking point with the inescapable reality of original sin and its effects in the life of the *animal rationale*. Humans become complicit with evil by using their mind, will, and heart, and for that reason their actions cannot be excused.

In conclusion, the philosophical understanding divides to portray humans either as angels with untapped potential by virtue of their autonomous reason or as brutes doomed because they are driven uncontrollably by passion and other subconscious powers. Recall that Luther's position on the *homo est animal rationale* was based not on the fundamental philosophical question of epistemology or ontology, according to what powers a human possesses, but rather theologically, on what he receives from God. When anthropology and soteriology meet, Luther dismisses powers inherent in the unregenerate and instead posits life as a gift from God. This premise has bearing on what theological anthropology offers to this discussion as its own particular contribution: the image of God.

4

THE THEOLOGICAL CONTRIBUTION TO ANTHROPOLOGY: THE IMAGE OF GOD

We find in Scripture a comprehensive and detailed description of humankind that distinguishes male from female and provides the structure or aspects of the human being, as Hoekema has traced through both Old and New Testament passages.[1] One additional aspect central to theological anthropology is the image of God itself. We open this discussion with the key text in Scripture, Gn 1:26–28, where the triune God expresses His intention to create the first couple:

> Let us make man in our image, in our likeness [בְּצַלְמֵנוּ and כִּדְמוּתֵנוּ; κατ' εἰκόνα ἡμετέραν καθ' ὁμοίωσιν (LXX); *ad imaginem similitudinem nostrum* (Vulgate)]. And let them have dominion . . . So God created man in his own image, in the image of God he created him; male and female he created them. And God blessed them. And God said to them, "Be fruitful and multiply and fill the earth and subdue it, and have dominion over the fish of the sea and over the birds of the heavens and over every living thing that moves on the earth."

From these words we know that a special relationship exists between God and humanity. Between the Creator and the first humans there is a similarity, a likeness, something they specifically have in common with Him (see Gn 5:1–3). The two terms indicating that relationship in particular are צֶלֶם (εἰκών; *imago*; *Bild*) and דְּמוּת (ὁμοίωσιν; *similitudo*; *Ähnlichkeit*). One could differentiate the two terms by saying that God created the human being in His shadow (צֶלֶם), the shadow that renders His image, and God created them in the likeness of His thoughts (דְּמוּת).

According to Irenaeus of Lyon, who is among the first to distinguish the *imago* and *similitudo*, the terms denote something different: צֶלֶם (εἰκών; *imago*) represents the remaining faculty of reason and the will, whereas דְּמוּת (ὁμοίωσιν, *similitudo*) is the ability to be in agreement with God's will (εὐθύτης, *rectitudo*), as was possible for Adam and Eve before the Fall while in the state of integrity. For Irenaeus, after the Fall neither side of the image can be restored fully in the human except through Christ and the Spirit. Since the image of God subsists substantively and truly only in Christ, humans participate truly in the image and similitude only as they participate dynamically in Christ.[2] The final loss of

1. Anthony A. Hoekema, "The Whole Person," in *Created in God's Image* (Grand Rapids, MI: Eerdmans, 1986), 203–26.

2. Irenaeus, *Against Heresies* 5.6.1, trans. A. Cleveland Coxe, ANF 1:315–578. See also Irenaeus, *Against Heresies* 5.16.2; ANF 1:544: "For in times long past, it was *said* that man was

the image at death is hell, or the eternal state of separation and forsakenness by God, whereas the possession of the image is heaven, or the eternal, immortal state of communion with God into which the believer grows more and more.[3]

MARTIN LUTHER AND LUTHERAN ORTHODOXY

Lutherans, in contrast, understand image and likeness as synonyms and thus have avoided a division.[4] After all, in verse 27 only one word, image ("in his image," בְּצַלְמוֹ), is used to summarize the previous verse that includes both aspects. Luther interprets it that way, translating verse 26 in German as "ein Bild, das uns gleich sei" (an image that is like us).[5] This understanding seems to reflect the position of the majority of modern exegetes, as the Keil/Delitzsch commentary claims:

> On the words "in our image, after our likeness" modern commentators have correctly observed, that there is no foundation for the distinction drawn by the Greek, and after them by many of the Latin Fathers, between εἰκών (*imago*) and ὁμοίωσις (*similitudo*), the former of which they supposed to represent the physical aspect of the likeness to God, the latter the ethical; but that, on the contrary, the older Lutheran theologians were correct in stating that the two words are synonymous, and are merely combined to add intensity to the thought: "an image which is like Us."[6]

Thus, the original man was created in the likeness of God's image so that in the human spirit the eternal fullness of God's qualities was reflected

created after the image of God, but it was not [actually] *shown*; for the Word was as yet invisible, after whose image man was created. Wherefore also he did easily lose the similitude. When, however, the Word became flesh, He confirmed both of these; for He both showed forth the image truly, since He became Himself what was His image; and He re-established the similitude after a sure manner, by assimilating man to the invisible Father through means of the visible Word."

3. According to Irenaeus, the human being who is rendered after the image and likeness of the uncreated God is "making progress day by day, and ascending towards the perfect, that is, approximating to the uncreated one." *Against Heresies* 4.38.3–4; ANF 1:521–22.

4. Pieper, *Christian Dogmatics* 1:516: "We should not assume that both the image and the likeness are two different terms. Rather, they may be used here as synonyms." Gerhard, *Theological Commonplaces* 11.1.16 (8–11:258); Härle, *Dogmatik*, 435.

5. *Lectures on Genesis*, 1535–45 (AE 1:68; WA 42:51.15–18): "Here Moses does not employ the word 'similitude,' but only 'image.' Perhaps he wanted to avoid an ambiguity of speech and for this reason repeated the noun 'image.' I see no other reason for the repetition unless we should understand it for the sake of emphasis . . ."

6. C. F. Keil and F. Delitzsch, *The Pentateuch*, Commentary on the Old Testament, vol. 1 (Peabody, MA: Hendrickson Publishers, 1996), 39. Similarly, H. C. Leupold, *Exposition of Genesis* (Grand Rapids: Baker Book House, 1950–53), 1:88–89: "The double modifying phrase, 'in our image, after our likeness,' requires closer study. It is in the last analysis nothing more than a phrase which aims to assert with emphasis the idea that man is to be closely patterned after his Maker. . . . To this must be added the fact that v. 27 considers the use of *tsélem* without *demûth* sufficient to express what God did, 'image' being used twice. . . . So we shall have to regard the second phrase, 'according to our likeness,' as merely supplementary to or explanatory of the first."

and foreshadowed. In the case of the first created humans, the image of God consisted not merely in the possession of a personality with an intellect and a will, but in a will and an intellect that were rightly oriented toward God. The relationship between God and man was perfect and man fully recognized God, doing what He desired. In other words, man lived in righteousness with God. Conversely, the loss of the state of integrity implies the total removal of the image of God, the דְּמוּת and the צֶלֶם.[7]

The plural possessive suffix "in our image, after our likeness" shows that man was created in the image of the triune God, of the glorious essence belonging to the three persons.[8] There is no indication that man was created according to only one of the persons of the Trinity, or after only the human nature of Christ[9] or only the divine nature of Christ. Though one might be inclined to think that God preconceived Christ's human form when creating Adam, the plural "let us" makes no such indication. Also, although Christ is the restoration of man's lost image, the fact that He took on the flesh and blood of man does not imply that man is now restored according to His flesh and blood. Pieper points this out: "According to 1 Cor. 15:45f., Christ is 'the last Adam' (man) and Adam 'the first man.' And, according to Heb. 2:14, Christ assumed flesh and blood of man; men were not patterned after the flesh and blood of Christ."[10] Thus Christ is the true and unique image of God: "The human Jesus, who is the eternal Son, is also the image of God as a human."[11] As we shall see, to underscore the distinction between Christ's image and that bestowed to the believer, the Lutheran dogmaticians define the former as *substantia* and the latter as *accidens*.

Luther notes in his *Lectures on Genesis* that at creation man existed in the state of integrity or innocence (*Unschuld*), and he possessed all the God-given gifts, powers, and attributes in a full and complete way. In short, beyond his physical life of eating and drinking like all other "beasts," he bore the image of God; he was God's counterpart. This is said only of the human and of no other creature.[12] Although Luther refrains from speculating on what the image of God might have been, he seems to identify it with the perfect relationship with God, a fulfillment of the First Commandment:

> In Adam there was an enlightened reason, a true knowledge of God, and a most sincere desire to love God and his neighbor, so that Adam embraced Eve and at once acknowledged her to be his own flesh. Added to these were other lesser but exceedingly important gifts—if you draw a comparison with our weakness—

7. Pieper, *Christian Dogmatics* 1:515; Luther, *Lectures on Genesis*, 1535–45 (AE 1:338; WA 42:248.16–17): "But through sin both the similitude and the image were lost."

8. Luther, *Lectures on Genesis*, 1535–45 (AE 1:58; WA42:43.38–41); Gerhard, *Theological Commonplaces* 11.6 (8–11:254); Pieper, *Christian Dogmatics* 1:515.

9. This position is commonly associated with Origen (*De Principiis*, 1.2.8, ANF 4:249).

10. Pieper, *Christian Dogmatics* 1:516.

11. "Der Mensch Jesus, der der ewige Sohn ist, ist auch als Mensch Bild Gottes." Peter Brunner, "Der Ersterschaffene als Gottes Ebenbild," in Brunner, *Pro Ecclesia* 1:86.

12. *Lectures on Genesis*, 1535–45 (AE 1:57; WA 42:42.36–43.6).

namely, a perfect knowledge of the nature of the animals, the herbs, the fruits, the trees, and the remaining creatures.[13]

Here the image of God is associated with a right relationship with God, with one another, and with the world. Luther adds to the image in Adam an ethical dimension, pointing to Adam and Eve's holiness:

. . . that Adam had it [the image in his being] and that he not only knew God and believed that He was good, but that he also lived a life that was wholly godly; that is, he was without fear of death or of any other danger, and was content with God's favor. In this form it reveals itself in the instance of Eve, who speaks with the serpent without any fear.[14]

We find an apparent analogy of this description in Luther's explanation of the First Commandment, that we are "to fear, love, and trust God above all things."[15] The relationship that Luther defines includes spiritual qualities of the true knowledge of who God is and what He desires and the ability to commit one's entire being to God in the form of fear, love, and trust in Him. That true relationship in man is located in the heart: "Therefore to have a god is nothing else than to trust and believe in that one with your whole heart."[16] Idolatry occurs when the relationship with God is broken: the heart turns away from God to things of this world, which replace God and the worship of Him.[17] With his anthropological perspective and Christological focus, Luther is not willing to ascribe to any human being on earth a neutral disposition in spiritual matters and in the relationship with God. One truly worships and honors only God or something else that replaces Him, which Luther identifies with various things, such as money and property,[18] learning, wisdom, power, prestige, family, honor,[19] and heathen images.[20] Above all he condemned what the theology of his time taught: that the conscience does not have to rely on God entirely but can seek "help, comfort, and salvation in its own works and presumes to wrest heaven from God."[21] Luther highlights that the restoration of the image of God in humans signifies an intimate relationship of fearing, loving, and honoring Him—not merely possessing such qualities but using them in an active relationship with God Himself. Thus, "fear and trust in God are the criteria of the *imago dei* by their presence, and of original sin by their absence."[22]

The theologian Johann Gerhard describes in a similar way the image in the state of integrity to which fallen humanity must be returned after the Fall:

13. *Lectures on Genesis*, 1535–45 (AE 1:63; WA 42:47.33–38).
14. *Lectures on Genesis*, 1535–45 (AE 1:63; WA 42:47.8–12).
15. SC I.2 (K-W, 351).
16. LC I.2 (K-W, 386).
17. LC I.21 (K-W, 388).
18. LC I.5–9 (K-W, 387).
19. LC I.10 (K-W, 387).
20. LC I.18–21 (K-W, 388).
21. LC I.22 (K-W, 388).
22. Braaten and Jenson, *Christian Dogmatics* 1:332.

"The image of God in man at first was the righteousness and holiness of truth . . . After the fall, men must be renewed in accordance with this."[23]

Gerhard identifies the original image primarily or principally as moral integrity:

> You see, the image of God consists primarily [κυρίως] and principally of the conformity of the rational soul and all its powers with God and with the Law of God, and of prescribed righteousness, holiness, and truth. Consequently, the light of wisdom and understanding shone in the mind, a consistent desire for good was in the will, delight and approval was in the heart, and complete submission free of any resistance was in all other powers. Tranquility of conscience, secure peace of mind, freedom from all pain and rebellion, eternal safety, and wholeness of all faculties were conjoined with this perfection of the soul.[24]

Gerhard then adds to that original image, "less principally and secondarily," the external privilege God handed to man, "the dominion over all other living things." Gerhard argues that the woman shares equally with man in possessing the principal image. However, with regard to dominion, understood as the image secondarily and less principally, the woman holds the image only derivatively, since the "high status properly befitted the man, for the woman had been made subject to the authority of the man."[25]

What is typical of Gerhard and later orthodox theologians is that they include as much as possible in their descriptions of the original image of God, probably in an attempt to sort out Luther's lengthy descriptions in his *Lectures on Genesis*. An example of this expansive outline of the image comes from the orthodox Lutheran theologian Nicolaus Hunnius (1585–1643), who lists seven points which comprise the image:

> The divine image denotes a state of perfection in which God delights, and in which human nature has been originaly [*sic*] created. This perfection consists in 1) a right perception of God and 2) His creation, 3) complete righteousness, 4) true holiness, 5) the liberty of the will, to do the good and to flee the evil, 6) in immortality, and 7) the domination over all the creatures.[26]

23. Gerhard, *Theological Commonplaces* 11.1.36 (8–11:266).

24. Gerhard, *Theological Commonplaces* 11.6.106 (8–11:301).

25. Gerhard, *Theological Commonplaces* 11.6.107 (8–11:301). In support of this distinction Gerhard cites 1 Cor 11:7–9. This distinction falls away, for example, in Pieper, who places the subordinate relation of the woman to man not in the image but in the order of creation; see *Christian Dogmatics*, 1:524. Augustine already had dismissed this derivative view: "For he [the author of Genesis] says that human nature itself, which is complete in both sexes, has been made to the image of God, and he does not exclude the woman from being understood as the image of God." See Augustine, *On the Trinity* 12.7.9–12, NPNFa 3:158–60.

26. Nicolaus Hunnius, *Epitome Credendorum: Containing a Concise and Popular View of the Doctrines of the Lutheran Church*, trans. Paul Edward Gottheil (Nuremberg: U. E. Sebald, 1847), 48.

For Hunnius the consequence of falling into sin is that the image of God with all its seven attributes is lost.[27] Johann Andreas Quenstedt divides up the list of what belongs to the image into a primary and secondary level:

> 1. Primary conformity with God located in his soul, (a) conformity of the intellect, (b) of the will, (c) of the sensuous desires.
> 2. Secondary conformity, located (a) in the human body: without suffering and without death, (b) outside of the human: dominion among lower creatures.[28]

Luther's statement in the *Lectures on Genesis* that to the image belonged "other lesser but exceedingly important gifts" allows Gerhard, Hunnius, and Quenstedt to claim that the image stands in relation to other, less central consequential or accidental qualities. When Quenstedt distinguishes between principal conformity and secondary conformity, the latter of which also pertains to the state of integrity, he has broadened the understanding of the image of God. Johann Wilhelm Baier (1647–95) thus speaks of the original image as having general (*generaliter*) and specific (*specialiter*) qualities because the image of God must be represented not only in spirit but also in the physical appearance, the body, which was the organ and willing bearer of the human spirit.[29]

In discussing what was lost of the *imago Deo* and what remains, however, Johann Gerhard is reluctant to dismiss certain attributes of the image after the Fall:

(1) The very essence of the human soul itself and its essential faculties, that is, mind, will, and memory, since they exist also in the unregenerate;

(2) General similarities to divinity, such as incorporeity, spirituality, intelligence, and free will: "All these things belong to the soul even after the fall";

(3) Human dominion over other creatures: "While the dignity of dominion over other creatures with which man was originally endowed was diminished and in many ways weakened as a consequence of the fall, yet some vestiges of it did remain";

(4) Moral principles: "We maintain that the image was not entirely lost. In fact, the work of the Law is still written in the hearts of men, even the unregenerate";

(5) The righteousness and holiness in which man was originally created: "Then it must be said that the image of God was lost indeed through the fall."[30]

---

27. Hunnius, *Epitome Credendorum*, 51.

28. Quenstedt, *Systema* II,2,1,5–8.

29. Johann Wilhelm Baier, *Compendium Theologiae Positivae: Adjectis Notis Amplioribus, quibus Doctrina Orthodoxa ad Παιδείαν Academicam Explicatur atque ex Scriptura S. Eique Innixis Rationibus Theologicis Confirmatur*, ed. C. F. W. Walther (St. Louis: Luth. Concordia-Verlag, 1879), 203–12.

30. Gerhard, *Theological Commonplaces* 11.9.129 (8–11:322). The early twentieth-century theologian Wilhelm Rohnert compiled the following list of attributes for the image: (1) wisdom; (2) holiness and freedom of the will, which meant Adam was able to sin (*posse peccare*) but he was also able *not* to sin (*posse non peccare*); (3) purity of the sensuous affects and complete

According to Johann Gerhard, the fifth aspect is lost in the Fall but will be received in Christ in the context of restoration.[31] The image of God is considered here not in the broad but in the narrow sense. As seen from Gerhard, Hollaz, Quenstedt, and others, the Aristotelian distinction between *substantia* and *accidens* helps to differentiate the image of Christ from the image of God in the human, namely, that in the human the image in the proper sense was not to be understood as a substance but rather as an accidental perfection. According to the Aristotelian categories, substance signifies something more than what is shared in a relationship with others. In that relationship it actually can become the "bearer" of one of the other qualities and exist with that quality on its own, whether the entity in question is a table, a human being, or a plant, whereas a nonsubstance-like entity, the *accidens*, cannot exist on its own but relies on another entity for its being, like a parasite living off a plant.[32]

Medieval theology adopted Aristotle's idea of the substance and promoted an ontological-metaphysical approach. The Aristotelian-scholastic metaphysical ontology underlying analogies impacts the human's understanding of his image and particularly of the way salvation is gained. The human is thought to have natural substance qualities that mirror God's, either his intellect and reason (*via antiqua*) or his will (*via moderna*), which he uses in the quest for salvation.[33] This substantive or ontological approach finds something constructive within the image of the individual human, irrespective of his actions or surroundings. Nature and grace, or differently put, anthropology and soteriology, come together.

Luther dismisses this metaphysical ontology that wishes to strike an analogy between God and His creation. He advances a different, nonsubstance-like relationship, a transcendental-personal relational concept enacted through soteriology. Analogy of being (*analogia entis*) now becomes an analogy between Christ and a believer, which is one not of ontology but of relation

harmony of all his powers and urges. In addition to these spiritual and moral qualities—which are all together called *justitia originalis*—are added as a natural outflow physical and external or consequential attributes. These attributes are the following: (1) superior qualities of the body and immortality of the body. The qualities of the body and its limbs were superior to those of all other animals. The human would not have had to die had he not sinned (*possibilitas non moriendi*), since death came as a consequence of sin (Gn 2:17, 25; 3:19; Rom 6:23). Also, he was free from all woes of the body (*impassibilitas*), from pain, illness, sweat from labor, and so forth (Gn 1:31; 2:17, 25); (2) dominion over creation, an image of the majesty of God, in whose stead the human should stand (Gn 1:26; 2:19). Rohnert, *Dogmatik der evangelisch-lutherischen Kirche*, 198. Polkinghorne, though sympathetic to evolution, lists next to language other traits: (1) self-consciousness, especially the ability to look far ahead into the future; (2) ethical intuitions of right and wrong and the ability to assume responsibilities that follow from these insights; (3) use of the conceptual tool of language; (4) exercise of rational skills, especially the scientific and mathematical abilities. See Polkinghorne, "Anthropology in an Evolutionary Context," 96–98. For additional and similar qualities, see Joel B. Green, *Body, Soul, and Human Life: The Nature of Humanity in the Bible* (Grand Rapids: Baker Academic, 2008), 45.

31. Gerhard, *Theological Commonplaces* 11.9.129 (8–11:322)

32. SD I.55 (K-W, 541).

33. Joest, *Ontologie der Person bei Luther*, 61.

enacted through faith (*analogia relationis*). This distinction is important for his understanding of the image: it is not a matter of possessing a substance prior to the event of grace but rather a relationship status between the Creator and His creation enacted through the Word and faith.[34] In an elaborate study entitled *Ontologie der Person bei Martin Luther*,[35] Wilfried Joest has shown that this pre-Reformation medieval-scholastic theology operating with an individual-substantive concept was strongly opposed by Luther.[36]

What is important here is that in the doctrine of salvation, to which the image of God is essentially connected, man possesses nothing, according to Luther, and brings nothing to the table. There are no *preambula fidei* that suggest there is a realm juxtaposed between the knowledge that comes through man's natural reason and the revealed understanding through faith, a realm in which man possesses the factual or rudimentary quality or qualities to be able to stand before God with natural endowed abilities to produce something by his own powers that he may consider *his*.[37]

It should be apparent that the image of God is not like a possession of man or a part of his essence. As we stated earlier, it is accidental in nature,[38] not substantive, for the latter applies only to Christ.[39] In a much higher way, Christ is the image of God (*imago Dei substantialis*). As the Son of God He is

---

34. Thus, when it comes to defining the image of God, Roman Catholic theologians, guided by the traditional ontology, miss in Luther's anthropology and image of God something that a human being possesses and owns even as God's grace comes to him. See Joest, *Ontologie der Person bei Luther*, 21–27.

35. Joest, *Ontologie der Person bei Luther*.

36. "The question of what a human *is* in view of grace and nature (in the sense of his essence) and thereby what his abilities are, is obsolete. The personhood of a human is always a relationship with God *in the making*, that is, in the making into which the human being is drawn, that God addresses him through the word and thereby opens up in him a disposition towards Him. This and not the equipping of substantive powers is what constitutes the personhood." ("Die Frage, was der Mensch in Natur und Gnade *ist* [im Sinne des Wesensbestandes] und *daher* im Vollzug von Beziehung vermag, ist als solche überholt. Das Personsein des Menschen ist je immer schon seine Gottesbeziehung *im Vollzug*; und zwar in einem Vollzug, in den der Mensch dadurch hineingezogen ist, daß Gott ihn angeht im Wort und ihm dadurch ein Verhalten zu sich selbst eröffnet. Dies und nicht eine Ausstattung mit Wesenskräften ist das Konstitutivum des Personseins.") Joest, *Ontologie der Person bei Luther*, 35.

37. Joest, *Ontologie der Person bei Luther*, 59. The existence of such a realm would also limit God's freedom according to Elert: "God does not face the world as one bound to it, but as its free Lord" (*Christian Faith*, 169).

38. "Imago Dei alia est substantialis, alia accidentalis. Illa est aeternus Dei Filius; quia totam essentiam Patris in se exprimit, modos subsistendi ab eo distinctus. a) Haec est, cujus accidentalis perfectionis infinitis Dei perfectionibus secundum modum capacitatis humanae conformes sunt." David Hollaz, *Examen Theologicum Acroamaticum, Universam Theologiam Thetico-Polemicam Complectens*, Pars II, Caput I (Holmiae; Lipsiae: Apud Godofredum Kiesewetterum, 1735), 501–2; Rohnert, *Dogmatik der evangelisch-lutherischen Kirche*, 197; Pöhlmann, *Abriß der Dogmatik*, 163.

39. Thus in contrast, as with the rest of Lutheran orthodoxy before him, the Lutheran theologian Friedrich Adolf Philippi (1809–82) also distinguishes between Christ's image and that of the human being: "Jesus is the image of God in full size [*Lebensgröße*], man is only a miniature image of the divinity." Friedrich Adolph Philippi, *Kirchliche Glaubenslehre*, vol. 2, *Die ursprüngliche Gottesgemeinschaft*, 2d ed. (Stuttgart: S. G. Liesching, 1867), 365.

the complete and perfect image (εἰκών) of the invisible God (2 Cor 4:4; Col 1:15), the reflection (ἀπαύγασμα) of His glory, and bears the very "stamp of His nature" (χαρακτὴρ τῆς ὑποστάσεως, Heb 1:3). In the Son the hidden God revealed Himself to the world in His original, absolute protoimage, whereas in the created man the image of God is represented in a derivative and relative fashion. This distinction is of great importance as we talk of a new relationship with the person of Christ into which the believer is drawn through the Word and His justification.[40] This discrepancy identifies the discussion about the image of God as a matter of soteriology;[41] and how salvation is received is in turn a matter of where that takes place, namely, in a missiological context where God's Word is preached to the nonbeliever.[42] The Christological and soteriological dimensions remain crucial: the true image of God found in Christ is received only through the encounter with God's Word.

The multidimensional descriptions of the image of God over the course of the church's history—from an early and medieval Christian association with possession of the will and reason, to perhaps a notion of upright posture, bodily integrity, and the ability to exercise dominion—would apply at best only to what some orthodox Lutheran theologians call the image in its broad sense. Orthodox Lutheran theologians such as Johann Wilhelm Baier, Johann Gerhard, and Johann Quenstedt and other Lutheran theologians after them[43] do not concede that God's image in man is wholly accidental, purely dependent upon its Source, but distinguish between a part of the image that has been lost and a part of it that remains. Genesis 9:6 and Jas 3:9 describe the human after the Fall as still possessing an intellect and will, and these passages thus assume

40. Thus, while we agree with the Eastern view that true humanity is found in that relationship with Christ and is not simply a biological reality, descriptions of that new relationship in Christ should be clarified when terms such as "ontology" and of course "divinization" are used. Statements such as those made by John Zizioulas, "Christ does not simply stand vis-à-vis each man, but constitutes the ontological ground of every man," exemplify that need. John Zizioulas, *Communion and Otherness: Further Studies in Personhood and the Church*, ed. Paul McPartlan (London: T&T Clark, 2006), 243. See here Marc Cortez, *Christological Anthropology in Historical Perspective: Ancient and Contemporary Approaches to Theological Anthropology* (Grand Rapids: Zondervan, 2016), 163–89.

41. Härle, *Dogmatik*, 437.

42. Georg F. Vicedom, *The Mission of God: An Introduction to a Theology of Mission* (St. Louis: Concordia Publishing House, 1965), 15. It is unclear why some missiologists assume the image still exists in humans, when it is brought to them through the Gospel. See Alan Hirsch and Lance Ford, *Right Here, Right Now: Everyday Mission for Everyday People* (Grand Rapids: Baker Books, 2011), 85.

43. For example, Wilhelm Rohnert: "The image of God in the wider sense (*imago Dei late dicta*), that natural image, exists as the rational thought and freedom of the will. It cannot be lost and belongs to the substance of the human; for if the ability to think and will is lacking, the human would stop being a rational being. This natural image remains in spite of the Fall and can be lost or clouded only by insanity (Gn 9:6; Jas 3:9; 1 Cor 11:7; Acts 17:28). —Here we are dealing solely with the image in the narrow sense (*imago Dei stricte dicta*), the moral image. It is the appended perfection to the human nature, the normal condition of the human after spirit and body that has been lost through the Fall." Rohnert, *Dogmatik der evangelisch-lutherischen Kirche*, 197 (my translation).

that humans retain some similitude with God. These Lutheran theologians give this dual or two-stage concept of the image its due attention—with the important clarification, however, that the assertion of a remnant image in the broad sense does not imply they are dismissing the total depravity of humans. In Gn 5:3, for example, Gerhard argues that Adam begetting Seth in his own image and likeness means that Seth received Adam's sinful image, "subject to sin, the wrath of God, the curse of the Law, and temporal and eternal death."[44]

Generally speaking, in contrast to Luther, the definition of the image of God in two distinct categories, one in its proper sense and the other in its wider sense, has a long tradition. In the teaching of the Roman Catholic Church and Eastern Orthodox churches, the image of God in its proper or narrow sense, ethically speaking, is considered completely lost, as man is totally depraved. But ontologically, in the wider or broad sense, the image is considered to remain, as man after the Fall remains man. But according to Luther's unitary view, that the image was once there but now has been lost implies God's prerogative to restore it. The image is affected so negatively by sin that it must be called the *imago diaboli* or *satanae*,[45] which implies its total loss. As one scholar noted, for Luther "the image of God refers to a total orientation of the human toward God, a total relationship. As such it cannot be divided or parceled out, as Aquinas was wont to do."[46] Or as another scholar pointed out, for Luther the image of God reflects a total dependency on God. In other words, everything in the human being, the spirit, heart, and conscience, is "not an anthropological given which then secondarily relates to God by means of faith. Rather, there is only one way in which human beings exist, by being in relationship with another person than the self, by means of 'relying' (*sich verlassen*)."[47] For Luther, the argument that the image of God still remains after the Fall (Gn 5:1, 3; 9:6f.; Jas 3:9) has little currency in the light of his focus on the restoration in Christ. For him the passages seem to speak rather to the "noble creature who once bore the image of God and in whom God would re-create this image through faith in Christ."[48] After all, he comments, if "remnant" is defined by a reasonable mind, then the devil himself would represent the truest image of God "since he surely has these

44. Gerhard, *Theological Commonplaces* 11.1.22 (8–11:259).

45. In his *Lectures on Genesis*, 1535–45 (AE 1:63; WA 42:47.22): "These and similar evils are the image of the devil who stamped them on us." Also in a sermon on Genesis, Luther writes: "Aber das selbe bilde [Gottes] ist nu untergangen und verderbet und an des stat des Teuffels bilde auffgericht" (The image of God is now gone and destroyed, and the devil's image emerged in its stead; my translation). *Über das erste Buch Mose. Predigten*, 1527 (WA 24:153.14–15); Peters, *Der Mensch*, 45, 194.

46. Braaten and Jenson, *Christian Dogmatics* 1:332–33.

47. Notger Slenczka, "Luther's Anthropology," in *The Oxford Handbook of Martin Luther's Theology*, ed. Robert Kolb, Irene Dingel, and Ľubomír Batka (New York: Oxford University Press, 2014), 216.

48. Pieper, *Christian Dogmatics* 1:519.

natural endowments, such as memory and a very superior intellect and a most determined will, to a far higher degree than we have them"[49] (Luke 4).

The Lutheran Confessions also follow Luther's forward-looking understanding of the image by holding to an image strictly speaking (*imago Dei stricte dicta*), which the Formula of Concord defines as "the image of God, according to which the human being was originally created in truth, holiness, and righteousness."[50] Consequently, in the Apology the loss of the image is defined as the loss of the state of integrity and moral image of God, which implies the loss of not only "a balanced physical constitution" (*aequale temperamentum qualitatum corporis*)[51] but also "a more certain knowledge of God, fear of God, and confidence in God, or at least the uprightness and power needed to do these things."[52]

The Apology affirms that the image consists of the following: a certain and true knowledge of God (*notitia Dei certior*), fear of God (*timorem Dei*), trust (*fiduciam Dei*), and a rectitude and ability (*aut certe rectitudinem et vim ista efficiendi*) "to grasp God and reflect God"[53] as a being "originally created in truth, holiness, and righteousness."[54] Thus, while the Confessions make a concession to the use of reason in running worldly affairs and credit that ability to the fallen human,[55] their view on the spiritual state of the human—that is, in his relationship with God—is that these rational powers are completely lost. There is no back door left slightly ajar, as there was in the two-stage concept of medieval times.[56]

49. *Lectures on Genesis*, 1535–45 (AE 1:61; WA 42:46.7–10).

50. SD I.10 (K-W, 533). The Lutheran Confessions do not make any distinction between the *imago Dei* in the broad and the narrow senses. They seem to hold that the image of God after the Fall has been lost. SD I.10–11 (K-W, 533–34).

51. The German text includes "perfect health in all respects, pure blood, and unimpaired powers of the body." Ap. II.17 (K-W, 114n20).

52. Ap. II.17 (K-W, 114). The German text is more elaborate: "Das Größte an solcher edler erster Kreatur ist gewesen ein helles Licht im Herzen, Gott und sein Werk zu erkennen, eine rechte Gottesfurcht, ein recht herzliches Vertrauen gegen Gott und allenthalben ein rechtschaffen gewisser Verstand, ein fein gut fröhlich Herz gegen Gott und allen göttlichen Sachen" (The greatest thing with that noble, first creature was a bright light in the heart, to recognize God and His work, a true fear of God, a right, cordial trust of God and in all things a righteous, upright mind, a pure, good, joyous heart towards God and all divine things). *Concordia Triglotta: The Symbolical Books of the Ev. Lutheran Church, German-Latin-English*, trans. and ed. F. Bente, W. H. T. Dau, and The Lutheran Church—Missouri Synod (St. Louis: Concordia Publishing House, 1921), 108, 109. This understanding is reflected also in Article II of the Augsburg Confession, "Concerning Original Sin," which identifies the post-Fall human condition as follows: "Since the fall of Adam all men who are propagated according to nature are born in sin, that is, without fear of God, without trust in God, and with concupiscence." AC II.1 (K-W, 37).

53. Ap. II.18–22 (K-W, 114–15).

54. SD I.10 (K-W, 533).

55. AC XVIII.4 (K-W, 233–34).

56. While this view is articulated clearly in the Confessions and Lutheran orthodoxy, the same cannot be said for Melanchthon, who from the 1530s on seems to entertain the third element, the will, next to the Word and the Holy Spirit as the causes for one's salvation. This is why the Formula of Concord raises the question of the causes of salvation and identifies only

Francis Pieper agrees with Luther. The reason and will of the fallen human are not, to use Pieper's words, an "idling motor" but rather running in darkness (1 Cor 2:14) and spiritually set against God (Rom 8:27).[57] "To call man the image of God because he possesses reason and will and leave out of consideration what he is to become in Christ is to stretch a point."[58]

The thought of calling rational capacities of some sort an *imago* remnant intensifies the tension between the Christocentric and pneumatological orientation and the philosophical approach touting rational powers. However, it is true that some continuity between pre- and post-Fall humanity must be maintained. If that were not the case, the human would have become something totally different after the Fall and a Manichean dualism would apply. That argument was leveled against Matthias Flacius, who maintained that original sin could not be understood as accidental to the human but only substantive.[59] So too with the image of God: though lost, it is returned to the human being in Christ without making him something different than he is. The Confessions make the point that some attributes are carried over after a person's conversion:

> Likewise, we reject those who concoct the idea that in conversion and new birth God creates a new heart and a new creature, so that the substance and essence of the old creature and especially the rational soul are completely annihilated and that a new essence of the soul is created of nothing. St. Augustine specifically criticized this error.[60]

This desire to establish continuity might explain in part the interest of Lutheran theologians to associate the image in the broad sense with the rational power as that which remains with a human structurally after his conversion. What certainly should not be brought into the discussion on the image is anthropomorphology.[61] The scriptural statement "Let us" provides a tempting avenue to lure us into thinking that humans resemble God Himself in physiognomy, that is, the temptation, as Gerhard puts it, to express the image "by the contour of the human body."[62] It is not helpful to associate with the image of God in the human some physical appearance of God, be it in an upright walk, a spirit which can communicate, differentiation of gender, or the dominion over earth.[63] Rather, God made the human as His own creation and according to His own design and placed him in a total relationship that exists in righteousness or holiness, proper worship, true faith, hope, and love.[64]

two—God's Word and the Holy Spirit—and dismisses the third element, the human mind or will. SD II.90 (K-W, 561). Peters, *Der Mensch*, 73.

57. Pieper, *Christian Dogmatics* 1:520.

58. Pieper, *Christian Dogmatics* 1:520.

59. SD I.33, 57, 60 (K-W, 537, 541–42).

60. SD II.81 (K-W, 559).

61. Within Christianity an anthropomorphic facet to the image of God is not very prevalent. See Philippi, *Kirchliche Glaubenslehre*, 367.

62. Gerhard, *Theological Commonplaces* 11.1.25 (8–11:260).

63. Härle, *Dogmatik*, 435.

64. Hermann Deuser, *Kleine Einführung in die systematische Theologie* (Ditzingen: Reclam,

The point here is that God is qualitatively different than humans, as can be seen from His aseity, even if metaphors can be used to compare Him to a human.[65] To speak of God in such picture-like, metaphorical categories is indeed helpful, even indispensable, but the issue is far deeper than some sort of physical resemblance with God, who is in fact the invisible God. Moreover, the image cannot be physical because God has no body and is given in Scripture a dynamic, relational reality when He is described as "spirit" (Jn 4:24) or love (1 Jn 4:8, 16).

In seriously considering both the categorical difference between God and humans and the relationship between God and humans, one could say that the image is a lived-out expression, a depiction or representation, yes, a true form of God's being. This description accurately captures the image of God in the context of the New Testament, where Jesus Christ is *the* image of God (2 Cor 4:4; Col 1:15; Heb 1:3). In Christ the true purpose and design of the human is fully realized, and so he is also the true image of God, or in Luther's words "a mirror of the Father's heart."[66]

THE BIBLICAL DATA: THE PROTOLOGICAL-ADAMITIC AND CHRISTOLOGICAL-ESCHATOLOGICAL ORIENTATIONS

Both negative and positive aspects of the appraisal of humanity have their roots in the Adam–Christ antitype structure in 1 Cor 15:21f., 45–49, and Rom 5:12–21, particularly in verse 19 in reference to disobedience and obedience. Consider the symmetry between the first and second Adams: God reacts to their actions inversely, declaring the human guilty because of Adam but righteous because of Christ.[67] Humans had been bearers of the image of Adam, but now will become bearers of the image of the new Adam. Luther points this out in his commentary on 1 Cor 15:23, that "it was not His will that we remain in sin and death, which would have happened if Christ had not come. Thus this is all sheer grace. Now we no longer suffer any harm from the fact that we die in Adam."[68]

This restoration also advances the concept of regression, or a return to the events of creation, which we could call protology or a protological orientation: the new image of Christ connects the believer to the original created image of Adam (Col 3:10: "Put on the new self which is being renewed in knowledge in the image of its Creator"). To become a believer is to become a second Adam. In Eph 4:24 the believer is "created to be like God," which hearkens back to Gn

1999), 69.

65. Pieper, *Christian Dogmatics* 1:515; Härle, *Dogmatik*, 435.

66. LC II.65 (K-W, 440).

67. In accordance with 1 Cor 15:45, Luther says: "Adam is a figure of Christ. The similarity consists in this, that just as through Adam sin came to all, so also Christ's righteousness comes to all who believe in Him." *Lectures on Genesis*, 1535–45 (AE 1:219; WA 42:163.33–35). See also AE 1:64; WA 42:48.6–10.

68. *Commentary on 1 Corinthians 15*, 1533 (AE 28:120; WA 36:563.30–33).

1:26–27. In Jesus Christ the concept of the image of God not only is provided with an eschatological perspective and the promise of growing ever more into His likeness, it also builds a bridge back to the first creation, to protology, and restores the believer in that original image that once was Adam's.[69]

The biblical texts discussing the image of God can be found in the Old and New Testaments. However, these texts require systematization, and upon closer review they fall into two categories. Some texts reflect what remains of the image from creation (a protological-Adamitic orientation), while others focus on its restoration in Christ (a Christological-eschatological orientation).

In Scripture we find the pattern of salvation history: the image of God was received perfectly in the state of integrity prior to the Fall, but in the Fall that image was lost, and its restoration occurs only through faith in Christ. This forward-looking or teleological understanding of the image of God being restored is defined Christologically. Through the reconciliatory work of Christ we "put on the new self, which is being renewed in knowledge [εἰς ἐπίγνωσιν] after the image of its Creator" (Col 3:10), "conformed to the image of his Son" (Rom 8:29, συμμόρφους τῆς εἰκόνος τοῦ Υἱοῦ αὐτοῦ), and are "created after the likeness of God in true righteousness and holiness" (Eph 4:24, κατὰ θεὸν ἐν δικαιοσύνῃ καί ὁσιότητι τῆς ἀληθείας). These texts, along with 2 Cor 3:18, Rom 12:2, and Phil 2:5, speak of a change (μεταμορφόω) into the likeness (εἰκών) of Christ, a conjoining of Christ and the believer understood as a renewal of the mind and thereby the attainment of a true knowledge of God.[70]

This scriptural trajectory that looks forward to the restoration of the image in Christ is balanced against scriptural accounts of the image being retained in some way after the Fall (Gn 5:1, 3; 9:6; Psalm 8; 1 Cor 11:7; and Jas 3:9). In some Scripture passages the image is attributed to fallen humanity, in others only in terms of restoration in Christ. Thus the two poles of orientation emerge of the image of God, one which refers to the beginning (*terminus a quo*) and the original pre-Fall image in Genesis, the other which reflects the process of renewal in Christ that will be perfected at the end of time (*terminus ad quem*). The protological-Adamitic orientation, which defines the image with reference to the creation of man, inclines toward a substantive or structural understanding of some kind, something that man possesses naturally, whereas the alternative, the forward-looking Christological-eschatological focus, focuses on a restoration brought about through a renewed relationship with Christ through His Word.

69. We should note that for many modern theologians the idea of regression does not apply, simply because they do not believe the historic Adam ever existed.

70. We concur with Bruce L. McCormack on this point: "We would be better off, I suspect, thinking of the work of the Holy Spirit in terms of an existential encounter of divine person with human person whose point of entry, if you will, is the mind." Bruce L. McCormack, "What's at Stake in Current Debates over Justification? The Crisis of Protestantism in the West," in *Justification: What's at Stake in the Current Debates*, ed. Mark Husbands and Daniel J. Treier (Downers Grove, IL: InterVarsity Press, 2004), 116.

THE DEBATE IN MODERN THEOLOGY

The debate among modern theologians begins with a relevant question from Albrecht Peters: "Is the image of God to be located in certain qualities or also in a 'part' of our essential humanity, or must it be described entirely from the standpoint of the relationship with God?"[71]

Peters points out two approaches to thinking about the image of God in humans: one that seeks to identify substantive or essential qualities in man, and one that looks forward to his restored relationship with God. Peters calls the first an ontological, substantive-materialistic (*seinshaft-materialen*) concept and the second an existential-relational (*existential-relationalen*) concept of the *imago Dei*.[72] Many modern (as well as past) theologians seek to adopt one of the two approaches, to combine them, or to go beyond any traditional thought and propose a wholly different concept. The three prevailing theological interpretations of the image advanced by various theologians are the substantive, the functional, and the relational views.[73]

Option One: The Substantive View

Noreen Herzfeld explains the approach adopted in support of the substantive view of the image of God as follows:

> Substantive interpretations tend to approach the question of what is the image of God in human beings from the bottom up, beginning with an examination of the human person and looking from there for what represents the highest and best in our innate nature, and what separates us from the rest of creation.[74]

Following this approach, the modern theologian Millard J. Erickson observes in a comment on Gn 1:26 that the image still has some bearing in defining humans after the Fall and that in a substantive way

> the image of God has not been lost as a result of sin or specifically the fall. The prohibitions against murder and cursing apply to the treatment of sinful humans as well as godly believers. The presence of the image and likeness in the non-Christian is assumed. If this is the case, the image of God is not something accidental or external to human nature. It is something inseparably connected with humanity.[75]

---

71. Peters, *Der Mensch*, 195: "Ist die Imago Dei zu lokalisieren in bestimmten Eigenschaften oder auch in einem 'Teil' unseres Menschseins oder muß sie ganz aus der Gottesrelation heraus beschrieben werden?" My translation.

72. Peters, *Der Mensch*, 195.

73. Millard Erickson has condensed the positions to three: the substantive view, the relational view, and the functional view (Millard J. Erickson, *Christian Theology*, 2d ed. [Grand Rapids: Baker Book House, 1998], 520–31). At times the categories "structural" or "teleological" are applied (Samuel H. Nafzger et al., eds., *Confessing the Gospel: A Lutheran Approach to Systematic Theology* [St. Louis: Concordia Publishing House, 2017], 1:332–36).

74. Noreen Herzfeld, *In Our Image: Artificial Intelligence and the Human Spirit* (Minneapolis: Fortress Press, 2002), 19.

75. Erickson, *Christian Theology*, 532.

Theological anthropologists follow the biblical idea that humans are something other than beasts (Psalm 8), even if at times the Bible seems to forgo that distinction to underscore man's brutal nature (e.g., Eccl 3:18–21). Bolstering the value and dignity of all humans in these theologians' view is the assertion that both those outside and those within the relationship with Christ possess an extant, structural image of God. Erickson asserts that God's image and likeness in the non-Christian is implicit in biblical accounts. What then could it be? One could argue with Augustine that, unlike animals, humans possess within their rational abilities also a degree of consciousness of the divine. They are endowed with a mind or *animus* that is also capable, though always imperfectly, of contemplation of God via general knowledge and revelation.[76] Reinhold Niebuhr agrees with Augustine on this point and suggests that all humans possess the potential for self-transcendency,[77] and that even the act of creating an idolatrous god, a rebellious reaction against the true, revealed God, demonstrates that humans are not animals. This is the argument many theologians—most of them—who follow Luther's teleological orientation wish to make and want to fall back on. Emil Brunner presses this point by citing a "formal structural responsibility."[78] Others offer similar approaches. Martin Kähler refers to the image of God as a "disposition . . . that includes the task of realizing it," implying that the human being as a personality has the ability (*Fähigkeit*) to step into a relationship with God.[79] Paul Althaus is less explicit that man possesses this ability innately but claims an endowment or constitution

76. According to Augustine, the human being finds himself in an "in-between status" as an integrated whole of mind, soul, and body who is above the beasts but "a little lower" than the angels and endowed with a mind or *animus* that is also capable of contemplation. Augustine added the idea that, unlike animals, humans possess within their rational abilities also a degree of God-consciousness. This dimension comes about through the intellectual contemplation of eternal things as opposed to the rational cognition of temporal things. Influenced by Neoplatonism, Augustine is less focused on a rational or intellectual capacity to form concepts of God than on a kind of mysticism believing that the human spirit reaches vertically to the mysteries of God, without ever being able to attain it apart from revelation. "Certainly it is great bliss to have a little touch or taste of God with the mind; but completely to grasp him, comprehend him, is altogether impossible." Augustine, *On the Words of the Gospel of John 1:1–3: "In the Beginning Was the Word and the Word Was with God and the Word Was God, Etc.": Against the Arians*, trans. Edmund Hill, in *Works of Saint Augustine* 3.4:209–23. See also Augustine, *On the Trinity*, 12.15.25 (NPNFa 3:165) and 12.7.12 (NPNFa 3:161).

77. Reinhold Niebuhr bases his insight in part on the Pauline tradition that the Spirit (רוּחַ, *ruach*, or πνεῦμα, *pneuma*) must be "conceived of as primarily a capacity for and affinity with the divine." Niebuhr, *Nature and Destiny of Man* 1:152, 157–58, 161–62.

78. "Likewise the distinction between a formal-structural responsibility which *cannot be lost*, and the responsibility which finds its fulfilment—materially—in existence in love, is such that it can only be derived from the false decision, from sin." Emil Brunner, *The Christian Doctrine of Creation and Redemption*, vol. 2 of *Dogmatics*, trans. Olive Wyon (Philadelphia: Westminster Press, 1952), 73; italics added.

79. "Anlage . . . , welche eine zu erfüllende Aufgabe in sich schließt." Martin Kähler, *Die Wissenschaft der christlichen Lehre von dem evangelischen Grundartikel aus im Abrisse dargestellt*, 2d ed. (Leipzig: Deichert, 1893), 262; quoted in Wolfhart Pannenberg, *Systematic Theology*, trans. Geoffrey W. Bromiley (Grand Rapids: Wm. B. Eerdmans, 1991–98), 2:228.

in the human being "in which man is destined for fellowship with God."[80] Oswald Bayer argues similarly:

> Accordingly being in the image of God is not completely lost but it is radically corrupt. It behaves like a radio receiver which still functions but picks up the wrong station: the community of communication is disrupted; the human can no longer hear or know God even if it wants to. It only picks up static.[81]

A Lutheran dogmatics text must of course also take into consideration Luther and the Confessions. In a claim that preserves this sense of uniqueness for humans, the Confessions state that after the Fall and before conversion "the human being is still a rational creature, which has understanding and will" in distinction to animals.[82] Moreover, these confessional sources introduce two more grounds for the value of humans. First, humans are still objects of God's love (Jn 3:16). The Confessions state that each person is loved by God and is a being in whom God begins His sanctifying work, a *modus operandi* that seeks the person's conversion based on the redemption in Christ. Even as sinner, a person remains human. Thus, the argument that original sin is an accidental and not a substantive reality helps to underscore that God loves humans in spite of their sin; were that distinction to fall away, God would have to shun the entire sinner.[83] Second, in regard to the *modus operandi* of one's conversion, the Confessions point to a passive capacity residing in all humans. This capacity indicates that humans are unique among life forms and indicates that God does not coerce anyone to convert as if a human being were a robot or a stone—even if Luther and the Confessions do not associate that capacity with the image.[84] Luther distinguishes humans from other life forms on the basis of this passive aptitude which cannot be found in trees or animals, and concludes: "For heaven, as the saying is, was not made for geese."[85] Although the human has lost the perfection of the image and righteousness of God through the Fall, still he retains, according to his humanity and contrary to the nature of beasts, the passive capacity to be converted. The emphasis here is on "passive," since the "human will is not active towards producing conversion."[86]

---

80. "*Verfassung* des Menschen, in der er *bestimmt* ist zur Gemeinschaft mit Gott; im zweiten, christologischen Sinne bezeichnet es die *erfüllte Bestimmung*." Paul Althaus, *Die christliche Wahrheit: Lehrbuch der Dogmatik*, 2d ed. (Gütersloh: C. Bertelsmann, 1949), 2:93. Pannenberg, *Systematic Theology* 2:227.

81. Oswald Bayer, "Being in the Image of God," *Lutheran Quarterly* 27, no. 1 (2013): 86.

82. SD II.19, 59 (K-W, 555). Pieper, *Christian Dogmatics* 1:519.

83. SD II.45 (K-W, 539).

84. SD II.23, 60, 71 (K-W, 548, 555, 557).

85. "But if the power of free choice were said to mean that by which a man is capable of being taken hold of by the Spirit and imbued with the grace of God, as a being created for eternal life or death, no objection could be taken. For this power or aptitude, or as the Sophists say, this disposing quality or passive aptitude, we also admit; and who does not know that it is not found in trees or animals? For heaven, as the saying is, was not made for geese." *The Bondage of the Will*, 1525 (AE 33:67; WA 18:636.16–22).

86. "The human will is not active towards producing conversion [*nihil confert*], but only experiences it [*tantum patitur, quod Deus in homine agit*]. . . . And that man does not assist in

Attempts among modern theologians to hold fast to a both/and structure inevitably invite a discussion similar to that held between Emil Brunner and Karl Barth, which ultimately reached an impasse. Brunner strongly emphasized the restoration of a relationship with God in Christ but stipulated that this restoration connects (*anknüpfen*) to something latent in the human being which he called the "formal-structural responsibility." He affirmed both a formal concept of the image, without attributing any spiritual powers to it, and a Christologically defined material one, which a human, "by the very fact that he is a sinner, no longer possesses."[87]

What he wished to say, and this echoes the invective of Paul against the Gentiles in Romans 1 and 2, is that because people know that God exists and what He wants from them and yet in sin reject Him, they are held accountable. Barth dismissed this position, however, claiming that Brunner could not have it both ways: he could not accept both the ontological idea of a formal remnant and the Christologically defined material one. Though his theological position was very similar to that of Brunner, Barth could not accept his idea that humans possess connective points and insisted that God's revelation finds no points of contact except the ones He Himself initiates.

To avoid any confusion or accusation of synergism, Brunner in his treatment on the image defined that formal capacity as *Wortmächtigkeit,* which could be translated as the "capacity for words" or the mere "capacity for speech." He explains it based on a concept of general revelation:

> The Word of God does not have to create man's capacity for words [*Wortmächtigkeit*]. He has never lost it, it is the presupposition of his ability to hear the Word of God. But the Word of God itself creates man's ability to believe the Word of God, *i.e.* the ability to hear it in *such a way* as is only possible in faith. It is evident that the doctrine of *sola gratia* is not in the least endangered by such a doctrine of the point of contact.[88]

Brunner felt unjustly criticized by Barth, who accused him of promoting *Offenbarungsmächtigkeit*, implying that he meant an unregenerate person had

---

his conversion but remains purely passive [*pure passive, tamquam subiectum patiens*] is owing to his condition after the Fall." Pieper, *Christian Dogmatics* 2:457.

87. Brunner, *Christian Doctrine of Creation*, 76. Emil Brunner references the formal concept of the image to Acts 17:28; 1 Cor 11:7; and Jas 3:9. The following quote explains well Brunner's distinction between the formal and material image: "We distinguish categorically: formally the *imago* is not in the least touched—whether sinful or not, man is a subject and is responsible. Materially the *imago* is completely lost, man is a sinner through and through and there is nothing in him which is not defiled by sin. To formulate it differently: as before, man is a person, *i.e.* he is in a derived sense that which God is originally. Yet he is not a personal person but an anti-personal person; for the truly personal is existence in love, the submission of the self to the will of God and therefore an entering into communion with one's fellow-creature because one enjoys communion with God. This *quid* of personality is negatived through sin, whereas the *quod* of personality constitutes the *humanum* of every man, also that of the sinner." Emil Brunner and Karl Barth, *Natural Theology,* trans. Peter Fraenkel (London: G. Bles, the Centenary Press, 1946), 24.

88. Brunner and Barth, *Natural Theology,* 32.

the "capacity for revelation." Brunner did not intend to advance that kind of natural theology, as the quote above proves, which is why he would not accept the term "remnant": it could imply that something good remains in the human being. Brunner gives the example of the knowledge of sin that comes before one is enlightened by the grace of God, when His laws are both comprehensible and incomprehensible: "Natural man knows them and yet does not know them. If he did not know them, he would not be human: if he really knew them, he would not be a sinner."[89]

The criticism against Brunner also targeted Augustine's concept of latent self-transcendence and those orthodox Lutherans who attribute to the human a formal, broadly defined image which is associated with the possession of reason and will. This discussion strives to maintain a proper distinction between between general revealed knowledge of God and special revelation through the Word of God. By keeping the two separate, yet giving each due consideration, Lutheran theologians as well would be criticized unjustly. For to speak of a remnant or broad image is not to imply that a human has an inherent power to initiate his own relationship with God. This capacity for a vague knowledge of God and what He wants is a capacity that has become perverted; without God's own initiative, that person remains spiritually dead. To phrase it biblically: "The natural person does not accept the things of the Spirit of God, for they are folly to him, and he is not able to understand them because they are spiritually discerned" (1 Cor 2:14).

While some who hold to a remnant image would like to reserve for the unregenerate some potential spiritual powers, that is not the case for Brunner and many orthodox Lutherans. Barth's criticism would target Luther himself and the Confessions, which did not speak of the image per se but still acknowledged, as we just observed, a passive capacity in the human being that distinguished "human beings from other animate or inanimate creatures," and "that human beings are creatures that can be converted."[90] In an attempt to distinguish himself from Barth's denial of "any sort of genuine revelation of God in nature," Brunner, according to Stanley Grenz, "presented a view of general revelation that he believed was fully consistent with the New Testament and the Protestant Reformers, especially Calvin and Luther."[91]

Brunner correctly attributes to Barth the following interrelated errors: the belief that the image of God was completely obliterated in the Fall, the denial of any sort of general revelation, the denial of God's grace of creation or preserving grace since this would contradict the oneness of the grace of Christ, the denial of a point of contact for the saving action of God, and the corresponding belief that the old man must be completely destroyed and replaced by the new

89. Brunner and Barth, *Natural Theology*, 31–32.

90. SD II.22–23 (K-W, 548n64).

91. Stanley J. Grenz and Roger E. Olson, *20th Century Theology: God & the World in a Transitional Age* (Downers Grove, IL: InterVarsity Press, 1992), 84.

man in conversion.[92] These errors must be rejected because they preclude a relationship with God: "there is no 'connective tissue' which ties human being to divine being, even by 'analogy.'"[93]

There are two reasons Barth dismisses the *analogia entis*. First, the analogy of being minimizes the entrenched hostility of the human, and second, it would limit God's sovereignty since it would make Him dependent on something outside of Himself.[94] "For the man who is with Jesus—and this is man's ontological determination—is with God," and the human being outside of God exists as a mere shadow of himself.[95] For Brunner the formal side of the *imago Dei*, namely, that which is retained in the human being even after the Fall, his capacity for words and his accountability before God, is the prerequisite for him to be addressed by God in the special revelation of the Spirit of God by and through the Word. These elements would underscore a human's exceptional status as a "kind" above all other creation, even when the material content of that formal structure is absent and only intuited in relation to Jesus Christ.[96] As Brunner argues, this "responsory actuality" (*responsorische Aktualität*) "makes out the essence of every human being, to be a subject, the capacity to hear and speak as well as responsible freedom, that elevates us above the rest of the created world."[97]

All those who like Brunner speak of a formal remnant of the image want to preserve aspects of both content and form, the relational analogy (*analogia relationis*) in terms of content or newly bestowed material and the substantial or formal remnant of the image via an analogy of being (*analogia entis*). This

92. Stanley Grenz notes that the harsh tone of Barth's response may have been in part a reaction to "the Nazi temptation into which many 'German Christians' were falling," that is, "their openness to natural theology." Grenz and Olson, *20th Century Theology*, 84.

93. Anderson, *On Being Human*, 76. Not only does Barth reject the Thomistic doctrine of analogy of being, he also dismisses general revelation or natural theology because he is guided by a singular concept of revelation. Thus, "one cannot ascend 'hand over hand,' by way of an 'umbilical cord,' from human being to the being of God." Karl Barth's claim is this: "Is it not palpable that we have to do with a clear and simple correspondence, an *analogia relationis*, between this mark of the divine being, namely that it includes an I and a Thou, and the being of man and female?" *Church Dogmatics* 3.1:96; Price, *Karl Barth's Anthropology*, 132ff.

94. See here Barth, *Church Dogmatics* 3/2:128. The debate would also include his famous response "Nein!" to Brunner in 1934. Karl Barth, *Nein! Antwort an Emil Brunner*, Theologische Existenz heute 14 (Munich: C. Kaiser, 1934); Emil Brunner, *Man in Revolt: A Christian Anthropology*, trans. Olive Wyon (Philadelphia: Westminster Press, 1947), 172ff. See Peters, *Der Mensch*, 121–22.

95. Barth, *Church Dogmatics* 3/2:136. Based on man's election of covenantal theology (*Gnadenbund*), Barth understands man's being in God as the only true ontological reality that sin cannot destroy: "Godlessness is not, therefore, a possibility, but an ontological impossibility. Man is not without God but with God. This is not to say, of course, that godless men do not exist. Sin is undoubtedly committed and exists. Yet sin itself is not a possibility but an ontological impossibility in man." With his focus on election and covenant established in Christ, the Second Adam, Barth's interest in subjective appropriation of grace through justification comes across as secondary, unlike Luther's strong focus on cross and the appropriation of grace. *Church Dogmatics* 3.2:142–50. See Peters, *Der Mensch*, 132, 135.

96. Brunner and Barth, *Natural Theology*, 23–24, 31; Peters, *Der Mensch*, 121.

97. Peters, *Der Mensch*, 121, 199.

idea of a remnant would help one imagine that there is something in the human with which God would be able to connect or build a relationship. As Grenz observes of Brunner:

> Recognition of such a bare, minimal awareness of God, he believed, is indispensable to the missions of church and theology, because it calls them to articulate the faith in a way that can be understood. While human thoughts and questions cannot determine the content of the gospel that the church proclaims, they must be taken into account in determining its manner of proclamation.[98]

As already mentioned, Luther's idea of capacity, though he did not call it the formal image, lends itself thus to the idea of Brunner's formal remnant. In this case, the image would not be seen entirely in a relational manner. A human's formal constitution, such as Brunner's *Wortmächtigkeit* or Luther's passive capacity, would then reinforce the idea that, unlike animals, humans are capable of a relationship with God. In this sense, while his concept of the image of God is relational, Brunner is not as anti-substantialist as Barth and as some scholars make him out to be. Not only is the idea of some connecting bond between God and humanity preserved; Brunner's view also retains a universal perspective, encompassing even those indifferent to God or in hostile rebellion against Him.[99]

There is a strong tradition of defining ontology of the human image apart from God's restoration in Christ, whether in reference to the capacity toward self-transcendence or to reason, will, or responsibility; all these attributes generally derive from the classical Aristotelian definition of the human being as an *animal rationale* (ζῷον λογον ἔχον) who is in possession of the life-giving "soul" (*anima vegetativa*). This ontology also looks back to the biblical creation narrative in an attempt to salvage for the human being some "leftovers" that have not been lost entirely through the Fall, as we saw with Gerhard.[100] From a scriptural point of view, that attempt is not without warrant. Texts like Gn 5:3 and 9:6, 1 Cor 11:7, Jas 3:9, and to a degree also Acts 17:28 all seem to affirm a surviving image for humans. The idea of the Word creating a response highlights a phenomenon common to all humans as created beings, namely, the unique capacity to hear and put together signs that we call language, whether such communication is spoken, written, signed, or conveyed otherwise. Luther declares that "there is no mightier or nobler work of the human than speech."[101]

98. Grenz and Olson, *20th Century Theology*, 84.

99. Erickson, *Christian Theology*, 530. I think that Millard Erickson treats Brunner unfairly, throwing Brunner entirely into Barth's camp as an anti-substantialist. If Brunner in his debate with Barth on nature and grace says anything, it is precisely in his argument for the image of God as structural or substantive at least to a degree.

100. "If the divine image is taken for inborn elements in us which are tenuous remnants of the divine image in the mind and will of man . . . then we again confess that the image of God has not been lost completely with respect to these tiny particles, because the work of the Law is still written even in the hearts of the unregenerate." Gerhard, *Theological Commonplaces* 11.9.129 (8–11:322).

101. *Preface to the Psalter*, 1528 (AE 35:254; WADB 10/2:101.13–15): "There is no mightier or

Unlike Barth, Luther does not dismiss the analogy of being entirely. As Brunner points out, the analogy of faith is preceded by the analogy of being, as illustrated in the example of speaking:

> When we say that we can only speak of God aright because God has spoken to us in His revelation, we have already made the tacit admission that there is a fundamental analogy between what "speaking" means in the divine and in the human sense.[102]

The capacities for speaking and hearing are central to humans' relationship with God and with one another. For Luther both capacities represent aspects of how one relates to God, and they are necessary for the proper posture before God and prerequisite for human survival.[103] To refuse to share one's faith and open one's heart to God and relate to Him one's joy or sadness as the saints do in the Psalter reveals spiritual muteness, because "the depths of the heart are not open, and what is in them does not come out."[104] And Gerhard Ebeling picks up from Luther that communicative nature of humans, stating, "The human being is ultimately not a doer but a receiver, because he lives from the Word."[105] Luther sees creation addressing all humans with a testimony of God's goodness, which demands their ability to hear and respond. Unfortunately, creation is deaf to God's address, so to speak, and unwilling to respond. This spiritual deafness is condemned by the Law, whereas the believer's response is foremost one of praise and thanks, a response enabled when he hears and receives the Gospel's promise. This view is what underlies Luther's statement: "For all of this I owe it to God to thank and praise, serve and obey him."[106] An intrinsic part of the communicative nature of humans is their possession and use of reason, which enables them to understand the words and process their meaning. Werner Elert connects that ability with the image of God:

> Man bears God's image in the sense that he is a creature endowed with speech just as God himself speaks. The ability to use language as a means of communication

---

nobler work of man than speech. For it is by speech, more than by his shape or by any other work, that man is most distinguished from other animals. By the carver's art even a block of wood can have the shape of a man; and an animal can see, hear, smell, sing, walk, stand, eat, drink, fast, thirst—and suffer from hunger, frost, and a hard bed—as well as a man." Experiences of the senses like feeling, hearing, hunger, thirst, and even the form (*Gestalt*) are for Luther not unique to humans.

102. Brunner, *Christian Doctrine of Creation*, 24; Peters, *Der Mensch*, 123–24.

103. This point should not be used to argue the degree or quality of hearing and speaking, as if to imply that the unborn or the deaf, because of their lack of speaking or hearing, are not in a relationship with God. That is neither Luther's intent nor ours.

104. AE 35:255; WADB 10/2:101.27–28.

105. Gerhard Ebeling, *Gott und Wort* (Tübingen: J. C. B. Mohr, 1966), 61; Peters, *Der Mensch*, 135.

106. SC II.2 (K-W, 355). Bayer comments on Luther's statement: "This describes everything about the human being that needs to be stated. He sees himself defined by a word that is addressed to himself, which calls him into life. His calling is now to respond; but he also must respond." Oswald Bayer, *Martin Luther's Theology: A Contemporary Interpretation*, trans. Thomas H. Trapp (Grand Rapids: Wm. B. Eerdmans, 2008), 173.

> distinguishes man from the lower creatures and establishes a "telling" likeness with his Creator.[107]

The communicatory powers of humans exceed those of all other creatures. The nature of these powers is unique to humans, as anthropologists and linguists generally seem to agree. According to Mortimer Adler, the human intellect and the unique ability to employ propositional language make a human exceptional, distinct from other animals,[108] for the human is the only sentence-making animal. He is "the only talking, the only naming, declaring or questioning, affirming or denying, the only arguing, agreeing or disagreeing, the only discursive, animal."[109] With his 'biolinguistic' approach Noam Chomsky famously claims that the command of language is part of the genetic make-up of humans, a species-specific possession unattainable by other animals such as apes.[110] But language is more than that: it is the means by which humans communicate, not only with others who also possess this unique ability but also with God. It is a mark of the special relation he has with his Creator.

All these ontological qualities could be understood at best as capacities of one kind or another; but though they may serve to justify an ontology for the image, such capacities have no status in soteriology. Their spiritual powers are nullified in view of the broken relationship with God, and since that communicatory ability with God is lost, it must be restored in Christ through faith before these faculties can be considered as valuable *coram Deo*.[111]

In all this discussion one caveat remains. For ethicists the substantive definitions of the human image, be it the rational power or the ability to communicate or to love,[112] do not satisfy. The ethicists' concern should remind theological anthropologists[113] not to lose sight of the ethical dimension.[114] For if

107. Elert, *Christian Ethos*, 26. Elert mentions the image in his dogmatics very briefly on two occasions, once pointing out its loss in the *status corruptionis* and elsewhere the transformation into the likeness of Christ. Elert, *Christian Faith*, 186, 318; Peters, *Der Mensch*, 143.

108. "At this moment, there are no scientific data infirmitive of the proposition that only man has a propositional language." Adler, *Difference of Man*, 113. He concludes, "I have called man's exclusive possession of propositional language the pivotal fact in this consideration of how men and other animals differ" (120).

109. Adler, *Difference of Man*, 112.

110. Noam Chomsky, *Language and Mind*, 3d ed. (New York: Cambridge University Press, 2006), 9. He agrees with Descartes on the uniqueness of human language.

111. Cortez, *Christological Anthropology*, 100.

112. In the early patristic era theologians were moving away from the Neoplatonic/Aristotelian rationalism and instead connected the image more and more with the passionate character of humanity that receives and mirrors the divine attribute of love. Irenaeus, John Chrysostom, and others emphasized that man is created to love rather than simply to think, deliberate, or act.

113. Werner Elert's theological anthropology is reflected not only in his dogmatics, *Christian Faith*, 30–68, but also in his *Christian Ethos*, 23–48. Helmut Thielicke as well should be noted for his strong ethical concerns, to which one was typically drawn in a post–World War II German situation.

114. A point we made previously in discussing the ethical dangers of the endeavor to create a superhuman through technology. Those ethical concerns involving technology are expressed

the image is understood as an ontological capacity, this understanding will lead humans, as history sadly has shown, to draw comparisons amongst themselves and then to elevate some over others. Consider, for example, outstanding thinkers or artists who exhibit superior capacities and powers. Compared to "ordinary" people including the unborn and the incapacitated, pejoratively called vegetables, these thinkers and artists are thought to be "more human" than those of lesser abilities. As a result of such comparisons, ethicists have brought into the debate about the image of God the question of the value of human life and its dignity, a development that should compel theologians to reassess their ontological descriptions of the image. The argument for a substantive, broader image still extant though marred serves to promote the value and protection of life, including that of the unborn, better than the refutation of an extant image.[115] On the other hand, those who like Luther hold that the image of God is no longer extant but is restored only in Christ maintain a position that also reinforces the value of life: it must be treasured in view of what it is to become. Pieper reminds us of this point:

> The only reason why God still concerns Himself with fallen mankind and preserves it—and for its sake also the world—is that, according to Scripture, He desires to renew fallen mankind to the image in which He originally created it (Colossians 3:10; Ephesians 4:24).[116]

From this perspective of God's desire and purpose for all of fallen creation emerges a realistic yet sobering view of who the human is outside of Christ. Having lost the image of God, he is set against the Gospel and against other humans. He no longer conforms to the righteous will of God. Any discussion about the image of God in post-Fall humans, outside of restoration and relationship in Christ, is not part of Luther's and Pieper's theological anthropology.

Option Two: The Functional Understanding Expressed through Regency

In the discussion of the image of God some exegetical treatments have shifted direction from an individual-substantive (structural or ontological) concept to a functional one that posits the image as a capability to rule over other life forms, animate and inanimate.[117] The question is no longer so much what we

---

by Noreen L. Herzfeld, *In Our Image*, and Gilbert Meilaender, *Neither Beast nor God: The Dignity of the Human Person*, 1st American ed. (New York: Encounter Books, 2009), among others.

115. Anderson, "Arguments Against Abortion": "Human beings are created in the image and likeness of God (Gen. 1:26–27; 5:1; 9:6). Bearing the image of God is the essence of humanness. And though God's image in man was marred at the Fall, it was not erased (cf. 1 Cor. 11:7; James 3:9). Thus, the unborn baby is made in the image of God and therefore fully human in God's sight."

116. Pieper, *Christian Dogmatics* 1:519.

117. Douglas John Hall, *Imaging God: Dominion as Stewardship* (Grand Rapids: W. B.

have within us but rather what we are to do. That perspective derives from the *dominium terrae* mandate, in which humanity's uniqueness and superiority is underscored in terms of function and abilities to rule and exercise dominion over the rest of creation. Here scholars argue that the so-called priestly writer (P) to whom they attribute Genesis 1 is informed by his immediate surrounding world like Egypt and Mesopotamia, where king and royalty generally represent their gods.[118] Applying some grammatical finesse to Gn 1:26, Gerhard von Rad and others argue that humans are invested with God's power to function as His representatives.[119]

This functional regency, exerting one's dominion, allows humans not only to follow what God has obliged them to do but also to use the earth as the means to ensure survival. This understanding bears a strong Lutheran component in calling for all humans to become God's agents, masks or channels of God, who in their vocations bestow His blessings on others, whether or not they are aware of it.[120] For exegetes like Gerhard von Rad and Hans Walter Wolff, that functionality comprises the image of God. The right to rule and the duty to do so are taken on in responsible fashion, not in selfish, high-handed arbitrariness.[121] According to von Rad, "the divine likeness is not to be found either in the personality of man, in his free Ego, in his dignity or in his free use of moral capacity, etc."[122]

In contrast to the first view, the individual-substantive perspective of the image within humans, which seems to be static and highlights intellectual rather than physical faculties, the second, the functional image of regency, makes two important observations. First, it allows a human to see himself as exercising dominion in a holistic fashion that includes all his skills, even his upright posture and walk. According to von Rad, "the Hebrews did not distinguish between the intellectual and the vital functions of the body"[123] and thus "one will do well to split the physical from the spiritual as little as possible."[124] Second,

Eerdmans, 1986).

118. Gerhard von Rad, *Old Testament Theology*, vol. 1, trans. D. M. G. Stalker (New York: Harper & Row, 1962), 146–47. According to Claus Westermann, however, who follows a relational concept, P's connection to his surrounding world is strictly a matter of conjecture. *Genesis: A Commentary*, trans. John J. Scullion (Minneapolis: Augsburg Publishing House, 1984–86), 1:153.

119. Gerhard von Rad prefers the translation of the בְּ in Gn 1:26 to read "as the image of God" rather than "in the image of God," because the former conveys the idea that the whole person and not just something in him serves as God's image. Gerhard von Rad, *Genesis: A Commentary*, trans. John H. Marks, rev. ed., The Old Testament Library (Philadelphia: Westminster Press, 1972), 56; Herzfeld, *In Our Image*, 23.

120. LC I.26 (K-W, 389).

121. Hans Walter Wolff, *Anthropology of the Old Testament*, trans. Margaret Kohl (Philadelphia: Fortress Press, 1974), 160. See also Hall, *Imaging God*.

122. Gerhard von Rad, "Εἰκών," in *Theological Dictionary of the New Testament.*, ed. Gerhard Kittel, Geoffrey W. Bromiley, and Gerhard Friedrich, trans. Geoffrey W. Bromiley (Grand Rapids: Wm. B. Eerdmans, 1964–76), 2:391; see also Herzfeld, *In Our Image*, 20–25.

123. Von Rad, *Old Testament Theology*, 153.

124. Von Rad, *Genesis*, 56; Herzfeld, *In Our Image*, 24: "It is the whole person, both physical and intellectual, that exerts dominion over the earth."

this view carries with it the understanding that humans do not act in their role as regents autonomously but serve as God's sovereign representatives.

Humans rule the world and are allowed to live from the life around them by taking it. In doing so, however, they often exploit this world. One of the drawbacks of this anthropocentric, even anthropomonistic, depiction of regency over creation is the temptation to be irresponsible stewards, which has resulted in what some call ecological imperialism.[125] Consequently, theologians have called for a more conscious sense of environmentalism.[126] In some cases these calls for a greater reverence for all of creation have gone to the extreme—whether motivated by religious, philosophical, or ecological factors—and have denied human superiority over the rest of creation. Often these concerns affirm an ecological monism which has dismissed the transcendent God and declared humans to consist of matter only, an ecological materialism also known as naturalism or physicalism.[127] If spirituality still plays a part in such thinking, the approach usually represents holistic traditions defined as pantheistic monism, such as the New Age movement, which is inspired by Eastern religions like Buddhism and ancient Gnosticism.

In this more inclusive approach, one that no longer recognizes the rule of humanity over creation and which thus denies the superiority of humans—their special status and honor as God's representatives—it is difficult to justify humans' special status and their right to destroy any life form, even those that might cause disease. By this logic humans would have to be considered either as one among equals (*pars inter pares*) or at best as first among equals (*primus inter pares*), which would be a self-chosen and thus arbitrary status. One must exercise caution in this discussion of regency to avoid either of two extreme positions, that of anthropocentricity, which leads to exploitation, and that of environmental monism. Theological anthropology falls between these two extremes and its proponents must argue clearly that humans exploit creation not because of the biblical dominion mandate but because of their habitual sinfulness.[128]

An additional ethical concern with this functional understanding of the image recalls one expressed with the first, ontological view. The functional understanding implies that humans must possess abilities to exercise dominion, which could lead to valuing one's status according to how well or badly a person exercises dominion and stewardship. In addition to noting these concerns, the Lutheran response would point out that the mandate to exercise dominion does not constitute the divine image but is an immediate consequence of possessing it.[129] The close proximity of "in our image" and "let them have dominion" in

125. Lynn White, Jr., "The Historical Roots of Our Ecological Crisis," *Science* 155, no. 3767 (10 March 1967): 1203–7.

126. *Together with All Creatures.*

127. Sire, *Universe Next Door*, 67.

128. Härle, *Dogmatik*, 427.

129. "Nevertheless, according to Genesis 1:26–28 it is accurate to say that the *dominium*

Gn 1:26 does not imply that the latter defines the former and thus confers identity on the first humans. Luther is radical in his conclusion that human sovereignty after the Fall is only a caricature of what it once was; it is nothing but a "mock sovereignty."[130] Humans at best can only strive to attain true and perfect functionality in exerting dominion, while realizing that because of their shortcomings and failures they will always fall short of fully grasping it.[131]

Option Three: Teleology, Relational and Non-Substantive Restoration through Christ

In contrast to the two previous positions, which define the image of God as a quality or capacity residing within humans, orthodox Lutheran theologians have made their case for the image as being accidental and relational, connecting it to Christ through whom and in whom the image finds its restoration.[132] This understanding builds on the important scriptural truth that all humans since the Fall are born outside of the original relationship with God and consequently are born without the natural ability to respond to and communicate with God. Only a return to the image of God endows the believer with that responsory-communicative ability.

But how does that restoration come about? Here the theology of the Word is imperative. The self is being appealed to and called out through the Word, which then leads to a response as an act of faith.[133] In essence this sequence reflects Luther's line of thought and that of many others. We have already noted Joest's point that personhood is relational with God, that a human being is drawn into relationship with God when He addresses him through the Word and thereby opens up in him a disposition toward Him.[134] This relationship and not the equipping of substantive powers is what constitutes the personhood.[135] In many ways, according to Bayer and Cortez, Luther's anthropology is "an anthropology of responding."[136] To exist means to be in constant dialogue with the Creator: "It is all that ordinary people need to learn at first, both about

---

terrae immediately arises from being in the image of God." Bayer, "Image of God," 83. Härle, *Dogmatik*, 437; Klaus Detlev Schulz, "Two Kinds of Righteousness and Moral Philosophy: *Confessio Augustana* XVIII, Philipp Melanchthon, and Martin Luther," *Concordia Theological Quarterly* 73, no. 1 (2009): 17–40, http://www.ctsfw.net/media/pdfs/SchulzTwoKindsofRighteousnessAndMoralPhilosophy.pdf.

130. Pieper, *Christian Dogmatics* 1:522.

131. Westermann supports the approach of Peters, *Der Mensch*, 200; *Together with All Creatures*, 23.

132. "Therefore the image of God cannot be in man unless he is renewed by the Holy Spirit. Now, that which is supposed to be acquired through a renewal cannot be possessed previous to the renewal." Gerhard, *Theological Commonplaces* 11.1.31 (8–11:265). Gerhard quotes Tertullian, "Christians are not born, but they become Christian," and Augustine, "Not generation but regeneration makes Christians." Peters, *Der Mensch*, 36, section 31.

133. Joest, *Ontologie der Person bei Luther*, 36.

134. Joest, *Ontologie der Person bei Luther*, 222, 224.

135. Joest, *Ontologie der Person bei Luther*, 34–35.

136. Bayer, "Image of God," 78; Cortez, *Christological Anthropology*, 98.

what we have and receive from God and what we owe him in return."[137] For Luther then, as Cortez puts it, that which most fundamentally identifies us as humans and distinguishes us from other creatures is not a particular ontology (for example, possessing an immaterial soul) or a unique capacity like reason. The distinguishing character comes to humans as "an independent—. . . transcendent—determination."[138] This observation can have a liberating effect "for those who tend virtually to identify humanity with creaturely existence, both in valuing themselves and in dealing with others."[139] All humans alike are to be addressed by God and necessarily respond.

According to Peter Brunner, God originally had placed the human in the communicative relationship by creating him as His counterpart, whom He addressed as "you."[140] This observation should have implications for the understanding of what it means to be human. The person, not to be confused with his personality, is and remains a person only in relationship to God, oriented around the constructs "I" and "You."[141] This Martin Buber–influenced dialogical personalism[142] has found many supporters who point to its origins in the creation narrative itself and note that it is born out of God's own desire to enter into a relationship with humans outside of Himself. As Peter Brunner puts it:

> The being as I is based on the fact that God lovingly addresses him at creation as thou. . . . In that God says thou to man, man becomes an "I." The personal relation between God and man, which God has established at the creation of man, is the center of the image of God.[143]

There's more to being human than being born, dying, eating and drinking, sleeping, propagating his species, or belonging to a certain race, and that "more" exists in the relationship with God and fellow humans. One author critically

137. LC II.24 (K-W, 433).

138. "Human beings are not distinguished from other creatures through a set of variables controlled by a 'genetic core,' but are differentiated from all other creatures on the basis of an independent— . . . transcendent—determination." Anderson, *On Being Human*, 28.

139. Anderson, *On Being Human*, 29.

140. Brunner, "Der Ersterschaffene als Gottes Ebenbild," 1:91.

141. Joest, *Ontologie der Person bei Luther*, 32. To prove his own position Joest quotes Friedrich Gogarten, *Der Mensch zwischen Gott und Welt*, 3d ed. (Stuttgart: Friedrich Vorwerk, 1956), 306.

142. Martin Buber, *I and Thou*, trans. Ronald Gregor Smith, 2d ed. (New York: Scribner, 1958), x, 134. A series of theologians such as Bonhoeffer and Barth invoked him. See Barth, *Church Dogmatics* 3/2:249; Anderson, *On Being Human*, 22; Herzfeld, *In Our Image*, 105n84; Boyd and Eddy, *Across the Spectrum*, 99.

143. "Das Ichsein des Menschen gründet also darin, daß Gott ihn in der Erschaffung als Du in Liebe anredet . . . Indem Gott so zum Menschen Du sagt, wird der Mensch ein 'Ich'. Die personale Relation zwischen Gott und Mensch, die mit der Erschaffung des Menschen gesetzt ist, ist die Mitte der Gottesebenbildlichkeit." Brunner, "Der Ersterschaffene als Gottes Ebenbild," 1:91.

observes: "When we say that being human is something we *have*—we 'own' it—then we are saying that we are human *apart from God*."[144]

Ultimately, "there is no escape from the divine Word that forms us in the image and likeness of God."[145] Scholars who follow this line of thought—such as Friedrich Gogarten, Dietrich Bonhoeffer, Peter Brunner, Gerhard Ebeling, and Wilfried Joest—dismiss the understanding of a human as being biologically already truly human and would argue that true humanity is found only in the newly enacted relationship with Christ through the Word. In contrast to the metaphysical, substantive descriptions, modern Protestant theologians have turned in the other direction, affirming in Luther an entirely new ontology that is dialogical, dynamic, responsory, and relational.[146] Dietrich Bonhoeffer said so in his treatment *Act and Being*, claiming in reference to Luther that only in Christ should anyone consider himself God's created being.[147] That new being in Christ is enabled through Word and Sacrament as a future event, of dying and rising with Christ, for those who still have their incurved being (*incurvatus in se*) in Adam.[148]

The idea that the image of God is received in a relationship with Him established through Christ and faith in Him means that the value of life for all humans, including the unborn, lies teleologically in their destiny and purpose. In his discussion over the unborn, Bayer presses the point that the human fetus "is granted personality from the start,"[149] whereas others like Anderson value a human fetus as "'potentially a person' and therefore already more human than non-human."[150] Both positions on the status of the unborn demonstrate that these theologians wish to locate in the creatureliness of a human fetus something inherently special, be it personality or the potential to become a person.[151] However, what both positions also state is that over all humans rests a

144. Michelle J. Bartel, *What It Means to Be Human: Living with Others before God*, Foundations of Christian Faith (Louisville: Geneva Press, 2001), 36.

145. Anderson, *On Being Human*, 83.

146. Other names associated with this Protestant position include Reinhold Seeberg, Erich Seeberg, Werner Elert, G. Gloege, and B. Langmeyer; see Joest, *Ontologie der Person bei Luther*, 28–34. To this list I would add Peter Brunner and Emil Brunner.

147. Dietrich Bonhoeffer, *Act and Being: Transcendental Philosophy and Ontology in Systematic Theology*, trans. H. Martin Rumscheid (Minneapolis: Fortress Press, 2009), 150.

148. Bonhoeffer, *Act and Being*, 158.

149. "Such a theological anthropology's immediate consequences for ethics are evident in a dispute with rival anthropologies—especially in view of the *imago Dei* prohibition of killing humans (Gen. 9:6) or with reference to bioethical debates. If it is correct that the embryo does not develop into a person but develops as a person, then it is granted personality from the start. The verb 'granted' indicates that personality essentially concerns recognition: the 'zygote' is clothed and illuminated with the dignity of personhood, independent of the position of its self-consciousness or the socially-construed majority view." Bayer, "Image of God," 80–81.

150. "*Normally*—and we must stress the word—we take it for granted that the process by which one human creature gives life to another creature is also a process by which a human person comes to be. This is certainly why, out of respect for human life, a human fetus is valued 'potentially a person' and therefore already more human than non-human." Anderson, *On Being Human*, 25.

151. This discussion on personhood draws in *Roe v. Wade*, 410 U.S. 113 (1973). The 1973

shortcoming and an incompleteness. Indeed, a pathological shadow and illness is cast over every human, something that deems humanity inadequate in its creaturely existence. For this reason theological anthropologists point forward, to varying degrees, to a restoration through God in Christ. Nature surrenders to grace. Albrecht Peters summarizes this forward orientation, espousing a line of thought similar to Luther's:

> We cannot fixate statically and ontologically the image of God in man, we can only circumscribe the image of God on its path forward towards Christ. To recount that event anew means to take Jesus Christ as the point of orientation. As being proleptic to the goal of the image for humans, he is the full revelation of the original image, certainly to a degree under the condition of estrangement. Here all theologians discussed thus far basically seem to be in agreement.[152]

Helmut Thielicke also follows Luther's forward orientation by suggesting that one starts with the "whither" and only then contemplates the "whence," since the "certainty of the divine likeness is thus grounded in our final relationship, in what we call our alien dignity."[153] Thielicke made these observations against the backdrop of the Third Reich, when part of humanity arguably had sunk to its lowest point, when biological origin and the value of life meant little to those in authority. His intention to place human dignity and value within the restored, vertical relationship between God and humans resonates with Luther's approach.[154] The impetus for this elevation derives from an event—justification—in which humanity, which is turned against God with conscience and heart, is called out through the Word from the inwardly focused state and turned outward in that receptive mode of listening.

A number of modern theologians favor a generic relational interpretation that opts out of the specific restoration that occurs through the Word. Karl Barth's version is of particular note. He sees the trinitarian relationship of oneness and love reflected in human relationships, especially in the intimate relationship between male and female in the form of husband and wife, which serves as a quintessential part of the image. Based on Gn 1:27 he engages an analogy, not along the lines of an ontology, which he rejected, but a relational one, an *analogia relationis*.[155] By going back to creation Barth introduces an

---

United States Supreme Court decision has called attention to the question of whether the unborn is a person legally. If it is, the act of abortion would have to be called murder. Ironically, the intentional killing of a pregnant woman is often treated as a dual murder case.

152. Peters, *Der Mensch*, 193.

153. Failing to do so, according to Thielicke, would invite ethical concerns: "If we base our dignity on our biological origin, we are simply made into more highly organized animals. If we base it on our immanent value, on our functional abilities, we are sacrificed to animality. For when we lose our usefulness, we lose our right to life. Only that relation establishes the inviolability of our humanity—only the fact that we are the children of God, the apple of His eye, bought with a price." Thielicke, *Being Human—Becoming Human*, 407.

154. Philip Edgcumbe Hughes, *The True Image: The Origin and Destiny of Man in Christ* (Grand Rapids: Wm. B. Eerdmans, 1989).

155. "It is not palpable that we have to do with a clear and simple correspondence, an

image in the form of a relationship with God, a dialogical anthropology, in which God is "addressing man as a Thou and making him responsible as an I, and that men themselves must stand and fall together as I and Thou, as man and woman."[156] This is the Barthian claim: it goes beyond the dialogical character of human relations and makes sexual differentiation an essential part of humanity and of the image of God—and many Reformed theologians follow the Swiss theologian.[157] "We hold that human sexuality at the creaturely level—that is, being male or female—is linked in some way to the fundamental polarity of being which is the imago Dei itself."[158] For these theologians it would not be enough to place this issue of co-humanity in the context of ethics alone, since that makes it appear an inferior or secondary concern flowing out of what seems to come first, namely, the self. To them this issue is more than an ethical concern: it is a part of how humanity is structured. They deduce this principle by applying the relationships evident in the Trinity to the image, which is "dynamic and relational . . . not borne by us merely individually, but also in a collective or communitarian fashion."[159] This principle implies that there is an ontological argument for co-humanity—living in community with others in mutual love, respect, concern, and responsibility—that precedes the ethical dimension, which each person must accept before becoming a conscious individual self.[160]

---

analogia relationis, between this mark of the divine being, namely, that it includes an I and a Thou, and the being of man, male and female. The relationship between the summoning I in God's being and the summoned divine Thou is reflected both in the relationship of God to the man whom He has created, and also in the relationship between the I and the Thou, between male and female, in human existence itself." Barth, *Church Dogmatics* 3/1:196. See also 3/2:286: "We cannot say man without having to say male or female and also male and female. Man exists in this differentiation, in this duality."

156. Barth, *Church Dogmatics* 3/1:200. Here Barth denies the original image as a state of rectitude of the soul or state of integrity as the reformers claimed, since for him such an original state before the Fall never existed. Claus Westermann, *Creation*, trans. John J. Scullion (Philadelphia: Fortress Press, 1974), 58.

157. Price, *Karl Barth's Anthropology*, 197; Stanley J. Grenz, *The Social God and the Relational Self: A Trinitarian Theology of the Imago Dei* (Louisville: Westminster John Knox Press, 2001), 141–82. Like Barth, Grenz draws an analogy between God's inner-trinitarian relations and the relation of humans with one another, especially in the relation of the sexes, even when God is considered to be without sex. Ray Anderson also follows Barth, *On Being Human*, 51: "The particular form of humanity in the image and likeness of God in its creatureliness is male and female, male or female." See also Thomas Siger Derr, review of *The Social God and the Relational Self: A Trinitarian Theology of the Imago Dei* by Stanley J. Grenz, *Journal of Markets & Morality* 5, no. 2 (2002): 464–66. Noreen Herzfeld's position echoes Barth's: "Rather, the image of God is found whenever two or three meet in authentic relationship. Computers cannot replace us, for each of us, as a participant in these relationships, is irreplaceable. In each moment when we follow Jesus' call to love God or to love one another, we imagine the Triune God in a unique way." Herzfeld, *In Our Image*, 94. Charles Sherlock, Millard Erickson, and Ray Anderson follow Barth slavishly on this point: Charles Sherlock, *The Doctrine of Humanity*. Contours of Christian Theology (Downers Grove: InterVarsity Press, 1996); Millard Erickson, *Making Sense of the Trinity* (Grand Rapids: Baker Academic, 2000); and Anderson, *On Being Human*.

158. Anderson, *On Being Human*, 86

159. Erickson, *Making Sense of the Trinity*, 85.

160. "This co-existence can be viewed as the radical structure of humanity itself. In

Humans are social beings and have been created to be together. God Himself considered the creation of Adam alone incomplete and hence created for him a partner (Gn 2:18, 22). This act does not mean, however, that now we should identify the image as co-humanity, and thus merely relational and communal, without first addressing the delivery system, Word and sacraments, that passes on the image of Christ. We cannot dissolve individual being into corporate being but must accept both as important aspects of humanity.[161] The latter is informed and shaped by the former. The individual person first of all must be differentiated as a person from other human beings and from nonhuman life in terms of both his physical and his spiritual existence. To Luther, the proper relationship with God and neighbor is Christologically defined and based on the specific event of justification, and that is what ultimately determines true humanity:

> True humanity thus comes into being as the human person is united with Christ in faith. Responding in unfaith, on the other hand, necessarily separates the person from Christ, fundamentally alienating the person from the only relationship in which we are constituted as true humans.[162]

Ignoring the event of justification and God's delivery system is contrary to a Lutheran understanding of the image. This is the Lutheran response to Barth's portrayal of Christ as the true image in whom all of humanity is included, some knowingly, others not.[163] From eternity God has acquitted humanity; thus the benefits of Christ's saving work extend to all.[164] True though the claim is that Christ represents man in his truest form, an accurate understanding recognizes that that image is restored through justification. As Cortez notes, "Since our standing *coram Deo* is always an act of grace, a relationship gifted to us by our maker, then human persons receive their essence, their very being, as a gift."[165] Since one's true humanity is a gift received through the Word, the image as righteousness—divine holiness and truth—also can be lost, which will have negative consequences for human relationships.[166]

The generic relational explanation of the image is an attempt to make the Trinity practical and relevant to the everyday lives of people. The late Roman

other words, existence as a human being is fundamentally existence with regard to the other." Anderson, *On Being Human*, 44.

161. Anderson, *On Being Human*, 46.

162. Cortez, *Christological Anthropology*, 98.

163. Grenz and Olson, *20th Century Theology*, 75.

164. Barth, *Church Dogmatics* 2/2:163: "In the election of Jesus Christ which is the eternal will of God, God has ascribed to man . . . election, salvation and life; and to Himself He has ascribed . . . reprobation, perdition and death." Grenz and Olson, *20th Century Theology*, 74–75.

165. Cortez, *Christological Anthropology*, 96.

166. "For man was created in the image of God, in the image of righteousness, of course, of divine holiness and truth, but in such a way that he could lose it, as he did lose it, moreover, in paradise and has now recovered it through Christ." *The Disputation Concerning Justification*, 1536 (AE 34:177; WA 39/2:108.6–9); Cortez, *Christological Anthropology*, 97.

Catholic theologian Karl Rahner advocated for this understanding,[167] and since then the trend has emerged to draw an analogy, direct or indirect, between human relationships and the inner-trinitarian communion of honor and love among Father, Son, and Spirit, in which people reflect God's nature by glorifying each other and working together in unison toward a common goal. This social model of the Trinity or social trinitarianism draws into human life the concept of perichoresis, a term traditionally used to explain that "the three persons commune intimately in the one God precisely by making room for one another, by coinhering equally one in the other, without any confusion."[168] For Leonardo Boff, and for others to a greater or lesser extent, social trinitarianism serves as an analogy or model for the way humans should relate with one another, within the church and the community in general, whether in marriage, in the extended family, or in society and its structures, and it provides thereby an implicit critique of the rampant individualism of Western cultures.[169]

To all this we respond that co-humanity, which started with God creating two where there had been only one (Gn 2:23), is understood essentially in relationships and not in singularity; it is not simply individualistic. Already in its original form, "existence as a human being is fundamentally existence with regard to the other,"[170] and once the basic social structure was in place Adam and Eve were directed toward the rest of creation through the mandate of dominion (Gn 1:27).[171] Only a cautious acceptance of this social and generic relational concept of the Trinity can be given, along with two objections. First, the ethical dimension of expressing such relationships meaningfully need not be inferred from analogy to the Trinity: Scripture offers not analogies but direct admonitions, such as in Eph 4:32–5:2 and 1 Pt 5:5.[172] Being in fellowship with others is certainly a created reality, an ontological part of human existence and not only an ethical issue. We are created for co-humanity, and thus the commands to nurture this co-humanity make sense. Lutherans would accept this understanding of relationships, that they are part of how humans have been

167. Karl Rahner, *The Trinity*, trans. Joseph Donceel (New York: Herder and Herder, 1970), 10–11.

168. Michael G. Lawler, "*Perichoresis*: New Theological Wine in an Old Theological Wineskin," *Horizons* 22, no. 1 (1995): 51.

169. Leonardo Boff, *Holy Trinity, Perfect Community*, trans. Phillip Berryman (Maryknoll, NY: Orbis Books, 2000), 7–8, 39–40, 75; Millard J. Erickson, *God in Three Persons: A Contemporary Interpretation of the Trinity* (Grand Rapids: Baker Books, 1995), 334–35, 343; Lawler, "*Perichoresis*," 58. For a helpful study engaging social trinitarianism critically see Earle D. Treptow, "Imitating the Trinity: A Proper Way to Make the Doctrine of the Trinity Practical?" *Wisconsin Lutheran Quarterly* 116, no. 3 (2019): 163–84.

170. Anderson, *On Being Human*, 44.

171. Anderson, *On Being Human*, 54: "Humanity as co-humanity means that the singularity of being a human person is determined by significant encounter with another human person. Thus, we argued, the social structure of co-humanity precedes and determines individuality, expressed as singularity. However, the intrinsic order of co-humanity is manifested in and through creaturely sexuality, so that singularity is experienced as either male or female existence."

172. Treptow, "Imitating the Trinity," 181.

created and are essential to their being, and then would point to ethics and not the inner-trinitarian relations to discuss how humans in their respective vocations live out these relationships. Such admonitions are intended to amend relationships that are impaired by sinful behavior, a purpose that would not apply to the inner-trinitarian relationships, which are not subject to change or sin.[173] Second, we cannot ascribe to the image of God the sexes of man and woman or the relationship to other humans in a communitarian or collective fashion.[174] If one argues that in creating man in His image God reflected His own inner-trinitarian relationships, then one must dismiss the idea that the image includes the male and female sexes, simply because God's trinitarian relationship is not to be understood as sexual. Karl Barth and those who follow him thus go too far with this claim, even if they think Gn 1:27 permits such a reading.[175]

Luther asserts that the analogy of being is preceded by an *analogia fidei* and *relationis* established through God's act of justifying the human. This relationality of a specific kind is brought about through the external act of justification in Christ. One is justified not by what he has in his possession but rather by what he receives from Christ through faith as a gift, an argument grounded in texts such as 1 Cor 15:44–49; 2 Cor 3:18; 4:4; and Rom 12:2.[176] It is hazardous to base one's justification on the ontological qualities of humans, because these lack specificity. One must move past the penultimate or proleptic focus to the ultimate categories of human life: being justified in Christ, living a life in Christ with a renewed heart and mind, and then living that life out in relationships. These are the building blocks for true humanity. Modern interpretations that omit this specific event of justification through

173. Treptow, "Imitating the Trinity," 180.

174. See for example Millard Erikson, *Making Sense of the Trinity*: "It is now important for us to ask about the implications of the understanding of the Trinity for the believer's relationship to other humans. Here I am working with the following thesis: God has created us in his image. That image, however, is not merely structural but also dynamic and relational, and is not borne by us merely individually, but also in a collective or communitarian fashion. If this is the case, then the relationships that obtain among the members of the Trinity furnish the key to the relationships that should be present between the believer and other believers, and quite possibly, other humans regardless of their spiritual condition. . . . Rather than one member of the Trinity being the source of the others' being, and thus superior to them, we would contend that . . . all three are eternally equal. . . . If we adopt this understanding of the relationship among the persons of the Trinity, what should be the implications for our own conduct? I would suggest that, if the relationship of the members of the Trinity to one another is intended to be a model for us to follow in relating to one another, then we will be concerned to function in a relationship of equality, of mutual respect, in which we understand that others are as important to God as we are, and treat them as equals" (84–85, 90).

175. Barth, *Church Dogmatics* 3/1:195–96. Wilfried Härle (*Dogmatik*, 436) concedes that the loving relationship between man and woman could hint at a possible reflection of the divine relationships as he ponders Barth's comments on Gn 1:27 and 5:1f. in *Church Dogmatics* 3.2:285–324.

176. *Lectures on Genesis*, 1535–45 (AE 1:65; WA 42:49.8–16). See also a sermon on 1 Cor 15:44–53 preached 1 February 1533 (WA 36:661.9–675.5). Peters, *Der Mensch*, 47.

which the image is restored—those that commit wholly to a generic relational explanation—miss Luther's point, as Marc Cortez explains:

> Of equal importance, though, is the fact that Luther did not affirm some kind of generic relationality, as if we could determine purely on the basis of human plurality or even sexual differentiation the kind of relationality that is in view. . . . Instead, Luther emphasized human relationships shaped by grace, faith, and responsibility as providing the necessary framework for human existence. It is only in this sense that Luther qualifies as a "relational" theologian.[177]

This teleological approach pointing to a restoration of the image in Christ affirms that the gift of the image becomes a reality for the believer here and now. Anderson provides a fitting description of that present change:

> It is like the restoration of sight to one blind from birth, like enabling one who is hopelessly deaf to hear, like calling Lazarus back out of the tomb into the bright sunlight of his own human life. Being in the image of God is being once again response-able in hearing and obeying the divine Word.[178]

While a full manifestation of the image awaits the believer upon Christ's return, it is important and comforting for the believer to be assured that this gifted character is present and not found only in-the-becoming as a future event.[179] Bayer points to the present tense:

> If the basis of the past and the future is the presence of God, then the human as addressed by God is not first and only in becoming but rather by virtue of the creatively present address (Ex. 20:2: "I am the Lord, your God") *already* in being.[180]

The anti-substantialist concept of teleology that considers grace as a restoration in Christ could be criticized for devaluing human life as such, for the teleological and salvation-historical interpretation of the image focuses on its restoration and not on its nature as a possession from creation. This point leads us back to the structural interpretation of the image. Cannot nature and grace be combined in some fashion, or are they inherently antithetical or mutually exclusive? Can we not establish an extant remnant image in humans

177. Cortez, *Christological Anthropology*, 101.

178. Anderson, *On Being Human*, 84. In the First Article sense, that relationship becomes one of thanksgiving. "We are in duty bound to love, praise, and thank him without ceasing, and, in short, to devote all these things to his service, as he has required and enjoined in the Ten Commandments." LC II.19 (K-W, 433). This is where Karl Barth follows Luther; *Church Dogmatics* 3.2:172.

179. We take note here of Wolfhart Pannenberg's approach in *Anthropology in Theological Perspective*, 48. Pannenberg is radical in teleology, separating himself completely from those who wish to maintain the image is an endowment from creation or bestowed at one's justification. Pannenberg seems to locate the restoration more in history than in salvation history, so that it takes on an evolutionary and processional character, never found but always a goal. See Thorsten Waap, *Gottebenbildlichkeit und Identität: Zum Verhältnis von theologischer Anthropologie und Humanwissenschaft bei Karl Barth und Wolfhart Pannenberg*, Forschungen zur systematischen und ökumenischen Theologie 121 (Göttingen: Vandenhoeck & Ruprecht, 2008), 27–28, 456.

180. Bayer, "Image of God," 81.

and thereby mollify some orthodox Lutherans who frequently hold fast to a broad sense of the image?

To an extent, the attempt to salvage a structural aspect of the image might find a solution in Luther's concept of a *capacitas passiva*, which points out what is unique to humans. Humans are not robots, they are above other created life, and they are not coerced in their conversion.[181] This recognition leads us to consider humans valuable because there is something they possess, albeit not actively: this response-ability to the Word of God or the capacity to respond (*Wortmächtigkeit*), though it be completely incapacitated. As demonstrated earlier, theologians like Niebuhr, Bayer, and Emil Brunner wish to stake a similar claim. This capacity comes as close as possible to what we may affirm as an image in the broad sense, one which applies to all of humanity. However, admitting such an inherent capacity does not imply that the Word appeals to an independent and natural spiritual power of man.[182] In other words, in this instance of spiritual transformation, capacity does not signify the ability to produce and direct the human will toward God.[183] Luther holds steadfastly and radically to a synthetic and monergistic understanding of the image only as *accidens* in the restored relationship with God through Christ. As a shattered clay pot is held lovingly by its potter who intends to restore it to its original shape, so humans are objects of God's love whom He desires to bring out of their broken existence. This radical approach must derive at least in part from Luther's rejection of the convoluted doctrine and understanding of salvation he encountered in philosophical and theological traditions, which he chose to put to rest once and for all.[184]

181. SD II.60, 64 (K-W, 555–56); Brunner, "Der Ersterschaffene als Gottes Ebenbild," 1:91–92.

182. Joest, *Ontologie der Person bei Luther*, 304. In his discussion on general revelation John Calvin appeals to an independent and natural spiritual power, a *sensus divinitatis* or *semen religionis* in every human being from birth onwards. John Calvin, *Institutes of the Christian Religion*, trans. Henry Beveridge (Peabody, MA: Hendrickson Publishers, 2008), 1:3.1–4.1:9–12. The term "semen" is used vaguely and its association with a concept of common grace requires further clarification. It seems that to Calvin, the semen carries only potentiality that never develops in reality because of human obduracy. This is not what the Lutheran Confessions mean by the passive capacity since they discuss it in the context of conversion, dismissing any spiritual attunement to God or true knowledge, for that is enacted only through the Word, apart from which there is only total corruption.

183. In this particular case, dismissing this power in humans rules out their initiative or causality for both proactive and responsive action, for even responsive capacity could be misinterpreted to mean that God is responsible merely to prompt man into activity and then leaves him on his own. That approach would be Arminian, which the church has rejected. See page 128 in this volume.

184. Similar explanations of soteriology emerged after Luther's death, such as in Methodism's appeal to a prevenient grace, which is rooted in Arminian theology. This appeal says in effect that divine grace precedes human decision but does not exclude human decision to effect one's own salvation. Jacob Arminius, *The Works of James Arminius, D.D.*, 3 vols. (Auburn, NY: Derby, Miller and Orton, 1853), 2:72; see Part 2.

5

THE STRUCTURE OF THE HUMAN

Theological anthropology also encompasses the important debate on the structure of a human being, or what a human consists of. This point is important since Scripture provides not only the distinction of humans as male and female but also names for the components of a human, such as a soul, spirit, flesh, and body (see Table 1). Thus it is helpful to engage this discussion because it speaks both to what humans have in common with other created beings on earth—their bodily existence—and to what distinguishes them as special and unique, namely, their possession of the soul. This dual perspective assumes a differentiation in humans of body and soul. At times Scripture reflects on what it means to be human from the perspective of our creatureliness, with hardly any differentiation from other creatures, as in this quote from Ecclesiastes (3:18–21):

Table 1. Biblical Words Describing Man

	OT Hebrew	NT Greek	English equivalent
Man as a Unity			
	אָדָם (adam)	ὁ ἄνθρωπος	individual, human being, or man
Man	אִישׁ (ish)		individual or husband
	אֱנוֹשׁ (enosh)	ὁ ἀνήρ	mortal, man, husband, or full-aged male
Woman	אִשָּׁה (ishshah)	ἡ γυνή	woman or wife
Aspects of Man			
Body	בָּשָׂר (basar)	Τό σῶμα	body
Flesh		ἡ σάρξ	flesh (physical or ethical sense)
Soul	נֶפֶשׁ (nephesh)	ἡ ψυχή	soul or life
Spirit	רוּחַ (ruach)	τό πνεῦμα	spirit, breath, or wind
Heart	לֵב (lebh)		
	לֵבָב (lebhabh)	ἡ καρδιά	heart, center or seat of feelings, volition, intellect

> I said in my heart with regard to the sons of men that God is testing them to show that they are but beasts. For the fate of the sons of men and the fate of beasts is the same. As one dies, so dies the other. They all have the same breath. And man has no advantage over the beasts; for all is vanity. All go to one place; all are from the dust, and all turn to dust again. Who knows whether the spirit of man goes upward and the spirit of the beast goes down to earth?

This text affirms the reality of death for all creaturely life, humans included, and lumps humans together with animal creatures who possess that "breath of life" (נִשְׁמַת חַיִּים) which will expire one day at their physical death. The word often used for "breath of life" is נֶפֶשׁ, commonly translated as soul, and we associate with that נֶפֶשׁ something humans have uniquely for themselves. If "soul" is understood as a mere breath of life that all creatures have in common, then human exceptionality is not easily argued. However, the word also may indicate something more: the concept of personality, which defines each human as a unique person, and also spirituality, the attunement of the soul's faculties to the transcendent. In *The Disputation Concerning Man* Luther operated with an understanding of humans as consisting of body and soul. However, contemporary views on anthropology seem to question whether this dualism should still be accepted or whether a monistically defined being is a better alternative, particularly in view of the weakness in the Platonic model of separating body and soul to the degree that they do not interact or relate with one another. Before engaging in that discussion we must examine ideas about the origin of the soul.

THE ORIGIN OF THE SOUL

Lutheran theologians have accepted the concept of *animal rationale* and located rational thought and the senses in the soul. This dual division of a human being into body and soul is now the standard approach, replacing a tripartite division of man into body, soul, and spirit. The spirit was considered the part of the soul which oriented one spiritually to things above, whereas the soul was associated with the individual's personality and sensory experiences dealing with worldly matters, those things below. While for Aristotle the soul is a generic term signifying the capacity all humans share and which brings about their activities,[1] he also assigned to every human a personality with character dispositions or personality traits. Through the active exercise of his mind, a person will seek to conform with the moral virtues of patience, modesty, courage, and righteousness and thereby distinguish himself in character from other humans.[2]

1. Aristotle, *On the Soul* 1:5.411b27–29, BWA 554. See also Melchert, *Great Conversation*, 331. In Theses 15 and 16 (AE 34:139; WA 39/1:175.32–35) of *The Disputation Concerning Man* Luther is skeptical of an agreement reached among philosophers on what the soul is, and he dismisses Aristotle as being deceptive and unclear to his hearers and readers.

2. *Nicomachean Ethics* 2.1.1103b21–26, BWA 952.

While most scholars have affirmed this dualistic anthropology which teaches that humans exist as body and soul, the origin of the soul itself continues to need clarification. A number of positions have been taken historically, three of which have been most common: traducianism, pre-existence, and creationism.

Traducianism

The doctrine of traducianism views the soul as passed on or transmitted through the seed (the sperm of the man). The word traducianism is derived from the Latin term *tradux* (root or shoot). Using the imagery of vine crafting, whereby the shoot propagates or transmits the vine plant itself, Tertullian argues in *De anima* 27[3] that when parents unite sexually, the soul—the immaterial—and the material body are generated or propagated. Parents are the originators of both body and soul. At conception the immaterial soul comes into being at the same time as the material body, yet not through (*ex*) conception but by means of it, *per traducem vel propaginem* (that is, by direct derivation, in their ordinary way of propagation), as a continuation of the seed in Adam. Thus, traducianism takes a more rudimentary approach than creationism by claiming that body and soul originate with the bodily sperm together with the traits of the parents' souls.[4] Just as the body passes on genetic characteristics, the soul and spirit likewise receive spiritual and intellectual traits from the preceding generations. The term "generationism" often is used to describe this transmission of positive and negative immaterial traits from one generation to the next.

The traducian position also is taken by Athanasius and Augustine. Modern Protestant advocates today include theologians such as Augustus H. Strong (Baptist), W. G. T. Shedd and Gordon Clark (Presbyterian), Lewis Sperry Chafer, Millard Erickson, Norman L. Geisler, Robert Culver, and Robert L. Reymond. Most theologians of the Reformation, including Luther, have accepted this theory. Luther reflects on his traducianistic position in his Table Talks: "The soul must be born out of corrupt matter and seed and must be created by God out of the matter of a man and a woman."[5]

The Lutheran Confessions also take the position that the soul came about through conception. The Formula of Concord states: "For God created not only the body and soul of Adam and Eve before the fall but also our body and

3. Tertullian, *On the Soul*, in *Apologetical Works*, trans. Edwin A. Quain, The Fathers of the Church 10 (Washington, DC: Catholic University of America Press, 1950), 242–45.

4. Heinrich Denzinger, comp., *Compendium of Creeds, Definitions, and Declarations on Matters of Faith and Morals*, ed. Robert Fastiggi and Anne Englund Nash for the English edition, 43d ed. (San Francisco: Ignatius Press, 2012), 303 (§ 1007), 641 (§ 3220).

5. "Since the soul was in that instance made with the body, so when a child is born today the soul is created together with the body, contrary to Plato. Although all others disagree, it's my opinion that the soul isn't added from the outside but is created of the matter of the semen." Table Talk No. 5230: *Luther Rejects the Pre-Existence of the Soul*, 1540, in Martin Luther, *Luthers Werke: Tischreden*, 6 vols. (Weimar: H. Böhlau, 1912–21), 5:18.12–24 (AE 54:401); hereafter cited as WATr.

soul after the fall."[6] This statement must be understood as follows: while the soul originates according to the laws of nature, it does not do so independent of or against God's watch; God is affirmed as active behind these processes when He lets them happen in a naturally ordered way. God's involvement and natural conception are not mutually exclusive: He uses this means within His mediated creation (*creatio mediata*). In the Small Catechism God is confessed as the creator and sustainer of human life: "I believe that God has created me together with all that exists. God has given me and still preserves my body and soul."[7] Together with Luther, the Confessions see God behind all that seems to come naturally to humans.[8]

The concern one might have with traducianism is that because the soul is viewed as a product of parental propagation, its connection to God and its simplicity and spirituality may be lost. The traducian position thus readily could succumb to materialism, yet the human soul is both immaterial and immortal. What the soul is and does goes beyond the capacity of matter and is dependent on God's causality. In the end, though, traducianism affirms God as the cause of the soul's existence and thus does not diminish the pro-life argument or facilitate an argument in favor of *in vitro* fertilization and cloning. Embryos too fall under God's providential care, and since life begins at conception, embryos should be recognized as having souls and should be regarded as full persons.

Traducianism can argue its case from Gn 5:3, where Adam "begot his son according to his image." This passage implies that parental generation took place, and thus Adam was the only one who received his soul directly from God. At his creation the Creator, God Himself, passed on the נִשְׁמַת חַיִּים (breath of life, Gn 2:7) directly and he became a living being or soul, נֶפֶשׁ. From then on the soul is transmitted by God indirectly through parental propagation. This position seems to be the one supported most fully by other parts of Scripture as well (Gn 1:28; Ps 51:7; Jb 14:4; Acts 17:24–26; Rom 5:12; Heb 7:10). Thus, traducianism bears deterministic thought, which seems to affirm no uniqueness to each individual.[9] Certain human behaviors of which Christianity is critical, like pursuing homosexual activity and modifying one's gender identity, in this view reflect not simply a person's lifestyle choices but proclivities received in conception, which have been programmed from before birth. However, traducianism would not go so far as to dismiss individuality and personal accountability for one's specific life choices; all that it conveys, as the Confessions repeatedly point out, is the gravity of the

6. Ep. I.4 (K-W, 488).

7. SC II.2 (K-W, 354).

8. "Thus we learn from this article that none of us has life—or anything that has been mentioned here or can be mentioned—from ourselves, nor can we by ourselves preserve any of them, however small and unimportant. All this is comprehended in the word 'Creator.'" LC II.16 (K-W, 432–33).

9. A. F. C. Vilmar and K. W. Piderit, *Dogmatik: Akademische Vorlesungen*, 2 vols. (Gütersloh: C. Bertelsmann, 1874), 1:349: "Immer aber liegt im Traducianismus die Gefahr nahe, dem Determinismus in die Hände zu fallen."

corruption of both body and soul "through carnal conception and birth from father and mother through the sinful seed."[10]

Pre-existentialism

The second position, pre-existentialism, holds that the life of the soul antedates the body. This idea originated with Plato and was supported by Philo and Origen; in more recent times it has been advanced by Immanuel Kant, Friedrich Wilhelm Schelling, Gotthold Ephraim Lessing, Johann Gottlieb Fichte, Friedrich Schleiermacher, Julius Müller,[11] and Mormonism.[12] This position maintains that in the beginning God created the soul before He created the visible world and Adam, and that at every conception of an individual the soul is handed down. Thus, the soul of every individual exists before the actual life of that person has begun. Until then the souls are thought to be stored in the heavenly sphere (*aether*) or in the unseen world of spirits (*limbus animarum*). Conception of a human invites or begs for the soul to come, so to speak. Here proponents seek to push aside original sin and its immediate imputation to all of humanity and salvage some room for personal freedom, such as the ability to choose to believe and the idea that an individual is sinless until he actually commits sin.

The Greek concepts of sin influenced Origen's theology. He taught that the soul exists prior to entering the body of a human being. In its pre-existent state the soul sins on a free and voluntary basis and thus enters the human body as a means of God's punishment and humiliation. Though the body or material form of life is not the cause of sin, it serves to punish the soul for its prior sins. We thus can understand Origen's thinking that the soul must focus on higher things and the body be mortified to release the soul, which after death will return to its purified state.[13]

---

10. SD I.7 (K-W, 533). Here the authors in reference to original sin reject creationism and seem to gravitate toward traducianism: "To this day and in this state of corruption, God does not create and make sin in us, but along with human nature, which God still in this day and age creates in human beings, original sin is transmitted through carnal conception and birth from father and mother through the sinful seed." See also SD I.28 (K-W, 536).

11. Julius Müller, a nineteenth-century theologian and professor, is best known for his two volumes on sin, *Die christliche Lehre von der Sünde* (2 vols.; Breslau: Josef Max, 1839), in which he revived Gnosticism's idea of humanity's fall before time.

12. The concept of premortal existence is an early and fundamental doctrine of Mormonism. Its founder, Joseph Smith, Jr., taught that human souls are pre-existent with God the Father and Jesus. Mormon doctrine holds that human souls are literally born of God the Father and a Heavenly Mother, one of the Father's plural wives. Spirits are seen as material beings made of finer, invisible matter. Blake T. Ostler, "The Idea of Pre-Existence in the Development of Mormon Thought," *Dialogue* 15, no. 1 (1982): 59–78. The pre-existence of the soul points also to Hinduism and reincarnation. In the Bhagavad Gita, considered by Hindus to be a sacred text, Krishna tells Arjuna, "Never was there a time when I did not exist, nor you, nor all these kings; nor in the future shall any of us cease to be" (2.12). Eknath Easwaran, trans., *The Bhagavad Gita*, The Classics of Indian Spirituality, 2d ed. (Tomales, CA: Nilgiri Press, 2007), 89.

13. One passage scholars often cite that speaks to the preexistence of the soul is in Origen's *De Principiis*, 2.9.1 (ANF 4:289–90), but that passage doesn't clarify whether the pre-existent soul

Scripture maintains, however, that sin entered the world through one man (Genesis 3; Rom 5:12–18), so a soul had nothing to do with bringing sin into the world. It should be clear that this position holds little ground in view of the scriptural evidence, which attests to the total corruption of every human (Ps 51:5; Rom 3:24). In view of Origen's teaching, belief in the soul's pre-existence was condemned as heresy in the Second Council of Constantinople (the fifth ecumenical council) in AD 553. The first of many anathemas spoken against Origen states: "If anyone asserts the fabulous pre-existence of souls, and shall assert the monstrous restoration which follows from it: let him be anathema."[14]

Creationism

The third position, known since Augustine, is today the one most commonly held among theologians. It can be traced back to the Greek philosopher Aristotle, who thought already in the fourth century BC that the soul comes from the gods above (θυράθεν) to the human. Creationism was taught further by Ambrose, Lucius Lactantius,[15] Jerome, some scholastics, Roman Catholic theologians, and mostly also Reformed theologians such as Calvin and Beza. This approach aims to correct or eliminate the materialistic aspect of traducianism. Creationists maintain that all those propagated after Adam also receive their soul directly from God, who repeats His first creative act with Adam by creating the נֶפֶשׁ directly also in his descendants. The parents can create the body only; God adds or infuses the soul. This position depends more on God's doing and conveys the idea of immortality: should a murderer kill a person, for example, he would destroy the body but not the soul. To be immortal, to belong to God and to be under His care and causality, serves as a source of comfort (Mt 10:28).

Creationism has become a controversial issue especially in the light of the current discussion regarding abortion and the question of when human life begins. In the past some theologians asserted that the beginning of human life, or ensoulment, takes place when the infant takes its first breath outside the womb. Aquinas stated that this infusion of the "rational" soul took place

---

is preembodied or not. A clearer text is found in *De Principiis* 1.7, Incorporeal and Corporeal Beings, 4 (ANF 4:263–64). Here Origen opts for a pre-existent, nonembodied state of the soul, which suffers when it becomes embodied: "If the soul of a man, which is certainly inferior while it remains the soul of a man, was not formed along with his body, but is proved to have been implanted strictly from without, much more must this be the case with those living beings which are called heavenly. . . . How could his soul and its images be formed along with his body, who before he was created in the womb, is said to be known to God, and was sanctified by Him before his birth?" Origen, *De Principiis*, 1.7.4 (ANF 4:263–64). Anderson, *On Being Human*, 90.

14. *The Anathemas against Origen*, NPNFa 14:318.

15. Lactantius (c. 240–c. 320), who follows the Platonic preference for the soul over the body, has much to say about the burden of the body on the soul and consequently suggests: "Whoever, then, prefers the life of the soul must despise the life of the body." Lactantius, *The Divine Institutes* 7.5, in *The Works of Lactantius*, trans. William Fletcher, Ante Nicene Christian Library 21 and 22, 2 vols. (Edinburgh: T&T Clark, 1871), 1:438, https://archive.org/details/antenicenechrist21robe/page/n438.

at the fortieth day of pregnancy for boys and the eightieth or ninetieth day for girls, a point at which the primary fundamental organs have been formed.[16] That position, called delayed hominization, has been replaced in Roman Catholicism today with the assertion of an immediate hominization, that is, that infusion occurs at conception. If any doubt exists about whether an embryo is a human being and one accepts a delayed hominization, one could argue still that the embryo is in a state of potency and will, and if the right environment is provided it will be born as a human being; one can still affirm a sacredness of life at conception and be against the abortion of embryos.[17] For "we should ascribe to the embryo a right that is specifically its own."[18] Though the positions of Aquinas and the Roman Catholic Church today are difficult to reconcile, this last point is still valid for the Roman Catholic encyclical *Humani Generis* (1938),[19] which does not dismiss evolution of the body[20] though it questions the factual basis of evolution (§§ 5 and 6). Even if the body's origin could come from pre-existent matter and could be studied (§ 36), the encyclical's interest is to preserve creationism for the soul: the soul originates from God.[21] However, the papal letter does not specify at what stage the soul comes into the human body and therefore remains unclear about whether the document maintains a delayed or immediate hominization. Since then the official Roman Catholic position of creationism[22] also has been bolstered to advocate for the unborn in all its stages, and consequently it rejects any attempts to depersonalize the unborn.[23]

One further concern raised against creationism is its susceptibility to Pelagianism or semi-Pelagianism: sin is understood only materially and so the

16. Fabrizio Amerini, *Aquinas on the Beginning and End of Human Life*, trans. Mark Henninger (Cambridge, MA: Harvard University Press, 2013), 77–78; McClain and Dilling, *Theological Anthropology*, 7. Aquinas's account of the beginning of human life and ensoulment is philosophical and not biological or medical (Amerini, *Aquinas*, 230).

17. Amerini, *Aquinas*, 229.

18. Amerini, *Aquinas*, 229.

19. Pius XII, *Humani Generis: Encyclical Letter of Pope Pius XII* (Washington, DC: National Catholic Welfare Conference, 1950).

20. Pius XII, *Humani Generis*, §§ 5, 6, 37; Stephen J. Pope, "Theological Anthropology, Science, and Human Flourishing," in *Questioning the Human: Toward a Theological Anthropology for the Twenty-first Century*, ed. Lieven Boeve, Yves de Maeseneer, and Ellen Van Stichel (New York: Fordham University Press, 2014), 17.

21. Pius XII, *Humani Generis* § 36.

22. "The Church teaches that every spiritual soul is created immediately by God—it is not 'produced' by the parents." *Catechism of the Catholic Church: Revised in Accordance with the Official Latin Text Promulgated by Pope John Paul II*, 2d ed. (Washington, DC: United States Catholic Conference, 1997), 93 (§ 366). That reference is based on Pius XII, *Humani Generis*; Denzinger, *Compendium*, 806–7 (§ 3896); Paul VI, *Apostolic Letter in the Form of* Motu Proprio: *Solemni hac Liturgia (Credo of the People of God) of the Supreme Pontiff Paul VI* (Vatican City: Vatican Publishing House, 1968), § 8; and Lateran Council V (1513; Denzinger, *Compendium*, 359–60 [§ 1440]).

23. See for example the instruction of the Roman Catholic Church's Congregation for the Doctrine of the Faith, *The Dignity of a Person: With Additional Resources: Dignitas Personae* (Washington, DC: United States Conference of Catholic Bishops, 2009).

flesh infects or corrupts the pure spirit coming from God, but never wholly or totally. Here some theologians question why the reverse might not be the case. "If the impure sin-stained body contaminates the pure, unstained soul by contact, why cannot the stainless soul disinfect the contaminated body?"[24]

A number of scriptural texts could be understood to support the claim that God creates the soul in the womb of the mother. The following texts speak of God creating the soul in the body: Nm 16:22; Jb 10:12; Ps 119:73; 139:15–17; Jer 38:16; Zec 12:1; Jn 5:17; and Acts 17:25. One main text supportive of the theory is Heb 12:9, to which Roman Catholic theologians often refer: here God is called the "father of the spirits" (πατὴρ τῶν πνευμάτων) in contrast to humans, who are spoken of as "fathers of the flesh."

In explaining the soul's origin, neither creationism nor traducianism wholly satisfies. Peter Lombard once said something that may serve as the final outlook on this topic: "In creating God infused (the soul) and in infusing He creates" (*creando infundit eas Deus, et infundendo creat*).[25] In conclusion, we would have to affirm one underlying premise: God is responsible for creating the whole person in the womb, both body and soul, just as He is said in many texts to create the growth of all plant life. Traducianism indirectly holds that position, since it places the origin of the soul in the context of God's conservation of the world (*conservatio mundi*) as continual creation (*creatio continua*).[26] If we combine ideas of traducianism and creationism, we could argue as follows: through the act of parental conception God's creative power (*concursus specialis*) brings forth a new human personality, albeit indirectly. The biblical text that most directly supports this view is Ps 139:15–17, which affirms that at conception a human person was formed with an identity, indicated in the first person. The psalm thus supports ensoulment at conception, even if it does not speak specifically to that point.

The debate on the transmission of original sin has elicited the creationist and traducianist approaches. Augustine is known to have changed his thinking on traducianism in response to Pelagianism, arguing that original sin is passed on through conception and brings a total spiritual corruption of will and reason, of the entire ensouled person. That contamination did not occur with Jesus Christ at His incarnation, however. He remained sinless even when He assumed human nature and His body and soul dwelt in the womb of His mother Mary. Both traducianism and creationism present an argument for Christ's sinlessness, but creationism may seem to some theologians to provide a better explanation, since it does not admit the propagation of the soul through human parents.[27]

A direct benefit from the discussion on the origin of the soul is the reinforcing of human exceptionalism. Reexaminations of Gn 1:26–28, 30, and

24. McClain and Dilling, *Theological Anthropology*, 90.
25. McClain and Dilling, *Theological Anthropology*, 81.
26. Vilmar and Piderit, *Dogmatik* 1:351.
27. McClain and Dilling, *Theological Anthropology*, 90.

Gn 2:7–8, 15–25 reveal the *modus operandi* or manner of a human's creation to be different from that of all other life forms. Through God's Word all animals were created immediately from basic geospheric elements of earth, water, and air (Gn 1:24). Yet God formed (וַיִּיצֶר) the human from the dust of the earth and breathed into his nose the breath of life (נִשְׁמַת חַיִּים), the principle of life, and through that breath the human became a living soul (נֶפֶשׁ חַיָּה), enlivened by the divine Spirit. This human soul did not emerge from the earth as did the rest of the animal world but was created through a divine act of God's breathing it into the body. Accordingly, the biblical account speaks of the human coming from flesh (בָּשָׂר) and "a living soul" (נֶפֶשׁ חַיָּה; Is 10:18).[28] Though he is "dust" (עָפָר; Gn 2:7; 3:19; Ps 104:29) he carries in him the "living breath" (נִשְׁמַת חַיִּים; Gn 2:7) and the "spirit" of God (רוּחַ). Since the soul owes its existence to the Spirit and has the Spirit's substance as the basis of its own existence, the soul exists and lives from the strength of the Spirit (Jb 33:4).

The human is a body–spirit being, and a complete being only in that combination or unity;[29] as little as the body can live without the soul at the basic level, still retaining the "breath of life" (נִשְׁמַת חַיִּים), so little does the soul have a place to stay without the body. Trends in society always have favored one component over the other: Platonism, asceticism, and Stoicism all seem to affirm soul or spirit over the body. Gnostic tendencies even today teach an escapism or irreverence for one's createdness.[30] Those discontented with their own body and sex may now explore and alter their physical constitution and sexual anatomy. If a genuine life truly existed only apart from the body because the body poses some form of hindrance to achieving true and full life, would not suicide offer a logical solution, as the Stoics concluded?[31]

The body, though coming from the earth and being earthly (ἐκ γῆς χοϊκος, 1 Cor 15:47), has an eternal component, serving as the temple for the soul and as the seed of the resurrection (1 Cor 3:16–17; 15:42–44). The entire unified human is the object of God's salvific work, including His eventual resurrection

---

28. Pöhlmann, *Abriß der Dogmatik*, 160.

29. Millard Erickson is a spokesperson for conditional unity, not monism, and speaks less of soul than of the unity of spiritual and physical elements, which still makes the human complex: "The spiritual and the physical elements are not always distinguishable, for the human is a unitary subject; there is no conflict between the material and immaterial nature. The compound is dissolvable, however; dissolution takes place at death. At the resurrection a compound will again be formed, with the soul (if we choose to call it that) once more becoming inseparably attached to a body." Erickson, *Christian Theology*, 556.

30. Peter M. Burfeind, *Gnostic America: A Reading of Contemporary American Culture & Religion According to Christianity's Oldest Heresy* (Toledo, OH: Pax Domini Press, 2014).

31. The Stoics were intent on reducing negative emotions like frustration, anger, grief, and disappointment, which result from setbacks and obstacles in one's life. Should these become overbearing, suicide was considered an appropriate path to freedom. However, the lust for death (*libido moriendi*), like the other passions and negative emotions, were to be avoided. William B. Irvine, *The Stoic Challenge* (New York: W. W. Norton & Company, 2021), 73. In fact, the rate of suicide in North America is higher than the rate of death from car accidents, which shows that many have lost the appreciation for the value of their own life.

from the dead, and never does one part act alone; the bodily functions are at the same time also functions of the soul and spirit. In German the distinction of *geistig* and *geistlich* is helpful: the former indicates the mere intellectual capacity of the soul, while the latter points to the awareness of God or one's spiritual disposition, which is unique to humans.[32]

DICHOTOMY OR TRICHOTOMY

Anthropological discussions inevitably lead to the question, "Of what is a person made?" This question invites an exploration of the distinctions of soul, body, and spirit and how they relate to one another. Without going into detail about the complex thoughts held by theologians over the centuries, we will give a brief overview of the two prevalent positions: the trichotomous view, which speaks about the body, spirit, and soul, and the dichotomous view, which refers to the body and soul. The discussion of this subject in theological anthropology reveals influences from the Greek tradition, particularly from the philosophers Plato and Aristotle. Plato's position in *Phaedo*, for example, is that the soul is the mark that distinguishes created life as human. Not only does the soul represent cognitive and intellectual features, it makes an inanimate thing animate and is imperishable and immortal as the body itself is not.[33]

Aristotle's soul–body "hylomorphism" (ὕλη, *hyle* or matter, and μορφή, *morphē* or form) is based on his understanding that something which exists (οὐσία) is a compound of matter and form. Thus, the form identified as soul is comprised of matter, the body.[34] A human being's body is matter and it needs a soul to live and perform vital functions. The matter, body, is subject in this life to change and deterioration, whereas the soul continues as a constant. For example, a person's body at seven years old is different from his seventy-five-year-old physique, but the soul maintains continuity between the two bodies. A body lives because of the soul, and after death a body no longer exists as it once did; the soul alone continues.[35]

According to the biblical account of creation there are three essential components of a human: the body that was taken from the earth, the spirit breathed into the body, and the living soul resulting from that act of God breathing in that spirit. These three components also are indicated in 1 Thes 5:23, where Paul uses Greek thought to speak about the human, distinguishing between spirit (πνεῦμα), soul (ψυχή), and body (σῶμα; "may your spirit and

32. Brunner, "Der Ersterschaffene als Gottes Ebenbild," 1:90.

33. Plato *Phaedo* 70b–c, 94b.

34. The soul–body hylomorphism applies to other entities as well: brick is matter to the form house, for example, or clay is matter to the form stone. Aristotle, *On the Soul* 2.1.412b5–7, 2.1.413a1–3, 2.2.414a15–18; BWA 555, 556, 559.

35. Aristotle, *On the Soul* 2.1.412b15–24, BWA 556. Christopher Shields, *Aristotle*, Routledge Philosophers (London: Routledge, 2007), 290–93. Also, Christopher Shields, "Soul as Subject in Aristotle's *De Anima*," *Classical Quarterly* 38, no. 1 (1988): 140–49.

soul and body be kept sound and blameless at the coming of our Lord Jesus Christ"). Hebrews 4:12 considers ψυχή and πνεῦμα next to one another ("For the word of God is living and active . . . piercing to the division of soul and of spirit"), as does 1 Cor 15:44: "If there is a natural body [σῶμα ψυχικόν], there is also a spiritual body [σῶμα πνευματικόν]." On the basis of these and other texts, including references to the three great realms of sin—the lust of the flesh, the lust of the eyes, and the pride of life (1 Jn 2:16)—some theologians view anthropology as trichotomous (tripartite); that is, man is made up of body, soul, and spirit. Here the soul (ψυχή, *psyche*; נֶפֶשׁ, *nephesh*) constitutes the particular life of a person; the body constitutes the lower, sensory factors, and the spirit (πνεῦμα, *pneuma*; רוּחַ, *ruach*) the higher, divine factor of life that all humans have beyond the strictly physical dimension. Herein lies the interest in arguing for a trichotomy of the human being or at least pointing out a body/soul dichotomy that speaks of a spirited soul: such distinctions reflect that humans, unlike the rest of creation, have an awareness of God, the center of their very being.[36]

Thus, soul in this sense would denote a human being who is aware of God and has the response-ability when God Himself enacts it in him through the Holy Spirit and the Word. We could argue from observation and experimentation that nonhumans also have the mental capacity to use an intellect of sorts, but what they lack is the distinct and unique human characteristic of an awareness of God and of the neighbor, including a self-consciousness. Of course, this unique feature can be lost in humans: the spirited soul can go insane or become diabolical in character by shutting itself off from God and from fellow humans, corrupting the image of God in a person, as Luther and others would argue.[37]

A trichotomous position was taken already by Plato and is supported particularly by theologians of the Eastern Orthodox Church. Luther also reflects this division in his earlier thinking in his *Magnificat*.[38] In the nineteenth century, theologians such as Hermann Olshausen, August Neander, Johann Tobias Beck, Leonhard Usteri, Heinrich August Wilhelm Meyer, Franz Delitzsch, Søren Kierkegaard, and August Vilmar revived this view; after that its significance waned among theologians.

The trichotomous view has been criticized for adopting Plato's inadequate structure of man as σῶμα, ψυχή, and νοῦς. Luther pointed out this deficiency in *The Disputation Concerning Man*, saying that philosophy or human wisdom

36. "Common to human and non-human at the creaturely level, the soul becomes differentiated in the human by spirit. The sign or mark of this differentiation is 'awareness' of God as the one who is the source and goal of one's own life." Anderson, *On Being Human*, 38. See also C. A. Beckwith, "Soul and Spirit, Biblical Conceptions of," in *The New Schaff-Herzog Encyclopedia of Religious Knowledge*, ed. Samuel Macauley Jackson (1908–14; repr., Grand Rapids: Baker Book House, 1949–50), 11:12: "Spirit is the condition, soul the manifestation, of life." See also Braaten and Jenson, *Christian Dogmatics* 1:333.

37. Anderson, *On Being Human*, 39.

38. *The Magnificat*, 1521 (AE 21:297–357; WA 7:539–604).

defines man as having the three divisions of "reason, sensation, and body." However, that trichotomous view falls short of the Christian trichotomy of body, spirit, and soul. So did Apollinaris's misrepresentation that was anathematized at the First Council of Constantinople in 381.[39] The challenge is to find the version of trichotomy that corresponds to Christian beliefs. The most compelling argument against trichotomy is the semi-Pelagian abuse of it, namely, asserting that sin has impacted the mind and soul but not the spirit. By contrast, Lutherans confess that original sin has infected the entire person; in other words, the spirit also is no longer attuned to God.[40]

Theologians of the Roman Catholic Church more often have taken a dichotomous view, asserting the dual division of man as body and soul or spirit. This concept is similar to that of the spirited soul already mentioned, which is dualistic but locates in the soul the attunement or awareness of God—the spirit—together with the intellectual capacity to navigate life here on earth. Martin Luther also took this position later in his life, after originally supporting a trichotomous division in his *Magnificat*.[41] Other nineteenth-century theologians in this tradition are Adolf von Harless, Karl Immanuel Nitzsch, Johann Christian von Hofmann, Gottfried Thomasius, Karl Friedrich August Kahnis, August Tholuck, August Hahn, Christoph Ernst Luthardt, and Franz Hermann Reinhold von Frank. In supporting the dichotomous position they cite a substantial number of biblical passages that testify to a human being's division into body and soul, or into body and spirit. A number of texts mention spirit and soul together or as synonyms, such as Ps 73:26; 84:3; Mt 6:25; 10:28; Acts 15:26; 20:10; Rom 7:15ff.; 1 Cor 5:3–5; 2 Cor 4:16 (ὁ ἔξω, ὁ ἔσω ἄνθρωπος); Jas 2:26; compare Mt 20:28 and 27:10; and Phil 1:27; Heb 12:23; 1 Pt 3:19; and Rv 6:9; 20:4. Soul and spirit cannot be separated neatly, but both represent the

39. See *The Seven Ecumenical Councils of the Undivided Church*, NPNFb 14:172–74. Apollinaris took the trichotomous view and then connected that to his Christological teaching. He appealed to the well-known Platonic division of human nature: body (σάρξ, σῶμα), soul (ψυχή ἄλογος), and spirit (νοῦς, πνεῦμα, ψυχή λογική). Christ, he said, assumed both the human body and the human soul or principle of animal life, but not the human spirit.

40. Vilmar and Piderit, *Dogmatik* 1:333–36.

41. *The Magnificat*, 1521 (AE 21:297–357; WA 7:539–604). Luther's last reference to the tripartite division is in his *Magnificat*. With the illustration of the tabernacle he makes his point that of the three, the spirit should be regarded the "highest, deepest, and noblest" part of a human being because it represents the dwelling place of faith and the Word of God. *The Magnificat*, 1521 (AE 21:303–5; WA 7:550.1–553.10). For other references to trichotomy in Luther see *Luthers Randbemerkungen zu Taulers Predigten*, c. 1516 (WA 9:99.36–40, 103.37–4.3); *Lectures on Romans*, 1516 (AE 25:62–66; WA 56:476.20–26); *In epistolam Pauli ad Galatas M. Lutheri commentarius*, 1519 (WA 2:510.2–5; 585.22–25). At first Luther was guided by texts such as 1 Thes 5:23 and Lk 1:46 ("My soul magnifies God, the Lord") and possibly influenced by theologians such as Origen, Jerome, or Augustine. Thus he started to take an initial trichotomous division of body (flesh), soul, and spirit (*corpus/caro-anima-spiritus*). In this scheme each division is represented respectively by the sensory (body, *homo sensualis*), the rational (soul, *rationalis*), and the spiritual being (spirit, *spiritualis*). See here Peters, *Der Mensch*, 36–37; also Wilfried Joest, *Ontologie der Person bei Luther*, 164–95; Reinhold Gallinat, "Der 'natürliche Mensch' nach Luther," *Lutherjahrbuch* 42 (1975): 33–51.

inner life of a human being and each points to a specific aspect of it. Here is how the distinction is generally understood today by the majority of exegetes and theologians:

> The Divine Spirit is the source of life, and its power is communicated in the physical, intellectual and moral sphere. . . . Soul, though identical with spirit, has shades of meaning which spirit has not; it stands for the individual: "Man is spirit, because he is dependent upon God. Man is soul, because unlike angels, he has a body, which links him to earth. He is animal as possessing *anima*, but he is a reasoning animal, which distinguishes him from the brute."[42]

Luther replaces the scheme of body (*sensus*), soul (*ratio*), and spirit with body and soul. For Luther, soul and spirit are not seen as two distinct components of a human; they point to the same animating source of life, though each fulfills its own functions. Luther understands spirit as the element in the human being that focuses on the eternal and invisible, his internal orientation toward God, or "the dwelling place of faith and the Word of God," as he identifies it.[43] In his interpretation of spirit as being connected to faith and God's Word, Luther goes beyond any Christian Platonic ideas that Origen taught and Augustine still professed. No longer can the spirit merely strive toward a higher idea or ideal through speculation or mysticism, but it is connected to God's revealed Word and faith in God.[44] The spirit is an immaterial element in the human and does not serve as a moral-intellectual capacity within the human that enables him to regain the relationship with God by his own efforts. Otherwise, "before we know it, faith is lost, and the spirit is dead in the sight of God."[45] Instead, the spirit's presence is an enactment of God, as Cortez concludes from his study on Luther: "The Spirit is the 'transcendental determination' of human life because the body/soul union is not a fixed possession but is something that must be continually established by God through the agency of the Spirit."[46]

Therefore, this spirit in the human should not be considered to be in a neutral state. Luther also posits that a spirit can be negatively disposed, where the relationship with God does not exist because this spiritual life has been taken captive by the powers of the devil. The final outcome of such a state is eternal death. All humans have a spirit, controlled either positively by the Spirit and Word or negatively by the spirit of the flesh. This polarity of spirit and flesh

42. McClain and Dilling, *Theological Anthropology*, 14, who reference here the Dutch Reformed theologian Herman Bavinck, *Reformed Dogmatics*, ed. John Bolt, trans. John Vriend (Grand Rapids: Baker Academic, 2003–2008), 2:628. See also Pieper, *Christian Dogmatics* 1:476–77.

43. *The Magnificat*, 1521 (AE 21:303; WA 7:550–51.28–30): "The spirit is the highest, deepest, and noblest part of man. By it he is enabled to lay hold on things incomprehensible, invisible, and eternal." See also Joest, *Ontologie der Person bei Luther*, 191.

44. *Bondage of the Will*, 1525 (AE 33:275; WA 18:774.39–42); Peters, *Der Mensch*, 38.

45. *The Magnificat*, 1521 (AE 21:304; WA 7:552.3–4); Joest, *Ontologie der Person bei Luther*, 191.

46. Cortez, *Christological Anthropology*, 154.

was a consistent theme for Luther, first in his *Galatians Commentary* in 1519,[47] then in the *Magnificat*[48] and his *Resolutions to the Leipzig Disputation*,[49] and especially in his *De servo arbitrio*.[50] In *The Freedom of the Christian* Luther expounds how spirit and flesh impact body and soul:

> Man has a twofold nature, a spiritual and a bodily one. According to the spiritual nature, which men refer to as the soul, he is called a spiritual, inner, or new man. According to the bodily nature, which men refer to as flesh, he is called a carnal, outward, or old man . . . Because of this diversity of nature the Scriptures assert contradictory things concerning the same man, since these two men in the same man contradict each other.[51]

The soul, on the other hand, represents the spiritual force that makes the body alive, works through it, and grasps the lower, earthly things. In the end Luther takes a dichotomist point of view as seen in Thesis 21 of *The Disputation Concerning Man* (1536).[52] The soul permeates the body, using the senses, and uses reason to rule over all other creation; the body serves as the organ of the soul, which communicates through the body. When Mary's "soul" magnifies the Lord, she displays that true attitude toward God, "that is, my whole life and being, mind and strength, esteem Him highly."[53] Thus, the soul becomes the fulcrum, the axis, for one's entire existence, drawing toward it everything that marks someone as human.

Both body and soul are kept and preserved by God. The soul, embracing both heart and conscience, is the deep inner seat of life and the body is its bearer. Were it not for the body/soul distinction, the two realms or two kingdoms would not exist, nor would the need to defend or contribute to society in a military role, or in any other vocation for that matter. To assert there is no distinction would be diametrically opposed to Luther's position.[54] The dichotomy of soul and body is important to recognize even in view of the theological criticism that it presents a "disembodied version of the image," which however Gn 1:26–28 does not seem to indicate.[55] The boundary between

47. *Lectures on Galatians*, 1519 (AE 27:153–409; WA 2:436–618).

48. *The Magnificat*, 1521 (AE 21:303; WA 7:550.26–27): "The nature of man consists of the three parts—spirit, soul and body; and all of these may be good or evil, that is, they may be spirit or flesh."

49. *Resolutiones Lutherianae super propositionibus suis Lipsiae disputatis*, 1519 (WA 2:388–435).

50. *Bondage of the Will*, 1525 (AE 33:214–15; WA 18:735.20–36.5).

51. *The Freedom of a Christian*, 1520 (AE 31:344; WA 7:21.12–15).

52. "Namely, that man is a creature of God consisting of body and a living soul, made in the beginning after the image of God, without sin, so that he should procreate and rule over the created things, and never die." *Disputation Concerning Man*, 1536 (AE 34:138; WA 39/1:176.7–9). He reflects a similar perspective in *Bondage of the Will*, 1525 (AE 33:225; WA 18:742.16–21).

53. *The Magnificat*, 1521 (AE 21:307; WA 7:554.20).

54. *Whether Soldiers, Too, Can Be Saved*, 1526 (AE 46:100; WA 19:629.14–15): "Since, then, there is no doubt that the military profession is in itself a legitimate and godly calling and occupation . . ."

55. Cortez, *Theological Anthropology*, 21.

soul and body is not impermeable, as if either body or soul remained unaffected by sin in the other component and continued to be a neutral entity. The plea to think of humans holistically in terms of well-being comes to theology from the medical field, and the need to consider every human's state of well-being or ill-being psychosomatically is critical.[56] The body and the soul (ψυχή) interact and mingle, and personality is influenced and affected by the genetic configuration as well as by external factors such as environment and social setting. The Christian belief in life after death also reflects a perspective that is holistic or unitary in a sense: resurrection is a phenomenon involving both body and soul, not a Platonic event in which the soul forever leaves the body.

The discussion on the composition of the human is long and complicated, and in this debate the understanding of the division of soul, body, and/or spirit is important, for it corrects modernity's single focus on body as matter, in denial of the soul and the transcendent realm.[57] Those who claim that humans evolved from matter can never adequately answer the nuances of biblical anthropology. Many human attributes go beyond the body, like the immaterial functions associated with personality and religious inclination. To attribute such functions to matter or to the body, as evolutionary monism suggests, falls short of what theological anthropology conveys.

In the end, whether humans reflect a bipartite (dual) or tripartite division remains a point of discussion. Both views find support in Scripture, and looking back in history, neither position was ever condemned officially by the church. With certainty it can be said that human nature is comprised of a body, a soul, and a spirit. Whether the soul and the spirit are one or are somehow distinct God did not choose to make abundantly clear in His Word. Whether we believe in a dichotomy or a trichotomy, every human must heed the following advice: offer your body as a living sacrifice (Rom 12:1), thank God for saving your soul (1 Pt 1:9), and worship God in spirit and in truth (Jn 4:23–24).

---

56. "Humans are to be treated as unities. Their spiritual condition cannot be dealt with independently of their physical and psychological condition and vice versa. Psychosomatic medicine is proper. So also is psychosomatic ministry. . . . The Christian who desires to be spiritually healthy will give attention to such matters as diet, rest and exercise." Erickson, *Christian Theology*, 557.

57. Eleonore Stump, "Resurrection, Reassembly, and Reconstitution: Aquinas on the Soul," in *Die menschliche Seele: Brauchen wir den Dualismus?* ed. Bruno Niederbacher and Edmund Runggaldier, Metaphysical Research 7 (Frankfurt: Ontos Verlag, 2006), 151–72.

6

PAST AND CONTEMPORARY DISCUSSIONS ON THE ORIGIN OF HUMANS

In this final chapter of Part One it is necessary to engage with prevalent views on the origin of humanity which have been raised in the modern era. Here theological anthropology relates to an area of anthropology called physical/biological anthropology, which "involves the study of human anatomy, non-human primates (primatology), and human origins."[1]

Some theories regarding the origin of humanity have come and gone in the light of new discoveries. However, one important discovery merits mention. In 1974 in the Afar region of Ethiopia, American paleoanthropologist Donald Johansen found fossilized bones that belonged to a single person. At his girlfriend's suggestion Johansen named the skeleton Lucy, after the Beatles song "Lucy in the Sky with Diamonds,"[2] to which they were listening at the camp. Scientists determined that Lucy was a female who lived 3.2 million years ago and theorized that she belonged to a premodern human (*Homo sapiens*) species they called *Australopithecus afarensis*. This particular species lived predominantly in the trees but also was able to walk upright on the ground.[3] Forty percent of Lucy's bone remains have been found, according to scientists the most complete remains predating modern man. She stood not much taller than three feet (one meter) and weighed around 66 pounds (30 kilograms).

Theological anthropology looks upon this story as one of many attempts to explain human origins with theories that are not based on the creation account in Scripture. One such theory originated with the biologist Charles Darwin, who believed that human life began millions of years ago and through natural selection and survival of the fittest has led to the species to which modern

1. Howell and Paris, *Introducing Cultural Anthropology*, 8. Other areas worthy of investigation are "archeology, linguistics, . . . and cultural or social anthropology." Howell and Paris, *Introducing Cultural Anthropology*, 6. See also "physical anthropology," *Merriam-Webster.com*, 2022, https://www.merriam-webster.com/dictionary/physical+anthropology.

2. Donald C. Johanson and Kate Wong, *Lucy's Legacy: The Quest for Human Origins* (New York: Three Rivers Press, 2009), 7–8.

3. In 2016 scientists and paleoanthropologists reported their new discovery regarding Lucy's cause of death: she must have died in a fall from a tree, which proves that she stems from tree-dwelling humanoids who evolved into bipeds that walked the African savanna. Her bone fractures show similarities to those found in humans today when they fall. Though many view Lucy as the missing link, not all scientists agree that she is in fact the direct predecessor of modern man, *Homo sapiens*. Carl Zimmer, "3.2-Million-Year-Old Mystery: Did Lucy Die in a Fall from a Tree?" *New York Times*, 30 August 2016, A14.

humans belong, *Homo sapiens*. For adherents of this theory the discovery of Lucy is most welcome because it affirms that modern humans have anthropoid progenitors. However, the idea that *Homo sapiens* emerged as the dominant and only surviving species of the human race continues to require some explanation from scientists.

In one of his recent books, *Sapiens*, Yuval Noah Harari argues that modern humanity's survival could be explained in two different ways. First, the replacement theory posits that the *Homo sapiens* killed others around them—the Neanderthals and the Denisova humans—in order to establish their dominance. They could not interbreed, so all humans stem from *Homo sapiens*. Modern man belongs to his own species. This replacement theory explains the dominance of *Homo sapiens* but bears a latent racist tone, one "of incompatibility, revulsion, and perhaps even genocide."[4] While the replacement theory was favored among scientists for a long time, its popularity gradually yielded by the early twenty-first century to that of a second possibility, the interbreeding theory. This theory suggests that about 70,000 years ago *Homo sapiens* spread from Africa to Arabia and from there to Eurasia and interbred with Neanderthals, so that today's Eurasians are not pure *sapiens* but a mixture of *sapiens* and Neanderthals. The Denisova humans also interbred with the Neanderthals and *Homo sapiens* to give rise to the modern Melanesians and Aboriginal Australians. Today the interbreeding theory seems to hold greater appeal than the replacement theory for scientists such as those studying at the Max Planck Institute of Evolutionary Anthropology,[5] who have found that up to 4 percent of the DNA unique to humans living in the Middle East and Europe is Neanderthal DNA.[6]

The interbreeding theory thus would re-categorize modern man and his predecessors. Now there is a larger genus called *Homo*, which includes the current *Homo sapiens* species, modern humans, but also the extinct species *Homo neanderthalensis* and *Homo denisova*.[7]

---

4. Yuval Noah Harari, *Sapiens: A Brief History of Humankind*, first U.S. ed. (New York: Harper, 2015), 14.

5. The following excerpt from a recent article entitled "Neanderthal DNA May Influence Human Traits" gives us an idea of the most recent opinions of evolutionists: "The study by scientists at the Max Planck Institute of Evolutionary Anthropology in Leipzig, Germany, also confirmed that some Neanderthal DNA found in people of non-African descent affects their skin and hair color, though not in any single direction. . . . Scientists have known for years that Neanderthals and modern humans interbred. About 2 percent of the DNA of people of non-African descent comes from Neanderthals, a species that became extinct about 40,000 years ago." "Neanderthal DNA May Influence These Human Traits," *CBSNews*, 6 October 2017, https://www.cbsnews.com/news/neanderthal-dna-may-influence-human-traits/.

6. Harari, *Sapiens*, 16.

7. Though *Homo sapiens* is today the only extant human species, the interbreeding theory claims there was a time when contemporary humans actually had brothers and sisters from the other two extinct archaic humans: "*Homo sapiens* has kept hidden an even more disturbing secret. Not only do we possess an abundance of uncivilized cousins, once upon a time we had quite a few brothers and sisters as well. We are used to thinking about ourselves as the only humans, because for the last 10,000 years, our species has indeed been the only human species

Set against the interbreeding theory is the biblical account of creation (Gn 1:27; 2:7, 21; as well as Acts 17:26), which serves as scriptural evidence that humans come from a single parent. That view, called monogenesis,[8] states that every human being is descended from a single couple named Adam and Eve, the protoplasts (the first created), as theologians sometimes refer to them. This understanding points not only to a bloodline that connects all nations regardless of their differences but also to a single spoken language. Both the common origin of all peoples and a single original language serve as important prerequisite information for the teaching of original sin that comes from a single human being, Adam, and also for the justification of all that comes through one person, Jesus Christ (Rom 5:18; 1 Cor 15:21–22, 45; 1 Tm 2:5).

Differences in the skulls that have been found—the features, skin color variations, hair, and so forth—have been cited as evidence against monogenesis, that the human race must have originated from more than one set of parents. Thus emerged the theory of polygenesis, with two alternative approaches: humans came to exist all over the world either in succession (pre-Adamism) or parallel to one another (co-Adamism). In the seventeenth century the pre-Adamite Isaac La Peyrère challenged biblical Adamism by claiming that there were already races of humans living before the creation of Adam, a position still popular today among some progressive evangelicals.[9] In this view Genesis 1 gives an account of the first creation of a human, and Genesis 2 follows with the report on the creation of Adam, the progenitor of the Jews. The co-Adamites, on the other hand, claim that there was more than one Adam, or small groups of men created at the same time in different places across the earth, and thus the different races were created separately. For example, when Thomas Harriot (1560–1621) and Walter Raleigh (1552–1618) explored the new world and came upon Native Americans, they could as advocates of co-Adamism argue for a different origin for them than for those who lived in Europe. Giordano Bruno (1548–1600), also a co-Adamist, could not imagine that the Jews and Ethiopians had the same ancestry but believed that they must have come from two separate Adams created by God.[10]

---

around. Yet the real meaning of the word human is 'an animal belonging to the genus *Homo*', and there used to be many other species of this genus besides *Homo sapiens*." Harari, *Sapiens*, 5.

8. Howell and Paris, *Introducing Cultural Anthropology*, 100.

9. Russell Grigg, "Pre-Adamic Man: Were There Human Beings on Earth before Adam?" *Creation* 24, no. 4 (2002): 42–45, https://creation.com/pre-adamic-man-were-there-human-beings-on-earth-before-adam.

10. Bruno is characterized by many authors as a martyr of science, attacked for taking a position called cosmic pluralism, which stated that there was an infinite number of Gardens of Eden. With statements like "I can imagine an infinite number of worlds like the Earth, with a Garden of Eden on each one," he challenged the mainline earth-centered cosmology of his time, the Ptolemaic view. Giordano Bruno, *Cause, Principle and Unity: And Essays on Magic*, trans. Robert de Lucca and Richard J. Blackwell, Cambridge Texts in the History of Philosophy (Cambridge, UK: Cambridge University Press, 1998), 92. Consequently he was tried by the Inquisition for heresy; one of the accusations was that he believed in multiple worlds. After seven years of imprisonment he was sentenced to death and was burned at the stake in Rome.

Genesis 1:27–28 could be bent to favor the co-Adamist position if the plural "them" were construed to refer not to a single couple but to multiple pairs: "So God created man in his own image, in the image of God he created him; male and female he created them. And God blessed them, and God said to them, 'Be fruitful and multiply, and fill the earth and subdue it.'" However, that interpretation would overturn the Old and New Testament concept of original sin committed by one man, Adam, and of redemption brought into the world by a single person, Jesus Christ—as stated earlier in reference to Rom 5:18; 1 Cor 15:21–22 and 45; and 1 Tm 2:5. In addition, it is not only the biblical account of the one man, Adam, but also that of Eve that favors a monogenesis, since she is called "the mother of all living" (Gn 3:20). This argument demonstrates that polygenesis cannot be treated as a matter of interpretation with hardly any theological consequences.

Since the emergence of Darwinism many (though by no means all) scientists agree that humankind could not have originated from a single created couple, one man and one woman. If Adam and Eve existed as historical persons, they maintain, they were members of a much larger population of the same species. Thus, *Homo sapiens* needs to be acknowledged as a species that at one time existed alongside other species belonging to the genus *Homo*, which can be traced back to a common ancestor but not to Adam and Eve. "Just 6 million years ago, a single female ape had two daughters. One became the ancestor of all chimpanzees, the other is our grandmother." Thus, "like it or not, we are members of a large and particularly noisy family called the great apes."[11]

From the perspective of the theory of evolution, if they existed at all, Adam and Eve were not created directly by God (*creatio ex nihilo*) but were two individuals in a long evolutionary chain that began about 13.5 billion years ago, "when matter, time and space came into being in what is known as the Big Bang." From then on matter and energy "started to coalesce into complex structures, called atoms, which then combined into molecules. The story of atoms, molecules and their interactions is called chemistry." Then, 3.8 billion years ago such molecules combined to form complex life forms called organisms, and about 70,000 years ago "organisms belonging to the species *Homo sapiens* started to form even more elaborate structures called cultures. The subsequent developments of these human cultures is called history."[12] The course of that history is mapped out as starting with the Cognitive Revolution 70,000 years ago, when the mind evolved into the form seen in today's humans. Next came the Agricultural Revolution about 12,000 years ago, when humans

William Boulting, *Giordano Bruno: His Life, Thought, and Martyrdom* (New York: Routledge, 2013), 262–79. Since 2004 Bruno's cause has been taken up by the anti-Christian Giordano Bruno Foundation in "Support of Evolutionary Humanism"; biannually it awards the Deschner Award (named after Karlheinz Deschner, a critic of Christianity), which was given to Richard Dawkins on 12 October 2007.

11. Harari, *Sapiens*, 5.

12. Harari, *Sapiens*, 3.

began to eat their own cultivated foods. Finally, the Scientific Revolution began just 500 years ago with the work of Nicolaus Copernicus (1473–1543), who claimed that the earth revolves around the sun—the heliocentric or sun-centered view of the cosmos—and it ended with that of Isaac Newton, who suggested that the world runs on universal laws and universal mechanics.[13]

To demonstrate that humans developed 70,000 years ago from a larger of group of species belonging to the genus *Homo* and then evolved into their own species would require that elusive missing link, fossilized evidence of a hypothetical transitional species reflecting our ancestors' progression from primitive "ape man" to modern *Homo sapiens*.[14] However, even if humans share some traits with certain apes, the conclusion cannot be drawn that the differences reflect mere gradations of development and that there is nothing special about the human species except for the cognitive ability that promoted it to the top of the food chain. The evolution of prosimians like lemurs into monkeys or monkeys into apes or apes into humans would require the addition of new genetic information into a genome.[15] Scientists have yet to observe and verify in nature that process in nonhuman primate (NHP) systems, for example by finding evidence of that transition from fossils.[16]

During the middle of the nineteenth century Darwin's theory of natural selection (the survival of the fittest) inspired other theories, one of which was that human development occurred completely spontaneously. Its leading advocate was Ernst Haeckel, whose theory of spontaneous generation (*generatio aequivoca*) from nonliving matter was popular among supporters of Marxism.[17]

13. Harari, *Sapiens*, 3. The popular narrative of history's linear development from primitivism to civilization, as presented by Harari and others, is contested by David Graeber and David Wengrow. They argue that this popular view stems from the Enlightenment and bases its theory more on ideology than on archaeological and anthropological evidence, which shows that a greater diversity of early human societies existed during the agricultural stage. David Graeber and David Wengrow, *The Dawn of Everything: A New History of Humanity* (New York: Farrar, Straus and Giroux, 2021).

14. The conclusions drawn by Darwin are often discriminatory and thus should be seen as leading to people's marginalization or oppression of one another. Some nineteenth- and twentieth-century Darwinists thought that all non-Caucasian people were apelike and therefore inferior to whites, a thought which stems from Darwin himself. Darwin, *The Descent of Man*, 156.

15. A genome contains an organism's complete set of DNA, including all of its genes and all of the information that determines or shapes that organism. In humans a copy of the entire genome—more than 3 billion DNA base pairs—is contained in all cells that have a nucleus.

16. Ola Hössjer, Ann K. Gauger, and Colin R. Reeves, "An Alternative Population Genetics Model," in *Theistic Evolution: A Scientific, Philosophical, and Theological Critique*, ed. J. P. Moreland et al. (Wheaton, IL: Crossway Books, 2017), 521. See also Casey Luskin, "Missing Transitions: Human Origins and the Fossil Record," in Moreland et al., *Theistic Evolution*, 437–74.

17. Marx himself stated: "The idea of the creation of the earth has received a severe blow . . . from the science which portrays the . . . development of the earth as a process of spontaneous generation. . . . *Generatio aequivoca* [spontaneous generation] is the only practical refutation of the theory of creation." Cited in Francis Nigel Lee, *Communism versus Creation* (Nutley, NJ: Craig Press, 1969), 68.

We mention this theory specifically because science has demonstrated, against both this theory and the subsequent theory of evolution, that life can come only from pre-existing life. In other words, evidence is yet to be found that non-life can lead to life, and for this reason many scientists, like microbiology professor Michael Behe, dismiss Haeckel's theory. "So it seemed to Haeckel," he states, "that such simple life, with no internal organs, could be produced easily from inanimate material. Now, of course, we know better."[18]

The conversation on the origin of the human being has yet to prove that life can emerge from inanimate material. In a scientific world in which facts speak for themselves, this lack of evidence hardly moves the proponents of Darwinism to question their own claims. They cling to the belief that between human and nonhuman animals there is either a difference in degree or a superficial difference in kind; and since a continuity between human and nonhuman life must exist, Darwin along with his followers "posit the required as-yet-unknown intermediaries in his evolutionary theory."[19] In his painting *The Discovery of Adam* (1891) the artist William Holbrook Beard draws a group of seven well-dressed primates standing on a beach looking down and discussing the origin of a tortoise-like creature on whose shell is written 200 000[0?] / BC / Adam. Beard's painting is a satire on Charles Darwin's *On the Origin of Species*, which had been published 32 years earlier in 1859. The civilized monkeys can no more believe that they descended from such a primitive "Adam" "than the artist and many of his contemporaries could accept that human beings evolved from apes."[20] Beard's satirical drawings encouraged Christians to become involved in the debate on the origin of humans. They "should take intellectual responsibility for making sense of and understanding issues important in making decisions influencing both the practice of science and the use of scientific advances."[21] This principle applies especially to areas in which all of human existence is reduced to matter and energy.[22]

---

18. Michael J. Behe, *Darwin's Black Box: The Biochemical Challenge to Evolution* (New York: Free Press, 1996), 24.

19. Adler, *Difference of Man*, xviii.

20. The painting (along with its description) is exhibited in the The Museum of Art, Toledo, Ohio.

21. Dorothy F. Chappell and David E. Cook, eds., Introduction to *Not Just Science: Questions Where Christian Faith and Natural Science Intersect* (Grand Rapids: Zondervan, 2005), 17. Lesslie Newbigin, *The Gospel in a Pluralist Society* (Grand Rapids: W. B. Eerdmans, 1989), 15–16, 21.

22. We take note of the Roman Catholic encyclical *Humani Generis* (1950), which on behalf of her members, "the children of the church," questions the factual basis of evolution (§§ 5 and 6) as well as the scientific hypothesis of polygenesis, which among many things would stand in opposition to the church's doctrine of original sin. Pius XII, *Humani Generis* § 37.

CONCLUSION TO PART ONE

In a discussion with physical/biological anthropology, theological anthropology offers an alternative story to the one that seems to capture society's thoughts on what it means to be human. That alternative story speaks of humans as God's creation, who having lost the image find their restoration in Christ, the true image. Structurally, all humans exist as body and soul and not merely as matter. They are spirited, ensouled bodies, upon whom God through the Word works His salvation. Thus, according to Albrecht Peters, we really have only two narratives from which to choose:

> Do we originate as individuals . . . from the cosmic evolution . . . and sink back into the rigors of death, or do we come from the gracious, blessed hand of the creator and proceed forward to meet the judge and savior?[1]

Theological anthropology points to the latter option and offers its answer to what it means to be human as *the* narrative. Though Christian anthropologists vary on many details of this story, they overwhelmingly stand united on the foundational principle that human existence is found in relationship with God. And this principle influences and shapes the understanding humans have about themselves: their origin (from where), their destiny (to where), their existence (why), and their purpose (for what). This principle thus also implies a difference in quality or kind between humans and all other animal life. Humans are endowed with a unique capacity upon which God works His salvation and with the intellectual ability to formulate a propositional language, both of which are indications of human exceptionalism.

There is a dual aspect to these unique capacities which distinguish humans. First is the ontological structure all humans possess because they are created with it. To this universal ontology belongs the bodily existence, to which we must add the soul—the possession of an intellect and a will, which though common to all humans are differentiated in their use—and communication through language. But these non-material qualities like soul and capacity for language are in the process of being developed over time through exposure to the external world. Thus, while personhood (*Personsein*) exists already as a universal reality, shaped by a body, sex, mind (brain), and soul with which humans are born, it develops and changes through the individual's lifespan and experiences. The argument that humans are mere social constructs or products

1. "Kommen wir als je einzelne . . . mit der kosmischen Evolution . . . und sinken in die Todesstarre zurück oder kommen wir letzlich aus der gütigen Segenshand des Schöpfers und gehen dem ewigen Richter und Erretter entgegen?" Peters, *Der Mensch*, 22.

of the surrounding world thus cannot dismiss the universal characteristics of personhood that mark the human from before birth.

Theological anthropology upholds both aspects of personhood and wishes to keep a balance between the two. Humans are seen as who they are and what they possess, but also for what they are to receive and become. In other words, personhood is not static but is always caught up in a process (*im Vollzug*) determined by the external reality of God's Word, which has the power to shape and transform the mind and activity. From a theological perspective, personhood is considered never to be fully developed or complete apart from its dependence on and determination by the external and transcendent reality of God's Word.

All humans struggle with the basic existential issues, such as aging, illness, and death, but some dismiss God from their lives in the hope that these struggles will go away or that their impact will be softened. If humans wish to define and explain their own existence in isolation from God, they will inevitably reach an epistemological and philosophical dead end. To those who are unwilling to bow their reason to the higher divine narrative, Pascal levels a harsh rebuke:

> Know then, proud man, what a paradox you are to yourself. Humble yourself, weak reason; be silent, foolish nature; learn that man infinitely transcends man, and learn from your Master your true condition, of which you are ignorant. Hear God.[2]

Luther adds an essential perspective to the narrative, both in his *Disputation Concerning Man* and in his *Commentary on Corinthians*, namely, that the believer finds joy and solace "that Christ has risen from the dead" and that "He will also awaken him and transport him from death and every misfortune to joy eternal."[3] For Luther, human existence is understood as outwardly focused, responsive, and eschatological; and that is so because it is in a relationship with God that is defined Christologically.[4]

2. "Pensées. Fragment 434," 143.
3. *Commentary on 1 Corinthians* 15, 1535 (AE 28:107; WA 36:543.31–44.19–20).
4. Peters, *Der Mensch*, 22.

PART TWO

THE TRAGEDY OF HUMAN EXISTENCE

7

SIN, NATURE, AND GRACE

Sin remains a force to be reckoned with as it affects every part of human life, for both the unregenerate and the regenerate. However, some distinctions apply between the two groups, which explains why theological anthropology adopts a threefold perspective on a human's condition. The first perspective looks at human existence in the light of the original creation prior to the Fall, a state that no longer exists. The second view approaches the unregenerate's condition and existence in terms of the ongoing ramifications of the Fall. The third perspective considers the human condition soteriologically, in terms of the renewal in Christ through justification and the reception of Christ's image. The second perspective on the unregenerate seems self-evident, since Scripture clearly attests to a natural person's depravity and corruption.[1] Nevertheless, theologians over the centuries have debated the depth to which sin affects the unregenerate. A similar discussion has gripped theologians within the third category, over the degree to which sin rules over a Christian's life. In other words, the discussions about sin or hamartiology have played no small part in dividing Christianity into movements and denominations, each with its own particular standpoint.[2]

There always have been debates over sin engaging a single critical question: is a human being's nature totally and essentially sinful and incapable of pleasing God, or is human nature instead neutral with regard to sin and grace and therefore able to operate with a freedom to choose to sin or not? This issue is at the heart of the relationship of nature and grace and shapes one's understanding of sin and salvation. It is important, then, for theological anthropology to establish a proper relationship of nature and grace. Many historical positions are contrary to scriptural evidence and require correction. We briefly note a few examples below, including Gnosticism, the ascetic monastic movement, the Platonic influences on Christianity, Manichaeism and Pelagianism, medieval theology, and finally the emergence of Arminianism in the seventeenth century.

1. Ps 51:5; Eccl 9:3; Rom 3:23; Eph 2:1–3.
2. Lutheranism and Calvinism share the principle that depravity is total.

HISTORICAL DEBATES

Gnosticism's unbiblical dualism, influenced by Greek philosophy, not only undermines the doctrine of Christ's true humanity, an issue addressed by John in his first epistle (1 Jn 1:1), but also impacts anthropology in general. This dualism stands in contast to a Hebraic anthropology which embraces both body and soul, in which the body is not deprecated in favor of the immortal soul. The great early church theologian Irenaeus of Lyon (c. 125–c. 202) opposed Gnosticism's erroneous positions as taught by Basilides and Valentinus. Writings such as his *Detection and Overthrow of the Pretended but False Gnosis* and his more popular work *Against Heresies* are especially important.[3] Against the anthropology of Gnosticism, which finds little value in the current human material condition and views it as a tragic accident for which people bear no responsibility, Irenaeus points out the possibility of sin and God's salvation plan: God created humanity with the intention that, once it had recognized in the Fall the difference between good and evil, it would grow gradually into the divine likeness on a road to deification, a perfect restoration in Christ.[4] Thus, unlike the Gnostics, who thought the current human condition was contrary to God's will, Irenaeus offers a system that allows humans to accept their fallen condition, assume responsibility, and seek perfection in Christ. Irenaeus explains that original sin is similar to a baby's fall while it is learning to walk. Without Christ the ability to walk as a Christian and grow in one's faith is not possible. Hopeful development rests on the incarnation of Christ, who as the Second Adam restores in Himself the relationship of humans with God, thus recapitulating what humans had lost and overcoming what held them in bondage.[5]

The negative assessment of matter, in this case the human body, found its appeal among many supporters. Unfortunately, it led to an unwarranted dualism that sees the body as finite and limited, even evil, and as imprisoning or entrapping the intellectual mind or soul or spirit. This low appreciation of the body led to one of two antithetical responses: either one resorts to asceticism and places the body under rigorous discipline or one takes to licentiousness, an unhindered hedonistic indulgence of the body which in this line of thinking would not impact one's spiritual relation to the Law of God.

By the middle of the third century this position had established itself as a movement called asceticism and was popularized by individuals like Anthony of Egypt (251–356) and Martin of Tours (d. 397). They proposed an alternative

3. See also Clement of Alexandria (c. 150–c. 215).

4. J. Patout Burns, ed. and trans., *Theological Anthropology*, Sources of Early Christian Thought (Philadelphia: Fortress Press, 1981), 3.

5. Irenaeus is known for the concept of recapitulation: "Thus, then, was the Word of God made man . . . God recapitulated in Himself the ancient formation of man, that He might kill sin, deprive death of its power, and vivify man." Irenaeus, *Against Heresies* 3.18.7; ANF 1:448.

lifestyle to that of society, which largely gravitates toward and progresses in evil and sinful behavior. Anthony of Egypt, often called the father of monasticism in Christianity, organized his disciples into a worshipping community and inspired them to lead a withdrawn life based on the evangelical counsel in Mt 19:21.[6] The Christian writer Sulpicius Severus (c. 363–c. 425) records detailed information about the life of Martin of Tours, including the rigorous discipline he imposed on his monk followers.[7] By establishing their own communities the ascetics believed they were following the commandments of God with great fidelity, in the hope of receiving the final heavenly reward.[8] Asceticism taught that man still possessed inherent natural powers or abilities; these were not completely destroyed by sin. With the use of reason a person could recognize the good and was free to choose it. This tendency toward self-imposed bodily discipline continued with medieval monasticism, with the pursuit of a life of self-denial and withdrawal from society combined with practices of fasting, almsgiving, and sexual abstinence. The reformers and the Lutheran Confessions took issue with such initiatives, as they were built on the false anthropological premise that one could be inherently or naturally capable in fulfilling these resolutions.[9]

In the third and fourth centuries the ascetic principles merged with a non-Christian, Platonic philosophical approach to give rise to Christian Platonism, whose proponents were Justin Martyr (c. 100–c. 165)[10] and Origen (c. 185–c. 254). To an extent these principles were reflected also in the theology of church fathers like Ambrose of Milan and Augustine, at least in his early philosophical treatises. Unlike the two previous examples of asceticism, in which the ability to make choices between good and evil is important, now the human spirit's natural capacity, his rationality and desire for union with God, serves as the resource for salvation. In this process the material condition of the human, which is subject to decay, is inimical to the spirit's development toward God, that "innate and inalienable drive of the human toward the divine."[11] Concupiscence, the inclination toward sin, draws a person's spirit away from seeking union with God. Matter and spirit serve as the two poles of human existence, and the key to Platonic Christianity is to resolve the tension between the two. To that end this movement affirms both God's grace

6. "If you would be perfect, go, sell what you possess and give to the poor, and you will have treasure in heaven."

7. Sulpicius Severus, *On the Life of St. Martin* 10, NPNFb 11:9.

8. Burns, *Theological Anthropology*, 4.

9. AC XX.19–22 (K-W, 55). "The poverty of the gospel . . . does not consist in the abandonment of property, but in the absence of greed and of trust in riches." Ap. XXVII.46 (K-W, 285). Moreover, monastic life should not think of such commitments as meritorious or even as vows that are possible to keep. Not only has monasticism been hypocritical about its vows, it has obscured Christ. Ap. XXVII.54–56 (K-W, 286).

10. Justin Martyr, *The First Apology*, in *Saint Justin Martyr: The First Apology, the Second Apology, Dialogue with Trypho, Exhortation to the Greeks, Discourse to the Greeks, the Monarchy, or the Rule of God*, ed. Thomas B. Falls, The Fathers of the Church 6 (Washington: Catholic University of America Press, 1965).

11. Burns, *Theological Anthropology*, 7.

and one's own efforts. God's grace helps in that "upward" process by reviving and nourishing the soul in its desire for union with God. Free choice is also encouraged in observing the commandments and exercising asceticism, "through which the Christian cooperates with the divine action and labors to free the gift of God within."[12] The liberation from the concupiscence of the flesh and the development of spiritual desire is aided through baptism, as a participation in the death and resurrection in Christ. In the end, physical death and resurrection bring the process to its completion. For example, in his *First Apology* Justin Martyr identifies Christ as the highest ordering principle of the universe, the λόγος (the Word), and asserts that those who believe in Christ will, with the use of their reason, have access to that principle. Christianity is seen to embody the true philosophy, and by being a Christian one can attain through the power of the Word the highest knowledge and reason.[13]

The affiliation with Neoplatonism, this stark dualism between body and spirit or soul, continued into the early medieval period. In a commentary on Pseudo-Dionysius, *Peryphyseon: The Division of Nature* (*Periphyseon: De Divisione Naturae*), the Irish theologian John the Scott or John Scotus Eriugena (c. 800–c. 880) claimed that humans are part divine and part animal: sin belongs to the animal nature, and through the heavenly gift of grace a human being moves away from sin and will return to God. By means of that divine grace a human being is enabled to rise above the needs of the body's senses; with his reason he will control his bodily appetite; through contemplation he will ascend from reason to ideas, and finally by intuition to God.[14]

In view of these positions, some theologians felt the need to identify human sin and fallenness as a given reality or prerequisite to conversations on salvation, in order to exalt the merits of Christ and not those claimed to be natural to a human being. To that end theologians like Ambrose took the orthodox stance on soteriology. He states in his treatise *Concerning the Calling of the Gentiles* the following concern:

> Redemption by the blood of Christ would become worthless and the preference for human works would not give way to the mercy of God if justification, which takes place by grace, were due to antecedent merits. For then it would be the worker's wage rather than the donor's gift.[15]

Any emphasis on human merits would in the end diminish Christ's feat on the cross; to affirm positively the human merit compromises the doctrine of salvation.

---

12. Burns, *Theological Anthropology*, 10.

13. Justin, *First Apology* 46 (p. 84).

14. Johannes Scotus Eriugena, *Peryphyseon: The Division of Nature*, trans. J. P. Sheldon-Williams and John J. O'Meara (Montreal: Bellarmin, 1987), 3–5.

15. *De vocatione [omnium] gentium* 1.17 (J. P. Migne, ed., *Patrologia Cursus Completus*, Series latina, 221 vols. [Paris: Garnier Fraher, 1844–], 51:670) as quoted in AC XX.14 (K-W, 55). It should be noted that this treatise is now generally attributed to Prosper of Aquitaine, not to Ambrose.

Though they all affirmed the reality of sin, theologians were not united in their description of the extent of original sin, that is, how far and how deep it reaches into the lives of every human being and the degree to which nature is in need of divine grace. Ultimately it was Augustine of Hippo (354–430) who established a conclusive definition of sin—and that mostly as a result of the Pelagian controversy.

Augustine broke with the traditions of both asceticism and Platonic Christianity, reinterpreting the structure of merit and reward. Though influenced by both movements, he articulated a far deeper sense of divine gratuitous and unmerited grace than either movement, setting it against the background of a strongly pronounced doctrine of human depravity. Augustine was moved to develop this anthropology and teaching about the human condition before God by the Donatists, and in particular by Pelagius and his disciple Caelestius, who was condemned by the Council of Carthage in late 411 or early 412.[16] Not only in his famous *Confessions*[17] does Augustine provide helpful material to explain his position but also in the treatises *The Grace of Christ and Original Sin*,[18] *Nature and Grace*,[19] *Grace and Free Choice*,[20] and *Rebuke and Grace*.[21] In these and other writings of his formidable corpus he treats themes of sin, grace, and freedom, and connected to these the question of predestination.

Pelagius, Caelestius, and others maintained a shallow understanding of sin, denying original sin and claiming that Adam's fall had no influence on later generations.[22] Adam's sin was not inherited by his descendants, they claimed, nor has it impacted human nature. Rather, every human being is born without guilt and with virtue, like Adam before the Fall. Humans possess the full and free ability to decide between good and evil. Sin is understood as an act of the free will, and death is a natural phenomenon since God created all humans as mortal beings. The passing on of sin through conception and birth is excluded, for that would contradict the idea that sin is a matter of conscious volition. The only universal truth concerning sin is that it exists in the powers of evil examples, in the perpetuation of habits, and in seduction. It is possible for sinless people to exist; and indeed there have been some. Consequently, there is no universal need for the forgiveness of sins. A human being does not even

16. The Council of Carthage passed nine canons condemning Pelagianism on 1 May 418; see Roland J. Teske, introduction to Augustine's *The Grace of Christ and Original Sin*, in *The Works of Saint Augustine: A Translation for the 21st Century*, ed. John E. Rotelle (Hyde Park, NY: New City Press, 1990–), 1.23:389–91 (hereafter cited as WSA). [Traditionally, eight canons are counted, since one canon is omitted in many manuscripts—Ed.]

17. Augustine, *Confessions* (WSA 1.1:1–416).

18. Augustine, *The Grace of Christ and Original Sin* (WSA 1.23:384–465).

19. Augustine, *Nature and Grace* (WSA 1.23:204–78).

20. Augustine, *Grace and Free Choice* (WSA 1.26:70–107).

21. Augustine, *Rebuke and Grace* (WSA 1.26:108–48).

22. Though Pelagius's treatise *On Nature* no longer exists as a separate document, it survives as quotations in his opponents' writings, such as in Augustine's *On Nature and Grace*.

need divine grace that leads to transformation or illumination of the intellect; such grace is of only relative or external value inasmuch as it facilitates the accomplishing of one's goals, boosts one's moral powers or will, and encourages genuine striving and virtue. This external grace, as one may call it, is provided in the divine will, the Law, and Christ's teachings and His example, and it serves to illuminate the mind but is not a new creation of the will.[23] With such statements Pelagius sought to confront the moral laxity of society which ran contrary to his very strict, rigid moralism and to affirm a natural, innate human ability to attain salvation.

Augustine's rebuttal can be summarized in four points. First, the sin of Adam may have been prompted externally by the devil but it occurred as a free decision, and as a consequence the sinful depravity of the first parents is transferred to their children through conception. All of humanity becomes the subject of Adam's fall; all humans bear a united and joint responsibility for the sin of Adam according to Rom 5:12, not by mere imitation but by propagation.[24] Second, the sinful state affecting all humans not only caused the loss of the image of God—a loss of the good[25]—but also brought with it concupiscence, that overbearing force of sinful, sensual, evil inclination against the Holy Spirit. This desire, which remains after baptism,[26] also includes the sexual lust (*libido*),[27] the inclination to love of self (*amor sui*) instead of love of God (*amor Dei*), and pride (*superbia*).[28] In this sinful state humans have lost their total freedom to pursue the good and instead are bound willfully to sin.[29] Third, the destruction caused by original sin is imputed to humans as real sin and guilt, bringing to each one punishment (death and suffering) and condemnation. For Augustine, the condemnation from Adam's fall extends even to infants, to every human, unless they have been joined to Christ in baptism. Indeed, the concept of original sin becomes key to insisting on the importance of infant baptism.[30]

---

23. See Philip Schaff, "Excursus on Pelagianism," NPNFb 14:229.

24. Augustine, *The Punishment and Forgiveness of Sins and the Baptism of Little Ones* 1.9–11 (WSA 1.23:38–40). Since Adam's sin is hereditary, passed on through propagation or procreation, Augustine brings to the discussion not only the role of the actual sexual act of procreation but whether "inheritance" also includes the passing on of certain biological (genetic) qualities from the parents to the child that is conceived. One may see here Brunner, *Christian Doctrine of Creation*, 103–7.

25. Called privation (*penness boni*), which is part of sin but not everything.

26. "The law of concupiscence, then, remains in the members, but, despite its remaining, its guilt is removed." Augustine, *Punishment and Forgiveness* 2.45 (WSA 1.23:110).

27. Augustine, *Punishment and Forgiveness* 1.57 (WSA 1.23:66–67); Augustine, *Nature and Grace* 40 (WSA 1.23:245).

28. Augustine, *Nature and Grace* 33 (WSA 1.23:241).

29. "Posse non peccare et mori" now becomes "non posse non peccare et non mori." Augustine, *Rebuke and Grace* 12.33 (WSA 1.26:132).

30. Augustine, *Punishment and Forgiveness* 1.21–25 (WSA 1.23:45–48). See also Augustine, *The Nature and Origin of the Soul* 1.11 (WSA 1.23:478). It might be worth noting that not all Lutherans agree with Augustine on this point. Johannes Bugenhagen, for example, condemns this teaching of Augustine and makes room for divine grace extending over those infants of Christian parents who die prior to their baptism, thereby following Luther's position. See Karl

Fourth, though all stand condemned by this sin, God in His sovereign grace has chosen before creation a number of people for salvation. Augustine affirms that God acts by His own autonomy and inscrutable choice and is not induced to act by someone or something outside of Himself. Thus, this absolute grace which is necessary for salvation is for the elect irresistible, and when granted also irrevocable, but it is unattainable for those not called by God according to His plan and who consequently sin by their own choice and deeds. On this last point Augustine affirms that God's will is inscrutable but not unjust (Rom 9:14).[31] For those who question God's judgment, Augustine suggests they surrender themselves to the testimony of Scripture, and "without murmuring against God" be content with the fact that they will not know "why God gives this [grace] to some and not to others."[32]

Augustine attempts to navigate between two sides of the issue, clarifying that God does not coerce, and that at the same time He does not simply respond to a natural ability or performance of the human. If conversion were a product of coercion, the human would be forced into something without willing it, like a robot caused to do something; whereas to say that God is responding to some quality or act in the human is to fall into the trap of semi-Pelagianism, allowing natural ability to creep in and undermine the concept of the gratuity and efficacy of God's grace.[33] With this clarification, Augustine's understanding of conversion is clear: because of the impotence of a human's natural powers, salvation is entirely an unearned, operative gift from God. The premise with which Augustine operates and which serves as the quintessence of his doctrine of grace is that "we live more safely if we ascribe everything to God, and do not attribute to him a part and to us a part."[34] Augustine thus concludes that grace does not contradict freedom but rather becomes its source.[35]

Augustine is of special note among these theologians who discuss issues related to anthropology and sin, since he was received positively in the sixteenth century by Luther. When others around Augustine seem either to trivialize sin or to dismiss its very existence, he comes to the fore in a most radical fashion by emphasizing original sin like no one before him. His theology is rooted

---

Hess, "The Faith of Unbaptized Infants in Bugenhagen's *On Unborn Children*," *Logia: A Journal of Lutheran Theology* 23, no. 2 (2014): 33. In his *Hodosophia Christiana* (1649) the orthodox Lutheran theologian Johann Conrad Dannhauer casts the net even wider than Bugenhagen (and Quenstedt) and would grant the same fate to heathen infants as to deceased, unbaptized infants of Christian parents. Emmanuel Hirsch, *Hilfsbuch zum Studium der Dogmatik: Die Dogmatik der Reformatoren und der altevangelischen Lehrer quellmäßig belegt und verdeutscht*, 4th ed. (Berlin: Walter de Gruyter, 1964), 348. One may follow Luther's thought on infant baptism in LC IV.47–63 (K-W, 462–64).

31. Augustine, *Sermon 27: On Psalm 96, and on the Words of the Apostle: "On Whom He Will He Has Mercy . . . "* 7 (WSA 3.2:108).

32. Augustine, *Rebuke and Grace* 19 (WSA 1.26:121).

33. Augustine, *The Grace of Christ* 1.52 (WSA 1.23:428).

34. Augustine, *The Gift of Perseverance* 6.12 (WSA 1.26:198).

35. Augustine, *Rebuke and Grace* 12.35 (WSA 1.26:134); Augustine, *The Grace of Christ* 1.52 (WSA 1.23:428); Augustine, "Letter 157: Augustine to Hilary" 10 (WSA 2.3:21).

particularly in the Pauline tradition, as he himself admits in his *Confessions*: "It was therefore with intense eagerness that I seized on the hallowed calligraphy of your Spirit, and most especially the writings of the apostle Paul."[36] There he found the true philosophy, particularly two insights which would impact Christian anthropology from then on: first, that God is the truth and exists as such on His own; second, that the weak and sinful human being cannot find God by his own strength. Central to those insights is the person of Christ as he encountered Him in the Bible, who was not only "a man of excellent wisdom and without peer" but the fleshly/incarnated Word, the savior of all, the source of grace.[37]

The church sided with Augustine against Pelagius and the Donatists. At the Councils of Carthage in 412, 416, and 418, and also at the Council of Ephesus in 431, Pelagianism was condemned as a heresy and Augustine's teaching was adopted. This development might have dealt a death blow to the extreme outright teachings of Pelagianism. However, the church soon had to contend with a milder form of Pelagianism that was not willing to embrace fully the consequences of Augustine's doctrine on sin and grace. Instead, this form taught that humans are by nature morally sick and weakened, wounded, but that they retain a residue of a good will and also the ability to dispose themselves favorably to God to receive from Him divine grace. A human being can and should cooperate with divine grace, they maintained, and in doing so can attain full righteousness and salvation. This assertion is an attempt to reconcile Pelagian synergism with Augustinian monergism. This so-called semi-Pelagianism was condemned at the Council of Orange in 529 but found its followers in the medieval church to such an extent that it became the basis for the Roman doctrine of salvation (soteriology), which the Council of Trent elevated to a church dogma.[38]

Among the scholastics of the Middle Ages, theologians such as Anselm of Canterbury, Peter Lombard, and Thomas Aquinas were indebted to Augustine as they built on his theology in various ways. One ensuing development was the division of grace. While Augustine assigns everything to the one grace as a gratuitous gift from God offering multiple effects, these theologians were interested in its bifurcation: the habitual grace of preparation and the actual grace of preservation, or as it is also known, the prevenient grace and subsequent grace. In that discussion, interest in anthropology, particularly in the psychology around the will of the human being, merged with the metaphysical study on the divine operation of grace. The focus was on how the human will prepares toward divine grace and how it transitions from evil to good, from resisting to cooperating. In search of answers "it was necessary to insert an ideal

36. Augustine, *Confessions* 7.27 (WSA 1.1:181).

37. Augustine, *Confessions* 7.25 (WSA 1.1:179).

38. H. J. Schroeder, trans., *Canons and Decrees of the Council of Trent* 6.5 (St. Louis: B. Herder, 1950), 31–32: "by freely assenting to and cooperating with that grace."

middle term between the two extremes, to place natura pura between natura lapsa and natura elevata."[39]

In his *Summa Theologicae* Aquinas proceeds with the section on Nature and Grace to demonstrate how humans respond to the two graces, the operating grace (*gratia operans*) and the cooperating grace (*gratia cooperans*). His thinking here is that grace is needed before and after justification. Before justification, grace prepares for justification, whereas the grace after justification ensures perseverence. This earlier grace is internal, habitual, infused, and associated with the divine operation within the will. This grace that is operative then combines with the actual grace that is *cooperans*.[40] For Aquinas the effects of grace follow a sequence. First, God enables someone to participate in the divine reality; second, God's grace causes the person's works to be regarded as deserving of merit; third, the reward of merit, eternal life, is the final effect of grace.[41]

Of the high and late scholastics, the Thomists (perpetuated by the Dominicans) were still more inclined to follow the Augustinian position, insisting that God must be the prime or first mover before a human can love and do good. This was not the case with the Scotists, named after Duns Scotus (1266–1308) and perpetuated by the Franciscans, or with Occamism, named after the Nominalist William of Occam (1285–1347). They followed the semi-Pelagian tradition by granting some positive response of natural human will, albeit a weak response prior to the first grace given.[42]

39. Bernard Lonergan, "St. Thomas' Thought on Gratia Operans I. Introduction," *Theological Studies (Baltimore)* 2, No. 3 (1941): 295–96.

40. Aquinas explains this twofold effect of grace as follows: "In this case there is a twofold action within us. There is an inward action of the will, in which the will is moved and God is the mover, especially when a will which previously willed evil begins to will good. We therefore speak of 'operative grace,' since God moves the human mind to this action. But there is also an outward action, in which operation is attributed to the will, since an outward action is commanded by the will, as we explained in Q. 17, Art. 9. We speak of 'co-operative grace' in reference to actions of this kind, because God helps us even in outward actions, outwardly providing the capacity to act as well as inwardly strengthening the will to issue in act." Thomas Aquinas, *Nature and Grace: Selections from the Summa Theologica of Thomas Aquinas*, trans. A. M. Fairweather (Grand Rapids: Christian Classics Ethereal Library, 1954), 129–30; Lonergan, "St. Thomas' Thought," 308.

41. "Again one human act follows on another: first there is the internal operation of the will; second there is external action which is a complement to willing." Lonergan, "St. Thomas' Thought," 315.

42. Within Roman Catholicism the Dutch theologian Cornelius Jansen (1585–1638) started the Jansenist movement, to which our oft-quoted philosopher Pascal also belonged. Jansen challenged the Roman semi-Pelagianism by pointing out the Augustinian tradition in his writing *Augustinus* (1640), dismissing the role of the free will in attaining God's grace. Jansenism emphasized original sin, human depravity, the necessity of divine grace, and predestination. The movement was short-lived. In 1653 Pope Innocent X condemned Jansenism as heresy on account of five points or propositions that were based on Augustine, especially their position on the human free will and efficacious grace, which contradicted the teachings of the Jesuit School. And in 1713 Pope Clement XI with the apostolic constitution *Unigenitus Dei filius* brought an end to the Roman Catholic toleration of the Jansenist teachings by declaring it a dissident religious movement. Clement XI, *Unigenitus Dei filius*, https://www.papalencyclicals.

Luther encountered this synergism in the doctrines of Nominalism as taught by William Occam and Gabriel Biel (1420–95) and in the humanism of Erasmus of Rotterdam (1466–1536). In his epistemology Occam is known to have distinguished between the spheres of faith and reason, and he recognizes reason's limitations in grasping certain matters of faith. Overall, however, he remains optimistic about reason's power to achieve understanding of many theological propositions. Luther disagrees, as his theses *Against Scholastic Theology* (1517) and the *Heidelberg Disputation* (1518) make clear. Luther sees natural reason as blinded by original sin and therefore unable to grasp certain supernatural truths. He also does not share Occam's optimism about the will's ability to contribute to one's salvation, judging Occam's position as semi-Pelagianism.[43] The Formula of Concord also identifies semi-Pelagianism with the "papists and scholastics," such as Peter Lombard, Gabriel Biel, and Erasmus of Rotterdam, who erroneously claim that "on the basis of their natural powers people can take the initial step toward the good and toward their own conversion and that, because they are too weak to complete it, the Holy Spirit then comes to the aid of the good that has begun on the basis of their own natural powers."[44] Melanchthon and Luther view this admission to natural human powers and the division of divine grace as a construct of medieval theologians that compromises justification by grace through faith. We recall Melanchthon's own account of the problem:

> They call it, 'initial grace,' which they understand to be a disposition [habitus] that inclines us to love God more easily. Nevertheless, what they attribute to this disposition [habitus] is of little consequence, because they imagine that the acts of the will prior to this disposition [habitus] and subsequent to this disposition [habitus] are of the same kind. They imagine that the will can love God, but that this disposition [habitus] nevertheless stimulates it to do so more willingly.[45]

Melanchthon expresses that this focus on the acts of the will prior to and after grace is one with which "they bury Christ so that people do not use him as a mediator and on account of him believe that they freely receive the forgiveness of sins and reconciliation."[46] He analyzes critically the distinction of the twofold grace and the merits of each: a merit of congruity and a merit of condignity. These are the works which emerge from the free will, done by someone who is still in a state of sin but nonetheless able to love God naturally (*facultas applicandi in se est*). Gabriel Biel, for example, claims that "by a good movement toward God elicited by the power of free will, the soul can merit the first grace *de congruo*."[47] God rewards this attempt by giving His first grace (*meritum de*

net/clem11/c11unige.htm.

43. B. A. Gerrish, *Grace and Reason: A Study in the Theology of Luther* (Eugene, OR: Wipf & Stock Publishers, 2005), 55.

44. SD II.76 (K-W, 558–59).

45. Ap. IV.17 (K-W, 122–23).

46. Ap. IV.18 (K-W, 123).

47. Denis R. Janz, *Luther and Late Medieval Thomism: A Study in Theological Anthropology*

congruo). Out of that initial move of grace, that initial infused grace, flows a stronger, grace-induced habit of love, by which someone can then perform condign merit for eternal reward (*meritum de condigno*).[48]

The semi-Pelagian element comes in through the notion of a partial loss through the Fall, which leaves behind a natural will that in this fallen state is weakened but not destroyed. A moral capacity remains that can still be used to please God (*naturalia in hominibus post lapsum manserunt integra*).[49] To these natural powers are added supernatural powers, such as holiness, immortality, wisdom, dominion of the earth, and so forth, as special gifts of grace. They are added supernaturally as a gift (*superaddita = donum supernatural externum ac accessorium*) to the human because they do not belong to the essence of a human. Thomas Aquinas, for example, suggests that the "superadded gift" (*donum superadditum*) was granted to humans before the Fall to do what God required.[50] Since this gift was lost through the Fall, it needs to be infused by grace after the Fall.

Luther argues against this: original righteousness is concreated; that is, it came with the creation of humans. It was not attached as a *donum superadditum* after Adam was created, "like some adornment, [that] was added to the human being as a gift, when someone places a wreath on a pretty girl."[51] "Therefore," Luther concludes, "they maintain about man . . . that although they have lost their original righteousness, their natural endowments have nevertheless remained pure, just as they were created in the beginning. But this idea must be shunned like poison, for it minimizes original sin."[52]

The Reformer insists that God is the sole initiator and provider of faith, of grace and forgiveness, without any contribution whatsoever from the human either in whole or in part, and thus he finds that this distinction of two graces and the merits is a cover tactic, "lest they appear to be outright Pelagians."[53]

The Roman Catholic position on original sin from the Council of Trent (1545–63) and then from the Vatican Council II (1962–65) can be summarized

(Waterloo, ON: Wilfrid Laurier University Press, 1983), 7. Gabriel Biel affirms the free will but is also intent not to compromise God's sovereignty and freedom to respond. While "God accepts the act of a person who does what is in his power as a basis for the bestowal of the first grace," he does so "not because of any obligation in justice, but because of his generosity. . . . Therefore God, because of his liberality, accepts this act of the removal of the obstacle and of the good movement toward himself and infuses grace into the soul."

48. K-W, 123n62.

49. Vilmar and Piderit, *Dogmatik* 1:343. See for example *Catechism of the Catholic Church*, 105 (§ 418).

50. Thomas Aquinas, *Man Made to God's Image*, trans. Gilby Thomas, vol. 13, *Summa Theologiae*, Ia. 90–102 (Cambridge, UK: Blackfriars, 1964), 109, (1.95.1.6): "From this it is plain that that primary submissiveness in which the reason put itself under God was not something merely natural either, but was by a gift of supernatural grace."

51. *Lectures on Genesis*, 1535–45 (AE 1:164–65; WA 42:123.39–40); Erickson, *Christian Theology*, 462: "like a suit of clothes that he could take off. It is rather the unitary person."

52. *Lectures on Genesis*, 1535–45 (AE 1:165; WA 42:123.40–24.2).

53. Ap. IV.19 (K-W, 123).

readily. The former council convened to condemn the beliefs of the Protestants and start the Counter-Reformation movement:

(1) Original sin is not so much a total corruption of the human nature as a *defectus iustitiae originalis*, a loss of the *dona supernaturalia*, which did not radically impact anything essential in the human being but is a reduction and weakening of a human's moral capacities.[54] And yet Adam's fall does cast a guilt (*reatus*) over all of humanity. However, this inherited guilt is removed through baptism.[55]

(2) The inborn sensual lust (*concupiscentia*) is not to be considered as a sin but as something indifferent in itself; it only causes or leads the free will to sin (*non per se et formaliter, sed causaliter, sed quia ex peccato est et ad peccatum inclinat*).[56] Even if the baptized still have a remnant desire to sin and an inclination toward evil, it may have no ill effect on them if they refuse to succumb to it; and those who come through victoriously will be rewarded gloriously.[57]

(3) Though the moral capacity of a human has been weakened, he still has the powers of the free will to decide between good and evil. The will is still strong enough to resist sensual lust, do the good, and work toward conversion.

(4) The two stages of grace also are affirmed, the prevenient divine grace followed by justifying grace itself, which includes "not only the remission of sins but also sanctification and renewal of the inward human through the voluntary reception of the grace and gifts."[58]

The teachings on original sin also impacted the Vatican Council II, as can be seen in the *Dogmatic Constitution on the Church* (*Lumen Gentium* 16). This document illustrates the consequences of denying original sin's inhibiting powers. For Lutheranism the claim of innocence characterized here as "through no fault of their own" does not exist. The idea of the unregenerate "sincerely seek[ing] God" also must be rejected, along with the concept of prevenient grace ("moved by grace").[59]

---

54. See here SD I.20 (K-W, 535; 535n31 with reference to the Council of Trent).

55. *Canons of the Council of Trent* 5.4–5 (Schroeder, *Canons and Decrees*, 22–23).

56. *Canons of the Council of Trent* 5.5 (Schroeder, *Canons and Decrees*, 23): "This concupiscence . . . the holy council declares the Catholic Church has never understood to be called sin in the sense that it is truly and properly sin in those born again, but in the sense that it is of sin and inclines to sin."

57. *Canons of the Council of Trent* 5.5 (Schroeder, *Canons and Decrees*, 23): "But this holy council perceives and confesses that in the one baptized there remains concupiscence or an inclination to sin, which, since it is left for us to wrestle with, cannot injure those who do not acquiesce but resist manfully by the grace of Jesus Christ."

58. *Canons of the Council of Trent* 6.7 (Schroeder, *Canons and Decrees*, 33).

59. "Those also can attain everlasting salvation who through no fault of their own do not know the gospel of Christ or His Church, yet sincerely seek God and, moved by grace, strive by their deeds to do His will as it is known to them through the dictates of conscience. Nor does divine Providence deny the help necessary for salvation to those who, without blame on their part, have not yet arrived at an explicit knowledge of God." *The Documents of Vatican II*, ed. Walter M. Abbott, trans. Joseph Callagher (Chicago: Follet Publishing Company, 1966), 35. See also Klaus Detlev Schulz, *Mission from the Cross* (St. Louis: Concordia Publishing House,

The Roman Catholic teaching on original sin differs from the Lutheran position in three respects. First, it differs in its scope since it exempts Mary as having been conceived immaculately, a belief Pope Pius IX officially declared a dogma on 8 December 1854 in the papal bull *Ineffabilis Deus*.[60] This doctrine had received support as early as 1180, favored especially by Duns Scotus and his followers, the Franciscans and the Jesuits, but was opposed by the Dominicans, such as Thomas Aquinas and his followers. Though the Lutheran Confessions obviously predate and thus do not address the official declaration, they nonetheless dismiss Mary's intercessory role and her merits since she is human like all others, not free of original sin.[61] According to Hollaz, this role assigned to Mary speaks not only against Rom 5:12 but also against Lk 1:46–48, where Mary includes herself among those in need of a savior.[62]

Second, the Roman Catholic position differs from the Lutheran one with regard to degree, since the spiritual, moral capacity has been weakened only but not totally corrupted, as the Lutherans in contrast claim.[63] Third, it differs with regard to the duration of original sin, maintaining that through baptism all of the original sin has been eliminated; what remains is only the "tinder" (*fomes*), nothing more than a neutral remnant. Lutherans carefully distinguish that baptism removes the condemning guilt of Adam's sin but its concupiscence remains, not as a "tinder of sin," as Roman Catholics understand, but as sin itself.[64]

These examples of the early church and medieval theologians and proceedings of the Council of Trent and Vatican II reveal how the topic of sin has a significant impact on theological anthropology. Complete agreement or consensus does not exist among the Fathers mentioned, which leaves the

---

2009), 291.

60. Pius IX, *The Bull "Ineffabilis" in Four Languages, or, The Immaculate Conception of the Most Blessed Virgin Mary Defined [. . .]*, trans. Ulick J. Bourke (Dublin: John Mullany, 1868).

61. Ap. XXI.27 (K-W, 241). The Council of Trent passed the following on Mary's relation to original sin: "This holy council declares, however, that it is not its intention to include in this decree, which deals with original sin, the blessed and immaculate Virgin Mary." Council of Trent 5.5 (Schroeder, *Canons and Decrees*, 23). Similarly also *Catechism of the Catholic Church*, 104 (§ 411).

62. Hollaz, *Examen Theologicum Acroamaticum*, 524.

63. SD I.60 (K-W, 542).

64. Ap. II.42 (K-W, 118). The Greek Orthodox position also gravitated toward semi-Pelagianism. This explains the Formula of Concord's rejection of John of Damascus's passage on conversion; see SD II.86 (K-W, 560), namely, the statements that "the human will is not idle in conversion but also does something" or that "God draws [those who come to Him], but he draws those who will it." The Greek church thus affirmed the semi-Pelagian tradition in one of its primary confessions, the *Orthodox Confession* or *The Catechism of Peter Mogilas*, 1643 (in Philip Schaff, *Bibliotheca Symbolica Ecclesiae Universalis: The Creeds of Christendom, with a History and Critical Notes*, 4th ed., 3 vols. [New York: Harper & Brothers, 1919], 1:58–61), which was endorsed by the Eastern patriarchs and the Synod of Jerusalem, 1672 (Schaff, *Bibliotheca Symbolica* 1:62–67). Jeremiah II, the Patriarch of Constantinople from 1572 to 1594, was asked to offer a response to the Augsburg Confession after receiving a copy in 1574 from two Tübingen professors and James Andreae. The patriarch's response in 1576 was unfavorable toward the Augsburg Confession and his comments were approved officially at the Synod of Jerusalem.

issue of what sin is somewhat inconclusive. According to Burns, a common agreement is lacking in three areas: "in explaining the initial state and vocation of humanity, in estimating the damage done in the Fall, and in describing the resources for recovery provided in Christ."[65]

Within Protestantism, semi-Pelagianism is often associated with the later teachings of Jacob Arminius (1559–1609), who opposed the Augustinian tradition in the theology of the reformers, particularly Calvin's position and that of the Belgic Confession,[66] namely, that all humans are born sinful and therefore cannot prevent their own sinning. However, the difference between the previously described semi-Pelagianism and Arminianism lies with the location of grace in the life of a person. Semi-Pelagianism holds that divine grace is needed for salvation, but it also affirms a natural freedom that precedes the giving of grace; thus, grace comes to a person only after the human will has taken the first steps. Arminianism teaches a more "Spirit-led" freedom, in which God Himself takes the first steps in the life of a person. To be sure, the two systems ultimately have in common a characteristic synergism, but Arminianism believes God must initiate with grace and semi-Pelagianism believes the human must initiate to receive the grace.

Arminius's followers, known as Remonstrants after the document The Remonstrance of 1610[67] which published their opinion in five points, were condemned by the Dutch Calvinists at the Synod of Dordrecht in 1618. That condemnation offered the well-known five points of Calvinism (later known as the TULIP principle), which teach the following: total depravity, unconditional election, limited grace or atonement of Christ for the elect only, irresistible grace, and perseverance of the saints.[68] Next to the Heidelberg Catechism and the Belgic Confession, this decision of the Synod of Dordt serves as the foundation of many Reformed churches. Dordt's rejection of Arminianism was not decisive, for today this belief system has nestled itself within Christianity in North America as a popular doctrine and is followed by denominations such as the American Baptist Churches USA, the United Methodist Church, the Wesleyan churches, the Pentecostal churches, and the Church of the Nazarene. Lutherans in North America who discuss theological anthropology should take note of this particular trend and context.

65. Burns, *Theological Anthropology*, 1.

66. Schaff, *Bibliotheca Symbolica* 1:502–8.

67. Schaff, *Bibliotheca Symbolica* 1:517–19.

68. Jean François Salvard, comp., *The Harmony of Protestant Confessions: Exhibiting the Faith of the Churches of Christ, Reformed after the Pure and Holy Doctrine of the Gospel, throughout Europe*, ed. Peter Hall, new ed. (London: John F. Shaw, 1844), 539–73.

THE LUTHERAN CONTRIBUTION: THE PROPER DISCOVERY OF SIN

Society's perception of sin reflects little of how the Bible and traditional theology understand it. For example, secular scientists and researchers create a narrative about humans from data gathered through empirical research, and in the process they will uncover at best only the symptoms of a far deeper problem that plagues humans. The disease itself, original sin, eludes their observation. Yet original sin is at the root of the negative experiences that weigh people down in their lives—unhappiness, anxiety, boredom, emptiness, restlessness, dissatisfaction, feelings of worthlessness, frustration.[69] The unregenerate's understanding of sin is reductionistic because the sin that inheres in human nature, that basic sin, is "unknown to the world."[70] Not only is it unknown, humans also intentionally ignore, doubt, and deny it, often blaming someone or something else because the source of sin is unbelief or the denial of God's Word. This is the penetrating truth the biblical account reveals about all humans and which they share with their first parents.[71]

The full discovery of sin's depth and its source, and the true knowledge of how it pertains to human life, come to us only through the revelation of the divine Word and when grasped in faith.[72] To demonstrate this point, the Formula of Concord closes Article I with the following observation in the explanation of original sin: "No philosopher, no papist, no sophist, indeed, not even human reason—no matter how keen it might be—can give the correct explanation."[73] Martin Chemnitz applies the four Aristotelian causes to sin, similar to what Luther did in his *Disputation Concerning Man*, to demonstrate the ignorance of the philosophers about sin:

(1) In regard to the *efficient* cause, theology teaches that the cause of sin is "the corruption of our nature and the tyranny of the devil 'working in the children of disobedience.'" The cause of sin is unknown to philosophers. They desperately try to avoid sin and yet have shameful lapses.

69. David J. Valleskey, *We Believe, Therefore We Speak: The Theology and Practice of Evangelism* (Milwaukee: Northwestern Publishing House, 1995), 95.

70. See *Exposition of the Fourteenth, Fifteenth, and Sixteenth Chapters of the Gospel of St. John*, 1537–38 (AE 24:342; WA 46:40.10–12). In an admonition to pastors on how to preach against usury, Luther makes a similar observation, that even if the world's governments think they have erased all sin, original sin as the source of all sin and the devil's work will remain ("so wird dennoch die Erbsünde die quelle aller sunden sampt dem teuffel bleiben"). *An die Pfarrherrn, wider den Wucher zu predigen, Vermahnung*, 1540 (WA 51:354.18–26). See also SD I.6 (K-W, 533n25).

71. Brunner, *Christian Doctrine of Creation*, 94.

72. "This inherited sin has caused such a deep, evil corruption of nature that reason does not comprehend it, rather, it must be believed on the basis of the revelation in the Scriptures." SA III.i.3 (K-W, 311). Anderson, *On Being Human*, 16: "It is a truth which comes by way of repentance and faith."

73. SD I.60 (K-W, 542).

(2) In regard to the *material* cause, theology sees that Scripture offers an objective rule for recognizing and judging sin, which is the divine will as revealed in the Ten Commandments. Philosophy instead sees sin as a vice which fights against the judgment of correct reason.

(3) In regard to the *formal* cause, theology points out from Scripture that sin embraces the entire unconverted human being, and that all works done without faith and outside of Christ are regarded as sin. Philosophy recognizes sin to exist only in its fruits, that is, in outward actions or in excess of evil desires.

(4) In regard to the *final* cause, theology sees it as "guilt worthy of divine wrath [and] bodily and eternal punishments unless there be forgiveness for the sake of Christ the Mediator." Philosophy at best considers sin as a torment of the conscience or perhaps some punishment after life.[74]

Outside of faith, the biblical message of original sin and the inherent desire to sin seem to have little explanatory power. According to Härle, the biblical narrative usually is met with indifference or suspicion: indifference, because the word "sin" has become an empty formula which carries little meaning and is used rarely; suspicion, because many people think the church uses the term deliberately to create in them a bad conscience and to control their lives.[75] The ethicist Robert Preston claims that a common criticism leveled against Christian ethics is that it never accepts human accomplishments "as is" but holds consciences accountable to a higher standard of "what ought to be." This constant reminder of human failure represses development and leaves humans at an immature level.[76] Modern humans think more positively of themelves and their accomplishments and are unwilling to accept Scripture's negative portrayal of human existence.

Even if the term "sin" has lost its meaning or explanatory power in society, it remains an enduring truth in Christianity's belief system and should not be replaced by an alternative term, which would sacrifice important aspects that the concept bears. "Sin" is of course a nomenclature that embraces multiple terms in the Old and New Testaments, each bringing out a specific nuance. In the Old Testament פֶּשַׁע (*pesha'*) means offense, crime, or rebellion, that is, resistance to the highest source of authority possible—God (Gn 31:36; Ex 34:7; Is 43:7; Jer 2:8). The word finds its equivalent in the Greek ἀσέβεια (*asebeia*) or παράπτωμα (*paraptoma*), for example in Eph 2:5. Then there is חַטָּאָה (*chata'ah*) or חָטָא—to miss (the mark or the way), to be lost in the dark, to fall off the set goal, or to overstep the standard or line God has drawn (Gn 4:6; 1 Sm 15:30; Ps 51:4; Ez 18:4). And last but not least, עָוֹן (*'avon*) indicates a misdeed, sin, or guilt caused by sin, or perversity, depravity, or iniquity (e.g. Ex 34:7; 1 Sm 15:2). Here sin is regarded as guilt or crookedness (Gn 4:13), which reinforces the

74. Martin Chemnitz, *Loci Theologici*, trans. J. A. O. Preus (St. Louis: Concordia Publishing House, 1989), 1:265.

75. Härle, *Dogmatik*, 456.

76. Ronald Preston, "Christian Ethics," in *A Companion to Ethics*, ed. Peter Singer, Blackwell Companion to Philosophy (Cambridge, MA: Blackwell Reference, 1991), 100.

understanding that sin originates from within, from a distorted and twisted human nature that is no longer what God wants it to be. In the New Testament sin is described predominantly as ἁμαρτία (*hamartia*; e.g., Rom 5:12)—not achieving the intended goal, committing an error, missing the mark, losing the original state. The apostle Paul has good intentions and aims for virtue, for example, but fails to reach it (Rom 7:15: "For I do not do what I want, but I do the very thing I hate"). A similar statement is made in Jas 4:17: "Whoever knows the right thing to do and fails to do it, for him it is sin." Paul observes that the sin of falling short involves all of humanity (Rom 3:23: "All have sinned and fall short of the glory of God"). Sin also is associated with παράβασις (*parabasis*) or παρακοή (*parakoē*), that intentional overstepping or disregard of the divine command, a transgression (Rom 5:14, 19). That disobedience is directed also against God, making humans "enemies" of God (Rom 5:10). Sin is not only disobedience, it is also described as ἐπιθυμία (*epithymia*), desire or covetousness (Rom 7:7).

The gravity of sin is also clear. Sin is described as injustice, ἀδικία (*adikia*), or unrighteousness, the antonym of δίκη (*dike*), the ancient Greek word for justice. Ἄδικος (*adikos*) is used to describe an unrighteous and unjust person. In distinction to ἀνομία (*anomía*), lawlessness, which highlights the offending act, ἄδικος draws attention to the person who commits it: an unjust person is one who breaks the Law (1 Tm 1:9). Thus, the sinner is guilty—bound, under obligation, subject to, or liable, all suggested by the Greek word ἔνοχος (*enochos*). Such connotations remind us that sin makes the transgressor liable to punishment beyond the unfortunate consequences it brings into his life, such as a broken humanity, a fallen world, or a disordered creation. In Mt 5:21–22 the Lord holds those who murder and those who are angry subject to judgment (ἔνοχος, *enochos*). The apostle Paul connects sin with its consequences, the fatal combination of Law and death (Rom 5:12). Luther is known to associate sin with death and the devil, or the three kinds of causes, "the flesh, the world, and the devil."[77]

Those who hear the Word of God will learn of sin's full impact and reality in their lives, and the posture of remorse over sin will shift from being contrived (attrition) to being genuine (contrition).[78] Specifically, the full extent of sin is uncovered only by the Law, which Luther calls "the thunderbolt of God, by means of which he destroys both the open sinner and the false saint and allows no one to be right but drives the whole lot of them into terror and despair."[79] The Law brings out the full reality of sin and death as the "wages of sin" (Rom 6:23) by functioning in its second use as a mirror. In this function, often called the *usus elenchticus* or *paedagogicus*, the Law reveals to a person that he does not live as the one he could and should be. As Luther puts it, "The foremost office

77. LC III.101–4 (K-W, 453–54).
78. SA III.iii.2 (K-W, 312); LC V.1–3 (K-W, 476).
79. SA III.iii.2 (K-W, 312).

or power of the law is that it reveals inherited sin and its fruits."[80] Because sin persists, the Law always accuses (*lex semper accusat*).[81] Since the Law represents God's will, each transgression against an individual law is a manifestation of the deeper underlying attitude of resisting God and attempting to usurp His throne. The human is God's enemy (Rom 5:10; Col 1:21), which makes him guilty before God. A rebellion against the Law is a rebellion against God.[82]

At the same time, the Law reveals that a person cannot free himself from that desperate situation. It reveals both what God desires a human to do and his inability to do it. He is not free to agree with the will of God but rather finds himself in a "bondage of the will" (*servum abritrium*). The only way out of that desperate situation is to find help from God.

The deficit the Law reveals is not merely quantitative but also qualitative. In terms of the former, we see our inability to keep the list of laws. However, should someone consider himself to have fulfilled the Law, as a "perfect" Pharisee might have done, he still cannot give his heart entirely to God. That is the qualitative aspect of the Law. Jesus Christ pointed to it in the Sermon on the Mount, and Luther does much the same in his explanations to the Second Table of the Decalogue, where the inability to escape from sin is revealed even for him who considers himself most righteous. The Law of God pardons no one, and in its second use it serves to reveal and judge the depth of sin in a person's heart ultimately as a lack of trust in God.[83] Sadly, if one were to cling to the Law, all one would see is the angry judge and one's condemnation which leads to death.[84] To escape that desperate impasse one must rely on the divine act of grace that is given through the Gospel alone.

The Law serves to make a human conscious of his dire situation and to make him recognize that he needs outside help, which comes from the Gospel. As Paul said: "So then, the law was our guardian until Christ came" (Gal 3:24). And Christ receives to Himself those who in their despair approach Him in true humility over their fallen state, as is laid out beautifully in the Lutheran hymn "Jesus Sinners Doth Receive."[85] The Law does not summon the human to pull himself out of his situation but rather to turn to Christ for help. This basic Lutheran proposition, that God accepts sinners, does not find widespread

80. SA III.ii.4 (K-W, 312).

81. One could qualify this statement: the Law accuses always but not only, since it also functions in its third use.

82. This rebellion against God is depicted well in the parable of the vineyard and the tenants (Mk 12:1–11).

83. In essence, sin is a failure to obey the First Commandment: "Again, throughout the following commandments, which concern our neighbor, everything proceeds from the power of the First Commandment." LC I.329 (K-W, 430).

84. For places in which Luther deepens the convicting nature of the commandments see LC I.182, 186–87, 223, 224, 230, 250 (K-W, 411, 416–17, 419); Peters, *Der Mensch*, 41.

85. The Lutheran Church—Missouri Synod, *Lutheran Service Book* (St. Louis: Concordia Publishing House, 2006), 609 (hereafter cited as LSB).

ecumenical agreement.[86] The dominant Lutheran understanding of grace is that it is not an endowment that demands but a gift. To keep the Gospel pure so that it does not become Law, and salvation a human's own feat, it is imperative to maintain the proper distinction and sequence of Law and Gospel.[87]

In terms of function and sequence, the Law precedes the Gospel since it serves as a means of the Holy Spirit to lead a person to the Gospel. For Lutherans it remains crucial that the Word of God maintain its function as *lex accusans* (the accusing Law), judging the human, revealing his sin, and then also comforting, forgiving, and lifting the human up through the Gospel. To Barth that sequence makes little sense. According to him, only through the Gospel can someone understand the content and demands of the Law.[88] His position once again raises the controversy over the purpose of the Law in contrast to the Gospel as discussed by Article V of the Formula of Concord. The Formula dismisses precisely the attempt to make the Gospel a means to penitence (a *doctrina poenitentiae*) instead of a proclamation of comfort of what Christ has done.[89]

The Lutheran distinction of Law and Gospel also is misunderstood when it is interpreted in a purely mechanical way or when the doctrine of Law is isolated completely from that of the Gospel. The Law serves as the means to drive a person to the Gospel, and in condemning him it performs God's penultimate purpose, not His ultimate intention of saving the sinner.[90] The believer, who is "simultaneously righteous and sinner" (*simul iustus et peccator*), remains as long as he lives under the condemnation of the Law but also under the promise of the Gospel—the dynamic of every Christian's life. By affirming

86. Daphne Hampson observes that "it would appear almost impossible for Catholicism to accept the basic Lutheran proposition, that God accepts sinners." Margaret Daphne Hampson, *Christian Contradictions: The Structures of Lutheran and Catholic Thought* (New York: Cambridge University Press, 2001), 99. Matt Jenson, *The Gravity of Sin: Augustine, Luther, and Barth on* Homo Incurvatus in Se (New York: T&T Clark, 2006), 65.

87. Michael Diener, *Gesetz und Evangelium: Grundsätzliches und Konkretes in 95 Thesen* (Kassel: Evangelischer Gnadauer Gemeinschaftsverband, 2017), 6 (Thesis 15).

88. "The one Word of God is both Gospel and Law. It is not Law by itself and independent of the Gospel. But it is also not Gospel without Law. In its content, it is Gospel; in its form and fashion, it is Law. It is first Gospel and then Law." Barth, *Church Dogmatics* 2/2:51. In a short monograph entitled *Evangelium und Gesetz* (Gospel and Law), Barth puts the Gospel before the Law: "Since the Law is in the Gospel, from the Gospel and directed towards the Gospel, we must, in order to understand the Law, first know the Gospel and not vice versa." Karl Barth, *Evangelium und Gesetz*, Theologische Existenz heute, neue Folge, 50 (1935; reprint, Munich: C. Kaiser Verlag, 1956), 4.

89. Melanchthon believed that the Gospel in the broad sense serves to lead one to penitence (*doctrina poenitentiae*). The section on the distinction of Law and Gospel in his *Loci Communes* gave rise to this controversy among Lutherans; see SD V (K-W, 581n154). The antinomian Johann Agricola is less the target in this article (more so in SD VI) than Melanchthon and the Philippists, who broaden the Gospel to include repentance; SD V.2 (K-W, 581). When a confusion of Law and Gospel occurs, "the merit and benefits of Christ are easily obscured, and the gospel is turned back into a teaching of law . . . This robs Christians of the true, proper comfort." SD V.27 (K-W, 586).

90. SA III.iii.5–8 (K-W, 313).

both realities in the life of a Christian, Lutheranism stands out as unique in its anthropology among others who claim to varying degrees that the Christian leaves sin behind rather than battling with it intensely every day of his life. This Lutheran affirmation also defines an authentic existence: a life lived out under God, but more specifically under His Word through its twofold operation as Law and Gospel, receiving relief and deliverance from the overpowering force of sin. Being justified is what it means to be a Christian and a true human in the eyes of God. In this relationship between God and the human, the Word of God elicits a divine–human communication. True communication between God and a human occurs in God's distinct acts of bringing about passive contrition through the Law and then also absolving him from his sin through the Gospel. Under God's Word a human is subject to two divine acts: "The first is our work and act, when I lament my sin and desire comfort and restoration for my soul. The second is a work that God does, when he absolves me of my sins through the Word placed on the lips of another person."[91] This interaction between God and humans, in which God elicits a response of passive contrition and faith, is specific to humans; they have a response-ability which reaches its pivotal point in the context of confession and absolution.[92]

In the Lutheran worship tradition we can see how these two divine acts come into effect: in the Confiteor, a form of prayer confessing sins, sin's impact is brought to every worshipper's attention.[93] In that context reflection about sin is not an abstract theological exercise but involves the personal life of every worshipping Christian. Confessing and being absolved of one's sins has become the ethos or distinguishing mark and guiding faith of a Christian community. Paul Althaus and Werner Elert especially have been forceful in pointing this out,[94] reaffirming that repentance is a daily occurrence, in line with Luther's opening statement in his Ninety-five Theses.[95] This ethos should govern every Christian's life, negatively by what it rules out, namely, sin; and positively by what it affirms—God's justification through Christ as forgiveness.[96] For we who exist here on earth in ensouled bodies have the flesh (σάρξ, *soma*) clinging to our bones, and as long as that is the case we are sinful and doers of

91. LC V.15 (K-W, 478).

92. When humanity is not defined as response-ability to God's Word it becomes a nebulous concept, and it is unclear how and at what level that response-ability occurs otherwise. Anderson, *On Being Human*, 41.

93. LSB 167: "If we say that we have no sin, we deceive ourselves, and the truth is not in us. But if we confess our sins, God, who is faithful and just, will forgive our sins and cleanse us from all unrighteousness."

94. Paul Althaus, *The Ethics of Martin Luther*, trans. Robert C. Schultz (Minneapolis: Fortress Press, 2007), 3; Elert, *Christian Ethos*, 7.

95. Thesis 1: "When our Lord and Master Jesus Christ said, 'Repent' [Matt 4:17], he willed the entire life of believers to be one of repentance." *Ninety-five Theses, or, Disputation on the Power and Efficacy of Indulgences*, 1517 (AE 31:25; WA 1:233.10–11); SC IV.4, on the significance of baptism (K-W, 360).

96. Elert, *Christian Ethos*, 217–25.

sin "in thought, word, and deed" (1 Jn 1:8–9).[97] Those who dismiss this reality in their lives, according to Luther, should "put their hands to their bosom to determine whether they are made of flesh and blood."[98] Sin cannot be denied outright, reduced, or marginalized as an impersonal or unnatural phenomenon. According to Anderson, we should "take it [sin] radically and seriously as an ontological aspect of personhood."[99] The apostle Paul observed about his own wrongdoing that "it is no longer I who do it, but sin that dwells within me" (Rom 7:17),[100] which the theologian R. C. Sproul (1939–2017) truthfully reflects in the following statement: "We are not sinners because we sin; we sin because we are sinners."[101] Blame and guilt are realities because this proclivity to sin resides in each of us even before we commit this or that sinful act.

The Word of God serves a positive function also in that it raises the question of the meaning of life. The Law prevents hypocrisy, which covers up blame and failure; it uncovers sin as more than an abuse of a societal convention; it has a transmoral function and serves as a transcultural authority that allows humans to revise their life.[102] Ultimately the Law lets humans know there is a Lawgiver above humanity in whom one can place one's trust and find guidance for one's earthly existence.

97. LSB 167.

98. LC V.75 (K-W, 474). Luther encountered a confessional system (today called Restitution in the Roman Catholic Church) that obliged Christians to recall only sins one actually had committed, with the intent to discern between mortal and venial sins, a practice which goes back to Thomas Aquinas. Recalling every sin is an impossible feat in the eyes of the reformers, and thus the person confessing should confess rather his sinful and corrupted state. SA III.i.3 (K-W, 311).

99. Anderson. *On Being Human*, 30.

100. See also Rom 7:14–15, 19.

101. R. C. Sproul, *What Is Reformed Theology? Understanding the Basics* (Grand Rapids: Baker Books, 2016), 137.

102. "Moral" here signifies conforming to mere societal conventions or laws passed by humans that are bound to time and locality, like customs. The Law by contrast is not created by society but serves as a transcendent authority. In his book *The Brothers Karamazov* Fyodor Dostoyevsky argues in the response of Mitya Karamazov to his brother Alyosha (part IV, book XI, chapter 4) against atheism and nihilism, that God is "He without whom one cannot live." This definition for the necessity of God is derived from morality: if God is not, "then everything is lawful" (or all things are permissible). Dostoyevsky, *Brothers Karamazov*, 640.

8

ORIGINAL SIN

It is important to turn briefly to Luther, the Lutheran Confessions,[1] and other theologians to see how they relate to four important topics associated with sin: the essence of original sin, its properties, its two causes, and its consequences—death and especially its impact on the free will.

THE ESSENCE OF ORIGINAL SIN: LOSS OF ORIGINAL RIGHTEOUSNESS AND AN ACTIVE DISPOSITION

The Lutheran dogmaticians have distinguished Adam's own personal sin from the sin that is transferred to all descendants. In that distinction, original sin is the inborn condition of moral corruption that has planted itself from the first parents into all their descendants through conception and birth, and has infested the entire human nature so thoroughly with sin that man is unable to perform any good; instead he is inclined toward evil and consequently falls under God's wrath.[2] Thus the first sin did not remain with Adam and Eve alone, but through natural conception or propagation is transferred universally from one generation to the next.

To describe the first sin and the depth of its impact on all of humanity we have used the terms original sin or inherited sin. However, these precise terms are not found in Scripture. Rather, Scripture conveys the idea of original sin in different ways to highlight its intrinsic nature in a human, such as "sin that dwells within me" (Rom 7:17); "sin which clings so closely" (Heb 12:1); "the law of sin that dwells in my members" (Rom 7:23); "evil lies close at hand" (Rom

1. Helpful presentations have been made in secondary commentaries: Gunther Wenz, *Theologie der Bekenntnisschriften der evangelisch-lutherischen Kirche: Eine historische und systematische Einführung in das Konkordienbuch*, De Gruyter Lehrbuch, 2 vols. (Berlin: Walter de Gruyter, 1996–98), 2:60–236; Holsten Fagerberg, *A New Look at the Lutheran Confessions (1529–1537)*, trans. Gene J. Lund (St. Louis: Concordia Publishing House, 1972), 125–43; Wilbert Rosin and Robert D. Preus, eds., *A Contemporary Look at the Formula of Concord* (St. Louis: Concordia Publishing House, 1978), 103–36; Wilhelm Walther, *Lehrbuch der Symbolik: Die Eigentümlichkeiten der vier christlichen Hauptkirchen vom Standpunkt Luthers aus dargestellt*, Sammlung theologischer Lehrbücher 9 (Leipzig: Deichert, 1924), 308–18.

2. "Original sin is the intimate and very deep corruption of the entire human nature destitute of original righteousness, arising from the fall of the first parents and propagated by them into all their descendants through carnal generation, making those who are not reborn to eternal life from water and the Spirit subject to the wrath of God and to temporal and eternal punishments." Gerhard, *Theological Commonplaces* 12.10.131 (12–14:94–95). See SD I.60 (K-W, 542).

7:21); "our old self" and "the body of sin" (Rom 6:6 and Col 3:9); "leaven" (1 Cor 5:6, 8); "the flesh" (Rom 7:18; Gal 5:16–19).

Studying these texts confirms an observation the Lutheran confessors made: sin in humans goes far beyond individual sins that are committed. To emphasize sin's depth it became customary to refer in the Latin to "original sin" (*peccatum* or *vitium originis* or *originale*), as did Augustine, the scholastics, and Article II of the Augsburg Confession, whereas in German the term "inherited sin" (*Erbsünde*), or even "chief sin" (*Hauptsünde*) or "root sin" (*Ursünde*), generally has been used.[3] The Formula of Concord also describes sin as a "horrible, dreadful, inherited disease" and "the root and fountainhead of all actual sins."[4] Thereby the Confessors wish to indicate its seriousness: it is the source from which "all other sins arise."[5] Original sin is not "only external, a simple, insignificant spot splashed on us."[6] To convey the grip it has on the entire person, Luther in the Smalcald Articles called it "person-sin" (*Personsünde*),[7] and to make the point that sin comes to all humans from Adam through an inheritance from which all other sins flow, Luther defines it in the same confession as the "chief sin."[8]

The Augsburg Confession places the article on sin immediately after Article I on God, to indicate that this sin deals with the loss of man's relationship with God. Sin is defined here as "sine metu, sine fiducia erga Deum et cum concupiscentia"—without fear of God, without trust in God, and with concupiscence.[9] Luther notes that sin is defined already in the First Commandment as a personal "lack of trust and faith of the heart." "It is," he says, "the trust and faith of the heart alone that make both God and an idol.... Anything on which your heart relies and depends, I say, that is really your God."[10] A human being does not fear Him who is holy and does not trust the one who is love. Original sin thus is a failure to keep the First Commandment, the "true honor and worship of God,"[11] and an attempt to replace Him with something else "in which the heart trusts completely."[12] The Apology adds that "the chief defects of human nature" are in "conflict especially with the first table of the Decalogue."[13] Then it describes a twofold aspect: original sin is not only "the absence of righteousness," the loss (*privatio*) of the "knowledge of God,

3. Originating first as "inherited sin," *Erbsünde*, in AC II.1 (K-W, 37); SD I.1 (K-W, 531).

4. SD I.5–6 (K-W, 533).

5. SD I.1 (K-W, 531).

6. SD I.21 (K-W, 535).

7. SD I.6, I.53 (K-W, 533, 540).

8. "Sin comes from one human being, Adam, through whose disobedience all people became sinners and subject to death and the devil. This is called the original sin or the chief sin." SA III.i.1 (K-W, 310).

9. AC II.1 (K-W, 37, 39).

10. LC I.2–3 (K-W, 386).

11. LC I.16 (K-W, 388).

12. LC I.10 (K-W, 387).

13. Ap. II.14 (K-W, 114).

trust in God, fear and love of God," but that loss is followed by concupiscence, an actual corrupted disposition (*habitus*) to rise up against God.[14] And this means that all unrighteous acts, such as "being ignorant of God, despising God, lacking fear and confidence in God, hating the judgment of God, fleeing this judging God, being angry with God, despairing of his grace, and placing confidence in temporal things," flow from the power of that evil desire or concupiscence.[15]

Lutheran orthodox theologians thus have insisted that original sin is not a mere loss of the ability to do good but also an active force driving man toward sin. They speak of both the negative and positive powers of original sin. The negative aspect has led to a loss (*defectus*), such as of love and trust for God, but this loss also is filled with a "positive" impetus to act against God (*affectus*).[16] The orthodox Lutheran dogmatician Hollaz offers a definition of original sin that expresses both the loss it incurs (negative) and its drive (positive):

> It is a *loss* of original righteousness joined with an active *evil inclination* that has corrupted the entire human nature originating with the Fall of the first parents and is transmitted through carnal propagation in all humans, making them inept at doing spiritual things, endowing them with a real propensity towards evil things, and becoming culpable of divine wrath and eternal condemnation.[17]

This definition lays out the truth that through the fall of Adam all of his descendants were infected by a state of corruption, including both the negative aspect of original sin as privation—a loss of the image and its qualities—and the "positive," active *concupiscentia* as evil desire. The twofold distinction corrects the one-sided interpretation of original sin as privation, that it is only a loss of something[18] with no "personal fault," which is taught in Roman Catholicism[19] and similarly by Ulrich Zwingli, who thinks this defect or disease is of itself "not sinful in the one who has it" and "cannot damn."[20] In contrast, the reformers

14. Ap. II.23–24 (K-W, 115). *Lectures on Genesis*, 1535–45 (AE 1:114; WA 42:86.17–30).

15. Ap. II.8 (K-W, 113).

16. The terms negative and positive may be misleading. Theologians of the sixteenth and seventeenth centuries commonly used these terms to mean that original sin is not a mere loss of something (negative or formal) such as the image but also includes an impulse, the concupiscence or desire (*böße Lust*) to do something (positive or material).

17. Hollaz, *Examen Theologicum Acroamaticum*, 518: "Peccatum originale est privatio iustitia originalis, cum prava inclinatio conjuncta, totam naturam humanam intime corrumpens, et lapsu primorum parentum derivate, et per carnalem generationem in omnes homines propagate, ipsos ineptos ad bona spiritualia, ad mala vero propensos reddens, reosque faciens irae divinae et aeternae condemnationis."

18. SD I.22 (K-W, 535).

19. The *Catechism of the Catholic Church* expressly states this about original sin: "Although it is proper to each individual, original sin does not have the character of a personal fault in any of Adam's descendants." *Catechism of the Catholic Church*, 102 § 405.

20. W. P. Stephens, *Zwingli: An Introduction to His Thought* (Oxford, UK: Clarendon Press, 1992), 74. This position also influenced his understanding of infant baptism—which he defended as an important practice—that since the child is sinful only when it does something sinful, there is no need to go to such lengths as to consider baptism a sacrament which removes original guilt.

such as Martin Chemnitz argue of concupiscence that it is not a neutral tinder (*fomes*) waiting to be incited by our will but "wars against the mind and holds it in captivity."[21]

The point of this discussion, then, is to highlight that sin in its essence includes both a negative and a positive sense: a loss or deprivation as well as an active rebellion or desire to sin. This loss is identified as a lack of righteousness, an important point to understanding properly what original sin is and what it is not. As a loss of righteousness associated with the inability to keep the First Commandment to trust, fear, and love God, original sin is a spiritual defect or loss that takes possession of the entire human being. It is not, as the words "hereditary" or "propagation" might suggest, a matter of conveying biological characteristics or qualities from one generation to the next, from parents to children. After all, "we inherit from our parents both good and bad qualities; from the biological point of view we inherit a 'blessing' as a well as a curse."[22] Nor does original sin imply that the sexual act of propagation is itself a sinful act. It is popular to bring elements of heredity and sex into the understanding of original sin, but this inclination distorts what original sin actually is: a spiritual loss of righteousness that is a godlessness and alienation from God. Some may think that in the Augsburg Confession this perspective is reflected in the statement "All human beings who are propagated according to nature [that is, born in the natural way] are born with sin."[23] In that case Melanchthon must have thought that not only is the seed sinful but so is the act of procreation, sexual intercourse, which consequently is also the producer of sin. That assumption seems unlikely, however, because all Melanchthon means to say is that at natural conception something the parents already have is passed on, namely, the spiritual corruption that affects the entire person.[24]

21. Martin Chemnitz and Johann Gerhard, *The Doctrine of Man in Classical Lutheran Theology*, ed. Herman A. Preus and Edmund Smits, trans. Mario Colacci et al. (Minneapolis: Augsburg Publishing House, 1962), 212; Ap. II.26, 35 (K-W, 116. 117).

22. Brunner, *Christian Doctrine of Creation*, 105. On this point I must agree with Emil Brunner that the term "hereditary" can be misleading if it leads us to associate with it naturalistic concepts that suggest we inherit biological characteristics, instead of seeing it as a failure in the relationship with God. See Brunner, *Christian Doctrine of Creation*, 106.

23. AC II.1 (K-W, 37).

24. The same applies to Luther: "But the Holy Spirit has a purer mouth and purer eyes than the pope. For this reason He has no misgivings about referring to the copulation or sexual union of husband and wife." *Lectures on Genesis*, 1535–45 (AE 1:238–39; WA 42:177.32). Like Luther, the Confessions take a subtle traducian rather than creationist position on the origin of sin, namely, that sin came into the world through propagation; but they stop short of calling marital propagation (the sexual act or desire for it) sinful, and they do not adopt the traducian position that at natural conception some material or biological substance is passed on as original sin, in addition to spiritual corruption. AC II.1 (K-W, 37); SD I.7, 28 (K-W, 533, 536). Chemnitz: "In marriage there are two elements, certain things which are good and exist by the order and institution of God, but there is also the element of desire in marriage, without which procreation would not take place, and because of this desire he says that infants are born in sin." Chemnitz, *Loci Theologici* 1:300. See also Braaten and Jenson, *Christian Dogmatics* 1:338–39.

THE PROPERTIES OF ORIGINAL SIN

There are three attributes of original sin, which theologians generally have called its properties (*affectiones*). First, it is universal or unrestricted in that all humans are born sinful (*propagabilitas universalis*). Second, it comprises total depravity since it has an inextricable connection with the human's nature and essence. It is a total corruption of this nature (*naturalis inhaerentia*), yet it is not substance but accident in the human. Third, it perseveres or is tenacious in that it persists and clings lifelong to a human (*tenacitas s. pertinax inhaesio usque ad mortem*), and though baptism removes the guilt of original sin, the inherited passion or desire remains in all believers.[25]

It is self-evident that the first property of original sin, its universal nature, impacts all humans; no one is exempt from it. An Old Testament scholar once used a metaphor to illustrate the aftermath of Adam's fall: sin spread exponentially like an oil spill in the ocean, so that it penetrates and ruins every part of human life.[26] This imagery describes the totality of sin from two perspectives. First, all humans without exception are affected by it, and second, sin is not left behind at any point in one's earthly life. Here it makes sense to speak of original sin as an inherited sin, that is, passed on from Adam to all people past, present, and future who are naturally born. Scripture texts supporting the principle of universality abound.[27] Here it is very important to point out that only Jesus, God's Son who became human, is exempt from all categories and effects of sin.

The second property of original sin, total corruption, was not self-evident but required lengthy debates among Lutheran theologians in the sixteenth century. Articles I and II of the Formula of Concord clarify the universality of sin over all humans and to what degree it corrupts the human. In contrast, while laudably trying to define the depth of sin Matthias Flacius erroneously identified sin with the human being, asserting it was the very substance, nature, or essence of a human. This claim implies, however, that God created sin when He created humans. As the Confessions furthermore point out, if this were true our body would not be separated from sin at the resurrection; and neither could Christ have become man without becoming sin.[28] True, sin belongs to a human's substance or being, but it does not constitute a human being's substance. It is accidental.[29] One may call sin a part of human nature only if one does not mean thereby that it is the substance or essence of a human or something that is capable of existing on its own. It is an accident that adheres

---

25. Johann Wilhelm Baier, *Compendium Theologiae Positivae*, 315–17.
26. Walther Zimmerli, *Grundriß der alttestamentlichen Theologie*, Theologische Wissenschaft 3, 2d ed. (Stuttgart: Kohlhammer, 1975), 149.
27. 1 Kgs 8:46; Jb 14:4; Ps 14:3; 143:2; Prv 20:9; Rom 3:22–23; 5:12; 5:18; 1 Jn 1:8–10; 5:19.
28. Ep. I.1–6 (K-W, 487–88); SD I.26–29 (K-W, 536–37).
29. SD I.57 (K-W, 541).

to a human's substance or essence, as one might say that "it is the nature of the snake to bite."[30]

The third property of original sin, its permanent reality in a human life, is indicated by Hollaz with Latin words such as *tenacitas* or *duratio*, which capture well the full impact of sin on a person's life. It is tenacious and persists, sticking to a person for as long as he lives on earth. Even though baptism removes the original guilt, it does not take away the material element, the persisting sin of concupiscence, which draws one toward sinning in deed.[31] As Luther would say, "We are in sin until the end of our life."[32]

The universality of sin and its powers over humanity, together with all its consequences and accompanying effects, is an undeniable truth. Its influence and persistence can be verified easily even with the youngest child, who already exhibits many errant behaviors before being subjected to outside influences or bad examples. Christian apologists have a simple task to depict the universal and persistent reality of sin: they can simply point to human history, where it is so evident. Moreover, such a survey also nullifies any thought or argument that naively insists humanity is progressing or evolving in the endeavor to avoid sin.[33] Sin will not go away; it is tenacious. Even poets and philosophers such as Thomas Hobbes and Sigmund Freud testify to humanity's inescapable entrapment by sin. This universal, total, and permanent sinfulness is thus a state, a *habitus*, into which all humans have been born, and which is connected inherently to each and every human's essence and nature. And yet an important clarification in the Confessions maintains that humans still remain human in spite of such corruption;[34] they have value even after the Fall, just as muddied water remains water[35] or a body remains human though attacked by leprosy, yet is not the same as it was before.

In summary, man's perversion through original sin is immense. With respect to reach it is universal, regarding degree it is a total corruption, and in terms of duration it persists with all humans as long as they live on earth. These properties bring to light the important principle in theological anthropology that all human powers have become so inhibited that no one can find salvation on his own terms.

---

30. Ep. I.21–25 (K-W, 490–91).

31. "[Luther] has always written that baptism removes the guilt of original sin, even if the 'material element' of sin, as they call it, remains, namely concupiscence." Ap. II.35 (K-W, 117). Scriptural texts in support of this include Gn 6:5; 8:21; Ps 51:5; 58:3; Rom 7:17; Heb 12:1.

32. *Lectures on Romans*, 1516 (AE 25:308; WA 56:321.2).

33. Definitive statements to that effect are made already by Hunnius, *Epitome Credendorum*, 55–57.

34. SD I.33 (K-W, 537). Likewise Hunnius, *Epitome Credendorum*, 57.

35. Rohnert, *Dogmatik der evangelisch-lutherischen Kirche*, 111.

THE CAUSES OF SIN

What then may have caused Adam to sin, or what are the causes of sin? Scripture denies that God holds any responsibility for the emergence of sin: He is not only omnipotent but also holy. Hollaz cites the prescience (foreknowledge) of God. God condemned Adam, but in that condemnation all humans are condemned since God foresaw that they too would consent to sin. In this way all humans are blamed for their sin and they, not God, are seen as the efficient cause of sin.[36] God does not cause sin or evil or condone it, nor is He responsible for it (Ps 5:5). The reason for sin must lie outside of Him (1 Jn 2:16); it exists in the will of the human, who has renounced his relationship with God and who is now under the seducing power of the devil, an outside influence (Jn 8:44). Because of this influence a human's will is prone to sin either consciously or unconsciously, with the result that the freedom he received is abused. This is the teaching of the Confessions and of the early Lutheran theologians. With regard to what actually causes the breaking of God's Law, for example, Quenstedt distinguishes the external cause from the internal one: "The external cause of this sin is first and foremost Satan . . . —The internal and efficient cause is man's intellect and will, and not a certain internal defect, but an accident by straying because of an external prompting and turning away from God."[37]

The Augsburg Confession states: "The cause of sin is the will of those who are evil, that is, of the devil and the ungodly. Since it was not assisted by God, their will turned away from God."[38] The Formula of Concord adds, "God is not a creator or author of sin" and "that our thoughts, words, and deeds are evil is in its origin a handiwork of Satan."[39] With reference to Augustine, Luther outlines three things that led to the fall of Adam. Most immediate was *concupiscentia*, the desire for the forbidden fruit. And Augustine shows that behind this desire was pride (hubris), the desire to be like God. Luther and Melanchthon go one step further and identify behind the pride the unbelief or (hermeneutical) doubt in God's command:[40] Adam doubted God's Word, whether He really meant what He forbade. So Luther offers a three-step approach to the Fall: *infidelitas* (unbelief or doubt), *superbia* (pride), and *concupiscentia* (desire),[41] on which he reflects in his *Lectures on Genesis*.[42]

Some modern theologians like Paul Tillich have picked up these three elements. In his *Systematic Theology* Tillich incorporates them into his central

---

36. Hollaz, *Examen Theologicum Acroamaticum*, 491.

37. Quenstedt, *Systema* II,2,1,51.

38. AC XIX (K-W, 53).

39. SD I.40, 42 (K-W, 538).

40. Thus, the Augsburg Confession in Article II mentions unbelief "without trust" as part of original sin. AC II.1 (K-W, 37).

41. See Peters, *Der Mensch*, 203. Luther seems to place emphasis on doubt or unbelief as the cause of Adam's fall, whereas Calvin emphasizes the disobedience or defection from God's command (*penness ab imperio Dei*). See Peters, *Der Mensch*, 91.

42. *Lectures on Genesis*, 1535–45 (AE 1:162; WA 42:122.10–19).

concept of estrangement from God: estrangement results from sin, where sin is "the personal act of turning away from that to which one belongs," so that "man as he exists is not what he essentially is and ought to be."[43] Thereby Tillich provides an existential description of sin as a broken relationship between two parties, in this case God and the human.[44] These three aspects—lack of faith or unbelief, hubris (pride), and desire—help to underscore the idea of an estranged existence. (1) Estrangement as unbelief means "the act or state in which man in the totality of his being turns away from God."[45] (2) Estrangement as hubris or *superbia* (pride) is the human's attempt to self-elevate, that is, "to make himself existentially the center of himself and his world."[46] (3) Estrangement as desire (concupiscence) is the hidden desire to be like God.[47] This last element signifies a comprehensive state of a human's temptation and quest toward "the possibility of reaching unlimited abundance."[48]

ORIGINAL SIN AND ITS CONSEQUENCES

The consequences of original sin are revealed in texts such as Gn 2:17 and 3:16–19. After committing sin Adam and Eve became the objects of God's wrath, for they had incurred guilt that deserved punishment, such as death, pain, toil, and evil of all kinds, and that led to their moral corruption. Scripture shows that the Fall impacted all of creation and not only humans; creation itself sighs under the curse of sin (Gn 3:17–18; Rom 8:19–23). In the light of these biblical descriptions the Formula of Concord calls all humans "by nature children of wrath."[49] The Augsburg Confession defines this original sin as "truly sin which even now damns" (*vere peccatum et damnans*).[50] Even if a human is not conscious of Adam's first sin and evil actions, this deed has two consequences which extend over all humans. First, from the legal aspect, because of Adam's sin all are condemned or declared guilty (λογίζεσθαι, forensically), and second, they are corrupted or defiled ethically or morally, which leads them to commit sin as Adam once did.

Why did God react as He did to Adam's sin in the first place? The first sin of Adam must be associated with a mindset that does not agree with God's essence

43. Paul Tillich, *Systematic Theology*, 3 vols. (Chicago: University of Chicago Press, 1951–63), 2:45, 46.

44. Tillich, *Systematic Theology* 2:39.

45. Tillich, *Systematic Theology* 2:47.

46. Tillich, *Systematic Theology* 2:49.

47. Tillich rightfully takes issue with the limiting of concupiscence to mere sexual desire, an identification which in turn affects the understanding of propagation, namely, that "hereditary sin" is rooted in sexual pleasure in the act of propagation. He also sees this desire as much more complex than Freud's concept of libido or Nietzsche's concept of the will to power. Tillich, *Systematic Theology* 2:52.

48. Tillich, *Systematic Theology* 2:52.

49. SD I.6 (K-W, 533), quoting Eph 2:3.

50. AC II.2 (K-W, 39).

and His expression of it. This contradiction with God is a violation against God. Important here is the Lutheran understanding of God's holiness and its absolute state. Measuring all humans against this essential attribute, God must hate all that disagrees with His being or essence, and He must reject it as a noble person hates the state of the total drunkard, regardless of the factors that may have contributed to his drunkenness. God abhors sin not because He cannot love it but because it disagrees with His entire immutable being.

Sin as Universal Condemnation—Forensic Imputation of Guilt

The guilt in which Adam and Eve found themselves led to their punishment, which is divine wrath and eternal damnation resulting in their spiritual, physical, and eternal death. This guilt and punishment is imputed to all their descendants (Rom 5:12).[51] This reckoning of unrighteousness is not a result or consequence of those descendants first having engaged in sin and disobedience but an imputation occurring immediately: we are declared unrighteous immediately because of our connection to Adam, and as a direct result of this declaration we become corrupt and engage in actual sin. This is the immediate understanding of imputation, an external objective declaration not based on our doing, but because of its extension to us we disobey the Lord's will.[52] We tend to be more familiar with this line of argument in its positive manifestation, the imputation of Christ's righteousness: we are declared righteous in Christ not because we have obeyed Him and the Law. Instead, Christ's righteousness is imputed to us and then we as holy saints obey. Quenstedt does not want to dismiss a mediated understanding of original sin but cites it in the context of the passing of Adam's sinful state to all through sexual propagation.[53]

The important point is that all humans already stand under God's wrath, are declared guilty, and are subject to His punishment prior to the clear manifestation of sinful deeds, those that humans commit themselves.[54] Adam's first sin and his guilt and judgment thus are extended to all humans. We distinguish here between objective guilt and subjective guilt.

---

51. "The punishment and penalty for original sin, which God laid upon Adam's children and upon original sin, is death, eternal damnation, and also 'other corporal' and spiritual, temporal, and eternal miseries." SD I.13 (K-W, 534). Hollaz: "Primum peccatum Adami, quatenus is ut communis parens, caput, stirps & repraesentator totius generis humani spectatur, omnibus ipsius posteris *vere* (a) *& justo* Dei judicio (b) ad culpam & poenam imputatur." *Examen Theologicum Acroamaticum*, 513.

52. Quenstedt, *Systema* II,2,2,113: "At posteri Adami per inobedientiam primi parentis facti sunt peccatores, teste Apostolo...Ut justi constituimur per imputationem justitiae Christi, ita injusti constitui sumus per inobedientiam Adami."

53. Quenstedt, *Systema* II,2,2,114: "Immediate nobis imputatur primum peccatum Adamaticum, in quantum exstitimus adhuc in Adamo. Mediate vero nobis imputatur peccatum Adami, scil. Mediante peccato Originali inhaerente, in quantum in propriis personis & individualiter consideramur."

54. Ps 5:5; Rom 6:23; Eph 2:3: "We were by nature children of wrath, like the rest of mankind."

The difference between objective and subjective guilt can be illustrated with a metaphor. Someone who inherits an estate will inherit the real debt that comes along with it and be sued even if he has not caused the debt directly. In the same way, the inherited sin becomes the guilt of the human even if he is not guilty of it directly, and God cannot ignore the reality that the human contradicts God's own being. There is with the human something that should not be there, a guilt of which he stands accused, that damns. Perhaps this is why the Formula of Concord uses the term *reatus* rather than *culpa* to refer to the more objective reality or state of the human, to imply that even if the responsibility for blame is not that clear, the human is nonetheless objectively guilty or in the state of being declared guilty.[55]

Because of Adam's sin, all humans also have become guilty and culpable before God and are condemned to death. Those who incur God's wrath and damnation are considered to merit receiving it. The Confessors anticipate the deterministic argument that inheriting guilt from Adam and Eve is undeserved and unfair. The Confessions thus present Adam's sin not as a foreign guilt but as that of all humans (Rom 5:12), since Adam was the moral representative of all of humanity. He bore the species of humanity, and his will and behavior against God is the will and behavior of all humans. The human race should not be understood as a conglomerate of independent individuals but as a united single body, an organic whole (Acts 17:26) in whom the will of the archfather Adam has been reproduced. With and through Adam all of humankind fell, is pronounced guilty, and is condemned.[56]

Whether we also have a responsibility for receiving that inherited guilt is left unaddressed in the Confessions. The Formula of Concord states that "because of this corruption and on account of the fall of the first human beings, God's law accuses and condemns human nature and the human person."[57] But it does not discuss the idea of a double guilt, that not only is the individual person corrupted but he also participated in the Fall with Adam.

In contrast to this understanding, many leading modern theologians have dismissed the concept of original sin as an inheritance or an imputation of guilt passed on from someone to others. They see the guilt falling upon humans as one they have earned by sinning themselves (mediated concept of sin and guilt), and not as a declaration pronouncing humans guilty prior to their actually engaging in sin (unmediated concept). First, these theologians take the hermeneutical position that the event of Adam's fall never occurred in history. Other biblical narratives fall under the same hermeneutical hatchet simply because what they say literally is incongruent with the worldview of

---

55. "That this inherited defect is guilt [or state of guilt (*reatus*)]"; see Latin text SD I.9 (K-W, 533).

56. Lazarus Spengler's hymn "All Mankind Fell in Adam's Fall" (LSB 562) is cited by the Confessors as testimony of man's total corruption. SD I.1 (K-W, 531).

57. SD I.6 (K-W, 533).

modern humans.[58] Second, for those who follow an existential line of thought like Paul Tillich, imposing a foreign element such as guilt from someone else's sin onto others without their own involvement or doing seems to them an unacceptable Hegelian-like universalism.[59] True, Tillich says, the reality of sin arises in everyone's life but it should not be viewed as an alien phenomenon "imposed" on humans as "external force"[60] through no fault of their own. It is simply there.[61] It is a "self-loss."[62] Third, according to Tillich and others, it would be unfair to treat Adam's situation as an ideal state of innocence before the Fall. The states of "Adam before the Fall" and "nature before the curse" are potential and not actual states. The actual state is the current existence in which the human finds himself along with the whole universe, and there is no time in which this was otherwise.[63] "The notion of a moment *in* time in which the human and nature were changed from good to evil is absurd and has no foundation in experience or revelation."[64] Theology should therefore drop terms like original sin or hereditary sin and proceed directly to describing "the interpenetration of the moral and the tragic elements in the human situation."[65] Similar views are shared in Braaten and Jenson's *Christian Dogmatics*[66] and by Wolfhart Pannenberg[67] and Karl Barth.[68] In his *Anthropology in Theological*

58. The first couple also experienced the Fall in space-time history. Groothuis, *Christian Apologetics*, 275.

59. Tillich, *Systematic Theology* 2:29, 37.

60. Tillich, *Systematic Theology* 2:60.

61. Tillich, *Systematic Theology* 2:30. As a result it is unclear what may have caused what he calls "the total estrangement from God." It just seems to be there as part of every human. Tillich, *Systematic Theology* 2:44–59, and also 2:29 and 2:57.

62. Tillich, *Systematic Theology* 2:60.

63. According to Tillich, "Orthodox theologians have heaped perfection after perfection upon Adam before the Fall, making him equal with the picture of the Christ. This procedure is not only absurd; it makes the Fall completely unintelligible. Mere potentiality or dreaming innocence is not perfection. Only the conscious union of existence and essence is perfection, as God is perfect because he transcends essence and existence. The symbol 'Adam before the Fall' must be understood as the dreaming innocence of undecided potentialities." Tillich, *Systematic Theology* 2:34. Thus the idea of a state of innocence or infinite freedom were not once actualized realities but "non-actualized potentiality." Tillich, *Systematic Theology* 2:33. Thus, "'Adam before the Fall' and 'nature before the curse' are states of potentiality. They are not actual states." Tillich, *Systematic Theology* 2:40; Schwarz, *Human Being*, 245–49.

64. Tillich, *Systematic Theology* 2:41.

65. Tillich, *Systematic Theology* 2:39.

66. Braaten and Jenson, *Christian Dogmatics* 1:328: "It is now universally held among theologians that the stories and concepts we have of Adam and Eve in paradise are legends and myths. The idea of humans living in a blessed primeval stage before the fall is looked on as poetical speculation, not history. It is sometimes argued that faithfulness requires our belief in a primeval condition of blessedness. Such an argument confuses faithfulness with the imposition of a mythical speculation on a modern historical outlook on human life."

67. Pannenberg, *Systematic Theology* 2:212, 263. See also Waap, *Gottebenbildlichkeit und Identität*, 397.

68. Pannenberg, *Anthropology in Theological Perspective*, 122; Karl Barth dismisses the Fall as a universal applicable event but still maintains it serves as a mirror reflecting every human being's doing. See *Church Dogmatics*, 4.1:509ff., 501; Schwarz, *Human Being*, 244, 246, 252.

Perspective Pannenberg concludes: "This being the case, we should renounce artificial attempts to rescue traditional theological formulas; one such attempt is the idea of an origin that is supposedly nonhistorical."[69] With their denial of the historicity of the Fall and by casting doubt on the actual transfer of guilt to all of humanity through this one-time event, these theologians gravitate more toward a mediated concept of sin even if they do not state explicitly that this is the case. Sin's power over humans simply exists without its cause rooted in Adam's fall as an historic event. Theologians like Paul Althaus and Emil Brunner also reject the traditional concept of sin as a transpersonal and transhistorical force because of their own attempts to demythologize the historic event of the Fall. For Althaus, the theological interest in Adam is as a symbolic reflection of all of humanity; he should not be understood as a historic or prehistoric first man. We are and represent in our sin one human being. Thus our sin is not caused by the first human being, but he reflects a universal problem.[70] Adam represents a collective "I" of all humans, who have in common the reality of sin. If we were to focus on Adam as a historic person and try to date the Fall, as Althaus argues, our guilt would not be our guilt and we should not be held responsible for it.[71] In the project of demythologizing Genesis 3 the event of the Fall loses the universal character of sin, and as a consequence it fails to explain fully the depth of individual or personal sin. The overall human predicament is existentialized to the point that the concept of sin is reduced to what humans themselves actually commit.

Neither does Werner Elert want to think of the relationship of evil and sin as one of the abstract moving to the concrete (*Abstraktum zum Konkretum*); he would rather declare its manifestation a mystery (*Geheimnis zu seiner Manifestation*). The mystery is that the abstract evil entered the world and becomes manifest in the reality of sin. It develops as its own transcendent power and then takes all humans into its service by causing them to sin. Elert speaks of "a synthesis of fate and guilt."[72] Original sin does not relieve a person of the evil and responsibility for it by pinning it on someone back in history; rather, the person is fatally connected to Adam like a fruit is to the root, and the person becomes sinful himself in his root Adam.[73]

We must balance between two extreme positions in order to contend with such modern theologians. We cannot resort to a fatalistic explanation of evil that seems to take the blame away from humans. That view is as one-sided as the belief that sin is merely a moral defect, an understanding which would grant free will to a human being. Sin must be viewed ontologically as a "being" and an "act," a "self-inflicted guilt" and also a "state of revolt."[74] As Luther puts

69. Pannenberg, *Anthropology in Theological Perspective*, 57.
70. Paul Althaus, *Die christliche Wahrheit*, 2:116; Pöhlmann, *Abriß der Dogmatik*, 189.
71. Pöhlmann, *Abriß der Dogmatik*, 189.
72. Elert, *Christian Faith*, 64.
73. Elert, *Christian Faith*, 64–65; Pöhlmann, *Abriß der Dogmatik*, 181.
74. Pöhlmann, *Abriß der Dogmatik*, 189.

it, "prior to any willing or doing on our part, we are sinful participants in the original sin of Adam."[75] For this reason we note the Confessions' intention to bring out precisely the point that original sin is not merely what the human does but also what it does in and through him. The human is not only the doer or subject of sin but also the object of sin that overcomes him and forces him to become the doer. Sin bears both a subjective and transsubjective nature. All humans participate in the sin of Adam, and at the same time they are recipients of his sin and punished with condemnation. Again, with and through Adam all of humanity fell. His fall was not simply an individual's fall but rather that of the entire human species.

The role of baptism is important here. Baptism removes the punishable guilt. However, the connection to Adam's fall does not go away after baptism but continues in the form of concupiscence, the desire to sin; it remains and leads to actual sins.[76] This fact does not diminish the value of the sacrament of baptism. This sacrament has accomplished its task in that the baptized no longer stands condemned before God. One important implication of this insight that all humans are guilty and condemned prior to the actual doing is the need for infant baptism, since deceased unbaptized children fall under condemnation. Most likely this is what Melanchthon also thought when he formulated in the Augsburg Confession in 1530 that original sin "damns and brings eternal death to those who are not born again through baptism and the Holy Spirit."[77] The Formula of Concord rejects the credobaptism of the Anabaptists, which claims an innocence for infants since they cannot hear the Gospel and hence do not have reasonable faith.[78] That rejection is still timely: the understanding of baptism as a washing away of original guilt is not shared by many Protestant Christians, such as Baptists who opt instead for adult baptisms at which they make "an outward public testimony of God's inward work."[79] This understanding is totally different from what the Confessions teach on the necessity of baptism. Children and infants do have faith[80] and should be baptized for their salvation

75. *Lectures on Romans*, 1516 (AE 25:277; WA 56:289.27–28); Jenson, *Gravity of Sin*, 54.

76. *Lectures on Romans*, 1516 (AE 25:259–61; WA 56:271.2–74.1).

77. AC I.2 (K-W, 39).

78. Ep. XII.6 (K-W, 520): Part of the Anabaptists' reason for supporting credobaptism is that they reject "the entire teaching of original sin and everything connected with it."

79. Boyd and Eddy, *Across the Spectrum*, 215.

80. "For . . . those who believe prior to baptism . . . have everything through the external Word that comes first." SA III.viii.7 (K-W, 322). Luther makes room for the possibility of deceased unbaptized and even stillborn children having faith through the hearing of God's Word. He would submit them to the almighty grace of God. In his *Lectures on Genesis* Luther also discusses the fate of Jewish infants who died uncircumcised, and submits the souls of those children and the unbaptized to God's almighty mercy: "Accordingly, the souls of those infants must be left to the will of the Heavenly Father, whom we know to be merciful." *Lectures on Genesis*, 1535–45 (AE 3:103; WA 42:621.34–36). To argue his case Luther points not only to God's mercy but to His absolute or extraordinary power, yet he quickly falls back on God's ordained power which is tied to baptism: "We must keep the ordered power in mind and form our opinion on the basis of it. God is able to save without Baptism . . . but in the church we must judge and teach, in accordance with God's ordered power, that without that outward Baptism

when the occasion is presented.[81] Should the discussion about an infant's faith lead nowhere, the imperative to baptize infants rests in the end on the Lord's mandate to baptize all (Mt 28:19).[82]

Sin as Total Corruption—Moral Ruin

The second consequence of Adam's sin is that the imputation of guilt leads to corruption. We have discussed aspects of corruption already under the properties of original sin. Here we seek to underscore what has been said about the spiritual corruption which also leads to the moral failure of a person. The imputation of guilt leads to moral ruin. As we saw previously, the reformers contended with a long tradition of theologians who held widely differing views on the degree of corruption of the unregenerate and his potential for supernatural reward, the divine grace. This issue required a great deal of attention and clarification. To that end the reformers unequivocally claimed total corruption, which implies that all faculties of the human—his reason, conscience, and will—are grasped and distorted so that in spiritual matters the unregenerate is considered dead and in no way capable of receiving through his own strengths supernatural reward. He is spiritually dead.

Total moral corruption means that nothing residing in the human is spared from corruption, including not only reason but also the conscience.[83] The reformers' understanding of total corruption led to their rejection of the concept of the synteresis, a supposed moral residual in the conscience that is able to grasp transcendental truths and thereby please God. This position, represented by Gabriel Biel, Pierre d'Ailly, and Duns Scotus, smacks of semi-Pelagianism because to them the synteresis (συντήρησις, derived from the Greek word συντηρέω, to keep or hold to) meant that the fallen human still has an inclination toward the good. He still possesses his original conscience and thus is able to make moral decisions between good and evil and against sin. In soteriology the synteresis was believed to be a natural resource and was appealed to with the maxim *facere quod in se est*. For Luther and the reformers to grant any validity to that concept would mean making a concession to synergism, and so they wholly dismiss the idea of a synteresis which inclines

no one is saved" (AE 3:274; WA 43:20–24). See also *Lectures on Genesis*, 1535–45 (AE 3:140; WA 42:648.10–12 and AE 3:143–44; WA 42:650.24–29).

81. For the distinction between absolute and ordained necessity of baptism, see Kurt E. Marquart, *The Saving Truth: Doctrine for Laypeople*, Truth, Salvatory and Churchly: Works of Kurt E. Marquart 1 (Ft. Wayne: The Luther Academy, 2016), 96–97.

82. "We bring the child with the intent and hope that it may believe, and we pray God to grant it faith. But we do not baptize on this basis, but solely on the command of God." LC IV.57 (K-W, 464).

83. On this point Roman Catholicism disagrees with the reformers. The *Catechism of the Catholic Church* denies total corruption. "It [original sin] is a deprivation of original holiness and justice, but human nature has not been totally corrupted: it is wounded in the natural powers proper to it." The *Catechism* then proceeds to dismiss the Reformation's concept of "radical perversion," 103 (§ 406).

the will toward good, albeit weakly.[84] Not much has changed in the Roman Catholic's affirmation of synteresis. The *Catechism of the Catholic Church* affirms the dignity of the conscience even in the fallen human: "Conscience includes the perception of the principles of morality (synteresis)."[85]

For Luther and the Confessions, all three areas associated with the soul, *conscientia* (conscience), *voluntas* (will) or *ratio* (reason), and *cor* (heart),[86] are affected by sin and set against God, and only through God's Word is the human converted. *Conscientia* becomes the place where God is encountered, where Christ and the Holy Spirit meet the believer, and through faith the conscience is set free from indictment. The conscience should not be understood as a faculty in which remnant power still resides but the place where God's judgment is encountered and felt, and which is then freed through divine pardon.[87] It endures the condemnation of the Law and receives the comfort and assurance of the Gospel. "Now my conscience is at peace; / From the Law I stand acquitted."[88]

For this reason we cannot imagine that neutrality toward evil exists in humans and thus also in their relationship with God. Only two options exist for us: either we believe His Gospel or we don't, either we love Him or we don't, either we fear Him or we don't. Since we do not have such neutrality, evil does not come to us humans only on occasion. We do not own evil; it owns us. It takes hold of our nature and influences our lives because we have been born into this existential conflict with God.[89] The Formula of Concord underscores this point, stating that "our entire nature and person is sinful, that is, totally and thoroughly corrupted in God's sight and contaminated by original sin with a spiritual leprosy."[90] While the Formula affirms a total corruption of the human nature by original sin, it calls for a proper distinction between nature itself and its corruption. The former "has taken up residence in this nature or essence and

84. Already in *Dictata super Psalterium*, 1513–16 (WA 4:1–462), Luther took issue with synteresis and dismissed its efficacy in the order of salvation: "To be sure, I admit that it is true that a person with this attitude can do and will some good things, but not all of them, for we are so entirely inclined to evil that no portion which is inclined toward the good remains in us, as is clear in the synteresis." *Lectures on Romans*, 1516 (AE 25:222; WA 56:237.5–8); Paul Althaus, *Paulus und Luther über den Menschen: Ein Vergleich* (Gütersloh: C. Bertelsmann, 1938), 51; Janz, *Luther and Thomism*, 12–13.

85. *Catechism of the Catholic Church*, 439 (§ 1780).

86. *The Magnificat*, 1521 (AE 21:303–4; WA 7:550.19–51.24); *The Sermon on the Mount*, 1532 (AE 21:235–36; WA 32:494.20–32); Peters, *Der Mensch*, 39.

87. See here Johannes Stelzenberger, *Syneidesis, Conscientia, Gewissen* (Paderborn: Ferdinand Schöningh, 1963), 94: "Conscientia ist ihm [Luther] nicht eine virtus operandi sondern iudicandi . . . Conscientia wird der Ort des Gottesverhältnisses, der persönlichen Christus und heiligen Geist-Begegnung. Endlich wird der Glaube als gute conscientia und Gewissensfreiheit erklärt." In *Ontologie der Person bei Luther* (212) Joest includes some references to Luther in his *operationes in Psalmos*, for example in Psalms 1 and 2.

88. Stanza 6 of the hymn "Jesus Sinners Doth Receive" (LSB 609); SD V.1 (K-W, 581).

89. Elert, *Christian Faith*, 174.

90. SD I.6 (K-W, 533).

corrupted it," but they "are not one and the same thing."[91] It clings to human nature like a parasite or leprosy. Applying the distinctions of *substantia* and *accidens*, the Formula rejects the idea that original sin is called *substantia* and instead calls it *accidens*, since it "does not exist in and of itself or is not a part of another independent essence."[92] In this sense the depth and objective power of original sin over humanity attaches to each person individually, yet without compromising its universal nature. This disposition of sin is particularly evident in the role of the will in the human as he goes through conversion.

Regarding the will, we affirm the truth that humans have not been born into Adam's sinful orientation as if it were a condition alien to them, but that the will already in its earliest stages is disposed to this hostile condition. All humans are implicated or declared unrighteous, which means original sin also is treated as a personal fault that even now condemns. Augustine says, appropriately, "We are not such uninvited" (*non inviti tales sumus*).[93] In other words, we ourselves are to blame for our moral failures because we willingly consent to sin. The moral implication of original sin is that we have become slaves to sin and love it; we are so of our own accord and are naturally inclined toward it.

Martin Luther dwells at length on this lack of a free will or reason, and in his Small Catechism he provides a summary: "I believe that by my own understanding or strength I cannot believe in Jesus Christ my LORD or come to him."[94] In *The Bondage of the Will* Luther argues that the will is bound as a consequence of the corruption of human nature. Likewise in the Smalcald Articles he rejects the idea "that the human being has a free will . . . to do good and reject evil" as "pure error and blindness."[95]

Melanchthon concurred with Luther on this issue, at least in the early period of the Reformation. In the Apology, for example, Luther's colleague also appeals to Augustine, referring to his books *On Nature and Grace* and *On Grace and Free Choice* to reject the Pelagian position on unregenerate reason and will in receiving the righteousness that saves.[96] However, he eventually gravitated toward a synergism and ascribed to the human "some cause in him who accepts, namely, in as far as he does not repudiate the grace offered."[97] This trend

91. SD I.33 (K-W, 537).

92. SD I.55 (K-W, 541).

93. Karl Immanuel Nitzsch, *System of Christian Doctrine*, trans. Robert Montgomery and John Hennen (Edinburgh: T&T Clark, 1849), 223.

94. SC II.6 (K-W, 355). The truthfulness of this statement is apparent when one compares it to Scripture: Gn 6:5; Ez 11:19; Jn 8:36; 15:5; Rom 6:20–22; 8:7; 1 Cor 2:14; 12:3; 2 Cor 3:5; Gal 5:1; Phil 2:13; Heb 12:2.

95. SA III.i.3, 5 (K-W, 311).

96. AC XXVIII.1–3, 8–9 (K-W, 51, 53); AC XX.13 (K-W, 55); Ap. IV.29–33 (K-W, 125).

97. Melanchthon's position on the free will in conversion has received much scrutiny and is found to be synergistic. Friedrich Bente contends that Melanchthon is "the father of synergism" among Lutherans, pointing to controversial statements he made on the three causes in his *Loci Communes, 1543*, trans. J. A. O. Preus (St. Louis: Concordia Publishing House, 1992), 96, 104. Bente states that Melanchthon's comments on Rom 9:6 in his *Commentary on Romans* (1532) are problematic too, namely this statement: "Divine compassion is truly the cause of

emerged within Lutheranism in theologians such as Victorin Strigel and caused some consternation among other Lutheran theologians. It was condemned by the Formula of Concord in its dismissal of the idea that the will or reason serve as the third cause in conversion, after the Word and the Holy Spirit.[98]

As the Confessors of the Formula laid out the *modus agendi* of the human's conversion, they refused to accept statements that suggest "that the human being has not completely died to the good in spiritual matters but rather is seriously wounded and half-dead,"[99] or the sentiment of John Chrysostom, who says that "the human will is not idle in conversion but also does something," if we understand "will" to mean the will of the unregenerate.[100] Instead, the Formula responds that the will of the unregenerate cannot do anything toward his conversion but that he remains purely passive,[101] since Scripture calls the heart "a hard stone"[102] or someone unbelieving "like a pillar of salt, like Lot's wife, indeed like a block of wood or a stone."[103] Against Flacius the Formula teaches that a human is not coerced or forced to convert but still possesses a *capacitas passiva*—which distinguishes humans from all other creatures—for God to work on and bring him to conversion.[104] As rational creatures, humans receive God's work on them differently than the way in which He accomplishes "his will in other, irrational creatures or in a stone or block of wood."[105] People who are not converted are those who stubbornly resist Him like a "wild, ferocious beast,"[106] since the Holy Spirit is not "given to those who resist him."[107] And yet the removal of resistance is entirely the work of the Holy Spirit, and the human remains totally passive (*pure passive*) when the Holy Spirit leads him to repentance and faith.[108] Against anyone who might want to attribute conversion to the will of the human, the Confessors argue that there are only

election, but . . . there is some cause also in him who accepts, namely, in as far as he does not repudiate the grace offered." Friedrich Bente, *Historical Introductions to the Book of Concord* (St. Louis: Concordia Publishing House, 1965), 197. In his 1540 edition of the *Commentary on Romans* Melanchthon omitted the controversial phrase "cause in him who accepts." See here Philipp Melanchthon, *Commentary on Romans*, trans. Fred Kramer, 2d English ed. (St. Louis: Concordia Publishing House, 2010), 8, 189. For an exhaustive study see Wolfgang Matz, *Der befreite Mensch: Die Willenslehre in der Theologie Philipp Melanchthons*, Forschungen zur Kirchen- und Dogmengeschichte 81 (Göttingen: Vandenhoeck & Ruprecht, 2001).

98. SD II.90 (K-W, 561). Shortly after Luther's death Victorin Strigel proposed that a person's natural powers to do the good had become only latent and could be incited again through the work of the Holy Spirit so that the will of the person actually cooperates at his conversion.

99. SD II.77 (K-W, 559).

100. SD II.86 (K-W, 560).

101. SD II.89 (K-W, 561); SD I.18 (K-W, 494).

102. SD II.19 (K-W, 547).

103. SD II.20 (K-W, 548).

104. SD II.60 (K-W, 555).

105. SD II.62 (K-W, 556).

106. SD II.19 (K-W, 547).

107. SD II.60, 82–83 (K-W, 555, 560).

108. SD II.83, 89 (K-W, 560, 561); and SD II.26, 52, 66, 71, 83 (K-W, 549, 554, 556, 557, 560).

two efficient causes in our conversion, the Holy Spirit and God's Word, not the will of the human.

The Formula argues further that one must attribute one's beginning, perseverance, and conclusion in the Christian calling to nothing but the Holy Spirit and God's Word and the gift of faith He provides, and definitely not to good works.[109] Once the Holy Spirit has begun the work of rebirth and renewal, the human can and should be cooperating with Him, "though still in great weakness."[110] This last statement should not be misconstrued to mean the will of the converted person cooperates alongside the Holy Spirit "in the way two horses draw a wagon together."[111] Such cooperation occurs not on the basis of the fleshly, natural powers but "on the basis of the new powers and gifts which the Holy Spirit initiated in us in conversion."[112] Where the Formula says the human "can accept the grace offered" or uses a similar phrase, it must be understood as speaking of the already converted person whose mind and heart have been changed.[113]

The Issue of Death

Through the Fall the first parents also fell into certain death, which implies that all humans have lost the right to an eternal and immortal existence with God. God could have ended the human creation right then and there, but in His mercy and eternal salvific will He decided to let the sinful human race continue. However, there are consequences. The wages of death (Rom 6:23; Ez 18:4, 23) that have followed all of humanity manifest themselves in three significant ways: spiritually, physically, and eternally.

First, there is a spiritual death because of sin: the separation of God and the human (in particular the separation of the sinner's soul from God). The umbilical cord, so to speak, that once joined the human with God now has been cut (Is 59:2; Eph 4:18), and the original harmony between the two has turned to hostile disharmony (Rom 8:7; Eph 2:16). For this reason all humans lack peace of mind over their sins and are burdened as well by the fear of death (Is 48:22; 53:5; Rom 8:6; Heb 2:15).

With this separation God no longer stands in the center of human life, so that sin enslaves and rules over the human (Rom 6:20; 8:2, 34; 2 Pt 2:19) and darkens his heart (Is 60:2; Jn 1:5; 1 Cor 2:14; Eph 4:17–18). In short, the human is focused on what his nature, that is, his flesh, wants (Rom 8:6). This spiritual death means that the good in the human has died; this calamity has estranged him from God and made him spiritually dead in his sin (Lk 15:32; Jn 5:24; Eph 2:1; Col 2:13; 1 Jn 3:14). The consequence of this spiritual death is

109. SD IV.34–35 (K-W, 579–80).

110. SD II.65 (K-W, 556); Ep. II.11 (K-W, 493).

111. SD II.66 (K-W, 557).

112. SD II.65 (K-W, 556).

113. SD II.83 (K-W, 560). See similar statements in AC XVIII.1–2 (K-W, 50). See also Ap. XVIII.4–6 (K-W, 233–34), SA III.i (K-W, 310–11), and SD II.26 (K-W, 549).

eternal punishment. Second, the physical death is also the suspension of the natural bond between body and soul, the point at which the body is separated from the soul. Even if death did not immediately set in at the time of the Fall, human life from the outset of sin followed the path of death, the course of slow decay (Pss 90:5–6; 103:15–16; 2 Cor 4:16). That gradual decay of the bodily existence would be felt in physical ailments of all kinds (illnesses and pain), which are the forerunners of death itself (Gn 3:16–19; Jer 2:19; Rom 1:18). As a result of sin the physical death has become the path all flesh must go (Gn 3:19; Heb 9:27). Non-humans also will experience death. Dying could be seen as natural in a sense, but it never should be viewed primarily as that. In general, human beings grapple with the reality of their physical death and seek different ways to suppress it. In *The Denial of Death* Ernest Becker sheds light on the psychological burden physical death has on human beings—how they have developed strategies to fend off awareness of their mortality and vulnerability while creating a feeling that they are immortal.[114]

Physical death is a divinely determined order of all creaturely existence. We are created mortal without the special gift of immortality with which Adam had been endowed originally, and he became mortal because of the Fall—a position which Calvin, Luther, and the Lutheran theologians took. Death is unnatural because humans are de facto sinners and therefore condemned to a physical death, as is all of creation. In this case we agree with Barth, who says: "We know the end of our temporal existence, our death . . . is an evil, an enemy of man. In the light of this fact there can be no doubt as to the unnatural and discordant character of death."[115] If "natural immortality" was a part of Adam that he lost, then physical death cannot be seen as natural; it is an enemy of human life which has dragged all other nonhuman creaturely life into it.

Third, humans alone among creatures die not only a physical death, but their passing leads to divine judgment, which becomes eternal death for the human who is under the penalty of sin. Eternal death is the eternal separation of the condemned sinner from the holy God, where the body and soul of the sinner are no longer with God. This death will afflict all the impenitent who reject the grace of God in Christ; their fate is eternal damnation (Mt 10:28; 24:41–46; Mk 8:44; 2 Thes 1:7–9; Rv 21:8). In this sense immortality will be part of all humans after their physical death but with polarized outcomes, either negative or positive. We emphasize this point in view of the numerous attempts to question and remove the penalty of eternal condemnation in one theory or another. Those who make concessions to universalism that would suspend these divergent outcomes would have difficulty providing compelling arguments for the church to continue her proclamation to those within and those outside the church.[116] Scripture remains silent as to whether God has a different plan in store

114. Ernest Becker, *The Denial of Death* (New York: Simon & Schuster, 1973).

115. Barth, *Church Dogmatics* 3/2:628. See here Anderson, *On Being Human*, 137–38.

116. The implications of universalism often are thought to impact only the missionary

for those who through no guilt of their own have not received the means of grace. In this case all heathens are judged according to the law they have set for themselves (Rom 1:18ff.), over and against those who consciously have rejected the grace extended to them when they heard the preaching of the Gospel.

---

enterprise of the church, but they reach far deeper than that by compromising the entire need for the church to pursue her kerygmatic sacramental activity. Millard J. Erickson, "The State of the Unevangelized and Its Missionary Implications," in John Mark Terry (ed.), *Missiology: An Introduction to the Foundations, History and Strategies of World Missions* (Nashville: B&H Academic 2015), 121–37.

9

THE ONGOING STRUGGLE WITH SIN

THE *HOMO INCURVATUS IN SE*

Our sinful human posture often is expressed as a curvature, describing a human who is turned inward to himself. This perception holds a prominent place in theological anthropology. Augustine discussed it,[1] and after him Luther drew attention to it with the following passage:

> The reason is that our nature has been so deeply curved in upon itself [*tam profunda est in seipsam incurva*] because of the viciousness of original sin that it not only turns the finest gifts of God in upon itself and enjoys them (as is evident in the case of legalists and hypocrites), indeed, it even uses God Himself to achieve these aims, but it also seems to be ignorant of this very fact, that in acting so iniquitously, so perversely, and in such a depraved way, it is even seeking God for its own sake.[2]

The incurved human being puts the self before anything and anyone else. He accepts no limits when it comes to pursuing his own advantage and benefit. Such a person stands as the quintessential sinful being, in contrast to someone who is focused on God and his neighbor, motivated by love. Luther called such a person *homo incurvatus in se*, "a man curved in on himself," a radical diagnosis of the human as formed or characterized by his egotism.[3] If the absence of sin would enable humans to truly love God and one another, then sin's presence is fundamentally a selfish occupation with oneself, both inwardly and outwardly. The "I" takes precedence over the "we" and the "you," and as a result a life that should be marked by the nurture of relationships suffers. Self-love stands in the way of this pure, extrinsic focus. Though the absence of love is the key issue, the church traditionally has pointed to seven cardinal sins which are indicative of the gripping power of the selfish "I," echoing Galatians (5:19–21): pride, greed, lust, envy, gluttony, wrath, and sloth. For Lutherans, sins go beyond the cardinal seven. Not only are there more acts of sin, each as deserving of condemnation as the other, but they are all born from a persistent drive toward sin, the very desire to sin.[4]

---

1. Augustine, *The City of God* 14.28 (WSA 1.7:136). The connection between Augustine and Luther on the incurvature is explored in Jenson, *Gravity of Sin*.
2. *Lectures on Romans*, 1516 (AE 25:291; WA 56:304.24–29).
3. Jenson, *Gravity of Sin*, 47.
4. *Lectures on Romans*, 1516 (AE 25:259; WA 56:271.14–15).

The metaphor *homo incurvatus in se* is helpful in addressing the problems that exist in a relational anthropology.[5] In this discussion it is important not to look at humans in substantive or existential ontologies alone but also in relationship to fellow humans, and of course to Jesus Christ. The believer has a new life in Christ (Col 3:3), a relationship built on faith and hope (*in fide* and *in spe*). In that relationship the righteousness of Christ is granted to us as a present possession but also in the hope for its full manifestation.[6] The *homo incurvatus* does not demonstrate simply an aversion toward God, he turns away from the true relationship found in Christ and shuts himself off from the grace of God. Thus, the opposite of curvature is standing in a true and real relationship with Christ.

On this last point Matt Jenson detects a distinction between Augustine and Luther in terms of the Christological focus of a human who is no longer captive to his incurvature. Whereas Luther reserves the believer's attention wholly for Christ and His humanity, acknowledging its instrumental soteriological significance on the cross,[7] Augustine reveals a Christological deficit, the lack of a continual fixed focus on Christ, hoping instead to achieve a vision beyond Christ's humanity, of God Himself: "Christ's humanity seems ultimately instrumental and of only temporary importance. . . . Our hope is in the day when his office of mediator will cease and we will participate in the divine life directly."[8]

In other words, for Augustine the incarnation does not factor fully throughout a believer's life. It serves as a kind of shortcut to becoming part of Christ's divine nature,[9] and once the way is paved, Christ's humanity and His office as mediator are no longer needed eschatologically to mediate the glory of God. According to Jenson, in the end "Christ remains a glorious *via* rather than the re-definition of Augustine's God."[10]

In answering the claim that an outward Christological focus is inadequate, we point to the whole person of Jesus, Christ the crucified in particular, who represents the full righteousness. Our hope for salvation and our human relationship with Christ do not bypass or take a shortcut by ignoring the human nature of Christ and His earthly ministry. Against Andreas Osiander the

5. Jenson, *Gravity of Sin*, 2, 4.

6. Jenson, *Gravity of Sin*, 58–59. Jenson uses the term "substantiation" to bring out the present reality of Christ's righteousness as a truly present reality and possession in the life of the believer; its possession, he says, rests on the existence of faith. A substantive ontology such as that taken by the Finnish School would teach otherwise, asserting an objective structure that is substantively present and that goes beyond one received through faith. By logical conclusion such an ontology loses sight of the sinner (*peccator*) in the *simul iustus et peccator*. Jenson, *Gravity of Sin*, 63n85.

7. Jenson, *Gravity of Sin*, 37.

8. Jenson, *Gravity of Sin*, 35; see Augustine, *On the Trinity* 1.10.20 (NPNFa 3:28). "Augustine can speak directly of deification without reference to Christ." Jenson, *Gravity of Sin*, 11.

9. Jenson, *Gravity of Sin*, 12; cf. Augustine, *City of God* 9.15 (WSA 1.6:294).

10. Jenson, *Gravity of Sin*, 43.

Confessors came to provide the correction that our righteousness is reckoned to us by the obedience of the total person of Christ, "who is at the same time God and a human being."[11] Throughout his earthly life the believer is dependent upon and embraces this Christ,[12] which is the point that matters in bringing a being out of the state of incurvature.[13] This continuing dependence on Christ is the remedy Luther prescribes for sinful humans.[14] Luther would focus the believer's attention consistently and exclusively on the entire and objective Christ, and for him nothing replaces faith: not desire, not perfection,[15] not any virtue.[16]

Incurvature is a constant threat and reality in a Christian's life because he is not free of sin; as a result, faith maintains an extrinsic focus on the cross for forgiveness and for the drowning of one's old Adam. "Such is life that one stands today and falls tomorrow."[17] Incurvature does not reflect the authentic human existence people are supposed to live. True existence is not achieved by narrowing one's focus to one's own self divorced from relationships with God and fellow humans. Psychology or psychotherapy that is built on treating a human with this approach limits the person's authentic existence to the "I" and does not encompass in any way other beings, especially God; such a view reflects a distorted interpretation of human existence. Only in his relationship to God and to other people is a human able to differentiate his own self. After all, God's will as expressed in the Ten Commandments is based around the sin of omission or active misconduct against God and one's neighbor. Sin results from the lack of love because the human has turned in on himself, replacing his love for others with the love for himself. This selfish, incurved posture of human beings is truly challenged only in the encounter with the Word of God, where the Law informs the sinner of his lack of love, of his broken relationship with God (First Table of the Law, Commandments 1–3) and with his neighbor (Commandments 4–10, the Second Table). The Gospel then reorients the believer from being inwardly focused on himself to focusing outside of himself in response to his neighbor's needs.[18]

11. SD III.58 (K-W, 572).

12. SD III.38–39 (K-W, 569).

13. The Confessors remain undeterred in this point: "We refuse to let ourselves be distracted from the principle point at issue here." SD III.29 (K-W, 567).

14. Jenson, *Gravity of Sin*, 48–49.

15. For this reason the Confessors reject those positions that have drifted partially or entirely from the theology of the cross, those that hold "that our righteousness before God does not depend upon the sole obedience and merit of Christ, but also upon our renewal and on the godliness of our own way of life before God" and "that a Christian, who is truly reborn through the Holy Spirit, can keep and fulfill the law of God perfectly in this life." SD XII.10, 33 (K-W, 657, 659).

16. *Heidelberg Disputation*, 1518 (AE 31:40; WA 1:354.19–22). See *Die Disputation de sententia: Verbum caro factum est (Joh. 1, 14)*, 1539 (WA 39/2:1–3), which proves that philosophy cannot fully grasp Christ's incarnation.

17. LC III.100 (K-W, 453).

18. Joest, *Ontologie der Person bei Luther*, 306–7: "Das Person-sein des Menschen ist darin

THE CONTROVERSY: ROMANS 7:14–25

Sin is not located on the periphery of human existence, identified as an ethical issue, a mere misconduct here or there that enters on occasion into the life of a person. The struggle with sin is neverending. Temptation from the world, sin, and the devil is constantly, daily attacking the Christian. Luther describes this reality well: "For we live in the flesh and carry the old creature around our necks," for "as long as we remain in this vile life, where we are attacked, hunted, and harried on all sides, we are constrained to cry out and pray every hour that God may not allow us to become faint and weary and to fall back into sin, shame, and unbelief."[19] As a result of this dialectic of sinner and saint existing in a believer as true realties, he stands wholly absolved through the Word and yet falls again because of sin: "For the flesh in which we daily live is of such a nature that it does not trust and believe God and is constantly aroused by evil desires and devices, so that we sin daily . . . in acts of omission and commission."[20]

Luther located this description of a Christian's struggle with sin in Rom 7:14–25. The question is whether he correctly reflects Paul's position. Many scholars clearly have thought otherwise. Paul Althaus, for example, points to a difference between the explanations of Paul and Luther. "According to Paul," Althaus claims, "a Christian is able to triumph persistently over his struggles with the flesh; he does not have to sin constantly. According to Luther, the Christian also sins daily and is in need of daily forgiveness."[21] Thus Althaus concludes that Luther's understanding of daily sin and daily forgiveness has no parallel in Paul.

This assertion bears significant implications for the entire Lutheran community, for it would mitigate in Paul's writings and life the burden of daily sin and forgiveness and challenge not only our reading of Rom 7:14–25 but also our own estimation of the severity of sin in our daily lives.

The suggestion that one has the natural ability to overcome temptation or not succumb entirely to it by one's own resources implies that one is willing

ausgezeichnet, daß es exzentrisch-responsorisch ist. . . . Es bedeutet, daß gerade die *Totalität* jenes Getragen-seins im fiat mihi des Glaubens ihre Entsprechung und Anerkennung findet." In his third chapter, on Centrality and Sin, Pannenberg uses two terms which are key to his anthropology. He speaks of the tension between selfhood as egotism, which he calls centrality (the ego/will over others), and the self's devotion to the other person and opennesss to the world, for which he uses the term exocentricity (the self for others). Pannenberg, *Anthropology in Theological Perspective*, 149.

19. LC III.102, 105 (K-W, 453–54).

20. LC III.89 (K-W, 452).

21. Althaus, *Paulus und Luther*, 69. In Althaus's interpretation of Romans 7, which parts with Luther and the tradition of Augustine, sin's impact on the life of a believer loses its severity. In his view Paul depicts the daily struggles of someone who is outside of Christ ("der Mensch ohne Christus"), for a Christian has left behind that sinful state ("der Sündenstand liegt zurück") and is able to overcome his battles with the flesh ("in dem Kampf mit dem Fleische können die Christen ständig siegen"). Paul Althaus, *Der Brief an die Römer*, Das Neue Testament Deutsch, vol. 6 (Göttingen: Vandenhoek & Ruprecht, 1953), 70.

to abandon theologically the full impact of sin on the life of a believer. The Lutheran Confessions take issue with the Anabaptists, "who deny that those who have once been justified can lose the Holy Spirit, and also [with] those who contend that some may attain such perfection in this life that they cannot sin."[22] Though they support the idea of growing and progressing in one's spirituality, the Confessions affirm that for a believer the battle between being a sinner and a saint never ends. This assertion derives especially from the understanding of concupiscence and its power. If one views concupiscence as a neutral force that becomes active only when provoked or tugged upon, as medieval theologians like Occam taught, this understanding makes room for the contention that a Christian battles less with sin than Luther claimed. For Luther that perspective offers a shallow interpretation of the active power of concupiscence as sin prior to all aberrant behavior. Instead, he radicalizes sin as a force that takes hold of a person and does not let go.

Luther's approach rests largely on Paul's description in Romans 7. In his *Lectures on Romans*, Luther depicts the Christian in 7:17–23 as a spiritual being struggling with concupiscence, the desire within him according to his carnal existence here on earth.[23] If anyone doubts who Luther understands the "I" to be in Romans 7, we read from *Against Latomus*, where he explains Rom 7:17:

> Who is this "I" who now does not do what it has just been said to do? It is the "I" which I spiritually am, because according to this "I," I am now looked at in terms of the grace which does not allow me to be looked at in terms of the sin which makes me carnal. Everything is washed away, and now there is a self different from the one before grace.[24]

Luther is drawing from tradition too in this specific interpretation, especially from Ambrose and Augustine.[25] Answering those who wonder how Paul as a baptized person could be engaged in this struggle, Luther builds on Augustine's concept that baptism extinguishes the guilt but that the proclivity to sin remains; thus Paul, like all Christians, is engaged in this battle with sin.[26] When the apostle states, "For I do not do the good I want, but the evil I do not want is what I keep on doing" (Rom 7:19), Luther understands the dilemma as Paul's motive or desire to produce works or to try to do them being confounded by his inability actually to accomplish the good, which is possible only through Spirit-induced love.[27] Luther does not deny this work of the Holy Spirit in the life of a believer, but his emphasis is on the Christian life that struggles with the desire to sin. Both realities, the negative and positive, exist simultaneously in the same person, not as "two successive stages but two different aspects, two

22. AC XII.7–8 (K-W, 45).
23. *Lectures on Romans*, 1516 (AE 25:62–66; WA 56:69.17–73.26).
24. *Against Latomus*, 1521 (AE 32:248; WA 8:120.36–40).
25. *Lectures on Romans*, 1516 (AE 25:261, 341; WA 56:273.6–74.2; 352.22–54.13).
26. *Against Latomus*, 1521 (AE 32:251; WA 8:122.1–21).
27. *Lectures on Romans*, 1516 (AE 25:64; WA 56:71.13–18).

contemporaneous realities, of the Christian life, both of which continue so long as the Christian is in the flesh."[28] Only this interpretation can hold chapters 7 and 8 together. "The new has not yet wholly swallowed up the old, there is still a significant degree of continuity between man's state prior to faith and his state under faith."[29] It is impossible for a Christian to live without sinning, even if he is no longer under the dominion of sin and the Law because of Christ.

In explaining the sinner-and-saint dialectic, Luther offers two helpful illustrations. The first is that of a sick person who is on the mend. The sick human, he points out, is the Levite lying at the side of the road in the parable of the Good Samaritan:

> When the Samaritan had poured wine and oil on his wounds, he did not immediately recover, but he began to do so. Thus, our sick human is both weak and getting well. Insofar as he is healthy, he desires to do good, but as a sick person he wants something else and is compelled to yield to his illness, which he himself does not actually want to do.[30]

Luther's second example is that of a house that is in disrepair and at the same time under construction:

> Suppose that a house which has fallen into disrepair is in the process of reconstruction, is then its construction and present condition one thing and its state of disrepair something else? It is one and the same thing. It can be said of the same house that because of its being under construction it is a house and that it is in the process of becoming a house, but because of its incompleteness it can at the same time be said that it is not yet a house and that it lacks what is proper to a house.[31]

In both illustrations Luther looks at the human as both a sinner and righteous here and now. He depicts a Christian not primarily as someone who progresses in his faith, leaving sin behind. A sick human is a sick human even when his remedy is underway. Yet because of the remedy provided, Luther is not wholly denying that a Christian is on the mend. A believer in Christ receives righteousness outside of himself (*extra se*, Rom 7:25). He is beginning to be healthy or is healthy in hope. But once a person is healthy he does not need the doctor: here the metaphors break down. Luther says that because concupiscence rears its ugly head, the saints are "like sick men under the care of a physician."[32]

---

28. C. E. B. Cranfield, *A Critical and Exegetical Commentary on the Epistle to the Romans*, The International Critical Commentary on the Holy Scriptures of the Old and New Testaments 28, 6th ed. (Edinburgh: T&T Clark, 1975–79), 1:356; Jürgen Roloff, *Neues Testament*, Neukirchener Arbeitsbücher, 4th ed. (Neukirchen-Vluyn: Neukirchener Verlag, 1985), 159; Werner Georg Kümmel, *Römer 7 und die Bekehrung des Paulus*, Untersuchungen zum Neuen Testament 17 (Leipzig: J. C. Hinrichs, 1929), 98.

29. James D. G. Dunn, "Rom. 7,14–25 in the Theology of Paul," *Theologische Zeitschrift* 31, no. 5 (1975): 270; Michael Paul Middendorf, *The "I" in the Storm: A Study of Romans 7* (St. Louis: Concordia Academic Press, 1997), 203, 208.

30. *Lectures on Romans*, 1516 (AE 25:340; WA 56:351.18–22).

31. *Lectures on Romans*, 1516 (AE 25:341; WA 56:352.13–17).

32. *Lectures on Romans*, 1516 (AE 25:336; WA 56:347.11–12).

Since Luther sees the Good Samaritan as Jesus, he wants the Christian always to be dependent on the Doctor and never separated from Him. Given that struggle, the mindset of a Christian always is attuned to God's gracious gift of righteousness bestowed from outside of himself through the Word, a point Luther intended to make with his famous last words: "We are beggars. That is true."[33] Since Luther insisted on this theological point, we consider Romans 7 a suitable paradigm depicting the state of a Christian believer.[34]

The point of contention, which in recent literature has been debated again,[35] is whether Rom 7:14–25 actually depicts a postbaptismal situation, as Luther so clearly stated above in *Against Latomus* and earlier in his *Lectures on Romans*. Does the "I" describe a Christian, including Paul himself, or does it refer to a person prior to his baptism and his coming to faith, and thus describe a situation in which he no longer finds himself? The question relates not only to the idea and power of concupiscence but also to the function or use of the Law. The Law is presented in this passage from a very negative perspective, as it convicts sin. The question for many scholars is whether that negative function of the Law applies also in the life of a Christian who has been freed from the Law's dominion and ultimate conviction. Of course, this is not entirely an antinomian issue but is related to the question on the use of the Law.

In the light of Paul's far more positive descriptions of a Christian in other passages such as Romans 6 and 8:1–4, 9–17, and Gal 2:20, some scholars have qualified the convicting nature of Romans 7.[36] It seems, they would say, that Paul does factor in the possibility of a Christian's disobedience against God and being judged by God (1 Cor 4:4), but not in the sense that a Christian remains enslaved to sin and under constant accusation. Phrases like "sold under sin" (Rom 7:14), "For I know that nothing good dwells in me" (v. 18), and "Wretched man that I am!" (v. 24) are not descriptions of a Christian as Luther would want him to be. Nicholas Thomas (N. T.) Wright's antipathy toward Lutheranism is well known, and as a proponent of the New Perspective on Paul he views Calvin as a more positive interpreter of Moses and the Old Testament Law as a "covenantal nomism," according to which the Law is not seen as negative once you are in the covenant relationship with God. According to Wright this view agrees with Calvin's interpretation, but not with Luther's, of Paul's relationship with the Law.[37]

33. *Luther's Last Observation Left in a Note*, 1546 (AE 54:476; WATr 5:318.2–3).

34. Jenson, *Gravity of Sin*, 52.

35. To be sure, debate on Romans 7 occurred also prior to 1900. Middendorf, *The "I" in the Storm*, 265–75.

36. And yet Rom 8:23 resonates with much of what Rom 7:24 indicates: this is a "not-yet" situation that implies a struggle for all of creation, including humans.

37. "If we have to choose between Luther and Calvin, we must in my judgment choose Calvin every time, for both theological and exegetical reasons." N. T. Wright, *Justification: God's Plan & Paul's Vision* (Downers Grove: IVP Academic, 2009), 73.

The New Perspective in this case is a Johnny-come-lately, for Paul Althaus had adopted this view previously, led by Adolf Schlatter, Ernst Käsemann,[38] Rudolf Bultmann, Werner Georg Kümmel, and Jürgen Roloff.[39] These all take Rom 7:14–25 to apply to a prefaith or prebaptismal status for Paul and all unregenerate generally. They assert that in this passage Paul is reflecting on his former pre-Christian state and how he dealt with life in sin. The "I" is the trans-subjective "I" of a pre-Christian, from the perspective of someone who is now in Christ. It is the "I" that identifies itself with Adam's sin of coveting in Genesis 3 (Rom 7:7ff.) and is convicted by the Law in the Tenth Commandment, "Thou shall not covet."

The Law does indeed convict the sinner; but does it convict him only in his prebaptized, non-Christian state? The verses immediately preceding the passage in Rom 7:9–11 present the Law of God as good, holy, and righteous (Rom 7:12), but also as revealing sin and convicting the sinner. This negative function of the Law reflects a negative nature inherent not to the Law itself but to the sinful person relating to it.[40] As the immutable and holy will of God, the Law cannot tolerate the sin of the human and so functions as the custodian, to reveal and condemn. This principle applies not only to the life of Paul before his conversion but to all people. Paul's apology of the Law, if one may call it that,[41] begins with Rom 7:9–11; the Law takes on a universal dimension that encompasses all people, the Jew living under the Law (Rom 2:1–29) and also Gentiles—all descendants of Adam (Rom 5:12–21). Once the Law enters the life of a Jew or a heathen, it brings to light the sin that had not been so apparent, as Paul confesses: "I was once alive apart from the law, but when the commandment came, sin came alive and I died" (Rom 7:9).[42]

Here we must note two points about the Law. First, what Paul does not say is that sin existed only once the Law was revealed. The Law does not cause sin and is not its source; it only reveals sin. Sin has been there since the beginning and determines the reality of humanity (see Rom 5:13: "Sin indeed was in the world before the law was given, but sin is not counted where there is no law"). According to Paul, sin originates with the human himself (Rom 5:12: "Sin came into the world through one man"). No further explanation of sin's origin is given, lest the human seek to excuse himself. In no way did the Law bring the

38. Ernst Käsemann, *An die Römer*, Handbuch zum Neuen Testament 8a, 2d ed. (Tübingen: Mohr, 1974), 193.

39. See here Karl Heinrich Rengstorf and Ulrich Luck, eds., *Das Paulusbild in der neueren deutschen Forschung*, Wege der Forschung 24 (Darmstadt: Wissenschaftliche Buchgesellschaft, 1964), 1–97.

40. See here SD IV.16, 23 (K-W, 577–78); Middendorf, *The "I" in the Storm*, 242, 262.

41. The question is whether rightfully to call it an apology as scholars do, since the Law is "put in its place" and given a role, yet a qualified one. Middendorf, *The "I" in the Storm*, 242, 262.

42. "'I was alive' apart from the law could only mean living apart from heightened awareness of the nature of sin and its consequences." Andrew John Bandstra, *The Law and the Elements of the World: An Exegetical Study in Aspects of Paul's Teaching* (Kampen: J. H. Kok, 1964), 137; Middendorf, *The "I" in the Storm*, 80.

reality of sin into this world; instead, it keeps all humans tied to sin and holds them in it. Its purpose is that "sin might be shown to be sin" (Rom 7:13). Thus Gal 3:24 now makes sense: the Law functions as a custodian (παιδαγωγός, *paidagōgos*) and slave master that keeps the human in custody until the coming of Christ and binds him to a conduct against God and lets him sin further, for every attempt of the human to keep the Law fails. The Law reveals all deeds as sin, since the acting subject is not the "I" that agrees with the will of God but rather sin itself.

Second, the Law that should serve as a positive means to salvation now has become the accuser and reveals the unholy state of the human. The Law objectively exposes the desperate situation of the human because he cannot fufill what God demands. With the coming of Christ the Law has no function to serve as savior (Gal 3:21): He brings salvation that no longer can be found in the Law. He has displayed an obedience fulfilling the demands of the Law by not sinning (Rom 10:4) and through His death took the judgment and curse formerly directed at us humans (Gal 3:10–14).[43] In this way Christ takes over the Law's place, and in its place He now becomes the goal and provider of God's righteousness.[44] It is important therefore to understand that the role of the Law has changed significantly: it no longer offers salvation; its demands have been fulfilled by Christ, and it cannot be regarded as the means to salvation. In the Adam–Christ typology of Rom 5:12–21, Adam has created a situation for all humans, one marred by sin, so now Christ through His obedience creates a new sphere of righteousness for all who belong to Him (Gal 5:19). The believer is brought into a relationship with Christ through the Holy Spirit so that he walks not according to the flesh but according to the Spirit, "in order that the righteous requirement of the law might be fulfilled in us" (Rom 8:4). This change leads also to a fundamental functional distinction between Law and Gospel: the Law does not promise salvation but places demands on the person, while the Gospel offers salvation as the promise of the gift of righteousness (Rom 3:21).

This description reflects an understanding of the verses prior to Rom 7:14–25, namely verses 7–11, that points to a past experience where those who did not know the Law or truly recognize their sin have come to recognize it because the Law now reveals it. However, it would be an error to assume that the situation described in verses 14–25 no longer pertains to the converted Paul, who speaks on behalf of himself and all Christians. Already the switch to

43. As also indicated in SD III.9, 56 (K-W, 563, 572).

44. Wright, *Justification*, 73. The point we need to add is that Christ's coming is also not a mere plan B but that He actually fulfilled the Law, God's own will. Paul himself points to the new era ("But now," Rom 3:21) as one where God Himself chose to come in Christ. Christ comes because sin entered into the world and the Law exposes God's displeasure with sin. This perception explains why God has revealed His wrath against humanity, of which Paul speaks (Rom 1:18ff.). There surely must be a reason for God's wrath, but Barth and Wright would have difficulty explaining it unless they agreed that God gave humans the Law as a rebuke for their sin.

the present-tense narrative leads us to understand that Paul is speaking of his current and not a past situation. Thus, the point Paul makes is that though all Christians are free from the dominion and final condemnation of the Law, they still battle with the reality of sin in their lives, and as a result the Law enters into its negative role of revealing and condemning that sin. In Luther's sense the condemning nature of the Law is more than a reality of a prebaptismal situation. In other words, the struggle is real and the Law's conviction of sin continues. In this function it serves in its "foremost office."[45] In an extensive presentation on the text Martin Luther concludes that the "I" cannot be an unbeliever, for that struggle against sin is "never heard of in the case of the carnal man,"[46] and thus he posits his famous description of a Christian's existence:

> The saints at the same time as they are righteous are also sinners [quod simul Sancti, dum sunt Iusti, sunt peccatores]; righteous because they believe in Christ, whose righteousness covers them and is imputed to them, but sinners because they do not fulfill the Law, are not without concupiscence, and are like sick men under the care of a physician.[47]

In this sense Rom 7:14–25 speaks to the life of every Christian, reminding him of his total dependence on Christ as his righteousness, making the life of a Christian not a pursuit of holiness in terms of fulfilling the will of God but acknowledging his need for the righteousness of Christ and the killing of the old Adam.[48] If a Christian's life were to be fashioned after the positive descriptions in Romans 6 and 8 alone, he would be tempted to shift his focus from Christ to his own self and his renewed abilities, opening the back door for the Old Adam to enter and inject a notion of self-achieved morality.[49] The Formula of Concord senses this danger and shuts the door that might support an antinomianism: "For this reason, too, believers require the teaching of the law: so that they do not fall back on their own holiness and piety and under the appearance of

45. SA III.ii.4 (K-W, 312).

46. *Lectures on Romans*, 1516 (AE 25:335; WA 56:346.15).

47. *Lectures on Romans*, 1516 (AE 25:336; WA 56:347.9–12).

48. Sanctification thus is not a striving of the self toward holiness, now that God has justified the sinner. That arrangement resembles a trade-off or pact with God: He acts first (justification) and then I do my part (sanctification). To be made holy is a gift; it means to be worked on by the Holy Spirit, which includes killing the Old Adam so that good works may flow. Read here Gerhard O. Forde, "The Lutheran View," in *Christian Spirituality: Five Views of Sanctification*, ed. Donald Alexander (Downers Grove, IL: InterVarsity Press, 1988), 13–32, 42–43.

49. Käsemann concludes otherwise. In the light of chapters 6 and 8, Rom 7:14–25 cannot even be descriptive of Paul's conversion experience ("nicht einmal als Inhalt der Bekehrungserfahrung des Apostels"). Käsemann, *An die Römer*, 192. Käsemann and others who take his position are not antinomians: to be that they would have to deny the Law's second use. But in understanding Rom 7:14–25 as pre-Christian they certainly soften the blow of its second use, because to them the reality of enslavement to sin is no longer so severe in a Christian's life. Kümmel concludes, for example, that in the light of Rom 8:1–4 a Christian no longer lives under the Law, thus he also no longer lives in bondage to sin ("Sündenknechtschaft"), *Römer 7*, 73. Thus he concludes that Romans 7 is a description of a non-Christian from the perspective of a Christian ("Denn es ist richtig, daß wir in Röm. 7 eine Schilderung des Nichtchristen vom christlichen Standtpunkt aus haben."), *Römer 7*, 138. See Middendorf, *The "I" in the Storm*, 203.

God's Spirit establish their own service to God on the basis of their own choice, without God's Word or command."[50]

But because Romans 7 is juxtaposed with chapters 6 and 8, the Confessions start off on a positive note. Since Christians are "born again . . . and set free from the law . . . , they live according to the unchanging will of God, as comprehended in the law, and do everything, insofar as they are reborn, from a free and merry spirit."[51] And yet they continue to reflect also the concerns of chapter 7:

> However, since believers in this world are not perfectly renewed—the old creature clings to them down to the grave—the battle between spirit and flesh continues in them. . . . To this extent they are never without the law, and at the same time they are not under the law but in the law; they live and walk in the law of the Lord and yet do nothing because of the compulsion of the law.[52]

The anthropological dualism portrayed in this quotation reminds the Christian of his continual battle with sin and encourages him not to succumb to it. As Paul himself knows in his current situation, the battle is real; thus he issues a twofold warning for Christians, to recognize first that they are unable to fulfill the Law's demands (and that they are thus always sinful), and second that they cannot rely on the observance of the Law as a way to obtain or maintain their righteousness (Rom 8:3–4). Fortunately, while the Law reveals this continual struggle and a Christian's susceptibility to sin, it no longer holds any condemnation over those who are in Christ (Rom 8:1). The righteousness of Christ, the mercy and grace of God as revealed through the Gospel apart from the Law, now makes the difference (Rom 3:28).[53]

In conclusion to this section, we hold that this interpretation of Romans 7 is not trivial but impacts a core issue of theological anthropology: that the believer lives his spirituality in the context of his justification and the forgiveness received because of Christ alone. In this view life thus reflects the daily reality of a *transitus* from sinner to saint and is shaped by Law and Gospel. The Law must remain to incite the believer to pray and to keep him spiritually thirsty and hungry for grace. According to Luther, to do away with the Law also would require us to abolish the Lord's Prayer and our petition "Hallowed be Thy name," since we would be holy already and not in need of holiness. The same stipulation would apply to the petition "Forgive us our trespasses," since they would no longer exist. The most important function of the Law would be its second use, the *usus theologicus*, that keeps the believer focused on Christ and the Gospel and never lets him fall back into a self-assured state that knows of no sin or knows only little of it.[54]

50. SD VI.20 (K-W, 590).
51. SD VI.17 (K-W, 590).
52. SD VI.18 (K-W, 590).
53. Middendorf, *The "I" in the Storm*, 264.
54. Wilfried Joest, *Gesetz und Freiheit: Das Problem des Tertius usus legis bei Luther und die neutestamentliche Parainese*, 4th ed. (Göttingen: Vandenhoeck und Ruprecht, 1968), 62.

In an incisive essay Martin Härle levels criticism against the anthropology of the New Perspective, which he claims drives a wedge between Luther and Paul by stating that Paul never understands the Law as negatively as Luther does. According to scholars like Sanders, Luther imposes on Paul the existential crises he himself experienced as a monk and makes Paul out to be anti-Jewish and a hater of the Law. Härle instead sees the reality of sin in the life of the believer as a reality shared by Paul and Luther. The *fomes concupiscentiae* (tinder of concupiscence) or passion is sin and not just "potentially the entryway to sin."[55] Reading Romans 7 in the light of that view, Härle observes that Paul and Luther hold a common understanding of sin's power. He concludes: "Thus, I find it hard to see any huge or fundamental difference between Paul and Luther on the relationship between being a Christian and sin."[56] Even if Romans 7 does not represent all that can be said about man and sin, it does frame anthropology in the light of justification, and in doing so offers a realistic perspective. This view, according to Härle, "localizes the issue of sin and justification in the human heart, the center of all emotions, will, and thought, a center which human beings themselves cannot control or change on their own, yet which determines their whole feeling, willing, thinking, and acting."[57]

This understanding of Romans 7 makes clear that justification must be the starting point of theological anthropology, a recognition that further shapes the interpretation of this passage. To frame the chapter in a preconversion/prefaith/pre-Christian context most likely ascribes to salvation a sanitizing effect, in which justification not only forgives the sin but actually removes it as a persistent force in the believer's life. As one scholar points out, sin's reality then is as unfortunate as a coffee stain on a shirt—an observation that recalls the Confessions' dismissal of the positions either that sin no longer exists in the life of reborn Christians or that they will not lose the Holy Spirit.[58] Moreover, the question arises: to what extent does the believer live under the cross and forgiveness if in his Christian life sin no longer grasps him? The forensic imputative concept, on the other hand, clearly upholds a life under the cross and a dependence on daily forgiveness. Justification wipes away sin and imparts forgiveness but does not remove the reality of sin, nor of God's Law which exposes it. While the believer remains engaged in a battle against sin all his life, he now is assured that he has the Holy Spirit on his side (Romans 8), and that by relying on the Spirit he will be vindicated of sin on the Last Day.

55. Härle, *Dogmatik*, 20; Jenson, *Gravity of Sin*, 54.

56. My translation. "Insofern fällt es mir auch hinsichtlich der Verhältnisbestimmung von Christsein und Sünde schwer zwischen Paulus und Luther eine erhebliche oder gar eine grundsätzliche Differenz festzustellen." Härle, *Dogmatik*, 19.

57. Härle, *Dogmatik*, 21.

58. AC XII.7–8 (K-W, 45).

THE DOMINION OF SPIRIT AND FLESH: BATTLE AND PROGRESS

These descriptions of a Christian caught in a struggle with sin raise the question whether or not he can progress in his spirituality. While a Christian continues to battle with sin throughout his life, is there not also a more positive aspect to his life, namely, a growth in righteousness and a decrease in sinful behavior? One would expect such growth in moral behavior as he abstains from certain acts of sin that were committed previously. After all, Luther intimates this point with the statement "Holiness has begun and is growing daily."[59]

The first consideration about sin's rule or power is that we must look at the human being holistically. Though we might be inclined to divide the person into two entities, on the one side the body battling with sin and on the other the soul free from sin, Luther in speaking of the dichotomy between spirit and flesh implies that they constitute one whole being (*totus homo*). In his *Lectures on Romans* Luther tackles Rom 7:14ff. and points out that where spirit and flesh are set in opposition, each applies to the entire person and his life: *caro*, or flesh "is a total lack of uprightness and of the power of all the faculties both of body and soul and of the whole inner and outer man."[60] One's body serves as the organ through which sin acts, taking hold of it and leading it to commit a wrongful act (Rom 6:6; Col 3:5). However, the source of sin is attributed neither to our sensual capacities nor to our earthly bodily nature; it must be located somewhere else. Hollaz says, "The primary seat of sin with its faculties, acts, and habit is the soul, and the secondary seat is the body."[61]

Likewise, Luther sees the entire person gripped by the Spirit and living in it. Using Paul as an illustration of this duality, Luther demonstrates how one lives in two different relationships, one under spiritual grace and one under carnal influence.[62]

In speaking of flesh we must discern properly between its different senses. Flesh can refer to everything that stands in opposition to the Spirit and therefore be treated negatively, or it can refer simply to the body in a more neutral sense.[63] This distinction is crucial when it comes to Christ's incarnation. When "the Word became flesh" (σάρξ, *sarx*; Jn 1:14; Rom 8:3) He became human by taking on a body, but this does not mean that Christ had flesh in the sense of the

59. LC II.58 (K-W, 438).

60. *Lectures on Romans*, 1516 (AE 25:299; WA 56:312.8–10). See also AE 25:332–33; WA 56:341.27–42.29.

61. Hollaz, *Examen Theologicum Acroamaticum*, 525: "Sedes primaria peccati originalis est anima cum facultatibus suis a): sedes secundaria est corpus cum suis membris." See also 498.

62. Here "is the one man Paul, who recognizes himself to be in two different relationships: under grace, he is spiritual, but under the law, carnal. It is one and the same Paul who is under both." *Against Latomus*, 1521 (AE 32:246; WA 8:119.14–16).

63. Luther looks beyond Paul at all of Scripture and offers these two important clarifications of a potential confusion about the body (σῶμα, *soma*) and its association with flesh (σάρξ). *Bondage of the Will*, 1525 (AE 33:215; WA 18:735.34–35).

negative force in a person dictated by sin, which makes a human "carnal, sold under sin" (Rom 7:14; cf. 7:19), working against God.[64] Specifically in reference to Paul's anthropology, Luther argues that the believer after baptism, like Paul, is subjected to a struggle between spirit and flesh. Flesh stands for "the 'old' or 'external' human *in toto* who is turned away in hostility to God." And spirit is "the 'new' or 'internal' human *in toto* who is friends with God."[65] Because of these two realities impacting his life, the believer finds himself on both sides of the battle, yet he always remains one and the same person, "the whole man."[66]

In almost deterministic fashion Luther describes a believer's spiritual struggle. There is no room to decide for himself, "no freedom of decision, no opportunity for self-determination,"[67] because for him a battle is taking place between two powers outside of his own self. In *The Bondage of the Will* (1525) Luther uses the famous illustration of a beast of burden lodged between two masters who are wrestling over it:

> Thus the human will is placed between the two like a beast of burden. If God rides it, it wills and goes where God wills, as the psalm says: "I am become as a beast [before thee] and I am always with thee" (Ps. 73:22 f.). If Satan rides it, it wills and goes where Satan wills; nor can it choose to run to either of the two riders or to seek him out, but the riders themselves contend for the possession and control of it.[68]

In the tradition of Galatians (especially chapter 5) and Romans (mainly chapter 7), Luther makes two contributions to anthropology. On the one side, he acknowledges with Paul the need not to underestimate the terrifying force of sin that resides as an incredible power in the heart of a believer. On the other side, he points to the believer's successful attempt, because of Christ's grace, to distance himself from sin and to act upon or against it. He describes the struggle between these two powers in order to warn the believer never to let his guard down and underestimate the alluring power of sin "which remains after baptism."[69] Both aspects pertain to the life of a Christian.

But which of the two predominates? Can the spirit rule over the flesh and control it? By being a spiritual person under grace, the believer is assured the final vindication over the shadows of death in spite of the powers of sin. Luther in his rebuttal *Against Latomus* (1521), in which he offers some of his central ideas on the relationship of sin and grace, Law and Gospel, and justification and sanctification, draws a distinction with references to Gn 4:7 and Rom 6:12 between "the sin which reigns" (*peccatum regnans*) and "the sin which does not reign" (*peccatum regnatum*).[70] He cites the penitential psalms and the

64. Rom 8:5–7, 12–13; Gal 5:16–20.

65. Jenson, *Gravity of Sin*, 67.

66. *Lectures on Romans*, 1516 (AE 25:340–41; WA 56:352.6).

67. Heiko A. Oberman, *Luther: Man between God and the Devil*, trans. Eileen Walliser-Schwarzbart (New Haven: Yale University Press, 1989), 219.

68. *Bondage of the Will*, 1525 (AE 33:65–66; WA 18:635.17–22).

69. *Against Latomus*, 1521 (AE 32:251; WA 8:122.36); Peters, *Der Mensch*, 41.

70. "At least this phrase, 'sin which reigns,' is not my invention, but is cited from Paul. Call

Sermon on the Mount to elaborate on the deep powers of sin and the strenuous warfare in which the Christian is engaged. Such sin can be overcome in the godly because God's mercy and grace abound. Because of the "magnitude of the gift and grace of God," evil thoughts, though just as strong in the godly as in the ungodly, do not damn the former as they do the latter. Both groups sin, but the godly have an antidote, the grace of God. Thus, "if grace were lacking, sin would truly damn, but now grace prevents it from damning evil nature."[71] Theologians such as Baier follow Luther on this point.[72]

Wilfried Joest further clarifies the two realities in the life of a Christian by distinguishing two stages in which a believer finds himself. This is a helpful distinction. The constant reality of sin in the believer's life as Luther described it belongs to the *transitus* stage, whereas the already existing renewal applies to the *progressus* stage. The idea of a *transitus* speaks to the believer's state in which he passively receives Christ's righteousness. This state is what Luther calls the existence as total sinner and as total saint at the same time, and the sinful Christian remains always dependent on receiving forgiveness entirely as Christ's righteousness. The *progressus* stage, on the other hand, relates to the idea of a progression in the moral or second righteousness, of "growing daily" in one's sanctification. Both aspects pertain, but the understanding of life as *transitus* dominates in Luther's theology over the idea of *progressus*. Luther remains adamant about sin's power and rule in the life of a Christian, pointing to David's fall into adultery, murder, and blasphemy against God—at which point faith and the Holy Spirit have departed.[73] In this *progressus* stage thus "we remain only halfway pure and holy,"[74] and consequently throughout the duration of our earthly life we remain wholly focused on the forgiveness received from God. Since the rise of pietism in the seventeeth century many Protestant theologians have approached Christian spirituality differently than Luther by affirming this second stage more strongly, claiming for saints a perseverance out of which they will never fall, or claiming that they are guilty and corrupt only when they

---

the other kind, which does not reign, by whatever name you please, although Gen. 4[:7] favors me: 'Its desire shall be under you, and you shall master it.' Here subjugated sin is certainly described. . . . If you consent to this [sin], you have made sin to reign, you serve it and have sinned mortally. From this point of view I have already recalled often enough what Paul says in Rom. 6[:12], and from this I will not allow myself to be separated. I say that they cannot deny that two evil things survive baptism, sin and its passions." *Against Latomus*, 1521 (AE 32:213–14; WA 8:96.20–34). See also this quotation: "Sin is here said to be conquered, even though rebellious, while in other places it is described as a reigning conqueror. It is everywhere absolutely the same, even though it does not everywhere have the same strength, or the same mode of acting or of being acted upon." *Against Latomus*, 1521 (AE 32:248; WA 8:120.24–26).

71. *Against Latomus*, 1521 (AE 32:252; WA 8:123.14–15).

72. In reference to Rom 6:12, Baier also states that in some people inherent sin rules and in others it does not. For the latter this is possible through the grace of God (*per gratiam Dei*), and they represent the liberated human (*homo liberior factus*) who does not walk according to the flesh but according to the Spirit (Rom 8:11). Baier, *Compendium Theologiae Positivae*, 318–19.

73. SA III.iii.44 (K-W, 319).

74. LC II.37–38 (K-W, 438).

choose to sin.[75] This focus on the second stage or the postconversion holiness shifts away from the principled Lutheran outlook on the first stage, that of finding righteousness before God as a gift through Christ.[76]

THE ISSUE OF THE UNFREE WILL OR ITS BONDAGE

An important question related to original sin's consequences is to what degree and at what level humans are in possession of free will as they live out their daily lives in this world. Was the Fall so destructive that it eradicated all ideas of freedom for humans, or do their actions still spring from a use of the free will? The postulate that humans have no free will is deterministic, a direction Lutheranism does not take because it rules out responsibility and accountability. Though it is often said that Luther's treatise on *The Bondage of the Will* tends toward a deterministic position, there is no indication that human responsibility and use of the free will "in things below" is dismissed. Luther's focus is on the "things above," "the things that lead to eternal salvation," and the spiritual implications for humans there.[77]

Some philosophers have indulged such a path, however, including Baruch (Benedict de) Spinoza (1632–77), who is known for taking a deterministic approach on the use of the free will according to his principle of immanent necessitarianism.[78] For him, "free choice" represents the possibility for a human to choose to act other than he actually did. He repudiates this idea of free choice and further dismisses any account of will or desire that would support a credible notion of free choice. "In the mind," he argues, "there is no absolute or free will; but the mind is determined to wish this or that by a cause, which has also been determined by another cause, and this last by another cause, and so

75. Michael S. Horton, "Are Churches Secularizing America?" *Modern Reformation* 17, no. 2 (2008): 43. According to George Barna in his book *The Second Coming of the Church*, "Eighty-two percent of Americans (and a majority of evangelicals) believe that Benjamin Franklin's aphorism, 'God helps those who help themselves,' is a biblical quotation. A majority believe . . . that 'if a person is generally good or does enough good things for others during their life, they will earn a place in heaven.'" George Barna, *The Second Coming of the Church* (Nashville: Word Publishing, 1998), 21–22. This analysis is corroborated by a study of American youth, whose spirituality is said to entertain a moralistic therapeutism in which "God wants people to be good, nice, and fair to each other" and "the central goal of life is to be happy and to feel good about oneself." See Christian Smith and Melinda Lundquist Denton, *Soul Searching: The Religious and Spiritual Lives of American Teenagers* (New York: Oxford University Press, 2005), 162–63.

76. Joest, *Gesetz und Freiheit*, 55–62; Oswald Bayer, *Martin Luther's Theology: A Contemporary Interpretation*, trans. Thomas H. Trapp (Grand Rapids: Wm. B. Eerdmans, 2008), 291.

77. *Bondage of the Will*, 1525 (AE 33:105; WA 18:663.12–18); Oberman, *Luther*, 224.

78. In *Ethics* 1p29 Spinoza defines necessity as follows: "Nothing in the universe is contingent, but all things are conditioned [one could also translate "have been determined"] to exist and operate in a particular manner by the necessity of the divine nature." This means that Spinoza's determinism, translated here as "conditioned," is defined by the immanent laws of nature or God. Benedict de Spinoza, *The Ethics*, in *The Chief Works of Benedict de Spinoza*, trans. R. H. M. Elwes (New York: Dover Publications, 1951), 2:68. Sections in the *Ethics* are given by part number, then the number of the definition (d) or proposition (p).

on to infinity."[79] The very idea of free choice is the illusory result of inadequate knowledge. "Men believe themselves to be free," he writes, "simply because they are conscious of their actions, and unconscious of the causes whereby those actions are determined."[80] That includes the "bondage" humans experience in the passions and emotions (desire, love, hate, fear) caused in them, which they passively endure.[81] Spinoza supports that determinism with an oft-quoted illustration in his *Ethics*:

> Thus an infant believes that of its own free will it desires milk, an angry child believes that it freely desires vengeance, a timid child believes that it freely desires to run away; further, a drunken man believes that he utters from the free decision of his mind words which, when he is sober, he would willingly have withheld: thus, too, a delirious man, a garrulous women, a child, and others of like complexion, believe that they speak from the free decision of their mind, when they are in reality unable to restrain their impulse to talk.[82]

Against this misconception Spinoza defines true freedom as the absence of any coercion to yield to an outside power or authority that contradicts one's own true being.[83] For Spinoza, God alone is the completely free being who does not contradict Himself in what He does, and He is the only free cause in the universe who determines everything else: "God acts solely by the laws of his own nature, and is not constrained by anyone."[84]

The issue that seems to be unaccounted for in determinism is that of personal responsibility. If our will is determined by external causes, and if all happens by necessity from the nature of God, then how are we accountable for our actions? How can we be said to have genuine autonomy over our behavior? From a Christian and ethical point of view, the whole concept of guilt is rooted in personal accountability.

Spinoza seems to be aware of that problem, and he attempts to answer by saying that God grants a certain degree of autonomy or freedom to humans: through the use of their reason they have a certain degree of causal power, but less than God's.[85] With the use of reason one can attain intuitive knowledge, a deepened knowledge of God or contentment of the mind, in what he calls the stage of blessedness. "The human mind cannot be absolutely destroyed

79. Spinoza, *Ethics*, 119 (2p48).

80. Spinoza, *Ethics*, 134 (3p2 Note).

81. Spinoza, *Ethics*, 168 (3p56).

82. Spinoza, *Ethics*, 134 (3p2 Note).

83. "That thing is called free, which exists solely by the necessity of its own nature, and of which the action is determined by itself alone. On the other hand, that thing is necessary, or rather constrained, which is determined by something external to itself to a fixed and definite method of existence or action." Spinoza, *Ethics*, 46 (1d7).

84. Spinoza, *Ethics*, 59 (1p17); Melchert, *Great Conversation*, 443.

85. Hannah Laurens, "Finite in Infinity: Spinoza's Conception of Human Freedom Explained through His Metaphysics," *Stance: An International Undergraduate Philosophy Journal* 5 (April 2012): 103.

with the body, but there remains of it something which is eternal."[86] He thus associates with the human mind a certain freedom to engage and attune itself metaphysically in speaking to God.[87]

This glimpse into the mind of a philosopher like Spinoza is indicative of how humans attempt to come to grips with the existence and extent of the free will. It is true that freedom in the absolute sense exists only with God. He possesses freedom in the highest sense because He has His existence from Himself (aseity), and we cannot claim that God would choose to be something else. That would contradict His entire being. No power can force God into desiring or doing something that would contradict who He is. In contrast, humans can have only relative freedom, because as created beings their living conditions have been set by God, and the parameters within which they act and make their decisions also have been arranged by God. As long as humans remained in these parameters arranged for them—and that would be only in their original state of innocence—they could want to do only what God wills and demands.

In philosophical theology, the discussion of the freedom to act and culpability distinguishes between formal and material freedom—the abilities to will and to do. In the material freedom the agent is able to carry out his will—he can effectuate the volition—whereas in the formal freedom the agent possesses free will apart from recognizing the choice. Adam before the Fall had formal freedom in a free will, for example, and material freedom in the further ability to act upon what he chose to do formally.[88] According to his formal freedom, however, he also had the freedom to choose not to go through with an action. Adam abused and thus forfeited his formal freedom by choosing not to obey God and thereby fell into sin. As a result, he broke the connection that existed between him and God and lost the image of God along with real freedom, so that materially also he was no longer free. Culpability was imputed fully to Adam because cooperation in this instance was free and willed (directly intended). He intended formally to cooperate with evil and then went through with it. Since then man is able neither to choose nor to enact the good over evil. He may have good intentions not to cooperate with evil, but materially he has lost the power to do the good and to will it and has become a slave to sin. The will of the unregenerate resembles the situation of a prisoner who has freedom in every way imaginable except for one: he lacks the freedom to be outside of prison.

86. Spinoza, *Ethics*, 259 (5p23).

87. "The human mind is part of the infinite intellect of God; thus when we say, that the human mind perceives this or that, we make the assertion, that God has this or that idea, not in so far as he is infinite, but in so far as he is displayed through the nature of the human mind, or in so far as he constitutes the essence of the human mind." Spinoza, *Ethics*, 91 (2p11 Corollary); Laurens, "Finite in Infinity," 107.

88. Kevin Timpe, *Free Will in Philosophical Theology* (New York: Bloomsbury Publishing, 2014), 7.

The reformers did not go so far as to deny the existence and use of the free will in certain realms of human life. The Formula of Concord warns against deterministic thought that aligns itself with the ancient heresy of the Stoics and Manichaeans, "that the human being does everything by compulsion" and that "the human will has no freedom or capacity to practice outward righteousness."[89] The Formula rejects that position and also dismisses the other extreme position, the Pelagian claim that the unhindered use of the will merits God's grace.[90] Lutherans thus maintain that the will is free to decide among various options that pertain to arranging matters here on earth.[91] It can decide for or against external righteousness, but not for the righteousness that pertains to one's standing before God. Here we must distinguish between the righteousness of God (*iustitia Dei* or *spiritualis*) and civil righteousness (*iustitia civilis*). The latter represents the "piety of the world" that is appreciated by humans or the "carnal righteousness" (*iustitia carnis*) that can be fulfilled by the unregenerate (*natura carnalis*) by virtue of his reason and in the doing of individual works. The former has value before God, it is taught by the Holy Spirit, it eludes the unregenerate, and from it good works flow.[92]

This topic of the impact of the Fall on the will of man has spurred numerous theological and philosophical discussions on the free will. Some perspectives gravitate toward determinism, while others are more sympathetic to indeterminism, which states that the will or cooperation is not compelled deterministically by events or other outside circumstances. Taking into consideration both causal and noncausal explanations for human decision-making, it is safe to say that in general and on a daily basis, humans operate with the understanding that they have causal control over their own acts and that their decisions flow out of their own deliberations. Such a belief cannot dismiss the reality of underlying causes and what neuroscientists and other scientists have to say about them, but it does indicate people perceive they can make choices that are in line with their beliefs, preferences, and goals.[93] What then would qualify as a freely made act or choice? Three conditions typically have to be met for an act to be done freely: (1) there is more than one alternative from which one may choose ; (2) the agent or author of the act chooses without coercion; and (3) the choice is not made randomly but deliberately as a rational act.[94]

---

89. SD II.74 (K-W, 558). Among the Stoics were the famous philosophers Seneca and Cicero, both of whom were known for their deterministic worldviews.

90. SD II.75 (K-W, 558).

91. Gn 4:7; Rom 1:20; 2:14; 10:3; Phil 3:6.

92. Ez 11:19; Jn 8:36; Rom 6:20–22; Gal 5:1.

93. George Musser, "Yes, Determinists, There Is Free Will: You Make Choices Even If Your Atoms Don't," *Nautilus* 072 (13 May 2019), https://nautil.us/yes-determinists-there-is-free-will-237396/.

94. Andrea Lavazza, "Free Will and Neuroscience: From Explaining Freedom Away to New Ways of Operationalizing and Measuring It," *Frontiers in Human Neuroscience* 10 (2016), https://doi.org/10.3389/fnhum.2016.00262.

Regarding points two and three, it would be hard to deny that often a person cooperates with evil either under coercion or randomly or unknowingly without an explicit intention. This explains the theological interest in taking a closer look at actual sins and categorizing them, for example, as either voluntary or involuntary. Beyond this context, studies of the human brain indicate the unconscious domain also may influence the will in decision-making. Yet it would be quite another matter to deny free will altogether in all of these three points, not only as a theoretical claim but also in reality within society. Given that God's providential watch over creation is real and that He uses the human will and reason to arrange civil matters here on earth, we affirm the freedom of humans in their daily lives. However, we do so with one qualification: God and man walk alongside and cooperate with one another, albeit in such a way that humans submit themselves to God that His "will [may] be done."

10

THE ACTUAL SIN, OR THE SIN WE COMMIT

In considering what causes humans to err, misbehave, or sin, we know that the source for such ill behavior is original sin manifesting itself as the internal desire called concupiscence. These sins that reveal ill conduct against God's will and Word are actual sins, and we could define them as those that each human being actually commits both inwardly and externally, in word, deed, thought, and desire,[1] intentionally and unintentionally, by omission and commission. Martin Chemnitz defines them as follows: "'Actual' sins are the many internal things which war against the Law of God, against which nevertheless the reborn fight, also the many sins of ignorance and omission."[2] Philipp Melanchthon brought against Eck in the Colloquy of Worms in 1541 the following definition for actual sin:

> Sin is a defect or inclination or action conflicting with the Law of God, offending God, damned by God, and making us guilty of the eternal wrath of God and of present and eternal punishments, unless remission should occur on account of the Son, the Mediator.[3]

BREAKING GOD'S LAW

The framework and basic premise of Genesis 3 is that sin is a transgression of a law placed before Adam and Eve. As Hollaz puts it: "The sin of the first humans is the transgression of the law in paradise which forbade them to eat from the fruit of the tree of the knowledge of good and evil."[4] This framework sets the stage for the understanding that every human sin breaks the Law of God; it is lawlessness (ἀνομία, *anomia*). First John 3:4 points this out: "Everyone who makes a practice of sinning also practices lawlessness; sin is lawlessness." This νόμος or Law that is transgressed is God's own will, His unshakable and

---

1. Chemnitz and Gerhard, *Doctrine of Man*, 206. Hutter is no different in his definition: "Actual sin is every action, whether internal or external, which conflicts with the law of God; as in the mind, doubts concerning God; in the will and heart, the flames of wicked desires; and in the members, all motions and actions contrary to the divine law." Leonard Hutter, *Compend of Lutheran Theology*, trans. by Rev. H. E. Jacobs and Rev. G. F. Spieker (Philadelphia: The Lutheran Book Store, 1868), 69.

2. Chemnitz and Gerhard, *Doctrine of Man*, 198.

3. Gerhard, *Theological Commonplaces* 13.1.5 (12–14:101).

4. Hollaz, *Examen Theologicum Acroamaticum*, 507. Hollaz also makes this point earlier: "Peccatum *formaliter* consistit in privatione conformitatis cum lege divina" (501; sin formally consists in the lack of conformity with the divine Law). My translations.

immutable order. The apostle Paul speaks of sin as disobedience (παρακοή; Rom 5:19) against the holy will of God.

This conflict with God's Word and its abandonment negatively affects all facets of life: how one relates to one's own body, to a marriage partner, to fellow humans, and to the nonhuman species. Luther paints in vivid pictures the consequences of Adam's sin as they pertain to Eve as child-bearer and to Adam in the management and support of the household.[5] He points out actual sins as those which transgress the Ten Commandments, such as

> unbelief, false belief, idolatry, being without the fear of God, presumption, despair, blindness, and, in short, not knowing or honoring God. Beyond that there is lying, swearing [falsely] by God's name, not praying or calling on God's name, neglect of God's Word, being disobedient to parents, murdering, behaving promiscuously, stealing, deceiving, etc.[6]

The theologian Nicolaus Hunnius aptly summarizes:

> In short: every thought, lust and desire, every word, gesture, and every work, whatever may be their name,—as soon as they are contrary to the law of God, or to the love of God, be it wilfully or unintentionally, or be they large or small etc.—they all together are, without any distinction actual sin.[7]

Martin Chemnitz offers further clarification as he describes the continuity between original sin as this transpersonal power and the corruption of all humans from which come personal sinful acts. In reference to Mk 7:18–23, which says that from within, out of the heart, proceed evil thoughts, foolish things, pride, adulteries, and so forth, Chemnitz writes: "Christ clearly distinguishes, therefore, between the storehouse, that is, the intrinsic or original cause, or the origin itself, and the actions proceeding therefrom."[8] His image of the storehouse underscores that all humans have something within, from which come forth acts of evil. The storehouse (original sin) and the sins which ensue (actual sins) are not separate phenomena, as he points out in a traditional description of the stages of sin:

> (1) the tinder, or the inherent depravity, which embraces also the defects; (2) the suggestions of thoughts and emotions, that is, when the original depravity is stirred by some inclination; (3) the delight therein; (4) the consent; (5) the act itself.[9]

Chemnitz elaborates: "Of these stages the first two belong to original, the remaining three to actual sin."[10] He concludes with two important points that would eliminate any confusion: "(1) Original sin is not an inactive thing (*res otiosa*). (2) In original sin there are always present at the same time actual sins."[11]

5. *Lectures on Genesis*, 1535–45 (AE 1:205; WA 42:153.10–29).
6. SA III.i.2 (K-W, 310).
7. Hunnius, *Epitome Credendorum*, 64.
8. Chemnitz and Gerhard, *Doctrine of Man*, 205.
9. Chemnitz and Gerhard, *Doctrine of Man*, 211.
10. Chemnitz and Gerhard, *Doctrine of Man*, 211.
11. Chemnitz and Gerhard, *Doctrine of Man*, 211.

All transgressions of the commandments, such as lying, swearing, not praying, disobeying parents, murdering, behaving promiscuously, stealing, and deceiving, are subsequent acts or "fruits" of that original sin.[12] This underlying corruption has penetrated so deeply our human nature or essence that when sin has been forgiven and we receive a new heart, as when we are baptized, the evil inclination remains within us. It can be removed or separated from our body completely only when we rise from death to eternal life.[13]

This disobedience or transgression of God's Law cannot be reduced to an outward act; it includes the inner disposition of the human being, a desire to place one's own will against God's will in the form of a rebellion (Ex 20:5; Rom 8:7).[14] For this reason the essence of sin, its nature, is more than a transgression of the Law and disobedience against God's command and will; it is also apostasy, an inner turning away from God and against God, a selfishness and infraction of the love for God, a rebellion and indignation, hatred toward and enmity against God, unbelief and pride. In short, it becomes a disposition that turns the total human against God. The Formula of Concord and orthodox Lutheran theologians who connect that disposition against God to the Law call sin "everything that opposes God's law."[15]

SIN'S MANIFOLD EXPRESSIONS

Though sin is essentially one, namely, lacking fear, love, and trust in God—to which Luther would connect each commandment—it appears in various forms. Every sin has its own individual character because each one is fashioned after the individual's will and desire. One need only speak to a forensic examiner to recognize that a sin like murder is approached by individuals in so many different ways. While some murders are premeditated and intentional, even the person who argues that he killed someone unintentionally is regarded as a murderer. Ultimately, all that which deviates from God's Law is called sin. Scripture speaks of sins committed willfully and those committed

---

12. SA III.i.2 (K-W, 310).

13. Ap. II.35–36 (K-W, 117–18); Ep. I.8–10 (K-W, 488–89).

14. τὸ ἑαυτοῦ ζητεῖν, 1 Cor 10:24: "Let no one seek his own good, but the good of his neighbor." Compare AC XIX (K-W, 53): "Their will turned away from God" ("avertit se a Deo"); "a perverse turning toward carnal things," Ap. XIX.25 (K-W, 115).

15. SD VI.13 (K-W, 589). Similarly, Nicolaus Hunnius: "All that, which forms the real source of a sin, and is as it were the beginning of the same, undeniably stands in opposition to the law of God. And that which stands in opposition to the law of God must certainly be sin" (Hunnius, *Epitome Credendorum*, 64). Calov calls it an illegal deformity from the Law ("Peccatum nihil aliud est, quam illegalitas, seu difformitas a lege"; Abraham Calov, *Theologia Positiva, Per Definitiones, Causas, Affectiones, Et Distinctiones, Locos Theologicos Universos, Succinte, Justoque Ordine Proponens: Ceu Compendium Systematis Theologici* [Frankfurt/Wittenberg: Johann Ludolph Quenstedt, 1690], II.2.4, 276), while Hollaz calls it an aberration from the divine Law ("aberratio a lege"; Hollaz, *Examen Theologicum Acroamaticum*, 501). Melanchthon likewise in his *Loci Communes* defines sin as "a defect or an inclination or an action in conflict with the law of God." Quoted in Chemnitz, *Loci Theologici* 1:264. See also Ap. II.3 (K-W, 112).

unintentionally. In Rom 7:16, 19 the apostle Paul states that he does those things that he does not want to do. Hebrews 10:26 speaks of willful sins, which indicates that there are also sins that are committed unintentionally and not willfully.

This distinction between sins committed unintentionally and those committed intentionally and willfully also implies that there are degrees of sins. Surely the sin committed unintentionally by someone who is regenerate is not as grave in the judgment of God as a sin committed willfully. In the Smalcald Articles Luther distinguishes between the regenerate who "still have and feel original sin and also daily repent of it and struggle against it" and the regenerate who "somehow fall into public sin." In the former case, the believers certainly sin but have the Holy Spirit who "does not allow sin to rule and gain the upper hand"; in the latter case, the believers allow sin to gain the upper hand and rule as David did by committing adultery and murder, which Luther concludes means that "the Holy Spirit and faith are not there."[16]

In this discussion we also encounter the distinction between mortal and venial sins in the regenerate. All acts against God's will are sinful regardless of how insignificant they may be. Whether a sin is venial or mortal is determined not by the act itself but by whether the person committing it is a believer or an unbeliever, as Luther points out in his *Lectures on Galatians*.[17] Venial sins are those committed by Christians but forgiven because of the sinners' faith and repentance, and those who have committed them remain in the grace of God. Mortal sins are those that lead to death because the unbeliever who commits them is without Christ and faith and thus remains unrepentant and does not desire forgiveness. As Chemnitz points out, however, a Christian also can commit a mortal sin by deciding to do something against his conscience, and when in full awareness of doing so he goes forward with it, "the Holy Spirit is driven out and faith is lost."[18] A venial sin occurs when a believer commits some evil work, yet immediately recognizes what he has done wrong, repents in sorrow, and in faith seeks forgiveness. Then the "faith and the grace of God have not been lost."[19] The famous episode between Nathan and David reveals this distinction. David is identified as having committed a mortal sin (2 Sm 12:5,

16. SA III.iii.43–45 (K-W, 319).

17. "To the believer, however, it is forgiven and not imputed, while to the unbeliever it is retained and imputed. To the former it is venial; to the latter it is mortal. This is not because of a difference between the sins, as though the believer's sin were smaller and the unbeliever's larger, but because of a difference between the persons. For the believer knows that his sin is forgiven him on account of Christ, who has expiated it by His death. Even though he has sin and commits sin, he remains godly. On the other hand, when the unbeliever commits sin, he remains ungodly." *Lectures on Galatians*, 1535 (AE 27:76; WA 40/2:96.9–13). See also Chemnitz, *Loci Theologici* 2:675.

18. Chemnitz, *Loci Theologici* 2:676. Drawing from Lombard and Augustine, Chemnitz lists the following steps that lead to the sinful act itself: "1. First, the evil suggestion, 2. The enticement, 3. The consent. Then the will agrees, 4. The planning or scheming, 5. The evil deed itself." Chemnitz, *Loci Theologici* 2:676–77.

19. Chemnitz, *Loci Theologici* 2:679.

7), not a venial sin, by willingly having committed adultery and then murdering the husband of Bathsheba. But after Nathan confronts him, he repents of what he has done and seeks forgiveness. At this point his premeditated sin, as grave as it was, becomes venial or pardonable.[20]

Finally, in the context of actual sins one generally also finds the discussion on the sin against the Holy Spirit, which is identified as one that cannot be forgiven. Why not? First, one would hold someone guilty of the sin only and insofar as he is able to articulate and understand what the true Gospel is and what saving faith is. Second, having acquired this true knowledge of how the Holy Spirit saves through the Word, the person denies it intentionally and wickedly. One thinks here mostly of those who do so by premeditation.[21] This sin then consists of "a premeditated denial and blaspheming of the acquired saving, heavenly truth, concerning the forgiveness of sins, wrought out by Christ."[22] When someone cuts himself off from the saving Word, it stands to reason that he cannot be forgiven or receive salvation. He will not hear the call to repentance and be forgiven; that is why it is called the unforgivable sin.

For an overview of actual sins we look at Johann Gerhard's detailed list or categories of sins. Though he focuses mostly on original sin, in Locus XIII of his *Theological Commonplaces*[23] he proceeds with the division of actual sins and elaborates on each one in the chapters that follow. Under the category of actual sins (*peccata actualia*), which he defines as acts that are done by a human, he comes up with the following list:

(1) Sins committed voluntarily (*peccata voluntaria*) and those not committed with volition (*peccata involuntaria*). "Of the latter (involuntary)," he says, "some are committed out of ignorance, and some, out of weakness; but the former (voluntary) are committed out of deliberate malice and stubbornness of the mind."[24] Gerhard refers to Gn 20:2; Rom 6:15; Gal 6:1; 1 Tm 1:13; Ti 3:10–11; and Jas 3:2 as examples of involuntary sins. Of course, the voluntary sins exceed in gravity those done involuntarily. But they too are forgivable "if one turns away from them through repentance."[25]

(2) Sins committed (*peccata commissionis*) and sins of omission (*peccata ommissionis*). "The basis for this division," Gerhard comments, "lies in the divine Law itself, which not only forbids evil but also commands good. Therefore surely one sins against the Law not only by committing evil acts but also by omitting good ones."[26] He cites texts such as Mt 25:42; Jas 4:17; and 1 Jn 3:17 as examples of sins of omission, and they will not go unpunished (Mt 25:30).

20. See here Luther's comments on David's situation in SA II.iii (K-W, 319).

21. One could think also of someone denying the truth out of the fear of death through persecution. But then, as in the case of Peter, that sin can be forgiven.

22. Hunnius, *Epitome Credendorum*, 70–71.

23. Johann Gerhard, *Theological Commonplaces* 13.5.19 (12–14:114).

24. Johann Gerhard, *Theological Commonplaces* 13.5.19 (12–14:114).

25. Johann Gerhard, *Theological Commonplaces* 13.6.22 (12–14:116).

26. Johann Gerhard, *Theological Commonplaces* 13.7.25 (12–14:117).

(3) Sins committed by turning away from God (*peccata*, committed *in aversione a Deo*) and those committed by turning toward creation (*peccata*, committed *in conversione ad creaturas*). "Formally turning away from God is distinguished from turning to created things, for the former is considered with regard to the goal from which one begins, while the latter is considered with regard to the goal to which one heads."[27] Jeremiah 2:13, for example, offers that distinction.

(4) Internal and external sins (*peccata interior* and *peccata exterior*, or *peccata interna et externa*). The former are committed internally through thought and the latter externally through word and deed. These are called "sins of the heart, mouth, and deed" (*peccata cordia, oris et operis*), and they demonstrate how sins come from within a person, from the heart (Mt 15:19) and progress outward to the actual sins being committed (Mt 5:21f.).

(5) Sins against God (*peccata contra Deum*) and sins against humans (*peccata contra homines*), which are defined in view of the object against whom they are committed. Those committed against God include those in the First Table of the Ten Commandments, the First, Second, and Third Commandments. Those committed against the neighbor are identified as sins by the Second Table of the Ten Commandments, the Fourth through Tenth Commandments. In essence, all sins are committed against God.

(6) Sins of the flesh (*peccata carnalia*) and those of the spirit (*peccata spiritualia*). This distinction resembles that in the previous category: spiritual sins are those committed against God (First Table of the Decalogue), sins of the flesh those committed against ourselves and the neighbor (Second Table of the Decalogue; Mk 12:30–31; 2 Sm 2:25).

(7) Secret sins (*peccata occultas*) and public sins (*peccata manifesta*). This distinction is self-evident. Gerhard here urges reflection on one's proper response to a secret sin that becomes public. While not all sins become public or are detected, a public sin also demands public response, which as Luther suggests should follow the rules laid down in Mt 18:15–20.[28]

(8) Sins that are venial (*peccata venialia*) and sins that are mortal (*peccata mortalia*). Gerhard states that because of the original depravity there are always actual sins, which in the unregenerate are all mortal.[29] However, in the regenerate he distinguishes between venial and mortal sins.[30] All sins are mortal because all elicit God's wrath, and yet we make a distinction: though the regenerate continues to commit sin, he does not let it rule over him (Rom

27. Johann Gerhard, *Theological Commonplaces* 13.8.29 (12–14:119).

28. LC I.276, 284 (K-W, 423, 424).

29. "Therefore in the unregenerate and unbelieving all sins without exception are and continue to be the sort of sins which are of their own nature, that is mortal." Johann Gerhard, *Theological Commonplaces* 13.20.101 (12–14:208).

30. "Some sin is venial not because it is worthy of pardon by its own nature but because God does not impute it to those who believe in Christ and who mortify sin." Johann Gerhard, *Theological Commonplaces* 13.20.101 (12–14:208).

6:12–14) but is willing to fight it and cleanses himself from it through daily repentance. This is not the case for a hardened sinner, who willingly and consciously parts from faith (1 Tm 1:19), actually enjoys sin, and lets it rule over him without any shame or fear. This person will incur God's wrath and judgment (Rom 8:13) and his sins are unforgiven. Certainly for such a person the way is still open to conversion. The gravest sin must be considered the sin against the Holy Spirit. It cannot be forgiven because the willingness to repent is lacking (Mt 12:31ff.; Mk 3:28f.; Lk 12:10; Heb 6:4–6; 10:26–29). This sin is a definite falling away from faith; it entails an arrogant persistence in being unrepentant and a denial of the truth received before from the Holy Spirit, combined with a deliberate rebellion and mocking of the Holy Spirit.

(9) Grave sin and light sins (*peccata graviora et leviora*), or greater and lesser sins. We would say with the Lutheran theologians that according to Mt 10:15; 11:20ff.; Jn 19:11; and 1 Tm 5:8 there are degrees of sins. The greater the understanding of the gravity of the sins, the stronger is the participation of the will, even if sin is in the end all the same. Especially grave are those sins that cry out to the heavens (*peccata in coelum clamantia*), such as murder, sodomy, oppressing the poor, and refusing to pay the workers a wage (Gn 4:10; 18:20; Ex 3:7, 22, 23; Jas 5:4).

SIN AND SOCIETAL STRUCTURES

Those who attempt to locate sin away from and outside of an individual in society and its structures no longer speak of it as an individual's personal aggression toward God. Rather, they point to sin as communal, manifest in structures that order and regulate the life of a community. The traditional view sees sin as endemic to every human being—Augustine's position and also Luther's, as well as that of modern theologians like Tillich, Barth, Brunner, and Pannenberg. They speak of sins as personal, though each to varying degrees.[31] The alternative approach that finds sin in corporate institutions and in social structures abandons this personal aspect of sin, and with it personal responsibility and accountability. Is there any validity to this approach? Undoubtedly, sin can be found beyond a personal context in society and politics, where laws and regulations are established to uphold the interests of certain people over against those of others. In the document "Instruction on Christian Freedom and Liberation," the Congregation for the Doctrine of the Faith articulates its understanding of social structures as follows:

> These are the sets of institutions and practices which people find already existing or which they create, on the national and international level, and which orientate or organize economic, social and political life. Being necessary in themselves, they often tend to become fixed and fossilized as mechanisms relatively independent of the human will, thereby paralysing or distorting social development and causing

31. Schwarz, *Human Being*, 242–54.

> injustice. However, they always depend on the responsibility of man, who can alter them, and not upon an alleged determinism of history.[32]

While sin moves legislators, whether they recognize it or not, to establish laws and regulations that permit people to engage in immoral acts, we cannot consider such laws and regulations simply in the abstract without also considering personal responsibility, namely, holding accountable specific people whose intent it is to corrupt and destroy the good. Examples of such corrupt established social structures abound, such as the Third Reich, the system of apartheid in South Africa, and Jim Crow laws in North America.

Since humans are sinful, one must also expect sin to infiltrate the social structures, whether formal (e.g., legal, institutional, political, or economic systems) or informal (e.g., language, customs, or social role). In either case, it is important not to see structural sin as something impersonal "out there" but to connect it also to personal responsibility and actual sins, for those who in concert create such laws and for those who cooperate and engage in them. One could even assert that structural sin, though "out there" and often established before one's time, is a reflection of sin that is also in oneself.[33] To address structural sin adequately, we need to begin with the individual person and his responsibility and accountability, since every human being bears the deeper depravity which then extends into actions and implications. If something can be gained from the philosopher Thomas Hobbes, it is this: he recognized and affirmed in his incisive *Leviathan* the deep disposition of sin and evil in every human that leads to broader evil and tragedy in society. Sin's destructive nature flows from individuals and manifests itself in societal structures and legislation.

To address structural sin, peaceful resistance becomes necessary. Understandably, people who seek to dismantle sinful social structures may deploy terms such as "liberation."[34] We should not forget, however, that institutions and laws are also necessary to uphold the orders of creation, such as structures of family and of government, and when these agree with natural law, they should be considered good and helpful. A person who pursues "freedom" in certain cases may be misled into thinking that freedom signifies liberation

---

32. Congregation for the Doctrine of the Faith, *Instruction on Christian Freedom and Liberation* (Washington, DC: United States Catholic Conference, 1986), para. 74. Brian Hamilton, "It's in You: Structural Sin and Personal Responsibility Revisited," *Studies in Christian Ethics* 34, no. 3 (2021): 360–80, esp. 364.

33. "The problem is that you think it's out there: and it's not out there. It's in you." Hamilton, "It's in You," 364.

34. "But in the liberation approach sin is not considered as an individual, private, or merely interior reality . . . The collective dimensions are rediscovered." Gustavo Gutiérrez, *A Theology of Liberation: History, Politics, and Salvation*, trans. Caridad Inda and John Eagleson, SCM Classics, rev. ed. (London: SCM, 2001), xix, xxvi, 174; Schwarz, *Human Being*, 255–56. Other terms often used to address sin in social structures are Critical Race Theory (addressing the relation of ethnicity, racism, and power) and cancel culture. Both are vague terms, the very ambiguity of which has escalated the debate over sinful social structures established in the past and those who have supported and may continue to benefit from them.

from every law and regulation. On the other hand, structural sins are not to be understood deterministically, in a way that would discourage any personal accountability for them. It is true that sinful structures can be intimidating, oppressive, and difficult to detect, or have attained some semblance of normalcy and wide acceptance so that they are hard to resist.[35] A deterministic approach, however, would deny human freedom and responsibility and negate the motivation to contribute personally to the betterment of society.[36] Humans living under such conditions, and especially Christians, have the obligation or responsibility of "both noncooperation with and active resistance against these kinds of structures of sin."[37] A more traditional term is conscientious objection. Such resistance can lead systems to change over time, dismantling some or all of their sinful structures and laws.

Wherever she sees structural sin in society, the Lutheran church has tried to address it by applying the principles of the two kingdoms or realms, yet her history shows she has never done so with unanimity. Two important rules apply here. First, abusive and sinful societal structures should not be attributed sweepingly to original sin and to some "vague and unaccountable group";[38] they exist because of errant and sinful behaviors of individual humans, that is, because of their actual sins. Second, the church's duty is to ensure that the actual sins of her own members are uncovered and addressed through the preaching of the Law, and then to encourage her members to contribute peacefully through their vocations toward improving societal structures and laws.[39]

THEODICY AND THE PROBLEM OF EVIL

The natural tendency for humans is to seek the cause of their misfortune outside of themselves, and often God is identified as the probable cause of evil and suffering. He becomes a scapegoat on whom humans place all the blame. However, there are three theological reasons He cannot be to blame. First, God could not have created sin or suffering in the human since His creation was called good. Second, He did not make prior contingencies for the human to fall. And third, He does not force the human to sin through temptation since He does not tempt (Jas 1:13–14).

Theological positions have arisen over time that undermine each of these arguments. The supralapsarian view of predestination, as held for example by Calvin, teaches that God destined events ahead of time, even the Fall.[40] Of course, for many Reformed this view sounds rather harsh, and so in Reformed

35. For example, the legality of abortion and gay marriage is based on the principles of rights and inclusivity.

36. Hamilton, "It's in You," 367.

37. Hamilton, "It's in You," 365.

38. Hamilton, "It's in You," 363.

39. Hamilton, "It's in You," 360–80.

40. For a discussion see Boyd and Eddy, *Across the Spectrum*, 15–46.

circles alternative, gentler teachings emerged, such as the infralapsarian view, in which God carries no blame for the Fall and sin but makes accommodations for humans after its occurrence. As we have noted already, we also take issue with the Arminian or open theist approach of Clark Pinnock and John Sanders, who maintain that God does not predestine everything but has left much to the freedom of the will, leaving humans to take responsibility for either their salvation or their damnation. In open theism it seems God is as surprised about future events as are humans themselves, or, simply put, the hand dealt at a poker game amazes God just as it does the player. This doctrine raises doubts about God's omniscience about future events.[41]

The debate about the cause of evil and its effects on all of humanity and creation raises a sensitive question with which many people have grappled: why would an almighty God, if He is almighty, not use His powers to prevent evil things from happening? The attempt to explain why a good God allows evil, or theodicy, naturally arises as people try to reconcile pain and suffering in human life with God's omnipotence and nature. His attributes of justice, love, and holiness are in particular focus so as to vindicate Him in the face of evil.

The alternative to wrestling with God is to dismiss Him outright. However, then humanity is left alone with this inexplicable and fateful power called sin. It makes the human's existence seem futile, his destiny dictated and ruled over by evil. There is no way out and no hope. This line of thinking has found its supporters in Sartre and Camus, both existential nihilists. That inescapability from evil has led Aleksandr Solzhenitsyn, though not a nihilist, to draw a parallel with human prisoners who cannot overcome evil; this fate has to be endured. The crushing reality of evil is that they can lead only a lemur-like existence headed on a path toward extinction.[42]

The existence of evil, grief, and suffering in this world can never be answered satisfactorily by a human being. In their lives humans deal with everyday contingencies and experience their own createdness that is beset with limitations. Consider for example disastrous events like the tsunami of 2004, for whose occurrence no human, by any account, can be blamed. Humanity is subject to its own limitations, forced to surrender itself to an omnipotent God who rules over the sea, the earth, the sky, and all that is below it. Given the fact that we are suffering and groaning in this world (Psalm 8), the temptation is to blame God in order to make sense of evil. The discussion around theodicy allows humans to engage God, at times seeking to confine Him to our human standards, domesticating Him as it were for consumers to appreciate, as if He could be presented to someone like a gift in a box.

---

41. Gregory A. Boyd, *God of the Possible: A Biblical Introduction to the Open View of God* (Grand Rapids: Baker Books, 2000); Clark Pinnock et al., *The Openness of God: A Biblical Challenge to the Traditional Understanding of God* (Downers Grove: InterVarsity Press, 1994); John Sanders, *The God Who Risks: A Theology of Providence* (Downers Grove: InterVarsity Press, 1998).

42. Pöhlmann, *Abriß der Dogmatik*, 194.

However, God cannot be boxed up. The prerogative of being totally free belongs to God alone. At the same time, He chose to have Himself bound to contingencies of this world through the incarnation of His Son. God too, then, experiences the pain humans go through, and thus any question raised about His nature and the existence of evil cannot escape the discussion of God's incarnation and death on the cross. It informs and sheds light on the question of why humans suffer and experience evil. This concern does not go away for Christians simply because they believe and confess God in their lives. In Christianity God reveals Himself as love, so the issue of suffering is even more of a problem for Christians. It is precisely God's love and majesty against which Christians measure what is seen and experienced as setbacks, suffering, and pain in a world that He created and preserves.

In his *Essays on Theodicy* the philosopher Gottfried Wilhelm Leibniz coined the term "theodicy" with reference to biblical texts such as Rom 3:4f. and Ps 51:6.[43] His intentions with this investigation were to see how God justifies His own actions on creation, with humans especially, in view of accusations brought against Him as creator and preserver of the world. Leibniz frames the issue as follows:

> The question is asked first of all, whence does evil come? *Si Deus est, unde malum? Si non est, unde bonum?* The ancients attributed the cause of evil to *matter*, which they believed uncreated and independent of God: but we, who derive all being from God, where shall we find the source of evil?[44]

Leibniz divides evil into three categories: it exists morally (*malum morale*), physically (*malum physicum*), and metaphysically (*malum metaphysicum*).[45] Leibniz assigns the existence of moral evil to the freedom of the human, who may choose the good but also evil. Evil is the negative byproduct of human freedom.[46] Physical evil flows from moral evil; it occurs as a consequence of the moral evil. This is the evil of punishment, which however in Leibniz's view can lead someone to do the good.[47] The metaphysical evil that limits the world and all creation does not encompass the unlimited possibilities of true freedom that God Himself possesses.[48]

As a result of this broader scheme addressing the question of how God relates to evil, Leibniz draws the conclusion that at times God permits evil to happen:

---

43. Leibniz submitted his *Essais de théodicée* in 1710; see Gottfried Wilhelm Leibniz, *Theodicy: Essays on the Goodness of God, the Freedom of Man, and the Origin of Evil*, ed. Austin Farrer, trans. E. M. Huggard, Rare Masterpieces of Philosophy and Science (New Haven, CT: Yale University Press, 1952); Härle, *Dogmatik*, 439.

44. Leibniz, *Theodicy*, 135 (§ 20).

45. Leibniz, *Theodicy*, 136 (§ 21).

46. Leibniz, *Theodicy*, 143, 184 (§§ 34, 111).

47. Leibniz, *Theodicy*, 137–38 (§§ 23–25).

48. Leibniz, *Theodicy*, 135–36 (§§ 20–21).

> As for evil, God wills moral evil not at all, and physical evil or suffering he does not will absolutely. Thus it is that there is no absolute predestination to damnation; and one may say of physical evil, that God wills it often as a penalty owing to guilt, and often also as a means to an end, that is, to prevent greater evils or to obtain greater good. The penalty serves also for amendment and example. Evil often serves to make us savour good the more; sometimes too it contributes to a greater perfection in him who suffers it, as the seed that one sows is subject to a kind of corruption before it can germinate: this is a beautiful similitude, which Jesus Christ himself used.[49]

In classical doctrinal terms, the issue discussed here follows the doctrine of God's providence (*providentia*), in which we hear how God keeps (*conservatio*) His world, how He participates and intervenes in all events (*concursus*) and in doing so guides and directs everything (*gubernatio*). Discussing God's providential care might be futile with those who have chosen to lead a life independent from God; they do not entertain the question of God's goodness despite the existence of evil. However, those who have consciously decided to live a life under God quarrel with Him over suffering in this world and in their personal lives. The biblical example of Job exemplifies much of that struggle. It may be that their consideration starts as a philosophical endeavor, but ultimately the answer to that question is surely theological, leading to contemplation of God, the struggle of Job, and the suffering and death of Christ. For there is not a direct correlation between sin and consequence, as there was in the Fall itself. In Job that immediate correspondence is questioned, for even the righteous and blameless person like Job suffers.[50] No cause is evident from his past behavior to justify his own suffering and encounter with evil (Jb 1:1; 9:21–22; 42:11). Similarly, in the New Testament the cause-and-consequence scheme breaks down. In John 9, for example, the blindness of the man Jesus heals has no cause from his past life, for "it was not that this man sinned, or his parents, but that the works of God might be displayed in him" (Jn 9:3).

At this point theology pushes beyond philosophy to Jesus Christ. For here God Himself suffers and endures the dilemma of theodicy. He, God the Father, "did not spare his own Son but gave him up for us all" (Rom 8:32), so that the Son before His death cries out: "My God, my God, why have you forsaken me?" (Mk 15:34). The cross itself raises this dilemma of theodicy. Our questions on the subject are silenced because they are subsumed into God's own dealings with His Son on the cross. What this means for humans is that we cannot expect intervention and relief from God as Greek tragedy would provide, by letting Him come down on a pulley (*Deus ex machina*) when a matter needs to be resolved. Humans must deal with God's omnipotence and majesty, which allow Him to do things His way, a way that is often inexplicable to us. In that sense, the challenge of theodicy remains unanswered and unresolved. The debate

49. Leibniz, *Theodicy*, 137 (§ 23).

50. Hermann Häring, *Das Problem des Bösen in der Theologie* (Darmstadt: Wissenschaftliche Buchgesellschaft, 1985), 23–28.

might be interesting but is ultimately futile, according to Elert, like one a person might have aboard a sinking ship. There is not much we can do as humans.[51] In Scripture, however, God breaks His own silence in coming down Himself and choosing to suffer in His own Son, Jesus Christ. Whatever pain humans endure, God endured also. God provides an answer in His Son, one that offers hope and consolation even in the midst of pain and suffering. A Christian may take a number of important elements into consideration as he ponders his own fate. The first principle must be that God the Creator is in control and rules. He can intervene and prevent suffering and evil, but He does so on His own terms. The second principle is that God the Redeemer has entered the world in His Son and has chosen to share suffering with humans. The third is that God the Sanctifier inspires us with faith and hope and the strength to work against evil and suffering. His children on earth are to withstand evil, and in doing so can prevent or at least alleviate some suffering.[52] This point is important, since the Lutheran Confessions state unequivocally that human sin directly or indirectly is the cause of evil.[53]

This dual approach to understanding God and His dealings with the world—considering that He acts both according to His majesty and according to His ordained will—brings to mind Luther's distinction between *Deus absconditus* and *Deus revelatus*, which the Confessions engage in Article XI on election.[54] For God displays mercy to some but hardens others, such as Pharaoh (Rom 9:14–18). He creates not only light and peace and prosperity but also darkness and disaster (Is 45:7). The devil, sin, and evil point to the omnipotent God, so that Luther himself would say about Psalm 117: "I must grant the devil his hour of godliness and ascribe devilhood to our God."[55] Yet in that struggle to reconcile opposites, Luther finds the revealed God—His love, grace, and faithfulness.[56] Here the dilemma of theodicy is no longer answerable in the abstract. For now our own cries join in with Job's—"For I know that my Redeemer lives, and at the last he will stand upon the earth" (Jb 19:25)—and with what the apostle Paul said: "Neither death nor life . . . will be able to separate us from the love of God in Christ Jesus our Lord."[57]

51. Elert, *Christian Faith*, 67.

52. Barth, *Dogmatik*, 453; Härle, *Dogmatik*, 439–55.

53. SD XI.7 (K-W, 642).

54. SD XI.52 (K-W, 649).

55. *The Commentary on Psalm 117*, 1530 (AE 14:32; WA 31/1:250.35–36).

56. "A profound understanding is required to grasp that God's grace and truth, or His love and faithfulness, rule over us and prevail. But it is comforting to him who can grasp it, if he is sure that all is God's grace and truth, even when it seems to be the opposite." *The Commentary on Psalm 117*, 1530 (AE 14:32; WA 31/1:250.28–31).

57. Romans 8:38–39, quoted in SD XI.48–49 (K-W, 648–49). Bonhoeffer echoes Paul's words when he famously states: "If we lose our lives in his service and carry our cross, we shall find our lives again in the fellowship of the cross with Christ." Dietrich Bonhoeffer, *The Cost of Discipleship*, trans. R. H. Fuller and Irmgard Booth (London: SCM Press, 1959), 80.

11

THE PHENOMENON OF SIN IN MAJOR RELIGIONS

One of the major changes Western society is undergoing is the shift from Christianity's central status in society to its marginalization. With that shift, the church is facing a context with which it is less familiar. Until recently it generally has been assumed, at least for Christians, that Scripture speaks the final word, offering the last authority on spirituality and morality, and that the story it tells is the prevailing dogma that the majority in society will heed. Alternative narratives of what it means to be human abound in other religions. In addition to secularization, Christians now are engaging with a wide range of religiously informed worldviews. As is commonly said, Western society has shifted from Jerusalem to Athens and seems to open itself up to such alternative stories. Systematic theology thus must respond not only to alternative positions within Christianity concerning who the human is, but also to positions held by religions such as Buddhism, Hinduism, and Islam. We shall respond by exploring the understanding of sin and fault in these other religions, and asking and answering two questions: How does the Christian concept of sin compare in this broader context with that of other major religions? How would those outside of Christianity describe the condition from which humans need to be saved?

SIN IN HINDUISM

We must immediately acknowledge that every religion pursues its own particular religious ends.[1] Therefore, all religions to varying degrees differ from basic Christian tenets on the subject of sin and salvation and from each another. In Hinduism, sin is identified basically as the failure of a person to recognize the divine and the oneness with God. This ignorance functions like a veil, so that the person confuses the temporary with the divine, identifies the impure with the pure, finds joy in evil, and believes that the body (non-soul) is the true self (*atman*).[2] In other words, this person is caught up in an everyday worldly and materialistic life and fails to look beyond it to the divine. This obliviousness is a human condition from which people wish to be freed,

1. We note here the comprehensive comparative study between Christianity and other major religions, Barth, *Dogmatik*, 511–24.

2. Harold Coward, *Sin and Salvation in the World Religions: A Short Introduction* (Oxford: Oneworld Publications, 2003), 89.

because in the end it prevents the final release (*moksha*).[3] Every human will go through repeated births, deaths, and rebirths to reach enlightenment, that eternal union or communion with the divine.[4] Instead of invoking divine grace for the forgiveness of sins, Hinduism encourages the exercise of human free will and choices so that the Hindu will not violate moral and ethical codes. Whatever acts a person performs, good or bad, will determine his future destiny, not only in this life but in those to come (reincarnation), and his current status likewise has been determined by past actions. The concept of karma (literally, action) is important here, "the notion that one's present fate, one's pleasure or pain, one's being a king or a slave or gnat, is the result of past action, especially in a former existence."[5]

The most widely used term for sin in Hinduism is the Sanskrit word *pāpa*, which describes wrongful actions against the laws of God that bring into one's life bad consequences, known as negative karma.[6] These laws are identified as (1) dharma, or moral order; and (2) one's own self. To escape that negative cycle, the Hindu should not reinforce a negative action in thought or deed, but with the use of his free will he should negate that bad karmic influence so that it loses its strength and eventually subsides altogether, even from one's own unconscious self. Good karmas that are stored in the unconscious self likewise can be reinforced and cultivated through right practice.[7] The unconscious self is like a huge granary or storage house from which both good and bad actions sprout. But the "unconscious contains not only all the karmic traces from actions and thoughts done in this life, but also in the life before this and so on infinitely, since in Hindu thought there is no absolute beginning."[8]

This understanding brings us to the idea of rebirth or *samsara*, a ladder of rebirth on which the Hindu hopes to advance upwards, assuming that he uses his free will to make the right choices. Increasing the amount of his good karma and decreasing evil karma will cause him to be born further up the ladder: "You reap what you sow." This cycle of karma (*karma samsara*) entails three stages: the lowest is the state of animals, which have no free choice and endure sufferings; the second stage is that of humans, who are supplied with free will to make right and good choices that eventually lead to the third stage of the final release, the *moksha*, being reborn as god to be with the divine Brahma. Once the last bad karma is removed, a person has no free choice any longer and simply enjoys the luxury of being in the state of god.[9]

One should note, finally, that for Hindus a human life, especially for the men of the household, ideally has four stages, each more conducive to

3. Coward, *Sin and Salvation*, 94.
4. Coward, *Sin and Salvation*, 107.
5. Sire, *Universe Next Door*, 156.
6. The term for committing grave offences is *aparadha*.
7. Coward, *Sin and Salvation*, 92.
8. Coward, *Sin and Salvation*, 92.
9. Coward, *Sin and Salvation*, 93.

promoting good karma than the preceding one. In the first stage a student learns to master the basic matters of his religion. In the second stage he becomes a householder and family man, has children, and fulfills important societal duties. This is a key stage for Hinduism, since those in this stage serve as the backbone of society. In the following stage he retires and devotes himself to the teaching of a guru. And in the final stage he becomes a guru, recluse, or holy wanderer waiting for the final release from rebirth, the *moksha*. Those who are familiar with the novel *Siddhartha* by Hermann Hesse,[10] a popular read in the 1960s, will see how the author follows three of these traditional stages of life for Hindu males: the student (*brahmacarya asrama*), the householder (*grihastha asrama*), and the recluse/renunciate (*vanaprastha asrama*).[11]

In Buddhism, which also embraces the concept, karma is connected to the elimination or cessation of suffering (*dukkha*) caused by desire. The way to stop suffering and its causes is to follow the eightfold path that lays out the proper karma of body, speech, and mind, which if followed leads to nirvana, the final stage in the cycle of rebirth, or *samsara* (literally, wandering).[12]

SIN IN ISLAM

In Islam, Muslims look for *najat* (salvation), the escape or deliverance from future punishment associated with the fires of hell, to enjoy the pleasures of paradise.[13] As the Qur'an puts it,

> O my people! Truly, this life of the world is nothing but a (quick passing) enjoyment, and verily, the Hereafter that is the home that will remain forever (39). Whosoever does an evil deed, will not be requited except the like thereof; and whosoever does a righteous deed, whether male or female and is a true believer (in the Oneness of Allāh), such will enter Paradise, where they will be provided therein (with all things in abundance) without limit (40). [40:39–40]

The way to salvation closely follows what Muhammad teaches in the Qur'an, namely, that a Muslim's life should be one of obedience and submission to Allah. Where Christians see the primary punishment for sin as a broken relationship with God, which manifests itself eternally in hell, and redemption through Christ as the solution, a Muslim attempts to escape the fires of hell by following

10. Hermann Hesse, *Siddhartha*, trans. Hilda Rosner, New Classics Series 34 (New York: New Directions, 1951).

11. Coward, *Sin and Salvation*, 94–95.

12. Malcolm David Eckel, "Buddhism in the World and in America," in *World Religions in America: An Introduction*, ed. Jacob Neusner, 4th ed. (Louisville: Westminster John Knox Press, 2009), 202.

13. Though the term *najat* is found only once in the Qur'an (40:41), it captures the basic goal of a Muslim, which is to escape punishment: "And O my people! How is it that I call you to salvation while you call me to the Fire!" *Interpretation of the Meanings of the Noble Qur'ān. In the English Language*, summarized in one volume by Muhammad Taqi-ud-Din Al-Hilali and Muhammad Muhsin Khan, 16th rev. ed. (Darussalam: Global Leader in Islamic Books, 2005), 472. All subsequent quotes from the Qur'an are from this edition.

God's guidance (*huda*) found in the Qur'an. Salvation and the way to prosper or succeed here on earth and in the next (*falāh*) depend on submission and obedience to the Qur'an. Muslims see sin (*dhanb, thanb*) as anything that goes against the commands of God (Allah). Islam teaches that sin is an act and not a state of being. The Qur'an does not teach that humans are flawed, dead to sin, and unable to use free will in the relationship with God. Muslims do not view Adam's sin as disobedience that comes over all of humanity. They can use their free will to choose to work together with God in creating a beautiful and moral world. As one scholar puts it: "Thus the human condition in Islam does not involve the recovery from a fall so as to regain some original state of glory, but rather entails the fulfilling of a set of obligations given by God in the Qur'an."[14]

The Qur'an teaches that "the (human) self is inclined to evil, except when my Lord bestows His Mercy (upon whom He wills)" (12:53), and that even the prophets do not absolve themselves of the blame (12:53). Muslims believe that *Iblis* (Satan) has a significant role in tempting humankind toward sin (e.g., 7:27; 17:61–64), of which there are several gradations. These include mistakes: *sayyia, khatia* (7:168; 17:31; 40:45; 47:19; 48:2); immorality: *itada, junah, dhanb* (2:190, 229; 17:17; 33:55); transgressions: *haraam* (5:4; 6:146); wickedness and depravity: *ithm, dhulam, fujur, su, fasad, fisk, kufr* (2:99, 205; 4:50, 112, 123, 136; 12:79; 38:62; 82:14); and *shirk*, or ascribing a partner next to God, as in idolatry and polytheism (4:48).

This list indicates what a Muslim seeking God's guidance (*huda*) in the Qur'an wants to avoid. Those who submit to and obey the Qur'an will move from darkness into light. They will move from lawlessness to a loving obedience, and especially away from polytheism to the one God, who on the Day of Judgment will lead them to heaven rather than hell.[15] One may sincerely repent to God for the wrongs committed and seek forgiveness, as stated in the Qur'an: "Our Lord! Forgive us our sins and expiate from us our evil deeds, and make us die (in the state of righteousness" (3:193); or, "Say: 'O 'Ibādī (My slaves) who have transgressed against themselves (by committing evil deeds and sins)! Despair not of the Mercy of Allāh, verily, Allāh forgives all sins. Truly, He is Oft-Forgiving, Most Merciful" (39:53). The mercy of Allah is invoked especially in not punishing a Muslim at the Day of Judgment and allowing the faithful to escape from hell to paradise. However, the basic premise is that humans can merit their own salvation, which is seen as a reward for those who were faithful. In this sense Islam functions as a "natural religion" that considers that humans are born with the natural ability and will intact, unaffected by original sin which they do not teach, and thus are able to choose their salvation.[16]

---

14. Coward, *Sin and Salvation*, 61.

15. Coward, *Sin and Salvation*, 59. Thus the concept of the Trinity and especially Christ's incarnation as God's Son, as God Himself, fundamentally goes against a Muslim's concept of God's oneness and transcendency. Christians are accused of *shirk*.

16. Frederick M. Denny, "The Problem of Salvation in the Qur'an: Key Terms and Concepts," in *In Quest of an Islamic Humanism: Arabic and Islamic Studies in Memory of*

SIN IN JUDAISM

Traditional Judaism considers sin a violation of any of its 613 commandments. While the Torah clearly lays out the will of God, this religion teaches that the people of Israel continue to act against what the Lord desires from them. Judaism teaches that to sin is a natural thing because no human is perfect and everyone has an inclination to do evil "from childhood" (Gn 8:21); the important thing is to try your best. God created "humans with free choice, to work with God by fostering harmony, or to go against God by pursuing selfish sinful ways. By choosing faithfulness to God, one finds life; by choosing sin one fosters disorder and death."[17] In this system sin has many classifications and degrees. Some sins are punishable with death by the court, others with eternal death, others with lashes, and others without such specified terms, but no sin with willful intent will go without consequence. Sins committed unintentionally are not considered sins, since you can't punish someone for something he did not know was wrong. Sins by error are considered less severe sins.

When the Temple still stood in Jerusalem, people would offer sacrifices for their misdeeds. The atoning aspect of *korbanot*, or the various kinds of sacrifices or offerings performed, is carefully circumscribed. For the most part, *korbanot* expiate only unintentional sins, sins committed because a person forgot that what he did was a sin. No atonement is needed for violations committed under duress or through lack of knowledge, and for the most part *korbanot* cannot atone for a malicious, deliberate sin. In addition, *korbanot* have no expiating effect unless the person making the offering sincerely repents of his actions before making the offering and makes restitution to any person who was harmed by the violation.

All willful sin has a consequence in Judaism. The completely righteous suffer for their sins in this world by humiliation, poverty, and suffering that God sends them and receive their reward in the world to come. Those neither completely righteous nor completely wicked repent of their sins in hell and thereafter join the righteous. The completely wicked cannot correct their sins in this world and hence do not suffer for them here but in *gehinnom* (hell). The very evil do not repent even at the gates of hell. Such people prosper in this world and receive rewards here and now, but they cannot be cleansed and hence cannot leave *gehinnom* because they don't repent, or can't repent. This world therefore can seem unjust when the righteous suffer while the wicked prosper. Many great thinkers have contemplated this apparent injustice, but God's justice is long, precise, and just. The Holocaust has caused many Jews to confront the dilemma of theodicy, the problem of how to understand suffering and evil in a world that God has created and ordered. For the modern Jew, the

Mohamed al-Nowaihi, ed. A. H. Green (Cairo: American University in Cairo Press, 1984), 197; Coward, *Sin and Salvation*, 63.

17. Coward, *Sin and Salvation*, 9.

human condition includes a wrestling with God in an imperfect world with the hope of ultimate redemption.[18]

In conclusion, common to all three religions—and this is the intention with this short review—is that sins are recognized as acts performed against principles or laws laid down. The deeper inclination of a human (concupiscence, AC II) that leads him to perform such sinful acts is not recognized by any of them, nor do they recognize the universal guilt and death that extends to all humans because of the first sin of Adam (Rom 5:12). In a dialogue with Judaism and Islam, Christians must bring out the reality of sin as original sin, the deep depravity that underlies the wrongful acts committed by every human. With Hinduism (and Buddhism), Christians share an understanding of guilt and could agree that desire brings upon people a lot of suffering, what Buddhism calls *dukkha*. However, Christian theology identifies this desire as original sin, and in contrast to Hinduism and Buddhism it needs to affirm beyond this transpersonal reality affecting humanity that each human individually is complicit in the fate that has overcome him. For Christians, humans do not go through the stages of life and achieve final freedom from suffering by appealing to one's free will and mastering one's subconscious impulses. True Christianity appeals to all Christians to assume responsibility for their actions in this world, but in their present spiritual life and at the end of life itself, salvation and life eternal is bestowed only through the suffering, death, and resurrection of Jesus Christ.[19]

THE MOTIVES BEHIND GOOD WORKS

Another issue to be considered is the human motivation behind charitable acts. Is a person motivated by some type of reward to perform charitable acts, or can such conduct be totally free of egotism and genuinely altruistic? By definition an act is altruistic if it is done to benefit the neighbor without any desire of reward for oneself, a description that pertains specifically to the motivation.[20] In other words, does curvature influence one's service toward the neighbor?

In the incisive study *Altruism in World Religions*, scholars researched whether altruism actually exists in Christianity and other religions, and they concluded that while all religions cultivate acts of welfare and charity, the concept of altruism does not apply to them because all include some beneficial consequence for the doer. These scholars agree that the motivation to do something for others entirely unselfishly and without any interest in reward

18. Coward, *Sin and Salvation*, 10.

19. Barth, *Dogmatik*, 514–16.

20. A scholarly working definition of altruism is the following: "Altruism is 'intentional action ultimately for the welfare of others that entails at least the possibility of either no benefit or loss to the actor.'" See Jacob Neusner and Bruce D. Chilton, eds., *Altruism in World Religions* (Washington, DC: Georgetown University Press, 2005), 191.

does not exist.[21] Thomas Emil Homerin claims altruism does not apply in Islam, for example, "because 'God has promised in the Qur'an to reward every good deed done by any person,'" and alms and almsgiving *(zakat/sadaqah)* form a pillar or central duty of the religion.[22] If this claim is true for Islam, then it is also true for other religions, and admittedly for some branches of Christianity. Since these all promise some kind of beneficial consequence for the actor in either this-worldly or otherworldly rewards, their acts of charity are not truly altruistic.[23]

Here Lutheranism stands apart even from other Christian denominations in its core understanding, unparalleled elsewhere, of grace and objective justification accomplished by Christ on the cross. Since the reward, the gift of grace, is received already prior to a believer's own actions, he will do charitable acts voluntarily and freely. While Luther did not use the term altruism, on a number of occasions he expressed the hope that every Christian's service to the neighbor would be offered in just this way, since a Christian "lives only for others and not for himself"[24]—rendered willingly and without any interest in gaining reward or merit from it.[25] This approach then opens the way for altruism, allowing the believer to receive salvation as a gift and to respond with an unselfishly motivated act toward the neighbor. Thus, neither reward nor fear of punishment are operative terms in the ethical approach Lutheranism takes.[26]

21. Neusner and Chilton, *Altruism in World Religions*, 193.

22. Neusner and Chilton, *Altruism in World Religions*, 67, 74, 84, 193.

23. Neusner and Chilton, *Altruism in World Religions*, 193.

24. *The Freedom of a Christian*, 1520 (AE 31:364; WA 7:64.15–16).

25. "This is a truly Christian life. Here faith is truly active through love [Gal. 5: 6], that is, it finds expression in works of the freest service, cheerfully and lovingly done, with which a man willingly serves another without hope of reward; and for himself he is satisfied with the fullness and wealth of his faith." *The Freedom of a Christian* (AE 31:365; WA 7:64.34–37). See also AE 31:367; WA 7:66.7–12.

26. In an investigation of the motivation of Christians, Ronald Preston concludes that Lutheranism takes a unique approach to Christian ethics, devoid of the concepts of reward or fear of punishment. Preston, "Christian Ethics," 91–105.

CONCLUSION TO PART TWO

In our discussion on sin we investigated multiple sources, from Scripture to modern theologians. We gained information about what we call sin: its origin, its power in taking humans captive, and its persistent drive that destroys the relationship between humans and God, and humans' relations with one another. Sin as a concept and as a term finds a home in the life of a Christian community. The common Confiteor, the acts of confession and absolution, sermons that distinguish Law and Gospel, and theological literature in general all proceed from the understanding that listeners are familiar with sin's meaning. For the most part, the term is accepted in the jargon of the church, and so it is still preached and taught.

This truth does not apply to the broader community. The Christian concept of sin is so specific and unique in content that it goes beyond the cultural and societal associations other faiths recognize as transgression and wrongdoing. For a number of reasons, society lacks a proper understanding of sin, and that fact certainly also influences how members of the church comprehend sin and deal with it in their daily lives. The church thus is obliged to translate sin's true meaning and do so vigorously and intentionally, sparing no energy in her efforts. The theologian Pöhlmann points out correctly that as long as the church defines sin in purely (trans)historical, causal, and biological categories, the modern man will have difficulty applying that information to his own life and in accepting it as a reality for himself here and now.[1] Humans in general perceive sin as something that they themselves have caused and by which they have impaired their own relations with others. Because of their own actions, they see themselves as culpable doers of sin rather than as objects or slaves of some outside force. In her proclamation the church must point out explicitly the wrongdoing, the actual sins, in the lives of people where guilt, fault, pain, anxiety, culpability, and disorder are experienced. She must do so while she continues to explain the historic origin, the cause, and the biological characteristics of original sin.

We are ready now to move on to the third and final part of this study: human involvement as being called out as God's stewards of this world in and under God's providential care. We will explore in greater detail what constitutes our involvement and cooperation with God as His stewards.

---

1. Pöhlmann, *Abriß der Dogmatik*, 198.

PART THREE

HUMAN EXISTENCE IN ACTION

12

ETHICAL APPROACHES TO CHRISTIAN LIVING

A Christian does not stand isolated from other human beings, and so the question arises: how does a Christian relate to the world around him, to creation, and to himself? How does the spiritual reality of being in relationship with God, possessing the image into which he has been restored, impact his outlook on daily life and in living out this relationship?

In answering those questions we begin with the three articles of the creed as Martin Luther explains them. We give each article its specific and valuable place in the life of a Christian: first, his createdness in body and his connection to people around him, including those of different ethnicity, religion, and social status as he assumes a specific vocation and role in society; second, his redemption through Christ, and third, his renewal in his spiritual life in the practice of worship, where God's means of grace are present. In each of these aspects an important theme is noticeable: whether in a Christian's bodily or spiritual existence, foremost is the reality or dimension of reception, which leads to a response through service and praise.[1]

Once the relationship with God is restored, the person is enabled to live out his faith toward others around him. In other words, co-humanity flows from the divine act of justification, and human conduct within those human relations belongs to the realm of ethics. Any role that Christians play in reaching out and ethically supporting their fellow humans is subsequent to and always proceeds from this initial gracious act.[2]

The following truths are therefore important: First, our humanity exists in a relationship with God, not outside of it. Second, humans are on the receiving end of this relationship. And third, they respond to God as thankful recipients of His gifts. They appreciate what they receive and so honor God rather than their own achievements. In this way, justification serves as the point of orientation for all of humanity, the vantage point from which humanity is considered.

LOVE AND IMPARTIALITY

Christians living among fellow humans thus must make an important shift in both attitude and behavior (Rom 12:2): while the individual comes first, as the one whose relationship with God is to be restored, upon its restoration he

1. For example, LC II.19 (K-W, 433); Cortez, *Christological Anthropology*, 98–99.
2. Cortez, *Christological Anthropology*, 97.

is asked to surrender that individual self for the good of the neighbor. In his treatise *The Freedom of a Christian* Luther is particularly devoted to making this ethical appeal. "I will therefore give myself as a Christ to my neighbor, just as Christ offered himself for me; I will do nothing in this life except what I see is necessary, profitable, and salutary to my neighbor," Luther repeatedly said.[3] Such behavior reflects Christ's sacrificial love on the cross, which motivates Christians to give themselves also sacrificially to others in service. For Luther, and later for Kierkegaard[4] and others like Bonhoeffer, the Christian's service to the neighbor is sacrificial, as Christ's was.[5]

One's motivation to serve the neighbor also comes from the understanding of who God is. Repeatedly Scripture reflects on God as impartial, making no distinctions based on the social and economic status of humans (Lv 19:5; Dt 1:17; 10:17; 2 Chr 19:7; Jb 32:21; 34:19). Christians are exhorted to model their lives after God's nature (Lk 20:21; 2 Cor 5:14; Phil 2:5), rejecting favoritism (Dt 16:19; 1 Tm 5:21; Jas 2:1–7). The Greek word for partiality is προσωποληµψία, a conflation of "receive" (λαµβάνοµαι, *lambanomai*) and "face" (πρόσωπον, *prosopon*) in Greek: literally, one "does receive a man's face" and thereby "brings judgment forward against someone" (πρόκριµα*)*. James prohibits Christians from adopting such an attitude toward others, as they "do not show favoritism" (Jas 2:1, 9). Peter's behavior in Antioch reflected partiality, for when other Jews came up from Jerusalem, he withdrew himself from the fellowship with the Gentiles (Gal 2:12).[6] However, in his mission to the Gentiles and foremost to Cornelius, Peter's appeal to impartiality took central place (Acts 10:34).

How should the important principles of love and impartiality shape a Christian's view and behavior today? It should impact his understanding of status and the role of merit, for one. In the divine relationship, no status is required, either of him or of others, to obtain the gifts from God (Rom 3:20). Christians are relieved of proving themselves before God and in the Christian community, and "relieved" likewise of judging others by their rank or other

3. *The Freedom of a Christian*, 1520 (AE 31:367; WA 7:66.3–5). See also in the same treatise AE 31:364–65; WA 7:64.14–37; *Two Kinds of Righteousness*, 1519 (AE 31:300; WA 2:147.15–23).

4. The inseparable connection of Christ with the the commandment of love and self-love is described by Kierkegaard in his book *Works of Love* with the metaphor of a wrestler. "But this *as yourself*—indeed, no wrestler [*Bryder*] can wrap himself around the one he wrestles as this commandment wraps itself around self-love, which cannot move from the spot." Søren Kierkegaard, *Works of Love*, trans. Howard V. Hong and Edna H. Hong, Kierkegaard's Writings 16 (Princeton: Princeton University Press, 1995), 18. In this discussion Kierkegaard deals primarily with the Christian understanding of *agape* love (ἀγάπη), built on the Lord's commandment in Mt 22:39 to love oneself, in contrast with erotic love (ἔρος) or preferential love (φιλέω).

5. Luther said similar things in a sermon on the Epistle of Romans (8:8ff.) preached on the Fourth Sunday after Epiphany in 1525, as he did in his sermon on the *Two Kinds of Righteousness*, 1519 (AE 31:299–300; WA 2:147:2–18): Christ as example and the command of love are deeply written in one's heart (WA 17/2:102.15–3.31).

6. See here the discussion of the term: Jouette M. Bassler, *Divine Impartiality: Paul and a Theological Axiom*, Society of Biblical Literature Dissertation Series (Chico, CA: Scholars Press, 1982).

status. This attitude stands in contrast to society's conventions, by which people treat one another according to status and merits and with a reciprocal justification that is understood in the active sense—expecting compensation and special treatment.

In certain stages of life, especially at its beginning and its end, humans are particularly vulnerable to society's discounting.[7] Treating others according to one's perception of their rank or status in society is an outgrowth of the idea that people should be rewarded for what they achieve, which by logic would deny any human with lesser accomplishments equal status and compassionate attention. In affirming and promoting the dignity and value of human life, Christianity rejects the valuing of individuals according to their rank and status, to which human societies are so receptive (Jas 2:1–11), and places in its stead the value, dignity, and equality of all humans. As one author puts it, "It was one of Jesus' central claims that all human beings, including the slow-witted, the untalented and the obscure, were beloved creatures of God—and hence deserving of the honour owed to every example of his work."[8]

Moreover, as Christians approach their own death they confront the stark reality that no one will be able to transfer his status and accomplishments to heaven: nothing of that which gave a human status and glory here on earth can be taken to the grave (Jb 1:21).[9] For this reason the Christian community serves as a beacon of light in the midst of a society that thinks and acts differently than it does.

This distinction does not mean that Christian communities are called to create their own ideal societies separate from others. The two-kingdoms approach to life encourages all Christians to participate actively in society within the ranks and structures humans have established. This principle also affirms rightful compensation based on production and success. But a Christian's perspective as he contributes to society through his vocation testifies that he operates with a sense of righteousness that is well aware of society's sometimes excruciating harshness toward people, as he helps temper or alleviate some of the woes that undermine a neighbor's dignity and self-worth.[10]

TREATING BEHAVIORAL SYSTEMS WITH CAUTION

These scriptural and Lutheran principles guiding theological anthropology contribute to a distinct portrayal of human and particularly Christian behavior in this world that would challenge other approaches. During the time of the

---

7. We shall return to this discussion in the conclusion of Part 3, where we highlight how social Darwinism often motivates society's censure of neighbors.

8. De Botton, though an atheist, acknowledges Christianity's unique approach patterned after Jesus. Alain de Botton, *Status Anxiety* (New York: Pantheon Books, 2004), 247.

9. "Naked I came from my mother's womb, and naked shall I return. The Lord gave, and the Lord has taken away; blessed be the name of the Lord."

10. De Botton, *Status Anxiety*, 251.

Reformation, Lutherans grappled with the first ethical system that invoked virtues and focused on the moral character of a person. This virtue ethic came from antiquity through Plato, Aristotle, and Stoicism, entering into the church through theologians such as Aquinas. Luther knew it well but met it with skepticism, since the four cardinal virtues of righteousness, prudence, fortitude (courage), and temperance (*iustitia, prudentia, fortitudo, temperantia*) were promoted as virtues to be discovered in an unregenerate person and to be attained through learning apart from God. Luther claims that such virtues come about only in the renewed relationship with God that results from faith in Him. Medieval theology, as through Aquinas, added to the classical four virtues three more—faith, hope, and love—which for Luther is equally problematic, since faith now also is categorized as a virtue rather than as a gift. If faith along with all other virtues can be taught and practiced, then according to Luther that "virtue" too is diametrically opposed to a theological ethic defined by justification.[11]

Of course, good behavior requires good people, and so the pursuit of a virtue like honesty or courage might be worthwhile to promote in society and at home. But Luther looks at the issue from the viewpoint of the source of an act: people become good only through an act of God, not by themselves. There is an alternative, Aristotelian-informed concept of justification which society in general adopts: that the human being justifies himself by demonstrating his innocence, understanding that God demands righteousness rather than giving it. That kind of justification remains only an "external" justification, not one created internally from the heart[12] and faith, and the works done are in agreement merely with human law and not with the Law of God.[13] To Luther the good works come along with the Spirit and the existence of faith, and they are expressed without coercion, totally voluntarily, motivated by love.[14] Love has the cheerful demeanor and spontaneous productivity of finding agreement with the will of God that surpasses the Decalogue of Moses.

The Lutheran Confessions agree in principle that the Spirit-filled person knows without the prodding of the Decalogue what is the good and true will of God.[15] But they were also willing to invoke the concept of necessity and the

11. Max Josef Suda, *Die Ethik Martin Luthers*, Forschungen zur systematischen und ökumenischen Theologie 108 (Göttingen: Vandenhoeck & Ruprecht, 2006), 54.

12. Luther understands the heart to be the seat of faith, and then also the emotional and cognitive domain. LC I.1–2 (K-W, 386).

13. Luther distinguishes between human law and the Law of God to indicate the difference between mere outward obedience and one that stems from faith: "God judges according to what is in the depths of the heart. For this reason, his law too makes its demands on the inmost heart; it cannot be satisfied with works, but rather punishes as hypocrisy and lies the works not done from the bottom of the heart." *Preface to the Epistle of St. Paul to the Romans*, 1522/1546 (AE 35:366; WADB 7:3.23–4.2).

14. *Preface to the Epistle of St. Paul to the Romans*, 1522/1546 (AE 35:368; WADB 7:6.12–26).

15. SD VI.6 (K-W, 588).

third use of the Law, saying that Christians "live and walk in the law of the Lord and yet do nothing because of the compulsion of the law."[16]

The Formula of Concord is realistic enough not to follow a pneumatological ethic that needs no table of the Law. Such an ethic seems to be reserved for the heavenly kingdom, whereas here on earth in the interim between Pentecost and Christ's return the believer will measure his conduct against the Law of God. There is a distinction in German between *Gesetz* (precept) and *Gebot* (mandate) in describing the Decalogue in a Christian's life. The former is the Law of God that accuses the conscience, whereas the latter describes the Decalogue as God's good and gracious will in the life of someone who no longer fears but still follows the commandments as rule and norm in his life.[17]

This understanding allows us to draw comparisons with other ethical systems. In contrast to a virtue- and merit-based (legal) approach, Luther posits an ethic formed by justification through faith and good works. His focus is on the ethics of faith leading to good works, rather than on a particular virtue achieved through human effort.[18]

Luther's approach is also critical of an ethical system that pursues happiness (εὐδαιμονία). Already in the *Nicomachean Ethics* Aristotle claims that the aim of the state should be to promote happiness for its people.[19] In *The Happy Life* (*De beata vita*) Augustine also puts forward a goal for humans, Christians included, which is to be happy; and "nobody can be happy without possessing what he desires."[20] Of course, he posits that true happiness (εὐδαιμονία) belongs to "whoever possesses God"[21] or whoever knows that his heart is devoted entirely to God. Here Augustine places faith, or the knowledge of the heart, over simple philosophical knowledge. Since God is the source of all ontological, moral, and logical truth, a soul is truly satisfied and happy once it is able "to recognize piously and completely the One through whom you are led into the truth, the nature of the truth you enjoy, and the bond that connects you with the supreme measure."[22] This complete package of happiness is rewarded, according to Augustine, with the beatific vision of God (*visio beatifica Dei*) as it is described in the sixth beatitude (Mt 5:8): "Blessed are the pure in heart, for they shall see God."[23]

---

16. SD VI.18 (K-W, 590).

17. SD VI.23 (K-W, 591); Adolf Köberle, *Rechtfertigung, Glaube und neues Leben* (Gütersloh: Gütersloher Verlagshaus Gerd Mohn, 1965), 147.

18. See here his *Treatise on Good Works*, 1520 (AE 44:25–26; WA 6:206.18–32); Suda, *Die Ethik Martin Luthers*, 54.

19. Aristotle, *Nicomachean Ethics* 1.3.1095a16–20, BWA 937.

20. Augustine, *The Happy Life*, trans. Ludwig Schopp, 2.10, in *The Happy Life; Answer to Skeptics; Divine Providence and the Problem of Evil; Soliloquies*, trans. Ludwig Schopp et al., The Fathers of the Church 5 (New York: CIMA Publishing Company, 1948), 57.

21. Augustine, *Happy Life* 2.22 (p. 70).

22. Augustine, *Happy Life* 4.35 (p. 83).

23. Augustine, *City of God* 22.29 (WSA 1.7:549).

Nowhere do we find Luther expressly formulating such a goal of happiness; his ethic instead is aligned with or conditioned by creation and the desire to fulfill one's duties toward the neighbor and society, to whom the Second Table of the Law points. A life led in faith and love is focused not on finding happiness but on serving neighbor and society with all that this entails, especially sacrifice and life under the cross.[24]

But Luther likewise would take issue with the deontological or duty-based ethical system of Immanuel Kant, which focuses on the imperative for behavior rather than its motivation. Though Luther did not know Kant's thinking, he did encounter some of its ideas in its pre-Kantian form from Stoicism and Cicero and from the great church father Ambrose's assimilation of nature and natural law to the Law of God. Kant's ethical theory has a strong focus on the rightness or wrongness of an action and not on the utilitarian approach that takes into consideration the result or consequences of an action.

But Luther most likely would see this principle of using reason to determine the morality of an act as an expression of natural law, which he affirmed on many occasions, particularly in his treatise *How Christians Should Regard Moses*.[25] Both the concept of unlimited freedom of the individual and the powers of reason are questionable premises for Luther. Freedom is qualified by the fact that a Christian is in a relationship with God and the neighbor and is bound always to consult God's Word. The fundamental ethical question is not what he wants for himself but rather what he can do for his neighbor. Kant's high estimate of reason, though put to good use in the civil realm, also is subject to error because of sin.[26]

Unfortunately, that devotion to individualism presents a challenge to living with others. The Enlightenment and Romantic era elevated individualism to an unprecedented level, making it atomistic, solipsistic, and self-sufficient, devoid of interest in the transcendent relationship with God and with others. An emphasis on one's rights, freedom, and choice emerged as a result, values which not only jeopardize any communal thought but also eclipse the very notion of God.[27]

In contrast to the contemporary world, which entertains multiple options for ethical conduct, theological anthropology encourages moral integrity built on God's Word. This principle does not permit an option in which ethics becomes merely situational, cutting one loose from a broader foundation. God's Word is not merely descriptive of human behavior but is also prescriptive,

24. This principle can be deduced from his works: *Two Kinds of Righteousness*, 1519 (AE 31:292–306; WA 2:145–52); *Treatise on Good Works*, 1520 (AE 44:15–114; WA 6:202–76); *Whether Soldiers, Too, Can Be Saved*, 1526 (AE 46:87–137; WA 19:623–62); *Temporal Authority*, 1523 (AE 45:75–129; WA 11:245–80); *Preface to the Epistle of St. Paul to the Romans*, 1522/1546 (AE 35; WA 56:5–532). Suda, *Die Ethik Martin Luthers*, 55.

25. *How Christians Should Regard Moses*, 1525 (AE 35:168; WA 16:380.19–25); *Against the Heavenly Prophets in the Matter of Images and Sacraments*, 1525 (AE 40:97–98; WA 18:80.15–81.17).

26. Suda, *Die Ethik Martin Luthers*, 56.

27. Sherlock, *Doctrine of Humanity*, 22.

inviting a deontological (*deon*: it is necessary) approach to ethics, one that addresses human conduct from the standpoint of what behavior is required since God is the Lawgiver. Since that Lawgiver has imprinted on the heart of all humans a knowledge of right and wrong (Rom 2:14–15), Christians approach non-Christians with the intent to solve ethical issues together.[28] There are thus elements of utilitarianism and teleology as John Stuart Mill (1806–73) and Jeremy Bentham (1748–1832) introduced them, in which humans act toward the common good of all and are mindful of the consequences of a decision. And yet the action proposed must not be chosen arbitrarily but should be measured against God's Word and what it prescribes.

Finally, Luther's understanding of the two kinds of righteousness is helpful in considering a Christian's behavior toward his neighbor. One of the paradigm's strengths is that it encourages a Christian's pursuit of the moral or second kind of righteousness without confusing Law and Gospel. For in his 1519 sermon on *Two Kinds of Righteousness* Luther distinguishes the first kind of righteousness—that of Christ, which comes from God as a gift through faith[29] and is received passively[30]—from the second kind. Since the second righteousness flows from the first, it can never infiltrate the first kind of righteousness. The second righteousness, the "product of the righteousness of the first type, actually its fruit and consequence," points the Christian to the neighbor rather than to himself, seeking not his own good but that of another.[31]

Here is an ethical system that corrects the premise of works-righteousness in Christian behavior by identifying a proper sequence, namely, that the rightful place of love and service in a Christian's life is after he has received the gift of Christ's righteousness.[32] This system also strongly affirms a Christian's focus away from his own self (*coram meipso*) and toward his neighbor. This distinction in focus is reflected by the *coram* categories, or the awareness of

28. "The good things we have from God should flow from one to the other and be common to all, so that everyone should 'put on' his neighbor and so conduct himself toward him as if he himself were in the other's place." *The Freedom of a Christian*, 1520 (AE 31:371; WA 7:69.1–3). In this regard, however, a divine command theory that claims all Old Testament laws are binding for Christians would not apply. Rather, because Christ fulfilled the Old Testament laws, Christians are to fashion their laws around the dual commandment to love God and neighbor, leaving room for them to assesss the situation and call for an action pursued jointly with those guided by natural law.

29. "Now it is certain that Christ or the righteousness of Christ, since it is outside of us and foreign to us [*extra nos et aliena nobis*], cannot be laid hold of by our works." Thesis 27 in Luther's *Disputation Concerning Justification*, 1536 (AE 34:153; WA 39/1:83.24–25).

30. *Two Kinds of Righteousness*, 1519 (AE 31:298; WA 2:146.14–17): "On the contrary, he who trusts in Christ exists in Christ; he is one with Christ, having the same righteousness as he. . . . This righteousness is primary; it is the basis, the cause, the source of all our own actual righteousness."

31. *Two Kinds of Righteousness*, 1519 (AE 31:300; WA 2:147.13–15).

32. Melanchthon is helpful here: "Therefore, after we have been justified and reborn by faith, we begin to fear and love God, to pray for and expect help from him, to thank and praise him, and to obey him in our afflictions. We also begin to love our neighbor because our hearts have spiritual and holy impulses." Ap. IV.125 (K-W, 140).

how he lives *coram Deo* (before God), *coram hominibus* (before people, i.e. the neighbor), and *coram mundo* (before the world, i.e., in his stewardship of animals, plants, and artifacts; Fig. 1). This three-pronged relationship is

Figure 1. The Two Kinds of Righteousness

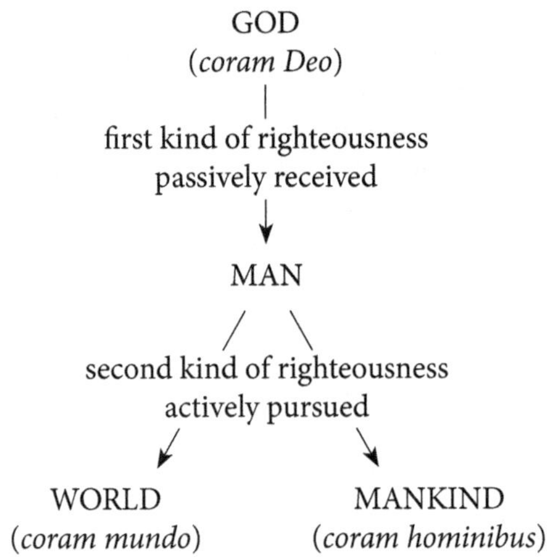

implied in the Ten Commandments: the relationship to God (*coram Deo*) in the first three, then to the neighbor (*coram hominibus*) in the remaining commandments; the last two also include animals and nonanimate belongings (*coram mundo*), which should not be stolen or coveted. According to Gerhard Ebeling, "the preposition *coram* allows for the fact that we humans, even in ontology, cannot exclude ourselves from our own being-with-others, and therefore also cannot discount our being-with-others, in whose relations and contacts we live."[33] And finally, the distinction between the two kinds of righteousness attends to Christian motivation. The motivation for practicing this righteousness toward the neighbor comes from being transformed into Christ's likeness (2 Cor 3:18) and then following His example (1 Pt 2:21). Just as He Himself did all things for us, not seeking His own good but ours only, so He desires that we act likewise toward our neighbors.[34] In the sermon on *Two Kinds of Righteousness* Luther bases his arguments on Phil 2:5: "Have this mind among yourselves, which is yours in Christ Jesus." What follows is the *exemplum* idea, what we may call "putting-on-the-mind-of-Christ" in a self-effacing or kenotic way.[35] Peter Brunner radicalizes a Christian stance as follows:

33. Gerhard Ebeling, "Luther's Understanding of Reality," *Lutheran Quarterly* 27, no. 1 (2013): 64. This understanding can be seen in Luther's Argument 5 in *The Disputation Concerning Justification*, 1536 (AE 34:162; WA 39/1:93.1–16).

34. *Two Kinds of Righteousness*, 1519 (AE 31:299–300; WA 2:146.20–47.18).

35. The *exemplum* or "mind of Christ" idea is reflected in *Two Kinds of Righteousness*,

> A Christian does not keep one eye on the work of Christ and the other on his good works. . . . The Christian fixes both eyes on his crucified and resurrected Christ. He is thus free from the aching anxiety about his salvation. . . . In this freedom he is liberated for a service to God and liberated for a God-sanctioned service to the neighbor.[36]

Sadly, a Christian's pursuit of the second righteousness is never perfect. The multidimensional *coram* relations do not exist in total harmony; they fall, "as experience shows, into a cacophony of shrill dissonance."[37] In that *coram* relationship the human find himself in the judgment seat before God, before others, and finally before himself (1 Cor 4:5). He confesses to God (*Deo confiteri*) his personal sinfulness (*confessio peccati*) and his shortcomings in the pursuit of the second righteousness. In this way, the first kind of righteousness is received as forgiveness and has an abiding presence in the life of a Christian. Properly understood, the distinction of the two kinds of righteousness never allows the "umbilical cord" to God to be severed.[38] As Luther puts it, "To have a God, as you can well imagine, does not mean to grasp him with your fingers, or to put him into a purse, or to shut him in a box."[39] To be human is to lay hold of God consciously and intentionally and cling to Him.[40]

From a Christian's perspective it almost makes sense to speak of a third kind of righteousness, one that proceeds from Christians as an ethical response of their faith in the redemptive love of the triune God, as Luther did early on.[41] But ultimately Luther concluded that since a Christian finds himself in society in the midst of non-Christians, he should relate to such neighbors by being mindful of the broader reign of God through natural law. The Christian has concerns similar to those of his unbelieving neighbor, who though outside of

---

1519 (AE 31:301; WA 2:147.34–38). For other places where Luther mentions the two kinds of righteousness, see *Sermo de Triplici Iustitia*, 1518 (WA 2:44.32–38); *Lectures on Galatians*, 1535 (AE 26:7–8; WA 40/1:45.24–47.14); *Disputation Concerning Justification*, 1536 (AE 34:162; WA 39/1:93.1–16); *Preface to the Complete Edition of Luther's Latin Writings*, 1545 (AE 34:336; WA 54:185.12–20).

36. Peter Brunner, "'Rechtfertigung' heute: Versuch einer dogmatischen Paraklese," in Brunner, *Pro Ecclesia* 2:139–40; Joest, *Ontologie der Person bei Luther*, 317.

37. Ebeling, "Luther's Understanding of Reality," 65.

38. This distinction underscores an understanding of justification as forensic and declarative in nature, rather than mystical or material. For unlike the latter understanding—the ontological transformation associated with divinization or theosis—the former demands a constant dependence on God's verdict and declaration. For a presentation of the former see Härle, "Die Entfaltung der Rechtfertigungslehre," 211–28; for insight into the latter perspective, which originated in the Finnish school, see Simo Peura, "Iustitia christiana in Luthers später Auslegung des Galaterbriefs (1531/1535)," *Lutherjahrbuch* 71 (2004): 179–210. See here also Robert Kolb, "Contemporary Lutheran Understandings of the Doctrine of Justification: A Selective Glimpse," in Husbands and Treier, eds., *Justification*, 153–76.

39. LC I.13 (K-W, 388).

40. LC I.15 (K-W, 388).

41. Luther offered a sermon on the three kinds of righteousness, *Sermo de triplici iustitia*, 1518 (WA 2:44.32–38). That threefold distinction gave way eventually to the now commonly recognized twofold distinction.

a relationship with God responds consciously to natural law.[42] In urging such civic engagement with one's neighbor based on this common understanding of natural law, Luther introduced a new understanding of how the church relates to society and temporal concerns. For the structure of the two kinds of righteousness is no theological trifle: it helps to counter the medieval tradition that still holds fast to a platonic division, considering that the things pertaining to the spirit or soul trump matters of the body and this world.

Luther confronted a tendency in his time to devalue temporal life and exalt the spiritual and mystical world. This inclination was evident with Erasmus of Rotterdam (1466 or 1469–1536)[43] and to a degree also with Philipp Melanchthon, who though attentive to classical Greek philosophical ideas such as Aristotle's promotion of an ideal society in *Nicomachean Ethics* was never quite able to embrace Luther's positive perspective on the worldly realm. According to Wilhelm Maurer, Melanchthon considers the spiritual realm of higher importance than society.[44] By contrast, Luther holds them as equally significant but on distinctly different terms, securing for each an important niche in the life of a Christian. While the one saves, the other provides an avenue for constructive and important human contribution. Luther's ethical perspective with the two kinds of righteousness provides a holistic approach to human existence that values both realms as equal. Where either is devalued, human life will be diminished.[45]

AFFIRMING OUR CREATEDNESS: THE EXAMPLES OF MARRIAGE AND FOOD

We have intimated that Christians are active in society as entire humans, in body and soul. As a consequence, Christians also enjoy the fruits of their labor and things that pertain to the bodily life here on earth. We have looked at anthropologies where the bodily existence, the fact of one's createdness, is subordinated to that of the spirit or mind. Throughout human history, which includes Christianity's history, a recurrent issue has been the attempt to deny or escape one's physical existence and its needs. Gnosticism and the asceticism of monasticism illustrate how these anthropologies have been unable to accept

42. Härle, "Die Entfaltung der Rechtfertigungslehre," 222; John S. Feinberg, "Luther's Doctrine of Vocation: Some Problems of Interpretation and Application," *Fides et Historia* 12, no. 1 (1979): 60; Cortez, *Christological Anthropology*, 108.

43. Desiderius Erasmus, *Enchiridion Militis Christiani: An English Version*, ed. Anne M. O'Donnell, Early English Text Society 282 (Oxford, UK: Oxford University Press, 1981). See Heiko A. Oberman, *Die Kirche im Zeitalter der Reformation*, vol. 3 of *Kirchen- und Theologiegeschichte in Quellen: Ein Arbeitsbuch*, ed. Heiko A. Oberman, Adolf Martin Ritter, and Hans-Walter Krumwiede (Neukirchen-Vluyn: Neukirchener Verlag, 1981), 25–27.

44. Maurer, *Historical Commentary on the Augsburg Confession*, 89.

45. Even the humanist Desiderius Erasmus struggled to value spirit and body equally. See Oberman, *Kirche im Zeitalter der Reformation*, 25–27; Arand and Biermann, "Why the Two Kinds of Righteousness?" 120.

the createdness of humans. To this day Lutheranism affirms human createdness in the midst of other beliefs that would disparage it. This stand sends a critical message to contemporary society, which perpetuates a message with Gnostic undertones that our bodies are far from what they should be and can be improved through medications, cosmetic surgery, diets, and enhancements of various kinds. The common person in society learns to flee from rather than affirm his own body, by being unhappy about it and/or by taking measures to change it.

The earthly body is the bearer of the soul, and one cannot divorce the two as though a human were designed to be a mere shadow of his true self. He is who he is as a created being, a recognition that should cause us all to consider what that bodily existence entails in terms of earthly possessions, desires and passions, our marriage partner, and also the fellow human being. (The Lutheran theologian Adolf Köberle ponders this question in an essay, the title of which can be translated as "The Joy of Bodily Existence."[46]) Accordingly, both Luther and the Confessions set the stage for affirming the bodily existence by addressing two concerns common to all humans: food and marriage.

In the Small Catechism Luther affirms that God is the creator of "body and soul: eyes, ears, and all limbs and senses; reason and all mental faculties."[47] Likewise, in the Large Catechism he states that God sustains His creation in body, soul, and life, members great and small, all senses, reason and understanding.[48] By this he means to say: God gave us the body, and wishes to have it honored. A person must recognize and treat the body according to God's design and the order or arrangement implicit in it (*Anordnung*). To that imperative belong two things: our bodies need food and clothing along with work. God created the body and gave for its nourishment and sustenance food, drink, clothing, house, and other resources. He wants us to maintain and look after it with great diligence and give flesh its due honor in time of need. He gave no one a body to maltreat, harm, or intentionally destroy it; He has created it for work and to fulfill its duties.[49] According to Luther it would be a rebellion against God not to make use of what He gave us, and resisting the demands of nature will not go unpunished. A person is wrong, for example, if he does not want to provide the body "with food and clothing for what it needs [*Notdurft*] so that he may live and work [*wirken möge*]" and instead "through frequent denial becomes sick and unfit for work." For abstinence from food "will cause his head to become crazy [*toll wirtt*] or ruin his stomach," and such a one "God will punish as murderer of his own body."[50] "For God does not

46. Adolf Köberle, "Die Freude am Leib," in *Die Seele des Christentums: Beiträge zum Verständnis des Christusglaubens und der Christusnachfolge in der Gegenwart* (Berlin: Furche-Verlag, 1932), 240ff.

47. SC II.2 (K-W, 354).

48. LC II.13 (K-W, 432); SD I.38 (K-W, 538).

49. *Wochenpredigten über Joh. 16–20*, 1528/29 (WA 28:208.34–36).

50. *Adventspostille*, 1522 (WA 10/1:18.12–14; 19.9–10.19–20); my translations.

want his orders and his creatures to be despised," but He wants people to use food and drink that He has created for the upkeep and sustenance of their bodies.[51]

In his *Lectures on Genesis* Luther points out that the world has been created for humans and humans have been created for the world. Humans must possess and use the things of this world, and they must work it, "build and preserve" it. Luther and the Lutheran Confessions emphasize this foundational insight on the value and significance of the human body and place it in the broader context of all physical existence in the world, in particular against the Roman Catholic ideal of monasticism.[52] Against the glorification of monasticism, Lutheranism points out that the body is not to be treated as something low or unworthy, even sinful, and consequently denied the pleasures of the world and the obligation to work in it. This inclination also is rejected repeatedly in Scripture, such as in Col 2:18–23, and thus a life separated from the world truly seems to be an "artificial," "humanly invented," or "superstitious religiosity" that attempts to pursue a life like that of angels, as if bodies did not exist.[53]

To abstain from the use of wine or meat or marriage sends the wrong message, implying that such things are displeasing to God and even condemned by Him.[54] On marriage, Melanchthon reasons as follows: because God wants humans to be "fruitful," He has made "human nature" such that one sex has a "natural affection" for the other sex. Since God has designed human bodies with this desire, we should look at it positively "as one belonging to our uncorrupted nature" and willed by God. "This love of one sex for the other is truly a divine ordinance" and the marriage of male and female "a natural right," that is "an order divinely stamped upon nature."[55] According to Luther, humans are corrupted and concupiscence should not tarnish procreation itself, which is "something good and holy that God has created."[56] It is important to distinguish between the nature created by God and the corruption of it through original sin.[57] Therefore, those desires or affections that seem less honorable to human opinion and which have been despised vehemently through the Roman elevation of celibacy are natural and not to be associated

51. Ap. XXIII.19 (K-W, 250); my translation.

52. There is the tradition within Roman Catholicism, stemming from St. Francis, that honors the sacramental character of creation by contemplating the divine in it; see J. Dudley Woodberry, Charles van Engen, and Edgar J. Elliston, eds., *Missiological Education for the Twenty-first Century: The Book, the Circle, and the Sandals: Essays in Honor of Paul E. Pierson*, American Society of Missiology Series 23 (Maryknoll, NY: Orbis Books, 1996), 76ff.

53. AC XXVII.14, 38 (K-W, 83, 87); Ap. XXIII.45 (K-W, 254).

54. Ap. XV.21, 29–30 (K-W, 226, 228).

55. Ap. XXIII.7–19 (K-W, 249–50); *The Babylonian Captivity of the Church*, 1520 (AE 36:99; WA 6:555.28–29).

56. *Lectures on Genesis*, 1535–45 (AE 1:237; WA 42:177.3–4).

57. "For God created not only the body and soul of Adam and Eve before the fall but also our body and soul after the fall, even though they are corrupted. God also still recognizes them as his own work, as it is written, Job 8[:8]." Ep. I.4 (K-W, 488); SD I.33ff. (K-W, 537).

with concupiscence.[58] This natural inclination to desire the other sex is truly a divine right, stamped upon nature, as modern theologians also would confirm.[59]

To clarify any misperception here that this claim might support promiscuity between humans or the prevailing social mores of Western society, we must insist on the point that this sexual activity is not understood as the pursuit of a single individual seeking to satisfy his or her own desires but "is tied closely to human relationships,"[60] and the relationship within which that activity is practiced is identified as marriage (Gn 1:28; Mt 19:6).

In this discussion the Confessions qualify the understanding of celibacy. Though it is commended by Paul as a "more excellent gift than marriage," the Confessions argue that it is seen so only because it is "less distracted by domestic activities" and can therefore "provide more time for praying, teaching, and serving." But celibacy serves more as the exception than the rule, reserved for those whom God has given the special gift of continence. For this reason God wants humans in general "to use the common law of nature which he has instituted. For God does not want his orders and his creatures to be despised."[61] Thus "God takes vengeance on those who show contempt for his own gift and ordinance, that is, those who prohibit marriage." One can see how the attempt to ignore what God has designed "undermines public morals and what vices and shameful lusts it has produced."[62] Since God "wants people to be chaste" and live pure and decent lives, they should use "the remedy he offers, just as he wishes to nourish our life when we use food and drink."[63]

Melanchthon approaches the matter of marriage and the satisfaction accompanying it in the same way as he would look upon other provisions God gives, such as food and drink, for which we thank God in prayer.[64] Luther unabashedly draws from this understanding a number of consequences for our bodily existence and its needs, some of which he recorded in a letter of 6 December 1525 to his friend Spalatin, who had entered into marriage recently.

58. "Human beings were created to be fruitful and that one sex should desire the other sex in a proper way. Now we are not speaking about our concupiscence, which is sin, but about that desire which was to have been in our uncorrupted nature, which they call natural affection [*natürliche Neigung*]. This love of one sex for the other is truly a divine ordinance." Ap. XXIII.7 (K-W, 249); similarly, Ap. XXIII.12–13 (K-W, 249).

59. Sherlock, *Doctrine of Humanity*, 208: "The wonder of conception, intended to be inseparably linked to an act of love, points to the goodness of sexual intercourse for both partners. Scriptural passages such as Genesis 2:15–24, and especially the Song of Songs, indicate that sexual activity, female and male, is a gift we are to receive with thanksgiving and careful delight."

60. Sherlock, *Doctrine of Humanity*, 208.

61. Ap. XXIII.16, 19, 38–40 (K-W, 250–53).

62. Ap. XXIII.52–53 (K-W, 255).

63. Ap. XXIII.19 (K-W, 250).

64. Ap. XIII.30 (K-W, 252).

Luther suggests that when Spalatin enjoys his wife Catherine's company in bed with sweet embraces and kisses, he thank and praise God for giving her to him.[65]

Luther is quite explicit in his descriptions, a situation that gives some observers occasion to accuse him of being overindulgent. A few centuries later, the Dominican Henry (Heinrich Seuse) Denifle (1844–1905) assessed Luther's comments as too profane, spawned by urges of evil lust, gluttony, and unruly passion such as were found otherwise only among the most corrupted people, and rarely at that. For example, by quoting an excerpt from Luther's letter to his wife Katharina, "I am gorging like a Bohemian and guzzling like a German, God be thanked for this. Amen,"[66] Denifle suggests that Luther was indeed a worldly man. But Denifle did not take into consideration that Luther's tone is humorous and thankful, for he had just overcome a spell during which he had been seriously worried about his poor appetite.[67]

At times Luther also cautions not to overindulge the body. In order that it not become rebellious and too passionate, he recommends that one discipline it on occasion without hurting or destroying it.[68] He suggests one do good works, as these were the true banner of light against binging, drinking, lewdness, quarreling, and belligerence (Gal 5:22).[69] In the end Denifle's scathing comments about Luther led nowhere. Scholars treated them as unfounded and biased.

Just as the bodily existence is embraced in God's order, so also is the entire natural social network into which we are placed. In this earthly life we should and must place ourselves under the course of nature as "divine ordinances."[70] Therefore, it is our obligation and duty to make use of every order and God-given law if we plan on achieving something. For example, although the Confessions grant God the prerogative to perform miracles,[71] and although they are also confident that our prayers can influence God and lead Him to perform a miracle,[72] they also demand we honor the natural law and orders set by God.

Melanchthon refuses to accept someone's rejection of marriage by reason of trusting in prayer to subdue his urges and be free of them.[73] We know that Scripture offers chastity as an alternative to promiscuity in

65. "Luther an Spalatin," 6 December 1525 (WABr 3:635.22–26 [Nr. 952]).

66. "Luther an seine Frau," 2 July 1540 (WABr 9:168.5–6 [Nr. 3509]). In an earlier letter to his wife on 29 July 1534 from Dessau, Luther bemoans the bad quality of beer and wine there and yearns for the excellent wine and beer back home and in addition his beautiful wife. He suggests that she send him his wine from the cellar and a bottle of beer, otherwise he will not visit Dessau again. "Luther an seine Frau," 29 July 1534 (WABr 7:91.7–13 [Nr. 2130]).

67. James Swan, "Heinrich Denifle: Catholic Interpreter of Luther," *Beggars All: Reformation & Apologetics* (blog), 2 May 2009, http://beggarsallreformation.blogspot.com/2009/05/heinrich-denifle-catholic-interpreters.html.

68. *Wochenpredigten über Joh. 16–20*, 1528/29 (WA 28:209).

69. *Adventspostille*, 1522 (WA 10/1:16.25–29).

70. Ap. XVI.6 (K-W, 232).

71. SD VIII.25 (K-W, 620).

72. For example, LC III.19 (K-W, 443).

73. Ap. XXIII.18–19 (K-W, 250).

this world.[74] But single Christians who want to be chaste and freed from the temptation of indecency and fornication should not expect a miraculous intervention from God, because He has chosen to provide marriage as the remedy to satisfy the natural urges and to allow one to live in a committed, loyal relationship.

What pertains to the natural law of marriage also can be said of all natural laws. A Christian can see himself guided in life by natural laws and measures considered reasonable, those we would think of as commonsense conventions. He conforms with such societal norms, assuming in the absence of evidence to the contrary that the legal code of a society is not gravely mistaken but has proven itself rationally over time and thus has been established as "natural." In the medical field, a Christian when ill will not readily disregard reasonable, commonsense methods of healing. He will consider carefully a broad consensus of the medical community in the light of the best available research, and not consider it idolatry but responsible stewardship to take into account what it provides and advises. He will take precautionary measures against eventualities, such as subscribing to a conventional health insurance and arranging his retirement plans, so that even though he trusts in God's miraculous powers, he will not expose himself unnecessarily and unreasonably to dangers.[75]

A Christian also will expect that those afflictions that come upon him through natural events can be explained by means of reason, even if they occur under God's providential care. As a general rule, he will not dismiss new findings and discoveries of scientists and historians that offer a natural explanation for an occurrence theretofore considered a miracle. Ultimately, what is important for Christians is to see all occurrences as coming from God's hands, even if He lets events unfold according to the so-called natural order of things and through conventions that are considered to be based upon reasonable, commonsense laws.

As a member of society, a Christian will not approach life around him in pioneer fashion, being suspicious of others around him or withdrawing from communal activities. Such measures would hardly enter a Christian's mind. Nonetheless, he could and should raise concern over this or that misdirected convention or practice, should he discover one in disagreement with God's will.

---

74. Sherlock, *Doctrine of Humanity*, 163, 166.

75. However, in the past many Lutherans were reluctant to embrace change, especially when it involved an issue about which they had moral reservations. Such was the case with mid-nineteenth-century Lutherans in America, where there is evidence of resistance to practices such card-playing, dancing, gambling, usury, installing lightning rods, even securing health insurance. Such hesitancy soon gave way to the embracing of new technologies, improved living conditions, and "indulgent" practices. While such changes might be seen as succumbing to Americanization, the openness to change itself is rooted in the nonconfrontational approach of Lutheran theology in indifferent or nontheological matters. See Carl S. Meyer, *Moving Frontiers: Readings in the History of The Lutheran Church—Missouri Synod* (St. Louis: Concordia Publishing House, 1964), 349–51.

There is a certain element of caution in a Christian's approach to and conduct within everyday life. After all, the Lord has likened His followers to Himself: as He was not of the world, neither are they of the world (Jn 17:14–19). This principle invites a discussion of the Christian's relation to both realms through which God rules in the world.

13

HUMAN EXISTENCE SET IN BROADER STRUCTURES

Previously we demonstrated how movements compromised a robust article of creation by resisting the idea that a human being is bound to flesh and physical existence for eternity. Our createdness impels us to assume social responsibility. The reformers were not set on compromising the Gospel and God's redemptive plan in Christ; they were embracing fully the article of creation and the principle that Christians and non-Christians live and work together in society in pursuit of common ethical issues for the welfare of society.

NEO-ORTHODOXY'S FLIGHT FROM CREATION

Gustav Wingren is known for a criticism of neo-orthodoxy which the title of his monograph *The Flight from Creation* already suggests: "The modern negation of the belief in creation has Karl Barth as its spiritual father: all others are secondary and have grown up in his shadow."[1]

Wingren's point is not that everything Barth says is wrong, but that his theology neglects the significance of creation and in the end offers little help in constructing a concept of social ethics which embraces all of humanity. When the Gospel is presented before creation and Law, all human arrangements and contributions of non-Christians are seen as either inadequate or of no ethical value. The idea that no morality exists for those outside of Christ, Wingren criticizes as assuming an "anthropological nihilism" and "ethical vacuum,"[2] a view he identifies as a dismissal of God's general revelation and the knowledge of natural law.[3]

1. Gustaf Wingren, *The Flight from Creation* (Minneapolis: Augsburg Publishing House, 1971), 20.

2. "Quite a different matter is the Barthian thesis that man without Christ lacks knowledge of the good. By taking that view, one starts in anthropological nihilism, in an ethical vacuum." Wingren, *Flight from Creation*, 73.

3. "Without the revelation in Christ, according to Barth, human life is an ethical vacuum, a nihil." Wingren, *Flight from Creation*, 70. It seems that Wingren's point sticks even if Barth spends a great deal of time on creation in his *Church Dogmatics*. The probable explanation for Barth's error is that he is reacting to theological positions taken during the 1930s and 1940s in Germany that seem to him to have been morally complicit with the regime's promotion of the German race according to the ideology of "race and blood," or *Volk*. Had the German Christians, Lutherans included, been less focused in their theology on created orders and natural law, they would have been more critical of the agenda of National Socialism. However, as Wingren and Lowell Green point out, the issue is more complex than that, and "national socialism's misuse

A Christologically defined anthropology can fall into the error of subjectivism, which ignores the created structures of human life into which an individual's life is placed. Albrecht Peters faults both Barth's Christomonism and Tillich's subjectivism for what he calls a "creation docetism."[4] He asserts that they both fall short of recognizing and acknowledging the divine care in First Article structures God has put in place and which precede each individual's existence.[5]

Luther also takes a Christologically defined existence as a basis for anthropology, but he pays respect to the Creator's design of the world, which conditions humanity for life here on earth. God is not only the author of certain structures and orders; He is also active behind and through them. God is not removed from this world; He is engaged in the present age. This awareness imprints onto our human existence some objectivity that avoids existentialism's solipsism, where a person imagines himself totally autonomous in shaping his own destiny.

On the opposite end of the spectrum from neo-orthodoxy's flight from creation is the position that takes the orders of creation in a far too rigid fashion, or so it appears. The theologian Paul Althaus is often the designated culprit. Althaus calls these defining orders *Ur-Offenbarung* or primordial structures, thereby promoting a natural anthropology that some scholars believe goes too far.[6] For it seems that according to his concept, humans can still operate satisfactorily in the eyes of God while remaining outside of that relationship with Him established through faith in Christ. It is as if those who live outside of Christ may exist happily and proceed as if nothing is wrong in their relationship with God.

According to Peters (and others), even though Althaus's dialectic of "yes" and "no" shows discernment of natural theology, he does not underscore sufficiently Paul's understanding of humans' own failure to perceive God and understand who they truly are, and that the curse of the Law continually looms

of the concept [of creation] does not provide a reasonable explanation for the behavior of contemporary theology." Wingren, *Flight from Creation*, 9. See also Lowell C. Green, *Lutherans against Hitler: The Untold Story* (St. Louis: Concordia Publishing House, 2007), 97–127.

4. Peters, *Der Mensch*, 134: "gewissen Schöpfungsdoketismus."

5. "The focus on the relationship God–man in Christ comes to the fore in Barth's No to a broader theology of the First Article" ("Die Konzentration auf die Relation: Gott–Mensch in Jesus Christus prägt sich aus in Barths Nein zu einer umfassenderen Theologie des ersten Glaubensartikels"). Albrecht Peters, *Der Mensch*, 132, my translation; see also 130, where he discusses Barth's rejection of the orders of creation. In that relationship to the outside world, the "self–world correlation" (*Systematic Theology* 1:16 and 3:34), Tillich lists eros, passion, feelings, and reason as the human elements which drive a person in this world and let him become creative. But in that list Tillich concentrates on the human spirit (*Geist*), noticeably marginalizing the bodily existence and its needs and relation to the world; *Systematic Theology* 3:35, 465–68. See also Peters, *Der Mensch*, 111.

6. Horst Georg Pöhlmann, "Das Problem der Ur-Offenbarung bei Paul Althaus," *Kerygma und Dogma* 16, no. 4 (1970): 242–58.

over their heads because of their sinful denial of God Himself.[7] Luther would not want confusion over creation issues to overshadow the primary article of justification, however, for justification itself places a Christian in a responsorial relationship with the world, and this article serves as a means to critically analyze all human attitudes and behavior.

Indeed, because of his promotion of the idea of primordial structures Althaus has been accused, as have other Lutheran theologians, of adopting the evangelically complacent attitude afforded by this construct. But whether this criticism of Althaus's use of primordial structures is justified must be considered in the context of his overall tenor. In his writing on *Die deutsche Stunde der Kirche*, Althaus is in fact realistic about the potential abuse of these structures: "All of us have certainly and will always come from God's primordial revelation in His creation. But we are all and always will be by nature heathen, who because of sin will abuse these primordial structures."[8] He is aware that because of the sinful nature of those within these structures, the structures themselves will be abused. We must concur with him that even in cases of such abuses, the structures themselves, like marriage, family, and government, do not merit dissolution. Abuse has to do primarily with the problematic behavior of incumbents in these institutions.

In the end, these structures or orders fulfill an important purpose and should not be discarded merely because of the sinful nature of their incumbents. They themselves serve a positive function, even though the Gospel as the final arbiter happens to stand in judgment over this or that incumbent. Althaus reflected on this as well: "We do not mean that the Gospel takes the place of all religions' traditions among nations; it rather steps into an association with them, and that not only in the negative, in the form of judgment."[9]

This discussion had a broader practical impact, including on Lutheran missionary Bruno Gutmann (1876–1966), who did precisely what Althaus's comment indicated: he stepped into an association with existing structures among the Chagga people at Mount Kilimanjaro. For him, "family, in its extended African form, age groups, elders, neighborhood, clan and tribe formed a network of relationships which was fundamental to all forms of life."[10] The three prevalent structures of extended family (or clan), neighborhood, and age group are what Gutmann calls primal bonds or ties (German: *urtümliche Bindungen*) through which and in which communal life among the Chagga is

7. Peters, *Der Mensch*, 152.

8. Paul Althaus, *Die deutsche Stunde der Kirche* (Göttingen: Vandenhoeck & Ruprecht, 1933), 45: "Wir kommen gewiß alle und jederzeit von Ur-Offenbarung Gottes in seiner Schöpfung her. Aber wir sind von Natur alle und jederzeit Heiden, welche die Ur-Offenbarung sündhaft mißbrauchen."

9. Paul Althaus, "Um die Reinheit der Mission," in *Mission und Theologie*, ed. Franz Wiebe (Göttingen: H. Reise, 1953), 52.

10. Timothy Edward Yates, *Christian Mission in the Twentieth Century* (Cambridge, UK: Cambridge University Press, 1994), 41; Bruno Gutmann, *Gemeindeaufbau aus dem Evangelium: Grundsätzliches für Mission und Heimatkirche* (Leipzig: Evangel.-Luth. Mission, 1925), 7.

experienced,[11] themselves a testimony to the creator God and thus structures acceptable to the missionary and to which his message connects. But this affirmation of a point of contact (*Anknüpfungspunkt*) established between the Word of God and human structures in society, as espoused by Brunner and Gutmann, Barth rejected with an explicit "No!" (*Nein!*), since to him these are not to be connected to the article of creation or to God the Creator. The revealed Word of God does not connect to something outside of God, for that would compromise God's sovereignty.[12]

In response to this last point, it is important to note that nothing exists outside of God, who created all. To say He binds His salvific activity to something outside of Himself, to that which exists already among humans, is not to say that He latches onto something that exists independently from Him. God connects His redemptive activity to what He has established through His creation. These orders are not thereby given salvific, redemptive quality, as though someone were saved automatically by belonging to or being situated in one of them. However, orders such as marriage and family help us recognize that God is operative in society in an orderly way and that His Law is being implemented to uphold society.[13] Through them God provides a structure for human existence, and above all these orders let us recognize the Aristotelian truth that humans are indeed social beings and exist for one another. Humans exist communally and relationally according to the principle "I am because we are,"[14] or as Gutmann himself puts it: "What you are, you are only through connectedness."[15] In view of this understanding, Lutheran anthropology cannot ignore "the social contexts to which the gospel is addressed."[16]

11. Gutmann pleaded for their protection from the onslaught of the encroaching European civilization, which threatened to destroy these natural bonds and thereby uproot the Chagga peoples' identity. Ernst Jaeschke, *Bruno Gutmann, His Life, His Thoughts, and His Work: An Early Attempt at a Theology in an African Context* (Erlangen: Ev.-Luth. Mission, 1985), 64–65.

12. Barth, *Nein!*; Brunner and Barth, *Natural Theology*, 11, 32, 54; Yates, *Christian Mission*, 43, 50.

13. We speak here of the Law functioning as *usus civilis*, "that through it external discipline may be maintained against the unruly and the disobedient"; see Ep. VI.1 (K-W, 502).

14. John S. Mbiti, *African Religions & Philosophy* (London: Heinemann, 1969), 108. See also John V. Taylor, *The Primal Vision: Christian Presence amid African Religion* (London: SCM Press, 1963), 50, 65, 117–21. This principle agrees with the common Zulu saying *Umuntu ungumuntu ngumuntu* (a human is a human through other humans).

15. Gutmann, *Gemeindeaufbau*, 15, 145. Gutmann's approach was shared by his contemporary Lutheran missionary Christian Keysser, who worked in Papua New Guinea before World War I. It seems that Bruno Gutmann's plea was overtaken by civilization's influence on the Chagga people. However, the fact that Lutheranism has grown so significantly in Tanzania speaks in favor of Gutmann's approach. Another charge leveled against his concept is that the Third Reich's nationalization program seemed to use vocabulary similar to his. However, that resemblance is truly coincidental and unfortunate, as Timothy Yates has shown. Yates, *Christian Mission*, 44.

16. Yates, *Christian Mission*, 56.

MALE AND FEMALE AS THE MOST BASIC STRUCTURE OF HUMAN RELATIONSHIPS

We have observed that the narrative of creation is helpful in our discussion of humanity in that it establishes the universal idea of co-humanity, or living in relationships. With co-humanity come structures such as family and marriage, extended family and kinships, vocations, and other social orders like government and authorities. One fundamental structure from creation that underlies all society is the distinction among humans of male and female (Gn 1:27). While we do not go so far as to draw implications from that distinction for the image or associate it with the inner-trinitarian movements (social trinitarianism) as some theologians do, we nonetheless affirm that the reality that there are two sexes, male and female, serves as an underlying principle for understanding how humans relate with one another.

If we speak of an ontology for humanity that is universally recognized across all cultures, it is that humanity is structured along the two categories of sex, male and female. This distinction is the primary or fundamental order of humanity, and every person experiences the world around him or her not only as a human but also according to his or her individual sex, as either male or female. Sexual dimorphism and the binary gender statuses correlate with God's creational intent.[17]

In his treatment *On Being Human* Ray Anderson makes the important point that from the primary ontological structure of male and female stem all other social relations, such as brother, sister, parent, child, husband, wife, and friend. The basic relationship or unit of husband and wife or that of parent and child is a consequence of the primary structure of sexual dimorphism.[18] This does not mean these secondary units are irrelevant to humanity. Life for every human begins and continues in the state of either male or female, and this fundamental structure or original form of human existence invites a host of additional social orders. From birth a society encourages a person's sex as female or male to be matched with an appropriate understanding of gender. Gender, anthropologists

17. Of course, transgender roles continue to blur the lines of male and female in societies but cannot erase the fact of the two sexual categories. The Philippines is known for its cross-dressers or transvestites, called *bakla*, but the West too has seen a surge in transgender identity. Howell and Paris, *Introducing Cultural Anthropology*, 91.

18. "To be sure, human existence is profoundly experienced in a multitude of social relations. Brother, sister, parent, child, husband, wife, friend—all these are forms of co-existence and thus manifestations of true humanity. But these are all secondary, not an intrinsic order of humanity. One does not have to be a brother or sister, husband or wife, in order to be human. But one does, according to our understanding of co-humanity, have to be either male or female. . . . All other social differentiations are included within the original determination in which human being is differentiated as male or female, male and female. The family unit—husband/wife, parent/child—is the basic social unit of humanity, but these social structures and relationships do not constitute the original form of humanity, nor therefore the true order of humanity. . . . For theological anthropology, therefore, marriage and family is a *secondary* order, made possible by the primary order of differentiation as male or female." Anderson, *On Being Human*, 51–52.

point out, is created in society. And yet, though it is culturally defined, gender helps to arrange humans according to their sex.[19]

A society which ignores sexual differentiation, however, causes confusion not only of relationships but also of the purpose for which male and female come into this world. This purpose, designed for both sexes, often is associated with procreation. To that end we should note first that from the beginning solitary existence fell short of what God intended (Gn 2:18: "It is not good that the man should be alone. I will make a helper fit for him"). The need to overcome man's solitary existence could not be met from the animal kingdom. And so God chose to separate humanity (אָדָם, adam) into man (אִישׁ, ish) and woman (אִשָּׁה, ishshah)—male and female persons who existed as a he and a she, copartners helping one another in the task of dominion over creation. And in spite of the sexual differentiation, the Bible stresses togetherness, that the two will become one flesh (Mt 19:6). This one flesh points to marriage, an exclusive relationship between man and woman that is complete in itself, according to the account of Gn 2:4–25. To this relationship then come children, growing out of the mandate to be fruitful and multiply. Sexual union for the purpose of procreation alone, the sole reason male and female exist in marriage, would limit the scope of that partnership and what it means to be fully human. The blessing of children also offers one sphere in which to exercise dominion, but being fully human does not depend on this blessing either.[20]

This distinction and its purposes provide the template for humanity, or at least the beginnings of it, that we affirm as having been established from creation, which precedes the birth of every human being as well the articles of redemption and sanctification. Individuals, male and female, step into structures like marriage, family, and vocation which exist by divine design. Because sexual dimorphism is the fundamental structure of humanity, the creator God has provided channels or orders, such as husband/wife and father/child, in which both sexes are placed and fulfill their distinct roles.

19. Paul suggests his own view on certain behavior and dress codes for women in that passage. There are thus across individual cultures some variations in what befits a particular gender; see Howell and Paris, *Introducing Cultural Anthropology*, 90–91.

20. "Procreation is thus a distinctive aspect of marital fruitfulness, but does not exhaust its meaning. This perspective is confirmed by Genesis 5:2, where humanity's being made in the image of God as male and female is reiterated, yet without mention of children. In the light of this, to limit the significance of gender to procreation is as restrictive as relating it only to sexual union; if the first is too narrow, the other is too hedonistic. On the one hand, being made as male and female (gender) is wider and deeper than sexuality. On the other, sexuality has procreation as a key purpose, a purpose which must not be rejected, but is not exclusive of others." Sherlock, *Doctrine of Humanity*, 40.

THE THREE ESTATES OF HUMAN ACTIVITY: *STATUS ECCLESIASTICUS, STATUS POLITICUS,* AND *STATUS OECONOMICUS*

Sexual dimorphism and the structure of male and female have always influenced the structuring of society. The three estates or states of society, memorably described in Geoffrey Chaucer's *Canterbury Tales* (AD 1385)—the church (clergy), nobility (and knights, or those who fought and ruled), and peasantry (everyone else, those who produced food and other commodities)—were defined from the perspective of males and their gender. The women were classified in categories of their own. Although they also were involved in the second and third estates and could join the first by their own choice, women were categorized into specific "feminine estates" based on their sexual activity with men: virgin (one who has never slept with a man), wife (one currently sleeping with a man), and widow (one who used to sleep with a man).

The arrangement of these traditional estates reflects the Aristotelian/medieval division of *domus* (*oikos*, home), *civitas* (*polis*, political and societal life), and *ecclesia* (church). These three social classes became known most commonly in medieval society as *oeconomia*, *politia*, and *ecclesia*, matched to the principle of three important duties: nourishing or feeding (German: *nähren*, which fell upon the peasants), defending (*wehren*, done mostly by the knights), and teaching (*lehren*, usually done by the clergy). Of course, these traditional divisions of society experienced a shift with the emergence of the mercantile class and intellectuals, those who achieved some wealth and rose above the rank of a peasant, and those who taught but did not belong to the church.[21] Over time, the possibility of choosing one's profession grew, as did the option to move from one profession to another. Societal and political systems also changed from monarchies to democracies.

While it is easier to trace Luther's comments on the two kingdoms or realms, to which he devoted specific writings, he did comment incisively and extensively on these three estates or hierarchies (*Stiftung*, *Ordnung*, and *Hierarchien*) in his *Confession on the Lord's Supper* (1528). He did so in order to dispel the idea that by belonging to one of these orders, especially to the order of the church, like a monastery, one is saved or guaranteed a special status before God.[22] Instead, in all three estates—the office of priest, the estate of marriage, and the civil government—people contribute equally with their good works toward the good of their neighbor.[23]

---

21. Ulrich Duchrow, *Christenheit und Weltverantwortung: Traditionsgeschichte und systematischer Struktur der Zweireichelehre*, Forschungen und Berichte der Evangelischen Studiengemeinschaft 25, 2d ed. (Stuttgart: Klett-Cotta, 1983), 502.

22. *Confession Concerning Christ's Supper*, 1528 (AE 37:365; WA 26:505.25–28).

23. Luther's comments on all three orders are worth noting here: "But the holy orders and true religious institutions established by God are these three: the office of priest, the estate of marriage, the civil government. . . . Above these three institutions and orders is the common

This important description of the three estates offers a glimpse into Luther's understanding. He upgraded these three structures or standings in social life by regarding them as institutions established by God and not merely as creations of society.[24] This understanding of institution comes from passages such as Rom 13:1–7 and Gn 1:26f., which oblige all of humanity to be fruitful and multiply, to serve as stewards over creation, and to prevent evil from taking over. The "table of duties" inserted in the catechisms offers advice to the incumbents of the three holy orders: in the church for bishops, pastors, and preachers; for governing authorities and other masters; and then for the family, for husbands, wives, and children. This pattern supports the understanding in the Augsburg Confession that the public order and marriage "are created and instituted by God and that Christians may without sin exercise political authority."[25] The divine character of these three standings is underscored further in the assertion that the Creator places or calls individuals to serve in these institutions in their respective positions or vocations (German: *Beruf*; Latin: *vocatio*, after the Greek word κλῆσις, "calling" in 1 Cor 7:20 and Eph 4:1).

Luther's anthropology underlies his reasoning on the three institutions. A human being exists in body and soul and thus has a relationship toward God (*coram Deo*), in which he receives spiritual righteousness through the Gospel, and a relationship toward the world (*coram mundo*), in which he actively promotes civil righteousness. Moreover, this approach has great bearing on Luther's understanding of the two kingdoms or two regiments, which is related to that of the three hierarchies: the hierarchies or estates of *politia* and *oeconomia* represent the worldly regiment and the church the spiritual regiment.[26] Within the *oeconomia*, the economic estate of trade and commerce, the household of the family and its relationship of master and servant serve as the nucleus from which flow all other services in the economy. The status of father and the family are upgraded to become the basic backbone of the *oeconomia*. Since marriage and family in Luther's view are God's basic arrangement in society, father- and motherhood represent God; for this reason parents, biological and nonbiological, all in their extended forms, must be honored regardless of their conditions.[27] Luther's teaching on the Fourth Commandment speaks to this extended concept of parents by identifying three kinds of fathers—fathers by blood, fathers of a household, and fathers of the nation—and also a fourth

order of Christian love, in which one serves not only the three orders, but also serves every needy person in general with all kinds of benevolent deeds, such as feeding the hungry, giving drink to the thirsty, forgiving enemies, praying for all men on earth, suffering all kinds of evil on earth, etc. Behold, all of these are called good and holy works. However, none of these orders is a means of salvation. There remains only one way above them all, viz. faith in Jesus Christ." *Confession Concerning Christ's Supper*, 1528 (AE 37:364–65; WA 26:504.30–5.17).

24. Duchrow, *Christenheit und Weltverantwortung*, 499, 502; Maurer, *Historical Commentary on the Augsburg Confession*, 85.

25. AC XVI.1–2, 5–7 (K-W, 48, 50).

26. Maurer, *Historical Commentary on the Augsburg Confession*, 86.

27. LC I.108–9 (K-W, 401).

category, the spiritual fathers.[28] From the fathers of blood flow parenthood and obedience to the parents, and by extension to schoolteachers and government and civil officials.[29] All of these must be given honor and respect.[30] This means there are people who rule over a person and who hold an authority over him that is derived from his true parents. These people are superiors, like masters and civil rulers, "whose duty it is to command and to govern."[31] Luther goes on to explain his point:

> Through civil rulers, as through our own parents, God gives us food, house and home, protection and security, and he preserves us through them. Therefore, because they bear this name and title with all honor as their chief distinction, it is also our duty to honor and respect them as the most precious treasure and most priceless jewel on earth.[32]

Those in the political realm (*politia*), namely, those who rule or stand in some kind of civil authority, and those in the economic realm (*oeconomia*) are to be guided by the proper use of reason in executing their God-given duty as stewards (Gn 1:26ff.).[33] On this point Luther comments that "God does not in the Scriptures teach us how to build houses, to make clothing, to marry, to wage war, to sail the seas, and so on."[34] Authorities in these realms are to be guided by reason, in part because both Christians and non-Christians participate in these two estates, whereas the third estate, the ecclesial estate, is filled by Christians alone. And since Christians understand that God is behind all three estates, they also should "'entreat [God] with prayers for all people.' From 1 Timothy 2[:1]."[35]

THE ORDERS OF CREATION

It is important to bring out this Lutheran interest in the structures and orders of human life because they have been lost in neo-orthodoxy's myopic focus on the relational, dialogical nature of human existence that is defined solely Christologically. That constriction raises the question of how non-Christians participate in God's providential care—those who, sadly, respond little to the First Commandment, and yet through whom God still works. We speak here of the orders of creation into which humans are placed and through which God directs the world through His Law and humans' natural knowledge.

---

28. LC I.158 (K-W, 408).
29. LC I.141–42, 150 (K-W, 405–6).
30. LC I.158 (K-W, 408).
31. LC I.141 (K-W, 405).
32. LC I.150 (K-W, 407).
33. Duchrow, *Christenheit und Weltverantwortung*, 504: "Daß Luther Wirtschaft (Haus und Ehe) und Politik eindeutig und ohne Abstriche zum Feld der Vernunft erklärt."
34. Martin Luther, "Epiphany," in *Sermons of Martin Luther*, trans. John Nicholas Lenker et al. (Grand Rapids: Baker Book House, 1988), 6:319. See also *Natural Knowledge of God*, 47.
35. SC VII (K-W, 367).

The idea of the orders of creation is built on Luther's theology of creation and the three estates, and generally it is considered to be the birth-child of nineteenth-century neo-Lutheranism, starting particularly with Adolf von Harleß, and then also taken up by Werner Elert, Paul Althaus, Friedrich Gogarten (1887–1967), Friedrich Brunstäd (1883–1944), Georg Wünsch (1887–1964), Gustaf Wingren (1910–2000), and Emil Brunner. These theologians reflect much of what Luther said about the instituted realms for society, in addition to biblical truths. Without scriptural support and faith in the Creator who instituted them, the talk about the orders of creation remains abstract, without any practical and concrete relevance.[36] Thus we will explore in Scripture the number of orders that exist and what details pertain to each of them.[37]

In line with Luther, we can identify three main orders: the order of family and household, the order of government, and the order of worship. First, we look at the order of the household, the family. The household as outlined by the Tenth Commandment in Ex 20:17 includes three sets of relationships: wives and husbands (Eph 5:24; Col 3:18: Ti 2:5; 1 Pt 3:1, 5); children and parents (Lk 2:51; Eph 6:1–3); and servants and masters (Ti 2:9; 1 Pt 2:18). The husband, whose head is Christ (1 Cor 11:3), is the head of the wife (1 Cor 11:3; Eph 5:23). Surprisingly, the call for a Christian wife to be subordinate to her husband does not focus on her obedience to him but on her respect for him as her head (Eph 5:22, 33; 1 Pt 3:2). Its purpose is for her to receive his love (Eph 5:24–27), and if she is married to an unbeliever, to gain his conversion (1 Pt 3:1–2). While the father is the head of the family, both parents are the heads of their children.

Following the way Jesus related to His parents (Lk 2:51), the subordination of children to their parents involves reverence (1 Tm 3:4) and obedience (Eph 6:1; Col 3:20) and leads to prosperity and longevity in the family (Eph 6:1–3). Since slaves are considered part of the family,[38] their status is similar to that of children. Their subordination to their masters also involves obedience (Eph 6:1; Col 3:20) and reverence (1 Tm 3:4), as well as acceptable behavior and utter reliability (Ti 2:9–10), and leads to Christ's approval and His reward (Eph 6:8; Col 3:24; 1 Pt 2:22). In all of these cases, the attitude of subordination results in the kind of behavior that is appropriate to the relationship.

Second, we consider the order of government (Rom 13:1, 5; Ti 3:1; 1 Pt 2:13). The subordination of Christian citizens to their rulers involves obedience with four kinds of good works (Ti 3:2): paying taxes, paying customs duties, showing respect for them, and honoring them (Rom 13:7). In these works Christians do exactly what all good pagan citizens do, but in addition they accept their rulers as God's agents, His ministers (Rom 13:4) and assistants (Rom 13:6). Through

36. Maurer, *Historical Commentary on the Augsburg Confession*, 119.

37. I am indebted to John Kleinig for helping me to refine this exegetical section on the orders of creation.

38. See Ex 20:17.

this subordination they receive benefits from God through their rulers and possess a good conscience before Him (Rom 13:3–5; 1 Pt 2:14). This second order, which includes paying taxes to authorities, implies the existence of the *oeconomia* in society.

Third, we explore the order of the church (1 Cor 14:40). There is an order of worship for humans that God has established at creation, the seventh day which God set aside and "appointed it for rest, and commanded it to be kept holy above all other days."[39] God's design and intention is to have humans occupy themselves with God's Word since, in Luther's words, "all our life and work must be based on God's Word if they are to be God-pleasing or holy."[40] Unlike other created life, all human life has a spiritual soul, and this order established by God proves that humans are endowed with a response-ability to God's Word. It is a testimony to self-transcendence as a mark of what is uniquely human that the Word of God approaches a person and establishes a response.[41] Within this established order, the head is the risen Christ (Eph 5:24; cf. Eph 4:15; Col 1:18; 2:19), who is placed under God the Father (1 Cor 11:3); subordinate to Christ are all the other ministries. In Eph 5:21, the participle ὑποτασσόμενοι could imply a general plea to all members for a reciprocal subordination of all to each another, ἀλλήλοις. But even if such a plea is intended, it does not mean that the proper order and the established leadership in the church should be ignored. Reciprocal subordination would involve, above all, subordinating oneself to the established church leadership as mentioned in Eph 4:11 and 1 Pt 5:5. Dismissing distinctions of leadership, sex, or profession is not indicated, as one might want to argue from Gal 3:28. This passage speaks to the equality of salvation, that everyone's righteous faith is equal in the eyes of God. The congregation is subordinate to God the Father in receiving life from Him (Heb 12:9; Jas 4:7) and to Christ in receiving its salvation (Eph 5:24; see 4:15–16). Its subordination involves adherence to God's Word (Rom 8:7) and the Gospel as confessed in the creedal statements of the church (2 Cor 9:13). The members of the congregation are subordinate to its leaders, such as elders, who teach God's Word (1 Cor 16:15–16; 1 Pt 5:5). This principle includes the silent subordination of all, women and men, to the men who teach God's Word in their congregation (1 Cor 14:34; 1 Tm 2:11). The purpose of subordination is to receive all that Christ gives to the church through His Word. Disorder and disrespect of others in the congregation results in confusion that compromises the reception of the Gospel's gifts.

Four points are worth noting here. First, the New Testament does not teach that there is a general universal order of creation. There are three specific orders. Adding others, such as land, race, or nation (*Volk*), has no scriptural support.[42]

39. LC I.80 (K-W, 397).

40. LC I.92 (K-W, 399).

41. Anderson, *On Being Human*, 41, 39.

42. Note that the ideology of National Socialism attempted to replace, not merely supplement, the traditional Christian belief by instilling a "new faith" in a supreme nation

Second, in the context of these orders, the proper stance is one of subordination. The Greek word for subordination in the above passages is *hypotassein* (ὑποτάσσειν)—a military term assigning a soldier to take his position in the line—and it is used in the context of the three basic orders God has ordained, two of which belong to the realm of creation, the world, and one of which belongs to the realm of salvation or redemption, the church. Peter's epistle demands that his readers subject themselves "for the Lord's sake to every human institution" (ἀνθρωπίνῃ κτίσει, 1 Pt 2:13). With the phrase "every human institution" he implies that the positions of rulers such as emperors and governors are not human inventions but divinely established positions of leadership, offices created by God for humanity.

In regard to the subordination of women in the order of the family and worship, the New Testament does not speak of the general subordination of all women to all men but only of their subordination in particular relationships, according to their station, such as wives to their husbands.[43] There is therefore no theological reason that women cannot be leaders in government or take on leadership positions in the business world.

Third, subordination means different things in different contexts and different relationships. While a woman may not speak as a teacher in the liturgical assembly, she may question her husband at home (1 Cor 14:33–35) and teach younger women to be good wives and mothers (Ti 2:3–5).

Fourth, subordination is not commanded blindly but is connected to and informed by the Word of God. Thus, if someone is asked to perform an act that shows noncompliance to or violates God's Word (Acts 5:29), in other words is called to commit a sinful act, that person should not subordinate himself but should conscientiously object. In the context of marriage, the demand for a Christian to refuse to comply with the Word may lead to divorce; for a citizen in the context of government or for a soldier in the army (such as in the case of a violation of just war theory),[44] biblical conviction may lead to conscientious objection. For a member in the church, noncompliance with God's Word may lead to resistance, that is, he will object if he discovers that what is taught or practiced in the church is contrary to God's Word; and for a worker in a profession this may lead to a nonviolent objection, or in an extreme case to abandoning that vocation.[45]

(*Volk*), one's race (*Rasse*), and its leader (*Führer*). Suda, *Die Ethik Martin Luthers*, 88.

43. See Pieper, *Christian Dogmatics* 1:524: "It is the plain teaching of Scripture that in relation to the man, the woman is in a position of subordination. Both the order of creation and the order established after the Fall assign her that position."

44. AC XVI.1–2, 5–7 (K-W, 48, 50); *Whether Soldiers, Too, Can Be Saved*, 1526 (AE 46:130–31; WA 19:656.22–57.10). Resistance to an insane ruler is permitted, but not to unjust tyrants, because the insane ruler would not "be considered a man since his reason is gone." *Whether Soldiers, Too, Can Be Saved*, 1526 (AE 46:105; WA 19:634.19–20).

45. For further reading, see Armin Wenz, "Natural Law and the Orders of Creation," in *Natural Law: A Lutheran Reappraisal*, ed. Robert C. Baker and Roland Cap Ehlke (St. Louis: Concordia Publishing House, 2011), 79–95.

LESSONS FROM LUTHER IN VIEW OF CONTEMPORARY CONCERNS

We live in a socially dynamic and changing world, and in many cases adjustments are made to the way past structures and orders have been upheld. We see this with marriage, where both spouses work and pursue careers often out of necessity to make ends meet; with the mobility of humans in society, which allows them to pursue better job opportunities; and with the arrangement of political life, where democracy has replaced monarchy.[46] Indeed, Scripture attests to such shifts in ruling structures, from a tribal system to a kingdom and eventually to the Roman Empire.[47]

For these reasons it becomes our task to ask the important question whether the understanding of estates and social classes or the orders of creation are still worth considering. It is difficult to dismiss these systems outright as irrelevant today, as mere social conventions and opinions of a time gone by, since they have have been rooted in scriptural truths. Thus, the Christian message to contemporary society includes an urgent call to realign its ways to how Scripture and traditional theological anthropology advise people to arrange their lives (Fig. 2).

Figure 2. The Two Kingdoms or Realms of God

We should note a number of important points. First, matters pertaining to the family, household, politics, and social life are common to all humans and consequently are subject to the laws of society. They are realms regulated by natural law, which is applied through the use of human reason and expert

46. Howell and Paris, *Introducing Cultural Anthropology*, 162.
47. Howell and Paris, *Introducing Cultural Anthropology*, 42, 149.

knowledge. As a contemporary scholar puts it, when it comes to human reason and natural law, one should not pummel unbelievers "with biblical texts whose authority they do not accept."[48]

Second, we should accept the fact that a degree of mobility may be unavoidable as a person pursues a number of occupations over the course of a lifetime. If God calls someone to a specific vocation,[49] then it may seem that to switch to another would violate that divine call. But in view of occupational mobility today, often due to economic necessity, this static view is difficult to defend. We also should allow the possibility that God calls a person multiple times. In that regard, Barth raises a valid question: "What right have we to exclude the possibility that the divine calling and man's corresponding obedience might one day transfer him altogether from his present sphere to another?"[50] The fact that we connect vocation to God places value on every occupation: it is more than a mere job, it is an important contribution to society's welfare.

Third, Luther holds marriage in high respect as divinely instituted by the Creator, "a godly estate" to be blessed, to be prayed for, and to be held in honor in every possible way.[51] Nonetheless, he denies it sacramental status and calls it "an outward, bodily thing like any other worldly undertaking."[52] He places marriage in the civil realm, where it is subject to the laws of the state.[53] Luther concedes three grounds for divorce: impotence, refusal to cohabitate, and especially fornication.[54] Any divorce based on other grounds is for him an abomination that still should be punished by death.[55] Neither are Christians spared challenges in marriage. After all, Luther concedes, "there are even among

48. Timothy L. Hall, "A Law for All Seasons: C. S. Lewis on Civilization & the Natural Order," *Touchstone* 22, no. 5 (2009): 29, http://www.touchstonemag.com/archives/article.php?id=22-05-024-f.

49. Vocation comes externally to a person in various ways: one's natural or biological skills might point him to a certain vocation, for example, as might the wishes of parents or other authorities. Thus the internal desire alone will not guarantee a successful vocation.

50. Karl Barth's question (*Church Dogmatics* 3.4:645) might not be the right one to put to Luther, although the Reformer also changed vocations.

51. *A Marriage Booklet for Simple Pastors* (1529) (K-W, 368, para. 3). "Marriage itself, being a divine institution, is incomparably superior to any laws, so that marriage should not be annulled for the sake of the law, rather the laws should be broken for the sake of marriage." *Babylonian Captivity of the Church*, 1520 (AE 36:99; WA 6:555.28–30). See also *A Sermon on the Estate of Marriage*, 1519 (AE 44:3–14; WA 9:213–19) and *The Estate of Marriage*, 1522 (AE 45:11–49; WA 10/2:267–304).

52. *The Estate of Marriage*, 1522 (AE 45:25; WA 10/2:283.8–9); *Babylonian Captivity of the Church*, 1520 (AE 36:92; WA 6:550.22–24); *Treatise on Good Works*, 1520 (AE 44:27; WA 6:207.15–22).

53. *The Estate of Marriage*, 1522 (AE 45:32; WA 10/2:289.3–7).

54. Luther based this conclusion on Mt 5:32; 19:9. *The Estate of Marriage*, 1522 (AE 45:30–35; WA 10/2:287.13–92.6); *Babylonian Captivity of the Church*, 1520 (AE 36:102; WA 6:557.35–36); Suda, *Die Ethik Martin Luthers*, 163–64.

55. *The Estate of Marriage*, 1522 (AE 45:32; WA 10/2:289.10–13); *Babylonian Captivity of the Church*, 1520 (AE 36:105; WA 6:559.20–23): "As to divorce, it is still a question for debate whether it is allowable. For my part I so greatly detest divorce that I should prefer bigamy to it."

believers married folk who are evil and worse than any heathen."[56] In the case of adultery, if both spouses are Christian they should seek to forgive each other even if this presents a great challenge.

Fourth, Luther's understanding of marriage and the practice of one's sexuality are closely related. He sharply dismisses sexual practices outside of wedlock as "fornication" and "knavery."[57] In his view, it is also impossible for someone to switch his or her sexuality, and marriage is meant to be between a man and a woman.[58]

Fifth, for Luther, marriage is for the purpose of assisting one another; it is of economic value. Luther's wife, Katharina, was a supportive helpmeet and ran a large household, which included six children (of whom two later died) in addition to frequent guests (who paid for their lodging), a number of servants, and a steady stream of visitors.[59] Katharina assumed roles that went beyond those of an average wife at that time, but nothing seems to indicate that Luther abandoned the patriarchal structure of marriage and family.

Sixth, in Luther's view, marriage also embraces family. By that we mean that he includes children, defining family from Gn 1:28.[60] Children belong to marriage, and it would not have crossed Luther's mind that a couple would choose to be childless. He so elevates marriage that he would be critical of a life led apart from marriage, in which one either remains single or chooses a same-sex partnership equated with the institution of marriage.[61]

Seventh, prominent in Luther's writings on marriage is the vocation of the parent, of father and mother. Parents know the challenges of raising children, yet for Luther the family is the place where the father and mother can practice their faith in word and deed, and they are obliged to see that their children are

---

56. *Babylonian Captivity of the Church*, 1520 (AE 36:93; WA 6:550.37–51.1).

57. Suda, *Die Ethik Martin Luthers*, 164–65.

58. *The Estate of Marriage*, 1522 (AE 45:17; WA 10/2:276.1–4): "Therefore, each one of us must have the kind of body God has created for us. I cannot make myself a woman, nor can you make yourself a man; we do not have that power. But we are exactly as he created us: I a man and you a woman."

59. In his twenty-one letters to his wife, Luther often teased her as "Lord" or "Master": "My dear beloved Lord Catherine Luther, doctor, preacher of Wittenberg" ("Meinem freundlichen lieben Herrn Katharina Lutherin, Doctorin, Predigerin zu Wittenberg"). "Luther an seine Frau," 4 October 1529 (WABr 5:154 [Nr. 1476]). Or "To the hands of my dear beloved housewife Catherine Luther of Wittenberg" ("Meiner herzlieben haußfrauen Katherin Lutherin zu Wittenberg zu handen"). "Luther an seine Frau," 8 September 1530 (WABr 5:608 [Nr. 1713]). Suda, *Die Ethik Martin Luthers*, 164.

60. *A Sermon on the Estate of Marriage*, 1519 (AE 44:8; WA 2:167.16–17): "A woman is created to be a companionable helpmeet to the man in everything, particularly to bear children." *The Estate of Marriage*, 1522 (AE 45:18; WA 10/2:276.21–22): "For this word which God speaks, 'Be fruitful and multiply,' is not a command. It is more than a command, namely, a divine ordinance [*werck*] which it is not our prerogative to hinder or ignore."

61. Ulrike Treusch, "Käthe und Martin: Das Verständnis von Ehe und Familie bei Martin Luther," in *Martin Luther—Aus Liebe zur Wahrheit: Die bleibende Bedeutung der Anliegen des Reformators für heute*, ed. Berthold Schwarz (Dillenburg: Christliche Verlagsgesellschaft, 2016), 391.

given a Christian upbringing.[62] Marriage, with the goal of procreating through the sexual union of husband and wife, is deeply embedded in humanity across all times and places, and it is given legal protection because posterity is ensured when humans receive one newly born into their midst, into a community or institution that we call family.[63]

62. LC Preface 4, 17 (K-W, 383, 385). See also SC VII: "The Table Blessing" (K-W, 364). But even this practice of eating together and praying has lost its place in many Christian homes.

63. *A Sermon on the Estate of Marriage*, 1519 (AE 44:8; WA 2:167.9–11). A universally acceptable definition of marriage may be this: "Marriage is a publicly recognized social or legal union that creates a socially sanctioned context for sexual intimacy, establishes (in whole or in part) the parentage of children, and creates kinship." Howell and Paris, *Introducing Cultural Anthropology*, 162.

14

HUMANS AS RESPONSIVE AND RESPONSIBLE COWORKERS OF GOD

There are many ramifications of belonging to a community. One that pertains to theological anthropology in particular is the understanding of stewardship or regency (Gn 1:26–28). We did not identify regency directly with the image of God but have argued that the two are closely tied. Regency embraces in the fullest sense every human being, especially the Christian who consciously acknowledges not only his standing as steward in this world but also his work as defined by the vocation into which God has called him to serve in this world. We may recall the stewardship duties given to humans: (1) be fruitful and multiply (Gn 1:28); (2) fill the earth; (3) subdue the earth; (4) rule over fish, birds, and animals of the land; (5) enjoy plants as food; (6) use the "garden," the earth, as their home (Gn 2:15); (7) be stewards over the earth; (8) name all animals (Gn 2:19–20).

STEWARDSHIP AND THE CONCEPT OF *CONCURSUS* AS COOPERATION

In his role as steward, each human assumes his own particular *Sitz im Leben*, his vocation, and so participates in God's providential activity over His creation. As stewards, humans are to be shepherds over creation, taking care of other life and nonorganic matter around them. The image of the shepherd is associated in the Bible primarily with pastoral ministry, where the person standing in the vocation of pastor is summoned to take care of his flock, his members (Acts 20:28). That imagery can be applied also to every Christian and to every human being, where a person's shepherding functions embrace his social circles, the family, and through work also his neighbor and the world. Today that stewardship over the world bears global ramifications. Nations have recognized that the impact of their stewardship in the world transcends geographical boundaries, as the nuclear disaster in Chernobyl and two world wars have demonstrated, and so a shared concern can be beneficial to all parties.

In his discussion with Erasmus of Rotterdam, Martin Luther points out that humans "in all things, even including the ungodly, cooperate with God."[1] The Latin term used here for the mutual work is *concursus*, which suggests a

1. *Bondage of the Will*, 1525 (AE 33:242; WA 18:753.32–33).

"running together" of God and humans. The term impresses on humanity the understanding that God exercises His providential care over His creation by acting through humans, every one of them. All humans cooperate with God, provided they pursue a legitimate vocation.[2] They do so only in the secondary sense (*causae secundae*), however; God alone acts as the prime agent in history. But how that cooperative relationship is perceived among people ranges from affirmation to a downright denial of it. Christians point to God in His providential care as being the triune God, while deism reduces the Trinity to a god with hardly any personality ascribed to him; naturalists believe humans act apart and independently from God, and pantheism points to the broader cosmic deity of which humans are a part.[3]

For theists, cooperation embraces the concept of God's continual work in creation (*creatio continua*), which occurs in the present rather than in the past, as *creatio ex nihilo* did. *Creatio continua* is ongoing as renewal and preservation of what God creates. Unlike those who dismiss God's interaction with His creation, Scripture depicts God as at work everywhere: "When you hide your face, they are dismayed; when you take away their breath, they die and return to dust. When you send forth your Spirit, they are created, and you renew the face of the ground" (Ps 104:29–30). And in Acts, Paul preaches that God is the one who "gives to all mankind life and breath and everything" (Acts 17:25). Luther says that "God alone does all things in and through me,"[4] and similarly in his *Magnificat* (1521) he reflects on the word "mighty" in Lk 1:49 as meaning not "a quiescent power. . . . But it denotes an energetic power, a continuous activity, that works and operates without ceasing."[5]

To that end God created humans as *primus inter pares*,[6] establishing a personal "I–you" relationship with humans, His creation (Gn 1:26), and assigning them to active duty. In underscoring the human part of "cooperation" and "co-ruling," God gave them this commission in the form of a blessing: "God blessed them. And God said to them, 'Be fruitful and multiply and fill the earth and subdue it, and have dominion over the fish of the sea and over the birds of the heavens and over every living thing that moves on the earth" (Gn 1:28).

Luther always maintains this continual involvement of God with man, though many theologians have attempted to impose their own philosophy of history on Luther without letting him have the final word.[7] In his church

2. Peters, *Der Mensch*, 122. For Luther two vocations are questionable, that of a prostitute and that of a monk.

3. Sire, *Universe Next Door*, 67.

4. "Allein Gott alles ynn mir thue und wircke." *Über das 1. Buch Mose: Predigten sampt einer Unterricht, wie Moses zu leren ist*, 1527 (WA 24:22.7; my translation).

5. *The Magnificat*, 1521 (AE 21:328; WA 7:574.29–30): "Ein wirckende macht und stettige tettickeit, die on unterlaß geht ym schwanck und wirckt."

6. Barth, *Church Dogmatics* 3/1:187, 198.

7. As Martin Seils demonstrates in his book *Der Gedanke vom Zusammenwirken Gottes und des Menschen in Luthers Theologie* (The thought of cooperation between God and man in Luther's theology), Beiträge zur Förderung christlicher Theologie 50 (Gütersloh: Gütersloher

postil, for example, Luther uses the image of a conduit (*Rohr*) or a channel (*Kanal*) to describe how humans receive good things from God and then pass them on down to the neighbor with love. And so in his orientation toward the world, the believer understands that he is placed there by God to receive His love and then pass it on. Vocation must be considered a "'station' instituted by God," "a channel for God's love to the world and his care of human beings."[8]

Luther acknowledges a human's cooperation but leaves no doubt who the actual subject is. Gustav Wingren, who devotes an entire chapter to cooperation in the context of vocation, observes: "Luther makes it clear that God's own love reaches out to others through Christians as channels."[9] In his commentary on the First Commandment in the Large Catechism, Luther treats human cooperation as proceeding from this relationship with God, not as a subject apart from Him.[10] From Luther's writings we learn three important things. First, God provides for and blesses all humans as they cooperate within God's orders at specific places—callings they should not abandon arbitrarily (1 Cor 7:17–20; Eph 4:1)—where they have been called as channels to pass on God's blessings to others. Second, since Christians are aware that they are ultimately mere recipients of God's blessings and then conduits of it, they respond favorably by honoring God in the right faith. Third, though all humans serve as God's channels, not all acknowledge the fact that they pass on what God hands down to them, nor are they faithful responders to the gifts from Him. Those actions come from faith, presupposing justification and the fulfillment of the First Commandment.

God serves as the subject and source for a human's cooperation, which raises the question whether it is appropriate and accurate to advance the concept of cooperation in the first place. It is true that a tendency can arise to be too one-sided in the matter, depicting the human merely as a means or a tool, which overlooks the partnership built on trust and faith in Him. Certain quotations of Luther may contribute to this tendency. He asserts, for example, that a human's will, though active, serves in God's hand simply by enduring, "just as a sword in its movement does not do anything but merely endures."[11]

On other occasions Luther articulates his position in a way that reflects a more active interpretation of humans in external works, where God is not alone in His doing but works together with humans. Ultimately, God Himself

---

Verlagshaus G. Mohn, 1962).

8. Gustaf Wingren, *Luther on Vocation*, trans. Carl C. Rasmussen (Philadelphia: Muhlenberg Press, 1957), 125.

9. Wingren, *Luther on Vocation*, 126.

10. "This forces us to recognize God's gifts and give him thanks, as this commandment requires." LC I.27 (K-W, 389).

11. On Ps 5:12 in *Operationes in Psalmos*, 1519–21 (WA 5:177.21): "Voluntas vero incarnata seu in opus externum effusa recte potest dici cooperari et activitatem habere, sicut gladius in suo motu prorsus nihil agit, mere autem patitur" (my translation); *Resolutiones Lutherianae Super Propositionibus suis Lipsiae Disputatis*, 1519 (WA 2:421.7–15).

remains the subject who acts through humans.[12] Luther likens this relationship to that of a lord and master to his own slave: the slave has the freedom to use his hands and feet, which the master cannot control in every detail, but that relative freedom connects the slave to the master even more. The master is much more effective if his subject is not dead but actually has the freedom to move and act.[13]

The underlying point is that God extends His service by committing Himself to people, which pertains to all aspects of His devotion toward the world. In terms of spiritual sustenance, He provides us the office of the Word, the ministry of His apostles, and the mutual consolation of all Christians, who share and comfort one another with the Word. This principle applies likewise to our bodily existence. "Thus he uses us human beings in both corporeal and spiritual governments, to rule the world and all that is in it."[14] In his *Treatise on Good Works* (1520) Luther explains why humans are needed as God's cooperators: though he admits that God has the power and ability to do these works by Himself, He "does not want to do it alone. He wants us to work with him. He does us the honor of wanting to effect his work with us and through us."[15]

Instead of approaching us in His "uncovered majesty," God comes with His mask before His face. "God clothes Himself in the form of an ordinary man who performs his work on earth. Human beings are to work, 'everyone according to his vocation and office'; through this they serve as masks for God, behind which he can conceal himself when he would scatter his gifts."[16] This understanding reflects the scriptural truth that "there are varieties of activities, but it is the same God who empowers them all in everyone" (1 Cor 12:6).

Martin Seils raises a further question on the topic of cooperation, asking how this concept relates to the Lutheran teaching of being saved and renewed by grace alone, by faith alone, and without works. Here we are reminded of the previous discussion on the two kinds of righteousness, since the first righteousness passively received corrects all merit-based thinking in cooperation. The understanding of *concursus* and cooperation then excludes the notion that such running together between humans and God earns anyone favor or occurs in a synergistic or semi-Pelagian sense. Moreover, the realm for such cooperation points to things below (*inferiora*), to matters that apply to people, not to those things considered as above (*superiora*), as Luther distinguishes the two realms in *The Bondage of the Will*.[17] However, matters that pertain to things

12. Wingren, *Luther on Vocation*, 137.

13. Wingren, *Luther on Vocation*, 124.

14. *The Prophecy of Johannes Lichtenberger in German, Carefully Edited*, 1527 (AE 59:180; WA 23:9.2–4).

15. *Treatise on Good Works*, 1520 (AE 44:52; WA 6:227.29–31).

16. Wingren, *Luther on Vocation*, 137–38; LC I.24, 26 (K-W, 389); see also LC III.72–73, 76–79 (K-W, 449–51).

17. Wingren, *Luther on Vocation*, 124.

above and those below should not stand in total separation.[18] The connection between these two realms is fluid: one flows logically into the other, since the believer who receives through faith his righteousness as a gift then turns to the neighbor with the love the Holy Spirit works through him. In this way the believer knows that in his role as cooperator he is still reliant on the Spirit's work of love in him.[19]

One important characteristic of humans as God's cooperators is the ability to communicate and respond so that they can interact with the world around them. We have learned from Luther, Emil Brunner, Elert, and Ebeling that a formal extant structure of the image of God exists for all people, which Brunner defines as a "capacity for words and responsibility." We can add that this capacity to hear and communicate is fundamental to functioning in interhuman relationships. Humans need this capacity to serve as stewards in the world. Humans are communicative, even if the same can be said in some sense of all other animal life. Humans are specially equipped for the service of stewardship. Through their sensory perception they become aware of and interact with the world around them. The ear picks up sounds and the mouth produces a response, whether speaking, laughing, singing, or crying. The human ability to speak and utter sounds that are then picked up by the ear and interpreted is truly the most remarkable feature of humans as they live in their relationships with one another and with God.[20] This capacity demonstrates that humans are created to be social beings, and every human to a greater or lesser extent shares this common creatureliness with all other humans on earth.[21] We would contradict our own character and purpose were we to lift ourselves out of that common creatureliness and pursue an isolated existence apart from the self–world–neighbor–God correlations. According to Bayer, this understanding should shape our attitude in the vocation we assume, since "the vocation of the human consists in responding with praise and thanks—sharing and passing on the gifts of God. . . . Theological anthropology is an anthropology of responding."[22]

18. Joest, *Ontologie der Person bei Luther*, 310.

19. Joest, *Ontologie der Person bei Luther*, 318.

20. Sherlock, *Doctrine of Humanity*, 224. Of course we also should point to all the other senses—sight, smell, touch, and taste—if we think of a human being holistically (225–27).

21. Christian Smith, *What Is a Person? Rethinking Humanity, Social Life, and the Moral Good from the Person Up* (Chicago and London: The University of Chicago Press, 2010). Smith, a sociologist, offers at least thirty causal capacities needed for subjective and objective human activity, such as consciousness, valuation, self-reflexivity, abstract reasoning, and truth-seeking (42–59). He observes: "Some other animals do possess some of these capacities, but usually at much lower levels of function and intensity. Other of these capacities are unique to human existence" (53).

22. Bayer, "Image of God," 78.

CREATION AND NEW-CREATION: TWO ACTIVITIES EXCLUDING HUMAN COOPERATION

From what Luther intimates in the First Article of the Large Catechism, we learn that God is the prime cause (*prima causa*) in creation and men are defined as cooperators (*cooperatores*) but never as co-creators (*concreatores*).[23] This distinction derives from the fact that they have received the status as stewards from God. Humans are second in command. Some theologians who are aware of this distinction would make the point that a human serves as a "created co-creator."[24]

This distinction between cooperation and co-creation makes sense as well in the spiritual realm. The Lord places a spiritual government of prophets, apostles, and pastors over all believers, and yet it is He who in the end is the subject of it all. He teaches, consoles, forgives, rebukes, and creates faith. In the reign of the Holy Spirit, the spiritual government cannot create a believer's faith, nor can the believer sustain himself in that faith. But this rule applies also to a human's bodily existence and to his cooperation with God in the world. In his *Bondage of the Will* Luther ponders the two divine acts of creation and sustenance: that through the creation of the world life came from nothing (*creatio ex nihilo*), and that life always remains a creation of God, both in becoming and in the state of being sustained by God alone. Though he affirms humans' cooperation, Luther also emphasizes its limits, since a human being "neither does nor attempts to do anything toward becoming a creature, and after he is created he neither does nor attempts to do anything toward remaining a creature, but both of these things are done by the sole will of the omnipotent power and goodness of God, who creates and preserves us without our help."[25]

By relegating humans to the status of cooperators rather than co-creators, Luther assigns them a crucial and important station in the context of God's created world. Of course, humans also produce things: farmers and owners of manufacturing companies see and define themselves as producers of material things for others. As much as this understanding pervades society, we still must think of all products made by humans in the end as products attributed to God's continual creation. The corn growing in the field, the apple sitting in the grocery store, and the automobile in the car lot are "creations" of humans, but in the end they point to God as the final cause who enables this creation. Unfortunately, those who hold to a humanist or naturalistic tradition and consider the world a closed system would see this principle as an interference or intrusion into their own doings.[26] The lack of the divine prerogative behind

23. Peters, *Der Mensch*, 121; Bayer, "Image of God," 81.

24. Braaten and Jenson, *Christian Dogmatics* 1:325.

25. *Bondage of the Will*, 1525 (AE 33:242–43; WA 18:754.1–4).

26. *Humanist Manifesto II*, in Kurtz, *Humanist Manifestos I and II*, 16; Sire, *Universe Next Door*, 70.

the verb "to create" was apparent already in the non-Christian Greco-Roman world. Because that culture did not embrace a single deity but a multitude of gods to whom various roles were ascribed, among these deities not even Zeus or Jupiter assumed the role of sole creator or providential caretaker. The Latin causal verb "to create" (*creare*, meaning "to let something grow") implies human activity: people are the causal agents who produce or procreate. This is the conventional understanding of the verb "to create." Yet Christianity wants to uphold the biblical worldview in which God the Creator assumes a special role in the act of creation, which is His creating something from nothing. Humans by contrast can create only from something that already exists (*creatio ex materia* as opposed to *creatio ex nihilo*). Even if the word "create" frequently is applied to human action, we still want to follow Peter Brunner and Werner Elert in pressing this theological distinction.[27]

In summary, we reiterate three important points:

(1) We cannot place ourselves in the right relationship to God, nor can we within that relationship offer any contribution toward the form or shape it takes. We can be in relationship with God only in the responsory role, to which God Himself opens us up, engages us, and lets us in. Toward God the self is simply receptive: it cannot place itself nor can it enact something.

(2) The self also is unable to place itself in the right relationship of love with the neighbor. We are drawn in to love the neighbor as we are drawn in in faith; the two acts are one and the same work of God. However, in this relationship of love we can contribute as cooperators by serving one another and thereby letting ourselves be used by God. In other words, in our relationship to the neighbor we move from reception to action (*rezeptiv-aktiv*). By being drawn into the love of God, we become active in our orientation toward the neighbor.

(3) In our own relationship to things and events we can exercise our personal freedom. We use our own rational powers to decide and act, invent and "create." On this level, to the *res* or the external things around us, we are able to decide and act (*setzend-einsetzend*). However, we are not to become engaged for the sake of doing something for our own selfish welfare or benefit. We are cautioned not to exercise our liberties in hedonistic ways but always to direct them to the neighbor and his well-being. We have been given all our abilities to engage the neighbor and promote his welfare.[28]

---

27. "Was auch immer die Kreatur an Wirkungen tätig hervorbringen mag, jede dieser Wirkungen . . . liegt in Gottes Hand und unterliegt seiner all-lenkenden und all-begrenzenden Macht." Peter Brunner, "Gott, das Nichts und die Kreatur," in Brunner, *Pro Ecclesia* 2:43; Elert, *Christian Ethos*, 204–5; Elert, *Christian Faith*, 166–70.

28. Joest, *Ontologie der Person bei Luther*, 319–20.

ALL HUMANS AS COOPERATORS OF GOD—EVEN THOSE OUTSIDE THE COMMUNITY OF FAITH

Theological anthropology addresses conventional human behavior in society from multiple perspectives or angles. It takes into consideration in particular the perspective of Christians, for whom the law of love serves as guide, and then also the perspective of all humans. No human seeks to live alone in the world, but because humans are social animals they come together and assume joint responsibility in this world. The difference between humans in general and the redeemed is that the latter are especially cognizant of being born into a web of human relationships and structures, and that in this context their ethical conduct is not chosen arbitrarily but is informed and prescribed by God. Moreover, Christians and non-Christians approach their ethical obligations from different perspectives. The law of reciprocity applies for both Christians and non-Christians, a rule which comes to the former via the Golden Rule (Mt 7:12; Lk 6:31; Rom 13:9) and to the latter through natural reason. To serve and love the neighbor seems to be a fundamental anthropological category that is universally known and practiced.

We Christians tend to see ourselves as God's cooperators in a different way than or in contrast to those who are not Christian. This inclination was intimated earlier in the suggestion of a third kind of righteousness which applies to Christians alone. But God's work in creation embraces the contribution of all humans, for which they are equipped with their reason and natural skills. This functional anthropology points to the qualities and obligations humans still possess after the Fall, which remain whether a person consciously acknowledges his role as cooperator in good faith or remains ignorant of his role under God. In the latter case, the Old Testament contains a number of examples in which God takes heathen kings into His service to punish or free Israel or uses heathen nations in the history of Israel. In the former case, conscious and faithful cooperation with God is evident among Christians, who act in accordance with Phil 2:12–13: "Therefore, my beloved . . . it is God who works in you, both to will and to work for his good pleasure."

Luther in his *Lectures on Galatians* (1535) distinguishes between the Law performed before justification and after justification, and then praises the contributions before justification of "many good men even among the pagans."[29] In His preservation and guidance of creation, God utilizes the reason of humans, expert knowledge in a subject matter, and the general law of the conscience in humans, and for that end He does not need the prerequisite of faith. We remember Luther's observation that even "the ungodly cooperate

29. Men "such as Xenophon, Aristides, Fabius, Cicero, Pomponius Atticus, etc.—performed the works of the Law and accomplished great things." *Lectures on Galatians*, 1535 (AE 26:123; WA 40/1:219.23–25).

with God."[30] Of course, such cooperation "is limited to the earthly realm, where outward rectitude counts."[31] Wingren explains that in the concept of vocation, the rule *in opere operantis* (that is, a work's effect does not depend on the agent's character or status) does not apply, and we have to reject a kind of Donatism,[32] which holds that in their vocations only Christians serve the good of the neighbor, while others do not. Wingren's point is that the belief or unbelief, goodness or wickedness of the person does not determine whether his work is effective or ineffective. The office or vocation enjoys relative independence from its incumbent. Thus "God works through the station, the office, which, as his creation, is good under all circumstances, regardless of the character of the incumbent."[33] God takes all humans into His service in the world. They serve the structures through their calling, whether they have faith in God or not. And those in faith who serve in such structures are not endowed automatically with special First Article skills because of their faith and trust in God. A dentist without faith in God might still have better skills for his profession than a Christian dentist. Christians cannot claim that because of their faith their aptitude exceeds that of non-Christians. The main difference between the two groups is that Christians consciously recognize that they stand in the service of God and that all blessings in their life come from Him.

In the Augsburg Confession as elsewhere, Lutheranism affirms that every human possesses reason, whether or not he is Christian.[34] In Luther's treatise on *Temporal Authority*, for example, he lauds the Duke of Burgundy's knowledge of God's natural law and his ability to judge between right and wrong. In this ruler Luther sees a non-Christian acting with a general knowledge of right and wrong by punishing one of lesser nobility for taking advantage of a married couple. Not only is this narrative vivid and captivating, it also provides great insight on the use of "untrammeled reason."[35]

Behind this narrative lies a tradition Luther also follows and by which Western society has lived since Aristotle and Cicero affirmed the concept.[36]

30. *Bondage of the Will*, 1525 (AE 33:242; WA 18:753.32–33). This does not mean that Luther abandoned his notion of what truly is considered a pleasing work in the eyes of God. In his *Treatise on Good Works*, 1520, he clarifies: "It is from faith as the chief work and from no other work that we are called believers in Christ. A heathen, a Jew, a Turk, a sinner may also do all other works; but to trust firmly that he pleases God is possible only for a Christian who is enlightened and strengthened by grace" (AE 44:25; WA 6:206.14–18).

31. Wingren, *Luther on Vocation*, 133.

32. AC VIII.2–3 (K-W, 43).

33. Wingren, *Luther on Vocation*, 134.

34. AC VIII (K-W, 51).

35. *Temporal Authority*, 1523 (AE 45:129; WA 11:279.35–80.15).

36. Aristotle deals with natural law theory in *Nicomachean Ethics* 5.1129a1–138b15, BWA 1002–22, and in his *Politics* 3.1.1274b32–288b6, BWA 1176–205. But according to Robert Radford, it was Cicero who first formulated the natural law theory summed up in this quotation from *The Republic* 3.33: "And there will not be different laws at Rome or at Athens, or different laws now and in the future, but one eternal and unchangeable law will be valid for all nations and all times, and there will be one master and ruler, that is God, over us all, for he is the author of this law, its promulgator, and its enforcing judge." Quoted in Robert T. Radford, *Cicero: A Study*

Thomas Aquinas in his *Summa Theologiae* points to natural law and human reason, connecting them to theology: "Whatever is contrary to the order of reason is, properly speaking, contrary to the nature of man, as man."[37] In both ancient and medieval accounts, the law of nature is held to be implanted in humans in some sense by God (or the gods). This law is the law of our nature and consists in the capacity for right reason. While belief in God(s) can vary, this premise gives both theists and Deists the sense that an essential part of society is a response to a knowledge of God's Law. This Law, Scripture testifies, God implanted in the heart of humans (Rom 2:14–15), and they can see from creation that He exists (Rom 1:19–23). This fact confers some objectivity on society's arrangement of life, especially in the passing of laws. In measuring themselves by the objectively moral Giver, the laws affirm His existence and the sense that they are constituted not merely culturally or by intuition. This is not to say that certain structures and laws passed by authorities will remain rigid. Luther refers to the *Sachsenspiegel*, a particular code of laws laid down for the people of Saxony for a specific time which were not applicable to the people outside of that state, just as the laws of Moses have their particular audience, the Jews and not the Christians.[38] Certain human customs upholding a specific law and the form of punishment decreed can change and have changed over time, whereas the Law itself remains unchanged. The law that society upholds concerns all citizens, both Christians and non-Christians.[39]

Christians and non-Christians have mutually agreed to work jointly in society, not creating separate worlds for themselves but being willing to collaborate, even if each holds a different set of commitments and worldviews. Examples abound where Christians and non-Christians work together on matters that concern the common good, including on moral issues relating to gender, artificial insemination, euthanasia, abortion, and same-sex marriages. These are all issues that affect society and not just the church. From a Lutheran perspective, the service of Christians contributes toward the improvement of society's condition, toward both individual and communal good; yet while they are active in society, Christians understand the manifest reality of sin and

in the Origins of Republican Philosophy (New York: Rodopi, 2002), 43.

37. See *Summa Theologica of St. Thomas Aquinas*, trans. Fathers of the English Dominican Province (New York: Benzinger Brothers, 1947), 316 (I–II, q.71, a2c).

38. Just as the *Sachsenspiegel* represents a set of laws only for the citizens of Saxony, so the laws of Moses belong to the Jewish people alone. However, unlike the individual casuistic laws of the Old Testament, the Decalogue stands out for its apodictic and noncausal prohibitions, and thus it seems to transcend time and situation, even when according to Luther all laws of the Old Testament apply only to the Jews. See Luther's *Against the Heavenly Prophets in the Matter of Images and Sacrament*, 1525 (AE 40:75–225; WA 18:37–214). According to Peters, the Decalogue itself, being apodictic and not casuistic, represents for Luther the paradigm of all laws inscribed on humans and thus retains its universal value and application for all humans, including Christians. Albrecht Peters, *Kommentar zu Luthers Katechismen*, ed. Gottfried Seebaß (Göttingen: Vandenhoeck & Ruprecht, 1990), 1:74.

39. Wingren, *Flight from Creation*, 26–27.

its evil. Instead of harboring utopian notions of an ideal and perfect society here on earth, Christians are level-headed and realistic about the world and society around them, waiting to be relieved someday of their earthly toils and labors, as the hymn "O Morning Star, How Fair and Bright" puts it.[40] Theological anthropology must accept that the *status corruptionis* continues to loom over creation, over people pursuing their profession in their calling, and that this condition will be removed only eschatologically at the end of human existence. Until then, the tension remains between a life which truly is led in proper response to God and one which is not.[41] Elert acknowledges the positive contribution of humans outside of Christ, but he also sees all human endeavors to improve society covered by the cloud of failure. Why is it, he asks, that the ideal society has not yet come into being, despite the devotion of all good people to their jobs and their unselfish participation in community betterment, while they refrain from every untruth and dishonesty and hurt, working constantly to improve the economic system and make the government more democratic?[42]

We see that theological anthropology integrates the discussion on man's relation to humanity in general with history, society, economics, culture, politics, and the environment. The discipline seeks an affirmation as well as a clarification of how God's involvement in all these sectors embraces the cooperation of humans. Christians find themselves placed under God in both realms or regiments of God's work, the spiritual and the physical, albeit in two different ways. In terms of God's reign in this world and our participation in it, we affirm that God's work in creation includes the involvement of all humans. This means that as Christians, we recognize and appreciate, as Luther did in *The Disputation Concerning Man*, the use and contribution of reason toward advances in technology and human civil life in general. We cannot be "monastic" in our attitude, that is, skeptical and diametrically opposed to advances being made in the worldly realm, whether in science, medicine, or technology.[43] Theological anthropology instead recognizes and affirms the value of science and technology, economy, and the social activity of both Christians and non-Christians.

40. "What joy to know, when life is past, / The Lord we love is first and last, / The end and the beginning! / He will one day, oh, glorious grace, / Transport us to that happy place / Beyond all tears and sinning!" LSB 395:6.

41. Elert instead sharpens the view on the reality of eternal death (*Todverfallenheit allen Menschseins*) becoming fully manifest at God's judgment over all (*weltumspannenden Gottesgericht*). Peters, *Der Mensch*, 145.

42. Elert, *Christian Ethos*, 140.

43. *Together with All Creatures.*

DENIALS OF ASSUMING A LIFE OF RESPONSIBILITY UNDER GOD

If we consider not only the possession of rationality but also its use, then humans in their role as stewards are confronted with an additional question: how do their accomplishments measure up? While a perfect balance or congruence once existed between possession and use of reason and abilities, it no longer does.[44] We are able to demonstrate easily and convincingly from empirical observation humanity's sin in human biology, psychology, cultural anthropology, and sociology.[45]

Concerned Voices

In his book *Orthodoxy* the apologist G. K. Chesterton states that original sin "is the only part of Christian theology which can really be proved."[46] Chesterton looks back at 3500 years of human history and states that sin is verifiable empirically, so its impact on human life can be studied easily.

Though freedom is given to humans here on earth, this privilege can be abused, particularly when it seeks to eliminate God. In Rom 1:18–32 the apostle Paul comments on this path of independence from God that humans choose and its negative consequences: "For although they knew God, they did not honor him as God or give thanks to him, but they became futile in their thinking, and their foolish hearts were darkened" (Rom 1:21). Since the Fall, God's wrath has been revealed over all, "against all ungodliness and unrighteousness of men" (Rom 1:18; 2:9ff.).[47]

This corruption of humans raises the question whether a universal ethic can be built on natural theology (*theologia naturalis*). These passages and others like Acts 14:15–17; 17:22–29; and Psalm 19 raise the issue of whether an ethic built on natural theology will be recognized and acknowledged by unregenerate humans. Any denial of a *theologia naturalis* would have difficulty refuting the scriptural proof text of Rom 1:18–2:18, in which Paul affirms unequivocally that "what can be known about God is plain to them, because God has shown it to them" (1:19).[48] From this exegetical point, the late orthodox Lutheran theologian Abraham Calov draws the conclusion that "of course the revealed knowledge of God is more complete than the natural knowledge, but it is no more firmly and certainly grounded in the testimonies of Scripture."[49]

---

44. Pieper, *Christian Dogmatics* 1:516.

45. Schwarz, *Human Being*, 250.

46. G. K. Chesterton, *Orthodoxy* (Garden City, NY: Image Books, 1959), 9.

47. Commenting on Romans, Douglas Moo observes: "*Every person* is 'without excuse' because every person—whether a first-century pagan or a twentieth-century materialist—has been given a knowledge of God and has spurned that knowledge in favor of idolatry, in all its varied manifestations." *The Epistle to the Romans*, The New International Commentary on the New Testament (Grand Rapids: W. B. Eerdmans, 1996), 98.

48. *Natural Knowledge of God*, 9.

49. Abraham Calov, *Consideratio Arminianismi* (1655), quoted in Preus, *Theology of Post-*

In Rom 1:29–31 the apostle Paul provides a catalogue of sins that seems to reveal progressive degeneration. The world that does not acknowledge God as its God and refuses to serve under Him invites chaos and unfettered perversion. Over the unregenerate gushes a tide of vices, from private to public immorality and a refusal to worship. In Rom 1:23 Paul speaks of the ultimate perversion, which is to replace the glory of God with false images. This perversion in turn evokes divine wrath, and Paul speaks repeatedly of God giving up such sinners to their vices (Rom 1:24, 26, 28), which means He releases them into a life dictated by flesh and chaos. Because humans abandoned God first and exchanged Him for idols, "He gave them up . . ."[50]

Which sins stand out today among people and society? In the encyclical *Laudato Si'* from June 2015, Pope Francis addresses the same issue in society today that Paul was addressing. The encyclical speaks to society's lack of appreciation for God's goodness as the creator God, and it states that people all originated from the hands of God the Creator and are sustained by Him.[51] Then the document becomes more specific about today's ills and provides a long list, including pollution and climate change, toward which humans contribute. It calls attention to the depletion of natural resources, especially water; the loss of biodiversity, particularly the destruction of the "lungs" of the world, the Amazon and African jungles; the decline in the quality of human life and the breakdown of society; and finally, global inequality between wealthier nations and poorer countries. The encyclical bemoans that despite the widespread global media focus on these issues, many people around the world remain wilfully ignorant about them or only superficially or not at all concerned, as if these events were not happening. *Laudato Si'* alerts humanity to the reality of how sin is impacting creation, the environment, in numerous ways as humans carry out their roles as stewards.

Perhaps a more serious and sinister depiction of sin was brought forward on 6 September 2015 at the International Conference of Confessing Communities (*Bekennender Gemeinschaften*), a group of concerned Christians in Germany. That conference adopted a noteworthy document called the Salzburg Declaration.[52] This document, authored by Lutheran theologians and praised

Reformation Lutheranism 2:21. The Lutheran Confessions affirm in a number of places the scriptural truth of general revelation and natural knowledge of the law. See for example SD V.22 (K-W, 585); AC XX.24–25 (K-W, 56). For an account of such affirmations by Luther, including in his *Sermon on the Second Book of Moses*, see *Natural Knowledge of God*, 42.

50. Ap. XIX (K-W, 53): "Since it was not assisted by God, their will turned away from God" (Latin text). See also LC III.83 (K-W, 451); SD XI.85 (K-W, 654).

51. Francis, *Encyclical Letter Laudato Si' of the Holy Father Francis: On Care for Our Common Home* §§ 76–77 (Vatican City: Catholic Church, 2015), http://w2.vatican.va/content/francesco/en/encyclicals/documents/papa-francesco_20150524_enciclica-laudato-si.html.

52. *Salzburger Erklärung: Die heutige Bedrohung der menschlichen Geschöpflichkeit und ihre Uberwindung: Leben nach dem Schöpferwillen Gottes: Eine theologische Wegweisung der Internationalen Konferenz Bekennender Gemeinschaften* (The Salzburg Declaration: present threats to human creation: life according to the will of God, the Creator) (Teterow, Germany: IKBG, 2015), http://www.ikbg.net/pdf/Salzburger-Erklaerung-Original.pdf. This document has

widely for its theological stance, takes a much closer look at human life and the ills it faces than does the previously mentioned papal encyclical. It calls for an "ecology for humans," in which people not only respond to disasters and mishaps around them but also become aware of who they are as God's created beings and what they are doing to themselves.[53] Humans are destructive not only of the environment but also of themselves. The document points out two grave dangers that could lead to the eradication of human life itself. First, in the midst of peace, humans are threatened with an unprecedented destruction of life at the hands of other humans, a concern that pertains especially to life at its beginning (before birth through abortion) and its end (through assisted suicide or euthanasia). Second, the foundational elements of what it means to be human, and thus human essence itself, are undermined through emancipatory ideologies such as feminism and genderism. Concretely, two fundamental elements are endangered. In peril, first, is the distinction of two sexes as God created them and desired them to become the foundation for marriage and family, and thereby also the dignity of humans as husband and wife and as father and mother. And second, at risk is the order of the creation of marriage and family along with the purpose of sexuality in creating new life, which are indispensable prerequisites for a dignified, humane society and civilization.[54]

The document clearly expresses a concern over the preservation of the human race and what is considered human. It points out two societal trends that correspond to the two dangers mentioned above. The concern over the treatment humans receive at the beginning and end stages of life is a response not only to the widespread taking of life in abortion and euthanasia but to many other related questionable practices. The other grave peril identified is the breakdown of the order of family and marriage and the departure from sexual dimorphism to include gender identity that is neither exclusively masculine nor feminine. This latter trend, the document observes, has next to the practice of same-sex unions[55] taken on an ideological trajectory, dismissing any discussion

---

not yet been translated into English. See also Werner Neuer, "Die Salzburger Erklärung," *CA: Confessio Augustana* 2 (2019): 49–56.

53. *Salzburger Erklärung* § 1.

54. *Salzburger Erklärung* § 3.

55. Same-sex unions must be judged in the light of 1 Cor 6:9–10 (v. 9: ἀρσενοκοῖται) and 1 Tm 1:9–10 (v. 10: ἀρσενοκοίταις), both of which describe men's offensive homosexual behavior with the term ἀρσενοκοίταις, a conflation of ἄρσενος and κοίτην, echoing what is said in LXX Lv 18:22 and 20:13. Paul thus is not saying something new, offering a revision or progressive reading of the Old Testament Jewish tradition, but he transfers this Jewish prohibition into the New Testament Christian community. The conclusive text is Rom 1:26–27, which condemns switching "natural" (φύσις) for unnatural relations. The debate around the meaning of φύσις is whether "by nature" refers to God's created order and Law or to the personal inclination or orientation of an individual and what he finds natural for himself. The latter reading is adopted by John Boswell in *Christianity, Social Tolerance, and Homosexuality: Gay People in Western Europe from the Beginning of the Christian Era to the Fourteenth Century* (Chicago: University of Chicago Press, 1980), which states that Paul is not condemning all same-sex attractions but rather those in heterosexual relationships for going against their own nature or inclination (111). Richard B. Hays clearly and correctly rejects Boswell's position as flawed, since Paul means

about what is morally right or wrong. It is an incisive observation. With the publication of *Gender Trouble* (1990)[56] by Judith Butler, the traditional view of sex and gender became an issue of debate, particularly as these categories are applied to women. Since then the discussion about sex and gender has only intensified in public and political discourse. Today the nonbinary or hypergender movement promotes an individual's exploration into gender according to the existential principle "You can become whoever you wish."[57] Such an assertion, we must note, disqualifies not only any discussion on anthropology and what proper personhood means but also Christology itself. For are we not to measure and evaluate our humanity in the light of Christ's sinlessness, of His being the most exemplary and only perfect person? His entire being and ministry on earth was to this very end: to demonstrate and practice moral righteousnesss according to the will of God.[58]

The Threat to One's Own Existence

The dimension of the threat to one's existence ought not be underestimated. One would expect society to retain a memory of past crimes committed against humanity on a large scale in the area of eugenics and thus refrain from certain practices. In the book *Du und das Leben* (You and Your Life), published in 1936 during the Third Reich, Karl von Frisch, a professor at the University of Munich, describes the goal to ensure humanity's health in a sinister way that reflects much of the motivation behind the evils of the Third Reich:

> On a very significant level, on that of promoting human health, the focus on the issue of selection dropped as culture's development rose. Humanitarian and medical sciences have allowed deviations to continue to exist, which would be eliminated mercilessly among wild tribes and free-range animals. An obese person and a blind person find their table decked the same as the other people. Weak children are saved at all costs, genetically handicapped are raised with care, and the insane are supported by the state on the backs of the healthy. The feeble can pursue their desires as can the clever. Yes, in particular they do it often without any inhibitions and no sense of responsibility with the result, as one well-known case

God's created order and not just one's personal proclivity. See Richard B. Hays, "Relations Natural and Unnatural: A Response to John Boswell's Exegesis of Romans 1," *Journal of Religious Ethics* 14, no. 1 (1986): 184, 194. For a helpful discussion see Denny Burk, *What Is the Meaning of Sex?* (Wheaton: Crossway Books, 2013), 200–205.

56. Judith Butler, *Gender Trouble: Feminism and the Subversion of Identity* (New York: Routledge, 1990).

57. One hypergender person's post reveals the wishes and openness to explore: "For me hyper-gender is about letting go of labels, dissolving the male-female binary, and exploring our capacity for new forms of relationships." Asmaa Guedira, "How My Coming-out and Job-out Led Me to Hyper-Gender," *Asmaa Guedira* (blog), 3 July 2016, https://medium.com/@asmaaguedira/hyper-gender-de11adc7e460; *Salzburger Erklärung* § 18 (p. 15).

58. "What's more, if Christ is (among so many other things) the most exemplary, but even more the most real, the most true person, and if we confess his sinless obedience to the Father as axiomatic, then to take sin as the primary locus for understanding personhood is to disqualify Christology (and, therefore, anthropology) from the discussion from the start." Jenson, *Gravity of Sin*, 188.

> demonstrates, that seventy-five living feeble-minded people can be traced back to one person five generations ago who had a genetic problem. What is lacking here is a healthy selection process. Unfortunately, it has given way to a favoritism for the inferior. . . . This development of these matters must surely lead to a deterioration of the human race.[59]

Today more than ever before, human life from the prenatal stage to its end is exposed to manipulation by others. Often such endeavors proceed under the guise of utilitarianism, which is guided by what is expedient and which promises, as von Frisch's quotation does, the betterment of society even if it involves the elimination of the weak and feeble. Underlying this approach is the influence of social and economic Darwinism, which leads people to consider themselves naturally better than those less able or less gifted.[60] Such inferior people should not be allowed to reproduce, nor be helped through mercy or by the government, as they would contaminate society even further. After all, helping them would reward them for their failure, which in turn would send a message to the "hard-working, industrious man that there is an easier path by which wants can be supplied."[61] Even their death, often premature, is considered beneficial to society. This principle of social Darwinism is reflected in industry magnate Andrew Carnegie's uncharitable views about welfare and mercy, despite his involvement in charitable works later in his life.[62]

In an essay published in *The New Yorker*, Michael Specter, an authority on the subject of genetic engineering, discusses the recent advances made in the area of genetic editing.[63] He describes the attempt to eradicate Lyme disease among Nantucket Island's citizens, of whom more than a quarter are infected. Lyme disease usually is passed on to humans by ticks, which themselves contract the pathogen from the white-footed mice (and especially their larvae) on which they feed. In changing the genetic configuration of these mice by implanting into their cells genes with stronger antibodies to Lyme, the disease eventually will be eradicated. This process of gene editing, CRISPR,[64] could alter the genetic destiny not only of mice but of all creation, humans included.

59. Karl von Frisch, *Du und das Leben: Eine moderne Biologie für Jedermann* (Berlin: Ullstein, 1936), 359; my translation.

60. De Botton, *Status Anxiety*, 68.

61. De Botton, *Status Anxiety*, 71.

62. His perspective comes through clearly in *The Gospel of Wealth* (1889): "Of every thousand dollars spent in so-called charity nine hundred and fifty of them had better been thrown into the sea." Andrew Carnegie, *The Gospel of Wealth and Other Timely Essays* (New York: The Century Co., 1901), 68. In his autobiography Carnegie disavows Christianity for social Darwinism: "Not only had I got rid of theology and the supernatural, but I had found the truth of evolution. 'All is well since all grows better' became my motto, my true source of comfort. Man was not created with an instinct for his own degradation, but from the lower he had risen to the higher forms. Nor is there any conceivable end to his march to perfection." *Autobiography of Andrew Carnegie*, ed. John C. Van Dyke (Boston: Houghton Mifflin, 1920), 327.

63. Michael Specter, "Rewriting the Code of Life," *The New Yorker*, 2 January 2017, 34.

64. CRISPR (pronounced "crisper") stands for Clustered Regularly Interspaced Short Palindromic Repeats, which are the hallmark of a bacterial defense system and which form the basis for CRISPR-Cas9 genome editing technology.

In mosquitoes, for example, the bearers of malaria, the genome could be genetically altered to create a mutation among them that would eventually block the parasite responsible for malaria while keeping the mosquito alive.

The potential of this procedure of genetic editing is life-altering and is becoming ever simpler, so that it can be conducted, if one wishes, in a basic laboratory. Genetic editing, scientists and biologists argue, bears potential for the betterment of creation and of humans, since it allows people to take initiative to offer a firmer guiding hand in creation and humans' development starting with their preborn state.[65] For Specter, who builds on evolutionary principles, genetic editing offers great benefits for humanity's future:

> For four billion years, evolution, driven by natural selection and random mutation, has insured that the most efficient genes would survive and the weakest would disappear. But propelled by CRISPR and other tools of synthetic biology, intelligent design has taken on an entirely new meaning, one that threatens to transcend Darwin—because evolution may soon be guided by us.[66]

As a result, twenty-first-century technological advances in medicine offer tremendous promise in a broad range of areas, especially for the human condition in its limitations and exposure to diseases. The prospects are alluring, but are they always guaranteed to bring positive outcomes? Genetic editing could mean the eradication or advantageous modification of certain species, from an optimistic human perspective. But in the example of mosquitos, concerns over the procedure itself might be raised: mosquitos also could be edited genetically by people with malicious intentions, for example to make them more aggressive toward humans or to "arm" them with perilous diseases. Outcomes depend in part on the character of those into whose hands these procedures are entrusted, and since all humans are sinful by nature, their work to improve humanity's condition must anticipate and seek to preempt the possibility of countless abuses, some of which could end catastrophically, as the Third Reich's genocide has shown.

Many medications are available that will alter bodily functions and affect the overall well-being of the ensouled body. All the modern diseases, plus fear, anxiety, stress, depression, loneliness, and guilt, can be mitigated through

65. We also should note the practice of prenatal diagnosis of unborn children and what is called preimplantation diagnosis, a profiling of embryos prior to implantation. The argument could be made that these screening methods can diagnose, and through genetic editing eliminate, life-threatening ills in the child in the womb or embryo, such as removing a single-gene disease linked to a heart disorder. According to Michael Cook, "It can be used not only for curing diseases but for 'enhancing' embryos with 'better genes.'" Yet the fact that even a human genome now can be edited has, according to Cook, significant ethical implications. One concern is that in the course of this research dozens of human embryos were created and destroyed before they had grown beyond a few days. This methodology poses the potential for a new form of eugenics. Michael Cook, "Human Embryos Modified to Eliminate a Single-Gene Disease," *BioEdge* (blog), 5 August 2017, https://www.bioedge.org/bioethics/human-embryos-modified-to-eliminate-a-single-gene-disease/12375.

66. Specter, "Rewriting the Code of Life," 34.

chemical compounds that promise an overall sense of well-being, peace, harmony, even mystical elation. There are also drawbacks to the use of some medications which otherwise may be beneficial, like opiates. One byproduct of what seems an endless and unwarranted use of opiates is a dramatic spike in a range of ailments, including psychosomatic and psychological disorders and life-threatening addictions.

Another technological advance that represents both benefit and danger is the harnessing of nuclear energy. While nuclear power offers an alternative energy source and nuclear weapons a deterrent to war, it also brings the potential for widespread harm and destruction. A power plant may suffer damage and leak radiation on a catastrophic scale, while nuclear arms are able to destroy large parts of the world's population and all creation, leading to concerns over their illegal trade and possession.[67] Nuclear energy along with medical advances and genetic engineering all have as downsides that they pose a threat to human existence, and that on a global scale.

67. The objective of the international Treaty on the Non-Proliferation of Nuclear Weapons (NPT), signed 1 July 1968, is to prevent the spread of nuclear weapons, to engage in peaceful cooperation in the use of nuclear energy, and to achieve nuclear disarmament. That treaty has been ratified by the (former) Soviet Union, the United States, the United Kingdom, and forty other countries. Countries that have not signed, such as North Korea and Pakistan, possess nuclear weaponry or plan to produce it in the near future.

CONCLUSION TO PART THREE

Lutherans are vulnerable to the attacks of modernism in understanding humanity's origin and role as steward, since they do not share the same convictions as the culture at large. The modern man and the secular forum see the Christian-biblical point of view of the human as opposed to science and hostile to a conversation devoted to the use of reason. Theological anthropology has taken note of this fact and has largely abandoned arguments from the article of creation, instead focusing discussion on soteriology—who the human is from the point of view of Christology and justification. This path has been taken by neo-orthodoxy in particular, an approach that has rendered all those who follow suit, including Lutherans, somewhat inept at discussing, outside of soteriology, the ethical issues concerning humanity's responsibility in creation and in the world.

For theological anthropology, humanity ultimately is defined Christologically and soteriologically. We committed ourselves especially to that observation in Parts One and Two. But Part Three has illustrated specifically the role of God within creation, the implications of living under God as stewards within His created orders of family and marriage, along with moral responsibility toward oneself and the world, concerns often left unaddressed by society. Without this narrative, however, humanity runs the risk of becoming a threat not only to the world around it but also to itself.

For this reason the Lutheran discourse on humanity's role as steward under God must be advanced in society in an attempt to correct its naturalistic anthropology. Lutheranism is well prepared for this task, even if its arguments in the sixteenth century were addressed to a different audience, one that elevated a spiritual withdrawal from human obligation and responsibility in the world. Against that perspective, Lutheran theology commits a Christian to the world, summoning him to leave his confinement and exchange the cell of a monastery for a secular calling known as vocation. For Luther, to pursue a vocation is a noble task, and so he regards the work of a house maiden (*Kindsmagd*), for example, as far superior to the self-chosen prayer life of a monk. Bringing that concept of vocation into an anthropology that is dialogical-responsory by nature calls due attention to the communicative relationship with God and with the world in which each human has been placed.

Humans are communicative or dialogical-responsory beings as they converse with one another and listen. Much of a Christian's apologetic task today is to emphasize the God–human relationship as foundational for human existence. In this way our theological anthropology does not remain abstract, floating above all immediate concerns, but approaches and engages a secular person with his largely forgotten relationship to God and to others in the context of vocation. Theological anthropology summons humanity to assume its role in creation as a conscious and intentional service toward the world and neighbor. It calls Christians to live a life in society alongside those who entertain and pursue non-Christian worldviews, and at this intersection to be willing to serve one another.

In the decades following World War II, theology paid hardly any attention to the creed's First Article on creation, and when it did, this seemed only an afterthought or a half-hearted attempt to address the article. As a result, a human without Christ was treated as one without knowledge of the good, an example of anthropological nihilism according to Wingren, for this thinking assumes an ethical vacuum in which humans outside of Christ have nothing in common with Christians.[1] Against neo-orthodoxy's dialectical theology, theological anthropology approaches the discussion of who the human is by affirming the article of creation, the divinely created orders, and speaks on behalf of all humans to their common createdness and their joint role as God's stewards or regents. Together Christians and non-Christians serve as God's cooperators and embrace a common ethos, based either on general revelation or on the New Testament ethic of love. Those who would dwell on the persecution of Christians or their status on earth as alien residents can easily lose sight of the important and special service of Christians as a community in society and the role each Christian assumes in his vocation in the world. Notions of persecution must be evaluated carefully in the light of those who truly suffer and have a right to claim victim status.

1. Wingren, *Flight from Creation*, 70 and 73.

CONCLUSION

THE IMPLICATIONS AND ROLE OF A LUTHERAN ANTHROPOLOGY

Theological anthropology dialogues with multiple nontheological disciplines, and it looks at them through the lens of the revelatory truth of Scripture. For the field to merit any theological credibility for preserving this revelatory truth, it must carefully select and filter information from nonbiblical sources. We have learned from Luther that a theologian must take this approach; total impartiality toward nonbiblical accounts will not do. Since Luther's lifetime, however, particularly with the ensuing Age of Enlightenment, information about who the human is has increased substantially, almost daunting the theologian with its vast scope. Luther's basic premise remains, though: information drawn a posteriori and from below stands under the critical surveillance of what comes to us a priori and from above, the revealed narrative in Scripture.

To put this in today's context, Luther would argue for a multilayered understanding of man that empirical sciences, built on the principles of naturalism, cannot recognize and explain, such as dignity, soul, the self, and personhood. In other words, just because the biblical account of the human includes certain things about man that scientific empiricists consider not material or directly visible, this does not mean that Scripture does not convey a reliable presentation of the human being and life. Thus theological anthropology should not bow to those scientific explanations of who a human is that in the end are reductionistic, limiting the evidence on who is human to what can be verified scientifically.[1]

Consequently, as a discipline theological anthropology offers not only a unique perspective; it also claims to provide the most comprehensive account of what it means to be human. Whether the world will be convinced by its arguments is in part a question for apologetics. This comprehensive story embraces important stations from the entire biblical account, starting with creation and the Fall and continuing with the death and resurrection of Christ, the new life found through justification which restores the human's relationship with the Savior, and a life shaped among neighbors and all created things. In

1. I borrow here some of the language of sociologist Christian Smith, who in line with cultural anthropologist Charles Taylor offers a helpful and comprehensive rebuttal of a reductionistic reading of scientific empiricists. See Christian Smith, *What Is a Person?* especially 90–115.

view of the final consummation as the last station for humans here on earth and because of sin's reality, theological anthropology paints a realistic and sober picture of human life and its accomplishments and dismisses utopian and idealistic portrayals of humanity.

In the biblical narrative, theological anthropology points to one particular divine act that is pivotal for humans. In his *Disputation Concerning Man* Luther presents us with a timeline of human existence that culminates in one's justification. This is the point at which the human can say he possesses the image, righteousness, knowledge, and spiritual aptitude. This act in turn initiates the dialogical-responsory relationship with God and fellow humans, which is sustained through the encounter with the Word and the Spirit. The human's total incurvature and non-response-ability toward God and fellow humans is broken open, and he is instilled with a new, outward-oriented focus. Theological anthropology is a Christologically defined anthropology in that the righteousness of Christ earned for all on the cross now comes to humans. Christ's death for the justification of all is the defining moment for who the human is in Lutheran theology, and the article to which all others are accountable. Thus one scholar rightly identifies the priorities for theological anthropology's conversation with nontheological disciplines:

> Non-christological perspectives are important, maybe even essential, for developing anthropologies that are both broad and deep, adequate to the complexity of the subject matter. Nonetheless, they cannot tell us about what it means to be human at the most fundamental level. Consequently they must be interpreted, even interrogated, by the Christological center of theological anthropology.[2]

A preliminary theological discussion was needed, however, to explore to what extent theological anthropology should be informed Christologically. Does the Christological focus in theological anthropology address the full scope of what it means to be human? In answering that question, this study proposes a robust trinitarian approach to anthropology that embraces the economy of the triune God in creation, redemption, and sanctification. Although in this outward economy of God all three persons participate equally, particular aspects of human life come into focus when creation is examined separately and subsequently connected to the acts of redemption and sanctification.

What are these particular aspects from creation? This article affirms God's daily care for humanity in providing all that is needed for life, so that a human first receives and then responds with praise and worship of the One who provides. Creation assigns humans the role of servants, so that in their work as His cooperators they function as masks of God Himself, obliging this world to affirm life in the particular orders of marriage, family, and government. A focus on creation sends a critical message to the world that it should respect

2. Cortez, *Christological Anthropology*, 222–23.

humanity's createdness, the body itself, in how a human treats both his own body and those of others.[3] The article of creation offers the opportunity to address a subject that pertains to all humans and to redress an individualism that has led society to become largely myopic and existentially solipsistic. This article focuses on concerns shared with other religions in the areas of physiology, illnesses, and common needs. It opens theological anthropology to other empirical sciences, such as medicine, biology, and technology, and learns from them, for example about the human form of communication, which for theological anthropology is evidence that humans are unique and special in kind in the animal world. Creation makes room for general revelation, shared morality, and common knowledge gained through reason among all humans, from which Christians also benefit. Being intentionally Christological does not mean we are Christomonistic,[4] reading the article of creation from the article of Christ's redemption and grace, an approach Gustav Wingren and other theologians identify as a shortcoming of neo-orthodoxy.

Eberhard Jüngel once defined a sinner as "a person without relations," and theological anthropology is aware of the constant danger that humans may be drawn out of relationship with God and others and fall back into a life of incurvature.[5] Instead, in a responsory-communicative and dialogical relationship with the triune God and with fellow humans, these relationships are enacted, renewed, and strengthened. And the church recognizes her central place in shaping and orienting human life toward God and others, where in the midst of fellowship the triune God does His work through the preaching of His Word and through baptism and the Lord's Supper. The trinitarian approach to defining humans recognizes their unique responsory capacity toward God and a life under His reign which fulfills itself in doxology (Is 38:18f.; Ps 6:6).[6]

Even when a trinitarian focus is taken in theological anthropology, the Christological orientation that centers on a life of forgiveness and restoration of the image in Him remains pivotal. This restrictive orientation admittedly does involve a certain exclusivity toward the rest of humanity who exist outside of Christ and the Gospel. The question thus frequently is raised: how can theological anthropology fully embrace all of humanity and at the same time reject the full humanity of those who are outside of Christ?[7] It is true that the biblical data support a Christological connection to the true *humanum*

3. Peter Singer, *Practical Ethics* (Cambridge: Cambridge University Press, 1993), 87; Jenson, *Gravity of Sin*, 189n1.

4. Cortez, *Christological Anthropology*, 223.

5. "Der Mensch . . . in der . . . selbstverschuldeten Beziehungslosigkeit." Eberhard Jüngel, "Hoffen, Handeln—und Leiden. Zum christlichen Verständnis des Menschen aus theologischer Sicht," in Beziehungsbereich. Perspektiven des Glaubens (Stuttgart: Radius-Verlag, 2002), 19. Jenson, *Gravity of Sin*, 191.

6. See the anthropology proposed by John Zizioulas, "On Being Other: Towards an Ontology of Otherness," in *Communion and Otherness*, 80; Cortez, *Christological Anthropology*, 185; Anderson, *On Being Human*, 182.

7. Jenson, *Gravity of Sin*, 190.

that centers on justification enacted through God's Word and to a renewed endowment of the image. The Bible defines true humanity in ways that seem "to exclude potentially large numbers of humans from being actually (or, at least fully) human."[8] One solution would be to open the theological floodgates, so to speak, by adopting a universalist or Christomonistic stance that would grant salvation to all humans, even to those who do not affirm Christ in their lives or who have not been justified through faith.

To a degree, this study's focus on embracing a robust Trinity to explain human life offers a solution to this dilemma, one perhaps not satisfactory to all but that at least acknowledges the creation of all life by the Creator and especially human life as creation's crown. From that point we advance Christ and the Holy Spirit as the fulfillment of such created life, because only through them can full humanity be restored following the Fall. To be sure, humans are humans already and not only human in the becoming. The unborn baby is a human life here and now and not just in the future, as both Bonhoeffer and Thielicke have pointed out. There seems to be something static, ontological, to human life that makes it special for what it is and not for what it will become in Christ. That the article of creation precedes Christology and the preaching of the Gospel offers some consolation in the face of an "exclusionary" definition of humanity, for this First Article allows us to speak of the value of all humans, whether Christians or not.

This sense of the inherent worth of all humans also influences a Christian's demeanor in society, where he affirms co-humanity. Living alongside many other humans is important, for separating from the world in order to protect himself from others is fundamentally still part of that selfish incurvature with which a Christian continues constantly to battle. But he is fed by God's Word and guided Christologically in his ethical stance, and he is called thereby to an active role through his vocation in the realm of the world, where his faith-informed anthropology is applied and lived out in service to others. There he is placed alongside other humans who serve humanity equally through their own particular vocations. These work together, Christians alongside nonbelievers, for the welfare of their neighbors as stewards of the human commission as well as the abilities with which they are endowed individually as God's created beings.

8. This is Cortez's observation of Luther and of others as well; see *Christological Anthropology*, 229.

BIBLIOGRAPHY

PRIMARY SOURCES

Abbott, Walter M., ed. *The Documents of Vatican II*. Translated by Joseph Callagher. Chicago: Follet Publishing Company, 1966.

Amerini, Fabrizio. *Aquinas on the Beginning and End of Human Life*. Translated by Mark Henninger. Cambridge, MA: Harvard University Press, 2013.

The Anathemas against Origen. In *Nicene and Post-Nicene Fathers*, edited by Philip Schaff, First Series, 14:318–19. Peabody, MA: Hendrickson Publishers, 2004.

Aristotle. *The Basic Works of Aristotle*. Edited by Richard McKeon. New York: The Modern Library, 2001.

———. *Metaphysics*. Translated by W. D. Ross. In *The Basic Works of Aristotle*, edited by Richard McKeon, 681–926. New York: The Modern Library, 2001.

———. *Nicomachean Ethics*. Translated by W. D. Ross. In *The Basic Works of Aristotle*, edited by Richard McKeon, 927–1112. New York: The Modern Library, 2001.

———. *On the Soul*. Translated by J. A. Smith. In *The Basic Works of Aristotle*, edited by Richard McKeon, 533–603. New York: The Modern Library, 2001.

———. *Physics*. Translated by R. P. Hardie and R. K. Gaye. In *The Basic Works of Aristotle*, edited by Richard McKeon, 213–394. New York: The Modern Library, 2001.

———. *Politics*. Translated by Benjamin Jowett. In *The Basic Works of Aristotle*, edited by Richard McKeon, 1114–316. New York: The Modern Library, 2001.

Arminius, Jacob. *The Works of James Arminius, D.D.* 3 vols. Auburn, NY: Derby, Miller and Orton, 1853.

Athanasius, *De Incarnatione*. In *Nicene and Post Nicene Fathers*, edited by Philip Schaff and Henry Wace, Second Series, vol. 4, 36–67. Reprint, Peabody, MA: Hendrickson Publishers, 2004.

Augustine. *The City of God*. Translated by William Babcock. In *The Works of Saint Augustine: A Translation for the 21st Century*, edited by John E. Rotelle, 1.6–1.7. Hyde Park, NY: New City Press, 1990–.

———. *Confessions*. Translated by Maria Boulding. In *The Works of Saint Augustine: A Translation for the 21st Century*, edited by John E. Rotelle, 1.1:1–416. Hyde Park, NY: New City Press, 1990–.

———. *The Gift of Perseverance*. Translated by Roland J. Teske. In *The Works of Saint Augustine: A Translation for the 21st Century*, edited by John E. Rotelle, 1.26:191–237. Hyde Park, NY: New City Press, 1990–.

———. *Grace and Free Choice*. Translated by Roland J. Teske. In *The Works of Saint Augustine: A Translation for the 21st Century*, edited by John E. Rotelle, 1.26:70–107. Hyde Park, NY: New City Press, 1990–.

———. *The Grace of Christ and Original Sin*. Translated by Roland J. Teske. In *The Works of Saint Augustine: A Translation for the 21st Century*, edited by John E. Rotelle, 1.23:384–465. Hyde Park, NY: New City Press, 1990–.

———. *The Happy Life*. Translated by Ludwig Schopp. In *The Happy Life; Answer to Skeptics; Divine Providence and the Problem of Evil; Soliloquies*, translated by Ludwig Schopp, Denis J. Kavanagh, Robert P. Russell, and Thomas F. Gilligan, 27–84. The Fathers of the Church 5. New York: CIMA Publishing Company, 1948.

———. "Letter 157: Augustine to Hilary." Translated by Roland Teske. In *The Works of Saint Augustine: A Translation for the 21st Century*, edited by John E. Rotelle, 2.3:16–39. Hyde Park, NY: New City Press, 1990–.

———. *Nature and Grace*. Translated by Roland Teske. In *The Works of Saint Augustine: A Translation for the 21st Century*, edited by John E. Rotelle, 1.23:204–78. Hyde Park, NY: New City Press, 1990–.

———. *The Nature and Origin of the Soul*. Translated by Roland Teske. In *The Works of Saint Augustine: A Translation for the 21st Century*, edited by John E. Rotelle, 1.23:451–542. Hyde Park, NY: New City Press, 1990–.

———. *On the Trinity*. In *Nicene and Post-Nicene Fathers*, edited by Philip Schaff, First Series, vol. 3, 17–228. Peabody, MA: Hendrickson Publishers, 2004.

———. *On the Words of the Gospel of John 1:1–3: "In the Beginning Was the Word and the Word Was with God and the Word Was God, Etc.": Against the Arians*. Translated by Edmund Hill. In *The Works of Saint Augustine: A Translation for the 21st Century*, edited by John E. Rotelle, 3.4:209–23. Hyde Park, NY: New City Press, 1990–.

———. *The Punishment and Forgiveness of Sins and the Baptism of Little Ones*. Translated by Roland J. Teske. In *The Works of Saint Augustine: A Translation for the 21st Century*, edited by John E. Rotelle, 1.23:18–139. Hyde Park, NY: New City Press, 1990–.

———. *Rebuke and Grace*. Translated by Roland J. Teske. In *The Works of Saint Augustine: A Translation for the 21st Century*, edited by John E. Rotelle, 1.26:108–48. Hyde Park, NY: New City Press, 1990–.

———. *Sermon 27: On Psalm 96, and on the Words of the Apostle: "On Whom He Will He Has Mercy . . ."* Translated by Edmund Hill. In *The Works of Saint Augustine: A Translation for the 21st Century*, edited by John E. Rotelle, 3.2:104–10. Hyde Park, NY: New City Press, 1990–.

———. *The Works of Saint Augustine: A Translation for the 21st Century*. Edited by John E. Rotelle. 43 volumes to date. Hyde Park, NY : New City Press, 1990–.

Artificial Intelligence: An Evangelical Statement of Principles. Nashville: Ethics & Religious Liberty Commission of the Southern Baptist Convention, 2019.

Baier, Johann Wilhelm. *Compendium Theologiae Positivae: Adjectis Notis Amplioribus, quibus Doctrina Orthodoxa ad Παιδεἰαν Academicam Explicatur atque ex Scriptura S. Eique Innixis Rationibus Theologicis Confirmatur*. Edited by C. F. W. Walther. St. Louis: Luth. Concordia-Verlag, 1879.

Barth, Karl. *Church Dogmatics*. Edited by G. W. Bromiley and T. F. Torrance. 4 vols. in 12 parts. Edinburgh: T&T Clark, 1936–77.

———. *Evangelium und Gesetz*. Theologische Existenz heute, neue Folge, 50. 1935. Reprint, Munich: C. Kaiser Verlag, 1956.

———. *Nein! Antwort an Emil Brunner*. Theologische Existenz heute 14. Munich: C. Kaiser, 1934.

Bonhoeffer, Dietrich. *Act and Being: Transcedental Philosophy and Ontology in Systematic Theology*. Translated by H. Martin Rumscheid. Minneapolis: Fortress Press, 2009.

———. *The Cost of Discipleship*. Translated by R. H. Fuller and Irmgard Booth. London: SCM Press, 1959.

———. *Ethics*. Edited by Eberhard Bethge. Translated by Neville Horton Smith. New York: Simon & Schuster, 1995.

———. *Letters and Papers from Prison*. Edited by Eberhard Bethge and translated by Reginald Fuller, Frank Clark, et al. 2d ed. New York: Touchstone Books, 1971.

The Book of Concord: The Confessions of the Evangelical Lutheran Church. Translated and edited by Theodore G. Tappert. Philadelphia: Fortress Press, 1959

Braaten, Carl E., and Robert W. Jenson, eds. *Christian Dogmatics*. Philadelphia: Fortress Press, 1984.

Brunner, Emil. *The Christian Doctrine of Creation and Redemption. Dogmatics,* Vol. 2. Translated by Olive Wyon. Philadelphia: Westminster Press, 1952.

———. *Man in Revolt: A Christian Anthropology*. Translated by Olive Wyon. Philadelphia: Westminster Press, 1947.

Buber, Martin. *I and Thou*. Translated by Ronald Gregor Smith. 2d ed. New York: Scribner, 1958.

Calov, Abraham. *Theologia Positiva, Per Definitiones, Causas, Affectiones, Et Distinctiones, Locos Theologicos Universos, Succinte, Justoque Ordine Proponens: Ceu Compendium Systematis Theologici.* Frankfurt/Wittenberg: Johann Ludolph Quenstedt, 1690.

Calvin, John. *Institutes of the Christian Religion*. Translated by Henry Beveridge. Peabody, MA: Hendrickson Publishers, 2008.

Camus, Albert. *The Stranger*. Translated by Stuart Gilbert. New York: Vintage Books, 1946.

Carnegie, Andrew. *Autobiography of Andrew Carnegie*. Edited by John C. Van Dyke. Boston: Houghton Mifflin, 1920.

———. *The Gospel of Wealth and Other Timely Essays*. New York: The Century Co., 1901.

Catechism of the Catholic Church: Revised in Accordance with the Official Latin Text Promulgated by Pope John Paul II. 2d ed. Washington, DC: United States Catholic Conference, 1997.

Chemnitz, Martin. *Loci Theologici*. Translated by J. A. O. Preus. 2 vols. St. Louis: Concordia Publishing House, 1989.

Chemnitz, Martin, and Johann Gerhard. *The Doctrine of Man in Classical Lutheran Theology*. Edited by Herman A. Preus and Edmund Smits. Translated by Mario Colacci et al. Minneapolis: Augsburg Publishing House, 1962.

Clement XI. *Unigenitus Dei filius*. 1713. https://www.papalencyclicals.net/clem11/c11unige.htm.

Concordia Triglotta. The Symbolical Books of the Ev. Lutheran Church, German-Latin-English. Translated and edited by F. Bente, W. H. T. Dau, and The Lutheran Church—Missouri Synod. St. Louis: Concordia Publishing House, 1921.

Congregation for the Doctrine of the Faith. *The Dignity of a Person: With Additional Resources: Dignitas Personae*. Washington, DC: United States Conference of Catholic Bishops, 2009.

———. *Instruction on Christian Freedom and Liberation*. Washington, DC: United States Catholic Conference, 1986.

Darwin, Charles. *The Descent of Man, and Selection in Relation to Sex*. Vol 2. London: John Murray, 1871.

———. *On the Origin of Species*. London: John Murray, 1859.

Darwin, Francis., ed. *The Life and Letters of Charles Darwin*. Vol. 1. London: John Murray, 1887.

Denzinger, Heinrich, comp. *Compendium of Creeds, Definitions, and Declarations on Matters of Faith and Morals*. Edited by Robert Fastiggi and Anne Englund Nash for the English edition. 43d ed. San Francisco: Ignatius Press, 2012.

Descartes, René. *Principles of Philosophy*. Translated by Valentine Rodger Miller and Reese P. Miller. Dordrecht: Kluwer Academic Publishers, 1991.

Dostoyevsky, Fyodor. *The Brothers Karamazov*. Translated by Constance Garnett. Chicago: Encyclopædia Britannica, 1955.

———. *Crime and Punishment*. Translated by Constance Garnett. New York: Random House, 1956.

Easwaran, Eknath, trans. *The Bhagavad Gita*. The Classics of Indian Spirituality. 2d ed. Tomales, CA: Nilgiri Press, 2007.

Erasmus, Desiderius. *Enchiridion Militis Christiani: An English Version*. Edited by Anne M. O'Donnell. Early English Text Society 282. Oxford, UK: Oxford University Press, 1981.

Eriugena, Johannes Scotus. *Periphyseon: The Division of Nature*. Translated by J. P. Sheldon-Williams and John J. O'Meara. Montreal: Bellarmin, 1987.

Francis. *Encyclical Letter Laudato Si' of the Holy Father Francis: On Care for Our Common Home*. Vatican City: Catholic Church, 2015.

Gerhard, Johann. *Theological Commonplaces*. Translated by Richard J. Dinda. Edited by Benjamin T. G. Mayes and Joshua J. Hayes. 13 vols. to date. St. Louis: Concordia Publishing House, 2006–.

Hegel, Georg Wilhelm Friedrich. *Lectures on the Philosophy of Religion*. Edited by Peter C. Hodgson. Translated by R. F. Brown, P. C. Hodgson, and J. M. Stewart. With the assistance of J. P. Fitzer and H. S. Harris. 3 vols. Berkeley: University of California Press, 1984–87.

Herbert, Edward, Lord of Cherbuy. *De veritate*. Reprint edited by Günter Gawlick. 3d ed. Stuttgart–Bad Cannstatt: F. Frommann, 1966.

Herder, Johann Gottfried. *Ideen zur Philosophie der Geschichte der Menschheit*. Darmstadt: Melzer, 1966.

———. *Outlines of a Philosophy of the History of Man*. Translated by T. Churchill. New York: Bergman Publishers, 1966.

Hesse, Hermann. *Siddhartha*. Translated by Hilda Rosner. The New Classics Series 34. New York: New Directions, 1951.

Hobbes, Thomas. *Leviathan*. Minneapolis: Lerner Publishing Group, 2018.

Hollaz, David. *Examen Theologicum Acroamaticum, Universam Theologiam Thetico-Polemicam Complectens*. Holmiae and Lipsiae: Apud Godofredum Kiesewetterum, 1735.

"Humanism and Its Aspirations: Humanist Manifesto III, a Successor to the Humanist Manifesto of 1933." Washington, DC: American Humanist Association, 2003.

Humanist Manifestos I and II. Edited by Paul Kurtz. Buffalo: Prometheus Books, 1973.

Hunnius, Nicolaus. *Epitome Credendorum: Containing a Concise and Popular View of the Doctrines of the Lutheran Church*. Translated by Paul Edward Gottheil. Nuremberg: U. E. Sebald, 1847.

Hutter, Leonard. *Compend of Lutheran Theology*. Translated by H. E. Jacobs and G. F. Spieker. Philadelphia: The Lutheran Book Store, 1868.

Internationale Konferenz Bekennender Gemeinschaften. *Salzburger Erklärung: Die heutige Bedrohung der menschlichen Geschöpflichkeit und ihre Uberwindung: Leben nach dem Schöpferwillen Gottes: Eine theologische Wegweisung der Internationalen Konferenz Bekennender Gemeinschaften* [The Salzburg Declaration: present threats to human creation: life according to the will of God, the Creator]. Teterow, Germany: IKBG, 2015.

Interpretation of the Meanings of the Noble Qur'ān. In the English Language. Summarized in one volume by Muhammad Taqi-ud-Din Al-Hilali and Muhammad Muhsin Khan. 16th revised edition. Darussalam: Global Leader in Islamic Books, 2005.

Irenaeus. *Against Heresies*. Translated by A. Cleveland Coxe. In *The Ante-Nicene Fathers: The Writings of the Fathers Down to A.D. 325*, edited by Alexander Roberts and James Donaldson, 10 vols., 1:315–578. Peabody, MA: Hendrickson Publishers, 2004.

Justin Martyr. *The First Apology*. In *Saint Justin Martyr: The First Apology, the Second Apology, Dialogue with Trypho, Exhortation to the Greeks, Discourse to the Greeks, the Monarchy, or the Rule of God*, edited by Thomas B. Falls. The Fathers of the Church, vol. 6. Washington: Catholic University of America Press, 1965.

Kant, Immanuel. *An Answer to the Question: "What Is Enlightenment?"* Translated by H. B. Nisbet. New York: Penguin Books, 2009.

———. *Grounding for the Metaphysics of Morals*. Translated by James W. Ellington. Indianapolis: Hackett Publishing Company, 1981.

Kierkegaard, Søren. *Either/Or: A Fragment of Life*. Translated by David F. Swenson and Lillian Marvin Swenson. Princeton: Princeton University Press, 1944.

———. *Fear and Trembling*. Translated by Alastair Hannay. Harmondsworth, England: Penguin Books, 1985.

———. *Works of Love*. Translated by Howard V. Hong and Edna H. Hong. Kierkegaard's Writings 16. Princeton: Princeton University Press, 1995.

Lactantius. *The Divine Institutes*. In *The Works of Lactantius*, translated by William Fletcher. Ante Nicene Christian Library 21 and 22. 2 vols. Edinburgh: T&T Clark, 1871.

Leibniz, Gottfried Wilhelm. *Theodicy: Essays on the Goodness of God, the Freedom of Man, and the Origin of Evil*. Edited by Austin Farrer. Translated by E. M. Huggard. Rare Masterpieces of Philosophy and Science. New Haven, CT: Yale University Press, 1952.

Lessing, Gotthold Ephraim. *Die Erziehung des Menschengeschlechts*. Leipzig: Evangelische Verlagsanstalt, 2018.

Locke, John. *The First & Second Treatises of Government*. Monee, IL: Pantianos Classics, 2021.

Luther, Martin. *D. Martin Luthers Werke. Briefwechsel*. 15 vols. Weimar: Hermann Böhlaus Nachfolger, 1930–78.

———. *D. Martin Luthers Werke. Die Deutsche Bibel*. 12 vols. Weimar: Hermann Böhlaus Nachfolger, 1906–61.

———. *D. Martin Luthers Werke. Kritische Gesamtausgabe*. 120 vols. Weimar: Hermann Böhlau and H. Böhlaus Nachfolger, 1883–2009.

———. *D. Martin Luthers Werke. Tischreden*. 6 vols. Weimar: Hermann Böhlaus Nachfolger, 1912–21.

———. "Epiphany." In *Sermons of Martin Luther*, translated by John Nicholas Lenker and others, 6:311–38. Grand Rapids: Baker Book House, 1988.

———. *Luther's Small Catechism with Explanation*. St. Louis: Concordia Publishing House, 1986.

———. *Luther's Works: The American Edition*. 82 vols. Edited by Jaroslav Jan Pelikan, Hilton C. Oswald, Helmut T. Lehmann, and Christopher Boyd Brown. St. Louis: Concordia Publishing House; Philadelphia: Fortress Press, 1955–86.

Mahler-Werfel, Alma. *Mein Leben*. Frankfurt/M: Fischer Verlag, 1960.

Malthus, Thomas. *An Essay on the Principle of Population*. London: J. Johnson, 1789.

Melanchthon, Philipp. *Commentary on Romans*. Translated by Fred Kramer. 2d English ed. St. Louis: Concordia Publishing House, 2010.

———. *Loci Communes, 1543*. Translated by J. A. O. Preus. St. Louis: Concordia Publishing House, 1992.

Meyer, Carl S. *Moving Frontiers: Readings in the History of The Lutheran Church—Missouri Synod*. St. Louis: Concordia Publishing House, 1964.

Migne, J. P., ed. *Patrologia Cursus Completus*. Series latina. 221 vols. Paris: Garnier Fraher, 1844–.

Miller, Arthur. *Death of a Salesman: Certain Private Conversations in Two Acts and a Requiem*. New York: The Viking Press, 1958.

Nietzsche, Friedrich. *Beyond Good and Evil: Prelude to a Philosophy of the Future*. Translated by R. J. Hollingdale. Harmondsworth: Penguin Books, 1979.

———. *Thus Spoke Zarathustra: A Book for All and None*. Translated by Walter Kaufmann. Modern Library Edition. New York: Random House, 1995.

Nitzsch, Karl Immanuel. *System of Christian Doctrine*. Translated by Robert Montgomery and John Hennen. Edinburgh: T&T Clark, 1849.

Oberman, Heiko A. *Die Kirche im Zeitalter der Reformation*. Vol. 3 of Kirchen- und Theologiegeschichte in Quellen: Ein Arbeitsbuch, edited by Heiko A. Oberman, Adolf Martin Ritter, and Hans-Walter Krumwiede. Neukirchen-Vluyn: Neukirchener Verlag, 1981.

Origen. *De Principiis*, Book II. Translated by Frederick Crombie. In *The Ante-Nicene Fathers: The Writings of the Fathers Down to A.D. 325*, edited by Alexander Roberts and James Donaldson, 10 vols., 4:239–382. Peabody, MA: Hendrickson Publishers, 2004.

Pascal, Blaise. *Pensées. The Provincial Letters*. Translated by W. F Trotter. New York: The Modern Library, 1941.

Paul VI. *Apostolic Letter in the Form of Motu Proprio Solemni hac Liturgia (Credo of the People of God) of the Supreme Pontiff Paul VI*. Vatican City: Vatican Publishing House, 1968.

———. *Kommentar zu Luthers Katechismen*. Edited by Gottfried Seebaß. 5 vols. Göttingen: Vandenhoeck & Ruprecht, 1990–94.

———. *Der Mensch*. Gütersloh: Gütersloher Verlagshaus Mohn, 1979.

Philippi, Friedrich Adolph. *Kirchliche Glaubenslehre*. Vol. 2, *Die ursprüngliche Gottesgemeinschaft*. 2d ed. Stuttgart: S. G. Liesching, 1867.

Pico della Mirandola, Giovanni. *Oration on the Dignity of Man*. Translated by Robert Caponigri. Chicago: Henry Regnery Company, 1956.

Pius IX. *The Bull "Ineffabilis" in Four Languages, or, The Immaculate Conception of the Most Blessed Virgin Mary Defined [. . .].* Translated by Ulick J. Bourke. Dublin: John Mullany, 1868.

Pius XII. *Humani Generis: Encyclical Letter of Pope Pius XII.* Washington, DC: National Catholic Welfare Conference, 1950.

Plotinus. *The Enneads* IV.8. Translated by Barrie Fleet. Las Vegas, Zurich, Athens: Parmenides Publishing, 2012.

Quenstedt, Johann Andreas. *Theologiae Didactico-Polemica, Sive, Systema Theologicum, In Duas Sectiones, Didacticam et Polemicam, Divisum.* Wittembergae: Johannis Ludolphi Quenstedii, 1701.

Roberts, Alexander, and James Donaldson, eds. *Ante-Nicene Fathers: The Writings of the Fathers Down to A.D. 325.* 10 vols. Peabody, MA: Hendrickson Publishers, 2004.

Roosevelt, Franklin D. "1941 State of the Union Address: 'The Four Freedoms'" (6 January 1941). Voices of Democracy.

Rousseau, Jean-Jacques. *The Social Contract.* Harmondsworth, Middlesex, England: Penguin Books, 1978.

Schaff, Philip, ed. *Nicene and Post-Nicene Fathers.* 14 vols. First Series. Peabody, MA: Hendrickson Publishers, 2004.

Schaff, Philip, and William Wace, eds. *Nicene and Post-Nicene Fathers.* 14 vols. Second Series. Peabody, MA: Hendrickson Publishers, 2004.

Seven Ecumenical Councils of the Undivided Church, The. In *Nicene and Post Nicene Fathers*, edited by Philip Schaff and Henry Wace, Second Series, vol. 14, 172–74. Reprint, Peabody, MA: Hendrickson Publishers, 2004.

Severus, Sulpicius. *On the Life of St. Martin.* In *Nicene and Post Nicene Fathers*, edited by Philip Schaff and Henry Wace, Second Series, vol. 11, 3–17. Reprint, Peabody, MA: Hendrickson Publishers, 2004.

Smith, Eliza R. Snow. *Biography and Family Record of Lorenzo Snow: One of the Twelve Apostles of the Church of Jesus Christ of Latter-Day Saints.* Salt Lake, UT: Deseret News Co., 1884.

Teilhard de Chardin, Pierre. *The Phenomenon of Man.* Translated by Bernard Wall. New York: Harper & Row, 1961.

Tertullian. *On the Soul.* In *Apologetical Works*, translated by Edwin A. Quain, 163–309. The Fathers of the Church 10. Washington, DC: Catholic University of America Press, 1950.

Thomas Aquinas. *Man Made to God's Image.* Translated by Gilby Thomas. Vol. 13. Summa Theologiae, Ia. 90–102. Cambridge, UK: Blackfriars, 1964.

——— *Nature and Grace: Selections from the Summa Theologica of Thomas Aquinas.* Translated by A. M. Fairweather. Grand Rapids: Christian Classics Ethereal Library, 1954.

———. *Summa Theologica of St. Thomas Aquinas.* Translated by Fathers of the English Dominican Province. New York: Benzinger Brothers, 1947.

Vilmar, A. F. C., and K. W. Piderit. *Dogmatik: Akademische Vorlesungen.* 2 vols. Gütersloh: C. Bertelsmann, 1874.

Walther, C. F. W. *Law & Gospel: How to Read and Apply the Bible.* Edited by Charles P. Schaum, John P. Hellwege, Jr., and Thomas E. Manteufel. Translated by Christian C. Tiews. St. Louis: Concordia Publishing House, 2010.

———. *The Proper Distinction between Law and Gospel: 39 Evening Lectures*. Translated by W. H. T. Dau. St. Louis: Concordia Publishing House, 1986.

SECONDARY SOURCES

Adler, Mortimer J. *The Difference of Man and the Difference It Makes*. 1967. Reprint New York: Fordham University Press, 1993.

Althaus, Paul. *Der Brief an die Römer*. Das Neue Testament Deutsch, vol. 6. Göttingen: Vandenhoek & Ruprecht, 1953.

———. *Die christliche Wahrheit: Lehrbuch der Dogmatik*. 2 vols. 2d ed. Gütersloh: C. Bertelsmann, 1949.

———. *Die deutsche Stunde der Kirche*. Göttingen: Vandenhoeck & Ruprecht, 1933.

———. *The Ethics of Martin Luther*. Translated by Robert C. Schultz. Minneapolis: Fortress Press, 2007.

———. *Paulus und Luther über den Menschen: Ein Vergleich*. Gütersloh: C. Bertelsmann, 1938.

———. "Um die Reinheit der Mission." In *Mission und Theologie*, edited by Franz Wiebe. Göttingen: H. Reise, 1953.

Anderson, Kerby. "Arguments Against Abortion." *Probe for Answers* (blog). 1 October 2014. https://probe.org/arguments-against-abortion/.

Anderson, Ray Sherman. *On Being Human: Essays in Theological Anthropology*. Eugene, OR: Wipf & Stock Publishers, 2010.

Arand, Charles P., and Joel D. Biermann. "Why the Two Kinds of Righteousness?" *Concordia Journal* 33, no. 2 (2007): 116–35.

Arrington, Robert L. *Western Ethics: An Historical Introduction*. Malden, MA.: Blackwell Publishers, 1998.

Atran, Scott. "Sam Harris's Guide to Nearly Everything." *National Interest*, no. 112 (March/April 2011): 57–68.

Bandstra, Andrew John. *The Law and the Elements of the World: An Exegetical Study in Aspects of Paul's Teaching*. Kampen: J. H. Kok, 1964.

Barbour, Ian G. *Issues in Science and Religion*. Englewood Cliffs, NJ: Prentice-Hall, 1966.

Barna, George. *The Second Coming of the Church*. Nashville: Word Publishing, 1998.

Bartel, Michelle J. *What It Means to Be Human: Living with Others before God*. Foundations of Christian Faith. Louisville: Geneva Press, 2001.

Barth, Hans-Martin. *Dogmatik: Evangelischer Glaube im Kontext der Weltreligionen: Ein Lehrbuch*. Gütersloh: Christian Kaiser, Gütersloher Verlagshaus, 2001.

Bassler, Jouette M. *Divine Impartiality: Paul and a Theological Axiom*. Society of Biblical Literature Dissertation Series. Chico, CA: Scholars Press, 1982.

Bavinck, Herman. *Reformed Dogmatics*. Edited by John Bolt. Translated by John Vriend. 4 vols. Grand Rapids: Baker Academic, 2003–8.

Bayer, Oswald. "Being in the Image of God." *Lutheran Quarterly* 27, no. 1 (2013): 76–88.

———. *Martin Luther's Theology: A Contemporary Interpretation*. Translated by Thomas H. Trapp. Grand Rapids: Wm. B. Eerdmans, 2008.

Becker, Ernest. *The Denial of Death*. New York: Simon & Schuster, 1973.

Beckwith, C. A. "Soul and Spirit, Biblical Conceptions of." In *The New Schaff-Herzog Encyclopedia of Religious Knowledge*, ed. Samuel Macauley Jackson, 11:12–14. 1908–14. Reprint, Grand Rapids: Baker Book House, 1949–50.

Behe, Michael J. *Darwin's Black Box: The Biochemical Challenge to Evolution*. New York: Free Press, 1996.

Bente, Friedrich. *Historical Introductions to the Book of Concord*. St. Louis: Concordia Publishing House, 1965.

Boff, Leonardo. *Holy Trinity, Perfect Community*. Translated by Phillip Berryman. Maryknoll, NY: Orbis Books, 2000.

Bostrom, Nick. "A History of Transhumanist Thought." *Journal of Evolution and Technology* 14, no. 1 (2005): 1–25.

———. *The Transhumanist FAQ: A General Introduction*. Version 2.1. Willington, CT: World Transhumanist Association, 2003.

Boswell, John. *Christianity, Social Tolerance, and Homosexuality: Gay People in Western Europe from the Beginning of the Christian Era to the Fourteenth Century*. Chicago: University of Chicago Press, 1980.

Boulting, William. *Giordano Bruno: His Life, Thought, and Martyrdom*. New York: Routledge, 2013.

Boyd, Gregory A. *God of the Possible: A Biblical Introduction to the Open View of God*. Grand Rapids: Baker Books, 2000.

Boyd, Gregory A., and Paul R. Eddy. *Across the Spectrum: Understanding Issues in Evangelical Theology*. 2d ed. Grand Rapids: Baker Academic, 2009.

Brunner, Emil, and Karl Barth. *Natural Theology*. Translated by Peter Fraenkel. London: G. Bles, the Centenary Press, 1946.

Brunner, Peter. "Der Ersterschaffene als Gottes Ebenbild." In Peter Brunner, *Pro Ecclesia*, 1:85–95. Berlin: Lutherisches Verlagshaus, 1962–66.

———. "Die Freiheit des Menschen in Gottes Heilsgeschichte." In Peter Brunner, *Pro Ecclesia*, 1:108–25. Berlin: Lutherisches Verlagshaus, 1962–66.

———. "Gott, das Nichts und die Kreatur." In Peter Brunner, *Pro Ecclesia*, 2:31–49. Berlin: Lutherisches Verlagshaus, 1962–66.

———. *Pro Ecclesia*. 2 vols. Berlin: Lutherisches Verlagshaus, 1962–66.

———. "'Rechtfertigung' heute: Versuch einer dogmatischen Paraklese." In Peter Brunner, *Pro Ecclesia*, 2:122–40. Berlin: Lutherisches Verlagshaus, 1962–66.

Bruno, Giordano. *Cause, Principle and Unity: And Essays on Magic*. Translated by Robert de Lucca and Richard J. Blackwell. Cambridge Texts in the History of Philosophy. Cambridge, UK: Cambridge University Press, 1998.

Bultmann, Rudolf. "The Meaning of the Christian Faith in Creation." In *Existence and Faith: Shorter Writings of Rudolf Bultmann*, compiled and translated by Schubert M. Ogden, 206–25. Cleveland: World Publishing Company, 1960.

———. "New Testament and Mythology (1941)." In *New Testament and Mythology and Other Basic Writings*, compiled, edited, and translated by Schubert M. Ogden, 1–43. Philadelphia: Fortress Press, 1984.

Burfeind, Peter M. *Gnostic America: A Reading of Contemporary American Culture & Religion According to Christianity's Oldest Heresy*. Toledo, OH: Pax Domini Press, 2014.

Burk, Denny. *What Is the Meaning of Sex?* Wheaton, IL: Crossway Books, 2013.

Burns, J. Patout, ed. and trans. *Theological Anthropology*. Sources of Early Christian Thought. Philadelphia: Fortress Press, 1981.

Burton, Robert. *The Anatomy of Melancholy*. Edited by Thomas C. Faulkner, Nicolas K. Kiessling, and Rhonda L. Blair. 6 vols. Oxford: Clarendon Press, 1989–2000.

Butler, Judith. *Gender Trouble: Feminism and the Subversion of Identity*. New York: Routledge, 1990.

Case, Amber. "Cyborg Anthropologist: We Can All Be Superhuman." *CNN Business* (blog). 5 December 2012. https://www.cnn.com/2012/12/05/tech/cyborg-anthropology-amber-case.

Chan, Dawn. "The Immortality Upgrade." *New Yorker*, 20 April 2016.

Chappell, Dorothy F., and David E. Cook, eds. *Not Just Science: Questions Where Christian Faith and Natural Science Intersect*. Grand Rapids: Zondervan, 2005.

Cherry, Kendra. "An Overview of Sigmund Freud's Theories," *Verywellmind* (14 February 2022), 3–4.

Chesterton, G. K. *Orthodoxy*. Garden City, NY: Image Books, 1959.

Chomsky, Noam. *Language and Mind*. 3d ed. New York: Cambridge University Press, 2006.

Collins, Francis S. *The Language of God: A Scientist Presents Evidence for Belief*. New York: Free Press, 2006.

Cook, Michael. "Human Embryos Modified to Eliminate a Single-Gene Disease." *BioEdge* (blog), 5 August 2017. https://www.bioedge.org/bioethics/human-embryos-modified-to-eliminate-a-single-gene-disease/12375.

Cortez, Marc. *Christological Anthropology in Historical Perspective: Ancient and Contemporary Approaches to Theological Anthropology*. Grand Rapids: Zondervan, 2016.

Coward, Harold. *Sin and Salvation in the World Religions: A Short Introduction*. Oxford: Oneworld Publications, 2003.

Craig, William Lane. "Historical Statements of the *Kalām* Cosmological Argument." In *The* Kalām *Cosmological Argument*, 1–50. Eugene, OR: Wipf & Stock Publishers, 2000.

———. *Reasonable Faith: Christian Truth and Apologetics*. Wheaton, IL: Crossway Books, 2008.

Cranfield, C. E. B. *A Critical and Exegetical Commentary on the Epistle to the Romans*. The International Critical Commentary on the Holy Scriptures of the Old and New Testaments 28. 6th ed. 2 vols. Edinburgh: T&T Clark, 1975–79.

Davies, P. C. W. "Physics and the Mind of God: The Templeton Prize Address." *First Things* 55 (August 1995): 31–35.

De Botton, Alain. *Status Anxiety*. New York: Pantheon Books, 2004.

Denny, Frederick M. "The Problem of Salvation in the Qur'an: Key Terms and Concepts." In *In Quest of an Islamic Humanism: Arabic and Islamic Studies in Memory of Mohamed al-Nowaihi*, edited by A. H. Green. Cairo: American University in Cairo Press, 1984.

Derr, Thomas Siger. Review of *The Social God and the Relational Self: A Trinitarian Theology of the Imago Dei*, by Stanley J. Grenz. *Journal of Markets & Morality* 5, no. 2 (2002): 464–66.

Deuser, Hermann. *Kleine Einführung in die systematische Theologie*. Ditzingen: Reclam, 1999.

Diener, Michael. *Gesetz und Evangelium: Grundsätzliches und Konkretes in 95 Thesen*. Kassel: Evangelischer Gnadauer Gemeinschaftsverband, 2017.

Duchrow, Ulrich. *Christenheit und Weltverantwortung: Traditionsgeschichte und systematischer Struktur der Zweireichelehre*. Forschungen und Berichte der Evangelischen Studiengemeinschaft 25. 2d ed. Stuttgart: Klett-Cotta, 1983.

Dunn, James D. G. "Rom. 7,14–25 in the Theology of Paul." *Theologische Zeitschrift* 31, no. 5 (1975): 257–73.

Ebeling, Gerhard. *Gott und Wort*. Tübingen: J. C. B. Mohr, 1966.

———. "Luther's Understanding of Reality." *Lutheran Quarterly* 27, no. 1 (2013): 56–75.

Eckel, Malcolm David. "Buddhism in the World and in America." In *World Religions in America*, edited by Jacob Neusner, 199–212. 4th ed. Louisville: Westminster John Knox Press, 2009.

Elert, Werner. *The Christian Ethos*. Translated by Carl J. Schindler. Eugene, OR: Wipf & Stock Publishers, 2004.

———. *The Christian Faith. An Outline of Lutheran Dogmatics*. Translated from the 5th ed. by Martin H. Bertram and Walter R. Bouman. Columbus: Lutheran Theological Seminary, 1974.

———. *The Structure of Lutheranism*. Translated by Walter A. Hansen. St. Louis: Concordia Publishing House, 1962.

Erickson, Millard J. *Christian Theology*. 2d ed. Grand Rapids: Baker Book House, 1998.

———. *God in Three Persons: A Contemporary Interpretation of the Trinity*. Grand Rapids: Baker Books, 1995.

———. *Making Sense of the Trinity*. Grand Rapids: Baker Academic, 2000.

———. "The State of the Unevangelized and Its Missionary Implications." In *Missiology: An Introduction to the Foundations, History and Strategies of World Missions*, edited by John Mark Terry, 121–37. Nashville: B&H Academic, 2015.

Esolen, Anthony M. *Out of the Ashes: Rebuilding American Culture*. Washington, DC: Regnery Publishing, 2017.

Fagerberg, Holsten. *A New Look at the Lutheran Confessions (1529–1537)*. Translated by Gene J. Lund. St. Louis: Concordia Publishing House, 1972.

Feinberg, John S. "Luther's Doctrine of Vocation: Some Problems of Interpretation and Application." *Fides et Historia* 12, no. 1 (1979): 50–67.

Fichte, Johann Gottlieb. *Foundations of Natural Right according to the Principles of the Wissenschaftslehre*. Edited by Frederick Neuhouser. Translated by Michael Baur. Cambridge Texts in the History of Philosophy. Cambridge: Cambridge University Press, 2000.

Forde, Gerhard O. "The Lutheran View." In *Christian Spirituality: Five Views of Sanctification*, edited by Donald Alexander, 13–32. Downers Grove, IL: InterVarsity Press, 1988.

Fraissl, David. "Horror Sapiens: Was Thomas Hobbes und die Fernsehserie 'The Walking Dead' gemeinsam haben—und was der große englische Philosoph vergaß." *Hohe Luft*, May 2016: 88.

Frisch, Karl von. *Du und das Leben: Eine moderne Biologie für Jedermann*. Berlin: Ullstein, 1936.

Gallinat, Reinhold. "Der 'natürliche Mensch' nach Luther." *Lutherjahrbuch* 42 (1975): 33–51.

Gerrish, B. A. *Grace and Reason: A Study in the Theology of Luther*. Eugene, OR: Wipf & Stock Publishers, 2005.

Gibson, David. "Jesuit Pierre Teilhard de Chardin's 'Conscious Evolution' Plays Role in American Nuns vs Vatican Debate." *Huffpost* (blog), 2 June 2014. https://www.huffpost.com/entry/teilhard-american-nuns_n_5374368.

Gogarten, Friedrich. *Der Mensch zwischen Gott und Welt*. 3d ed. Stuttgart: Friedrich Vorwerk, 1956.

Graeber, David, and David Wengrow. *The Dawn of Everything: A New History of Humanity*. New York: Farrar, Straus and Giroux, 2021.

Graham, Elaine L. "The 'End' of the Human or the End of the 'Human'? Human Dignity in Technological Perspective." In *God and Human Dignity*, edited by R. Kendall Soulen and Linda Woodhead, 263–81. Grand Rapids: Wm. B. Eerdmans, 2006.

Green, Joel B. *Body, Soul, and Human Life: The Nature of Humanity in the Bible*. Grand Rapids: Baker Academic, 2008.

Green, Lowell C. *Lutherans against Hitler: The Untold Story*. St. Louis: Concordia Publishing House, 2007.

Gregory of Nyssa. *On the Making of Man*. New York: Aeterna Press, 2016.

Grenz, Stanley J. *The Social God and the Relational Self: A Trinitarian Theology of the Imago Dei*. Louisville: Westminster John Knox Press, 2001.

Grenz, Stanley J., and Roger E. Olson. *20th Century Theology: God & the World in a Transitional Age*. Downers Grove, IL: InterVarsity Press, 1992.

Grigg, Russell. "Pre-Adamic Man: Were There Human Beings on Earth before Adam?" *Creation* 24, no. 4 (2002): 42–45.

Groothuis, Douglas R. *Christian Apologetics: A Comprehensive Case for Biblical Faith*. Downers Grove, IL: IVP Academic, 2011.

———. "Deposed Royalty: Pascal's Anthropolocial Argument." *Journal of the Evangelical Theological Society* 41, no. 2 (1998): 297–312.

Guedira, Asmaa. "How My Coming-out and Job-out Led Me to Hyper-Gender." *Asmaa Guedira* (blog). 3 July 2016. https://medium.com/@asmaaguedira/hyper-gender-de11adc7e460.

Gutiérrez, Gustavo. *A Theology of Liberation: History, Politics, and Salvation*. Translated by Caridad Inda and John Eagleson. SCM Classics. Rev. ed. London: SCM, 2001.

Gutmann, Bruno. *Gemeindeaufbau aus dem Evangelium: Grundsätzliches für Mission und Heimatkirche*. Leipzig: Evangel.-Luth. Mission, 1925.

Hall, Douglas John. *Imaging God: Dominion as Stewardship*. Grand Rapids: Wm. B. Eerdmans, 1986.

Hall, Timothy L. "A Law for All Seasons: C. S. Lewis on Civilization & the Natural Order." *Touchstone* 22, no. 5 (2009): 24–29.

Hamilton, Brian. "It's in You: Structural Sin and Personal Responsibility Revisited." *Studies in Christian Ethics* 34, no. 3 (2021): 360–80.

Hampson, Margaret Daphne. *Christian Contradictions: The Structures of Lutheran and Catholic Thought*. New York: Cambridge University Press, 2001.

Harari, Yuval Noah. *Homo Deus: A Brief History of Tomorrow*. Translated by the author. New York: Harper, 2017.

———. *Sapiens: A Brief History of Humankind*. Translated by the author. New York: Harper, 2015.

Häring, Hermann. *Das Problem des Bösen in der Theologie*. Darmstadt: Wissenschaftliche Buchgesellschaft, 1985.

Härle, Wilfried. *Dogmatik*. Berlin: De Gruyter, 2000.

———. "Die Entfaltung der Rechtfertigungslehre Luthers in den Disputationen von 1535 bis 1537." *Lutherjahrbuch* 71 (2004): 211–28.

———. *Systematische Philosophie: Eine Einführung für Theologiestudenten*. Munich: Christian Kaiser Verlag, 1982.

Harris, Sam. *The Moral Landscape: How Science Can Determine Human Values*. New York: Free Press, 2010.

Hays, Richard B. "Relations Natural and Unnatural: A Response to John Boswell's Exegesis of Romans 1." *Journal of Religious Ethics* 14, no. 1 (1986): 184–215.

Herzfeld, Noreen L. *In Our Image: Artificial Intelligence and the Human Spirit*. Minneapolis: Fortress Press, 2002.

Hess, Karl. "The Faith of Unbaptized Infants in Bugenhagen's *On Unborn Children*," *Logia: A Journal of Lutheran Theology* 23, no. 2 (2014): 31–42.

Hirsch, Alan, and Lance Ford. *Right Here, Right Now: Everyday Mission for Everyday People*. Grand Rapids: Baker Books, 2011.

Hirsch, Emanuel. *Hilfsbuch zum Studium der Dogmatik: Die Dogmatik der Reformatoren und der altevangelischen Lehrer quellmäßig belegt und verdeutscht*. 4th ed. Berlin: Walter de Gruyter, 1964.

Hirschberger, Johannes. *Geschichte der Philosophie*. 12th ed. 2 vols. Freiburg: Herder, 1980.

Hoekema, Anthony A. *Created in God's Image*. Grand Rapids: Wm. B. Eerdmans, 1986.

Hood, Bruce M. *The Self Illusion: How the Social Brain Creates Identity*. Oxford: Oxford University Press, 2013.

Horton, Michael S. "Are Churches Secularizing America?" *Modern Reformation* 17, no. 2 (2008): 42–52.

Hössjer, Ola, Ann K. Gauger, and Colin R. Reeves. "An Alternative Population Genetics Model." In *Theistic Evolution: A Scientific, Philosophical, and Theological Critique*, edited by J. P. Moreland, Stephen C. Meyer, Christopher Shaw, Ann K. Gauger, and Wayne Grudem, 503–22. Wheaton, IL: Crossway Books, 2017.

Howell, Brian M., and Jenell Williams Paris. *Introducing Cultural Anthropology: A Christian Perspective*. Grand Rapids: Baker Academic, 2011.

Hughes, Philip Edgcumbe. *The True Image: The Origin and Destiny of Man in Christ*. Grand Rapids: Wm. B. Eerdmans, 1989.

Husbands, Mark, and Daniel J. Treier, eds. *Justification: What's at Stake in the Current Debates*. Downers Grove, IL: InterVarsity Press, 2004.

Irvine, William B. *The Stoic Challenge*. New York: W. W. Norton & Company, 2021.

Jaeschke, Ernst. *Bruno Gutmann, His Life, His Thoughts, and His Work: An Early Attempt at a Theology in an African Context*. Erlangen: Ev.-Luth. Mission, 1985.

Jansen, Cornelius. *Augustinus*. 1640. Reprint, Frankfurt am Main: Minerva, 1964.

Janz, Denis R. *Luther and Late Medieval Thomism: A Study in Theological Anthropology*. Waterloo, ON: Wilfrid Laurier University Press, 1983.

Jenson, Matt. *The Gravity of Sin: Augustine, Luther, and Barth on* Homo Incurvatus in Se. New York: T&T Clark, 2006.

Joest, Wilfried. *Gesetz und Freiheit. Das Problem des Tertius usus legis bei Luther und die neutestamentliche Parainese*. 4th ed. Göttingen: Vandenhoeck & Ruprecht, 1968.

———. *Ontologie der Person bei Luther*. Göttingen: Vandenhoeck & Ruprecht, 1967.

Johanson, Donald C., and Kate Wong. *Lucy's Legacy. The Quest for Human Origins*. New York: Three Rivers Press, 2009.

Jones, Peter R. "The New Spirituality: Dismantling and Reconstructing Reality." *Modern Reformation* 17, no. 3 (2008): 24–29.

Jüngel, Eberhard. "Hoffen, Handeln—und Leiden. Zum christlichen Verständnis des Menschen aus theologischer Sicht." In *Beziehungsbereich. Perspektiven des Glaubens*, 13–40. Stuttgart: Radius-Verlag, 2002.

Kähler, Martin. *Die Wissenschaft der christlichen Lehre von dem evangelischen Grundartikel aus im Abrisse dargestellt*. 2d ed. Leipzig: Deichert, 1893.

Käsemann, Ernst. *An die Römer*. Handbuch zum Neuen Testament 8a. 2d ed. Tübingen: Mohr, 1974.

Keil, C. F., and F. Delitzsch. *The Pentateuch*. Commentary on the Old Testament, vol. 1. Peabody, MA: Hendrickson Publishers, 1996.

Kelsey, David H. "Human Being." In *Christian Theology: An Introduction to Its Traditions and Tasks*, edited by Peter C. Hodgson and Robert H. King. London: SPCK, 1998.

Kenny, Anthony. *Faith and Reason*. New York: Columbia University Press, 1983.

Köberle, Adolf. "Die Freude am Leib." In *Die Seele des Christentums: Beiträge zum Verständnis des Christusglaubens und der Christusnachfolge in der Gegenwart*. Berlin: Furche-Verlag, 1932.

———. *Rechtfertigung, Glaube und neues Leben*. Gütersloh: Gütersloher Verlagshaus Gerd Mohn, 1965.

Kolb, Robert. "Contemporary Lutheran Understandings of the Doctrine of Justification: A Selective Glimpse." In *Justification: What's at Stake in the Current Debates*, edited by Mark Husbands and Daniel J. Treier, 153–76. Downers Grove, IL: InterVarsity Press, 2004.

Kölreuter, Joseph Gottlieb. *Vorläufige Nachricht von einigen das Geschlecht der Pflanzen betreffenden Versuchen*. Leipzig: Gleditsche Handlung, 1761.

Kraft, Charles H. *Anthropology for Christian Witness*. Maryknoll: Orbis Books, 1996.

Kreeft, Peter. *Christianity for Modern Pagans: Pascal's* Pensées *Edited, Outlined, and Explained*. San Francisco: Ignatius Press, 1993.

Kümmel, Werner Georg. *Römer 7 und die Bekehrung des Paulus*. Untersuchungen zum Neuen Testament 17. Leipzig: J. C. Hinrichs, 1929.

Laurens, Hannah. "Finite in Infinity: Spinoza's Conception of Human Freedom Explained through His Metaphysics." *Stance: An International Undergraduate Philosophy Journal* 5 (April 2012): 97–109.

Lavazza, Andrea. "Free Will and Neuroscience: From Explaining Freedom Away to New Ways of Operationalizing and Measuring It." *Frontiers in Human Neuroscience* 10 (2016).

Lawler, Michael G. "*Perichoresis*: New Theological Wine in an Old Theological Wineskin." *Horizons* 22, no. 1 (1995): 49–66.

Lee, Francis Nigel. *Communism versus Creation*. Nutley, NJ: Craig Press, 1969.

Leupold, H. C. *Exposition of Genesis*. 2 vols. Grand Rapids: Baker Book House, 1950–53.

Lewis, C. S. *Mere Christianity*. New York: HarperCollins, 2000.

Lewontin, Richard. "Billions and Billions of Demons." *New York Review of Books* 44, no. 1 (9 January 1997): 28.

Lloyd, Robin. "Like Humans, Other Apes Plan Ahead," *Live Science Newsletter* (17 June 2008).

Lonergan, Bernard. "St. Thomas' Thought on Gratia Operans I. Introduction," *Theological Studies (Baltimore)* 2, no. 3 (1941): 289–324.

Luskin, Casey. "Missing Transitions: Human Origins and the Fossil Record." In *Theistic Evolution: A Scientific, Philosophical, and Theological Critique*, edited by J. P. Moreland, Stephen C. Meyer, Christopher Shaw, Ann K. Gauger, and Wayne Grudem, 437–74. Wheaton, IL: Crossway Books, 2017.

Lutheran Church—Missouri Synod. *Lutheran Service Book*. St. Louis: Concordia Publishing House, 2006.

McClain, Alva J., and David R. Dilling. *Theological Anthropology*. Lafayette, IN: Kensington Theological Academy, 2015.

McCormack, Bruce L. "What's at Stake in Current Debates over Justification? The Crisis of Protestantism in the West." In *Justification: What's at Stake in the Current Debates*, ed. Mark Husbands and Daniel J. Treier, 81–117. Downers Grove, IL: InterVarsity Press, 2004.

McGrath, Alister E. *Mere Apologetics: How to Help Seekers and Skeptics Find Faith*. Grand Rapids: Baker Books, 2012.

Marquart, Kurt E. *The Saving Truth: Doctrine for Laypeople*. Truth, Salvatory and Churchly: Works of Kurt E. Marquart 1. Ft. Wayne: The Luther Academy, 2016.

Matz, Wolfgang. *Der befreite Mensch: Die Willenslehre in der Theologie Philipp Melanchthons*. Forschungen zur Kirchen- und Dogmengeschichte 81. Göttingen: Vandenhoeck & Ruprecht, 2001.

Maurer, Wilhelm. *Historical Commentary on the Augsburg Confession*. Translated by H. George Anderson. Philadelphia: Fortress Press, 1986.

Mayer, F. E. *The Religious Bodies of America*. St. Louis: Concordia Publishing House, 1954.

Mbiti, John S. *African Religions & Philosophy*. London: Heinemann, 1969.

Meilaender, Gilbert. *Neither Beast nor God: The Dignity of the Human Person*. 1st American ed. New York: Encounter Books, 2009.

Melchert, Norman. *The Great Conversation: A Historical Introduction to Philosophy*. 4th ed. Boston: McGraw-Hill Higher Education, 2002.

Middendorf, Michael Paul. *The "I" in the Storm: A Study of Romans 7*. St. Louis: Concordia Academic Press, 1997.

Moltmann, Jürgen. *The Crucified God: The Cross of Christ as the Foundation and Criticism of Christian Theology*. Translated by R. A. Wilson and John Bowden. New York: Harper & Row, 1974.

———. *Man: Christian Anthropology in the Conflicts of the Present*. Translated by John Sturdy. London: SPCK, 1974.

Monaghan, John, and Peter Just. *Social and Cultural Anthropology: A Very Short Introduction*. Oxford, UK: Oxford University Press, 2000.

Moo, Douglas J. *The Epistle to the Romans*. The New International Commentary on the New Testament. Grand Rapids: Wm. B. Eerdmans, 1996.

More, Max. "The Extropian Principles, v. 3.0." *The Published Data of Robert Munafo* (blog). Last updated 26 March 2020. https://mrob.com/pub/religion/extro_prin.html.

Moreland, J. P., Stephen C. Meyer, Christopher Shaw, Ann K. Gauger, and Wayne Grudem, eds. *Theistic Evolution: A Scientific, Philosophical, and Theological Critique*. Wheaton, IL: Crossway Books, 2017.

Moriarty, Michael. *Pascal. Reasoning and Belief*. Oxford: Oxford University Press, 2020.

Müller, Julius. *Die christliche Lehre von der Sünde*. 2 vols. Breslau: Josef Max, 1839.

Müller, Max. *Lectures on the Science of Language*. 5th ed. London: Longman, Green, and Co., 1866.

Nafzger, Samuel H., John F. Johnson, David A. Lumpp, and Howard W. Tepker, eds. *Confessing the Gospel: A Lutheran Approach to Systematic Theology*. Vol. 1. St. Louis: Concordia Publishing House, 2017.

The Natural Knowledge of God: In Christian Confession & Christian Witness. A Report of the Commission on Theology and Church Relations of The Lutheran Church—Missouri Synod. St. Louis: The Lutheran Church—Missouri Synod, 2013.

"Neanderthal DNA May Influence These Human Traits." *CBSNews* (blog). 6 October 2017. https://www.cbsnews.com/news/neanderthal-dna-may-influence-human-traits/.

Neuer, Werner. "Die Salzburger Erklärung." *CA: Confessio Augustana* 2 (2019): 49–56.

Neusner, Jacob, and Bruce D. Chilton, eds. *Altruism in World Religions*. Washington, DC: Georgetown University Press, 2005.

Newbigin, Lesslie. *The Gospel in a Pluralist Society*. Grand Rapids: Wm. B. Eerdmans, 1989.

Nida, Eugene A. *Message and Mission: The Communication of the Christian Faith*. New York: Harper & Brothers, 1960.

Niebuhr, Reinhold. *The Nature and Destiny of Man: A Christian Interpretation*. Vol. 1. New York: Charles Scribner's Sons, 1964.

Oberman, Heiko A. *Luther: Man between God and the Devil*. Translated by Eileen Walliser-Schwarzbart. New Haven: Yale University Press, 1989.

Ostler, Blake T. "The Idea of Pre-Existence in the Development of Mormon Thought." *Dialogue* 15, no. 1 (1982): 59–78.

Pannenberg, Wolfhart. *Anthropology in Theological Perspective*. Translated by Matthew J. O'Connell. Philadelphia: Westminster Press, 1985.

———. *Systematic Theology*. Translated by Geoffrey W. Bromiley. 3 vols. Grand Rapids: Wm. B. Eerdmans, 1991–98.

Peura, Simo. "Iustitia christiana in Luthers später Auslegung des Galaterbriefs (1531/1535)." *Lutherjahrbuch* 71 (2004): 179–210.

Pieper, Francis. *Christian Dogmatics*. 4 vols. St. Louis: Concordia Publishing House, 1950–57.

Pinnock, Clark, Richard Rice, John Sanders, William Hasker, and David Basinger. *The Openness of God: A Biblical Challenge to the Traditional Understanding of God*. Downers Grove, IL: InterVarsity Press, 1994.

Pöhlmann, Horst Georg. *Abriß der Dogmatik: Ein Repetitorium*. 3rd ed. Gütersloh: Gütersloher Verlagshaus Gerd Mohn, 1980.

———. "Das Problem der Ur-Offenbarung bei Paul Althaus." *Kerygma und Dogma* 16, no. 4 (1970): 242–58.

Polkinghorne, John. "Anthropology in an Evolutionary Context." In *God and Human Dignity*, edited by R. Kendall Soulen and Linda Woodhead, 89–103. Grand Rapids: Wm. B. Eerdmans, 2006.

———. *The Faith of a Physicist: Reflections of a Bottom-Up Thinker*. Princeton: Princeton University Press, 1994.

Pope, Stephen J. "Theological Anthropology, Science, and Human Flourishing." In *Questioning the Human: Toward a Theological Anthropology for the Twenty-first*

Century, edited by Lieven Boeve, Yves de Maeseneer, and Ellen Van Stichel, 13–31. New York: Fordham University Press, 2014.

Preston, Ronald. "Christian Ethics." In *A Companion to Ethics*, edited by Peter Singer, 91–105. Blackwell Companion to Philosophy. Cambridge, MA: Blackwell Reference, 1991.

Preus, Robert D. *The Theology of Post-Reformation Lutheranism*. Vol. 2, *God and His Creation*. St. Louis: Concordia Publishing House, 1970.

Price, Daniel J. *Karl Barth's Anthropology in Light of Modern Thought*. Grand Rapids: Wm. B. Eerdmans, 2002.

Radford, Robert T. *Cicero: A Study in the Origins of Republican Philosophy*. New York: Rodopi, 2002.

Rahner, Karl. *The Trinity*. Translated by Joseph Donceel. New York: Herder and Herder, 1970.

Rauschenbusch, Walter. *A Theology for the Social Gospel*. New York: Abingdon Press, 1917.

Rengstorf, Karl Heinrich, and Ulrich Luck, eds. *Das Paulusbild in der neueren deutschen Forschung*. Wege der Forschung 24. Darmstadt: Wissenschaftliche Buchgesellschaft, 1964.

Rohnert, Wilhelm. *Die Dogmatik der evangelisch-lutherischen Kirche: Mit Berücksichtigung des Dogmengeschichtlichen zunächst den bekenntnistreuen Geistlichen und den Theologie-studierenden dargeboten*. Braunschweig: Wollermann, 1902.

Roloff, Jürgen. *Neues Testament*. Neukirchener Arbeitsbücher. 4th ed. Neukirchen-Vluyn: Neukirchener Verlag, 1985.

Rosin, Wilbert, and Robert D. Preus, eds. *A Contemporary Look at the Formula of Concord*. St. Louis: Concordia Publishing House, 1978.

Ruse, Michael. *Can a Darwinian Be a Christian? The Relationship between Science and Religion*. Cambridge: Cambridge University Press, 2004.

Sacks, Oliver. *The Man Who Mistook His Wife for a Hat: And Other Clinical Tales*. New York: Simon & Schuster, 1998.

Salvard, Jean François, comp. *The Harmony of Protestant Confessions: Exhibiting the Faith of the Churches of Christ, Reformed after the Pure and Holy Doctrine of the Gospel, throughout Europe*. Edited by Peter Hall. New ed. London: John F. Shaw, 1844.

Sanders, John. *The God Who Risks: A Theology of Providence*. Downers Grove, IL: InterVarsity Press, 1998.

Sanneh, Lamin O. *Translating the Message: The Missionary Impact on Culture*. 2d ed., revised and expanded. American Society of Missiology Series 42. Maryknoll, NY: Orbis Books, 2009.

Sartre, Jean-Paul. "Existentialism." In *A Casebook on Existentialism*, edited by William V. Spanos, 275–96. New York: Crowell, 1966.

Schaeffer, Francis A. *The God Who Is There: Speaking Historic Christianity into the Twentieth Century*. Chicago: InterVarsity Press, 1968.

Schaff, Philip. *Bibliotheca Symbolica Ecclesiae Universalis: The Creeds of Christendom, with a History and Critical Notes*. 4th ed. 3 vols. New York: Harper & Brothers, 1919.

———. "Excursus on Pelagianism." In *Nicene and Post Nicene Fathers*, edited by Philip Schaff and Henry Wace, Second Series, vol. 14, 229–30. Reprint, Peabody, MA: Hendrickson Publishers, 2004.

Scheler, Max. *The Human Place in the Cosmos*. Translated by Manfred S. Frings. Evanston, IL: Northwestern University Press, 2009.

Schleiermacher, Friedrich. *The Christian Faith*. Edited by H. R. Mackintosh and J. S. Stewart. London: T&T Clark, 2004.

Schroeder, H. J., trans. *Canons and Decrees of the Council of Trent*. St. Louis: B. Herder, 1950.

Schulz, Klaus Detlev. *Mission from the Cross*. St Louis: Concordia Publishing House, 2009.

———. "Two Kinds of Righteousness and Moral Philosophy: *Confessio Augustana* XVIII, Philipp Melanchthon, and Martin Luther." *Concordia Theological Quarterly* 73, no. 1 (2009): 17–40.

Schwarz, Hans. *The Human Being: A Theological Anthropology*. Grand Rapids: Wm. B. Eerdmans, 2013.

Seils, Martin. *Der Gedanke vom Zusammenwirken Gottes und des Menschen in Luthers Theologie*. Beiträge zur Förderung christlicher Theologie 50. Gütersloh: Gütersloher Verlagshaus G. Mohn, 1962.

Sherlock, Charles. *The Doctrine of Humanity*. Contours of Christian Theology. Downers Grove, IL: InterVarsity Press, 1996.

Shields, Christopher. *Aristotle*. Routledge Philosophers. London: Routledge, 2007.

———. "Soul as Subject in Aristotle's *De Anima*." *Classical Quarterly* 38, no. 1 (1988): 140–49.

Singer, Peter. *Practical Ethics*. Cambridge: Cambridge University Press, 1993.

Sire, James W. *The Universe Next Door: A Basic Worldview Catalog*. 5th ed. Downers Grove, IL: InterVarsity Press, 2009.

Slenczka, Notger. "Luther's Anthropology." In *The Oxford Handbook of Martin Luther's Theology*, edited by Robert Kolb, Irene Dingel, and Ľubomír Batka, 212–32. New York: Oxford University Press, 2014.

Smith, Christian. *What Is a Person? Rethinking Humanity, Social Life, and the Moral Good from the Person Up*. Chicago and London: The University of Chicago Press, 2010.

Smith, Christian, and Melinda Lundquist Denton. *Soul Searching: The Religious and Spiritual Lives of American Teenagers*. New York: Oxford University Press, 2005.

Smith, James K. A. *How (Not) to Be Secular: Reading Charles Taylor*. Grand Rapids: Wm. B. Eerdmans, 2014.

Smith, Wesley J. *A Rat Is a Pig Is a Dog Is a Boy: The Human Cost of the Animal Rights Movement*. New York: Encounter Books, 2012.

Solzhenitsyn, Aleksandr. *A World Split Apart: Commencement Address Delivered at Harvard University, June 8, 1978*. Translated by Irina Ilovayskaya Alberti. New York: Harper & Row, 1978.

Soulen, R. Kendall, and Linda Woodhead, eds. *God and Human Dignity*. Grand Rapids: Wm. B. Eerdmans, 2006.

Specter, Michael. "Rewriting the Code of Life." *New Yorker*, 2 January 2017, 34–43.

Spencer, Herbert. *Principles of Biology*. Vol 1. London: Williams and Northgate, 1864.

Spinoza, Benedict de. *The Ethics*. In *The Chief Works of Benedict de Spinoza*, translated by R. H. M. Elwes, 2:43–271. New York: Dover Publications, 1951.

Sproul, R. C. *What Is Reformed Theology? Understanding the Basics*. Grand Rapids: Baker Books, 2016.

Stelzenberger, Johannes. *Syneidesis, Conscientia, Gewissen*. Paderborn: Ferdinand Schöningh, 1963.

Stephens, W. P. *Zwingli: An Introduction to His Thought*. Oxford, UK: Clarendon Press, 1992.

Stump, Eleonore. "Resurrection, Reassembly, and Reconstitution: Aquinas on the Soul." In *Die menschliche Seele: Brauchen wir den Dualismus?* edited by Bruno Niederbacher and Edmund Runggaldier, 153–74. Frankfurt: Ontos Verlag, 2006.

Suda, Max Josef. *Die Ethik Martin Luthers*. Forschungen zur systematischen und ökumenischen Theologie 108. Göttingen: Vandenhoeck & Ruprecht, 2006.

Swan, James. "Heinrich Denifle: Catholic Interpreter of Luther." *Beggars All: Reformation & Apologetics* (blog). 2 May 2009. http://beggarsallreformation.blogspot.com/2009/05/heinrich-denifle-catholic-interpreters.html.

Symons, Xavier. "The Risk of a Transhumanist Future." *BioEdge* (blog). 5 August 2017. https://www.bioedge.org/bioethics/the-risk-of-a-transhumanist-future/12371.

Taylor, Charles. *A Secular Age*. Cambridge, MA: The Belknap Press of Harvard University Press, 2007.

Taylor, John V. *The Primal Vision: Christian Presence amid African Religion*. London: SCM Press, 1963.

Thielicke, Helmut. *Being Human—Becoming Human: An Essay in Christian Anthropology*. Translated by Geoffrey W. Bromiley. Garden City, NY: Doubleday & Company, 1984.

Tillich, Paul. *Systematic Theology*. 3 vols. Chicago: University of Chicago Press, 1951–63.

Timpe, Kevin. *Free Will in Philosophical Theology*. New York: Bloomsbury Publishing, 2014.

Tindal, Matthew. *Christianity as Old as the Creation*. London, 1730. Reprint, Stuttgart–Bad Cannstatt: Frommann-Holzboog, 1967.

Together with All Creatures: Caring for God's Living Earth. A Report of the Commission on Theology and Church Relations of The Lutheran Church—Missouri Synod. St. Louis: The Lutheran Church—Missouri Synod, 2010.

Treptow, Earle D. "Imitating the Trinity: A Proper Way to Make the Doctrine of the Trinity Practical?" *Wisconsin Lutheran Quarterly* 116, no. 3 (2019): 163–84.

Treusch, Ulrike. "Käthe und Martin: Das Verständnis von Ehe und Familie bei Martin Luther." In *Martin Luther—Aus Liebe zur Wahrheit: Die bleibende Bedeutung der Anliegen des Reformators für heute*, edited by Berthold Schwarz, 381–91. Dillenburg: Christliche Verlagsgesellschaft, 2016.

Valleskey, David J. *We Believe, Therefore We Speak: The Theology and Practice of Evangelism*. Milwaukee: Northwestern Publishing House, 1995.

Vicedom, Georg F. *The Mission of God: An Introduction to a Theology of Mission*. St. Louis: Concordia Publishing House, 1965.

Von Drehle, David. "How Gay Marriage Won." *Time*, 8 April 2013.

von Rad, Gerhard. "Εἰκών." In *Theological Dictionary of the New Testament*, edited by Gerhard Kittel, Geoffrey W. Bromiley, and Gerhard Friedrich, translated by Geoffrey W. Bromiley, 2:381–97. Grand Rapids: Wm. B. Eerdmans, 1964–76.

———. *Genesis: A Commentary*. Translated by John H. Marks. Rev. ed. The Old Testament Library. Philadelphia: Westminster Press, 1972.

———. *Old Testament Theology*. Vol. 1, translated by D. M. G. Stalker. New York: Harper & Row, 1962.

Waap, Thorsten. *Gottebenbildlichkeit und Identität: Zum Verhältnis von theologischer Anthropologie und Humanwissenschaft bei Karl Barth und Wolfhart Pannenberg*. Forschungen zur systematischen und ökumenischen Theologie 121. Göttingen: Vandenhoeck & Ruprecht, 2008.

Walther, Wilhelm. *Lehrbuch der Symbolik: Die Eigentümlichkeiten der vier christlichen Hauptkirchen vom Standpunkt Luthers aus dargestellt*. Sammlung theologischer Lehrbücher 9. Leipzig: Deichert, 1924.

Wenz, Armin. "Natural Law and the Orders of Creation." In *Natural Law: A Lutheran Reappraisal*, edited by Robert C. Baker and Roland Cap Ehlke, 79–95. St. Louis: Concordia Publishing House, 2011.

Wenz, Gunther. *Theologie der Bekenntnisschriften der evangelisch-lutherischen Kirche: Eine historische und systematische Einführung in das Konkordienbuch*. 2 vols. De Gruyter Lehrbuch. Berlin: Walter de Gruyter, 1996–98.

Westermann, Claus. *Creation*. Translated by John J. Scullion. Philadelphia: Fortress Press, 1974.

———. *Genesis: A Commentary*. Translated by John J. Scullion. Minneapolis: Augsburg, 1984–86.

White, Lynn, Jr. "The Historical Roots of Our Ecological Crisis." *Science* 155, no. 3767 (10 March 1967): 1203–7.

Wingren, Gustaf. *The Flight from Creation*. Minneapolis: Augsburg Publishing House, 1971.

———. *Luther on Vocation*. Translated by Carl C. Rasmussen. Philadelphia: Muhlenberg Press, 1957.

Winner, Langdon. "Resistance Is Futile: The Posthuman Condition and Its Advocates." In *Is Human Nature Obsolete? Genetics, Bioengineering, and the Future of the Human Condition*, edited by Harold W. Baillie and Timothy K. Casey, 385–411. Basic Bioethics. Cambridge: MIT Press, 2004.

Wolff, Hans Walter. *Anthropology of the Old Testament*. Translated by Margaret Kohl. Philadelphia: Fortress Press, 1974.

Woodberry, J. Dudley, Charles van Engen, and Edgar J. Elliston, eds. *Missiological Education for the Twenty-first Century: The Book, the Circle, and the Sandals: Essays in Honor of Paul E. Pierson*. American Society of Missiology Series 23. Maryknoll, NY: Orbis Books, 1996.

Woodhead, Linda. "Apophatic Anthropology." In *God and Human Dignity*, edited by R. Kendall Soulen and Linda Woodhead, 233–46. Grand Rapids: Wm. B. Eerdmans, 2006.

Wright, N. T. *Justification: God's Plan & Paul's Vision*. Downers Grove, IL: IVP Academic, 2009.

Yates, Timothy Edward. *Christian Mission in the Twentieth Century*. Cambridge, UK: Cambridge University Press, 1994.

Zimmer, Carl. "3.2-Million-Year-Old Mystery: Did Lucy Die in a Fall from a Tree?" *New York Times*, 30 August 2016, A11–14.

Zimmerli, Walther. *Grundriß der alttestamentlichen Theologie*. Theologische Wissenschaft 3. 2d ed. Stuttgart: Kohlhammer, 1975.

Zizioulas, John. *Communion and Otherness: Further Studies in Personhood and the Church*. Edited by Paul McPartlan. London: T&T Clark, 2006.

SACRED SCRIPTURE INDEX

LUTHERAN CONFESSIONS INDEX

NAME AND SUBJECT INDEX

www.ingramcontent.com/pod-product-compliance
Lightning Source LLC
LaVergne TN
LVHW010052110826
845155LV00028B/308

* 9 7 8 1 9 3 5 0 3 5 4 6 6 *